Diversity and Community

For Mary

Diversity and Community

An Interdisciplinary Reader

EDITED BY
PHILIP ALPERSON

Blackwell
Publishing

Editorial material and organization © 2002 by Blackwell Publishers Ltd
a Blackwell Publishing company

350 Main Street, Malden, MA 02148-5018, USA
108 Cowley Road, Oxford OX4 1JF, UK
550 Swanston Street, Carlton South, Melbourne, Victoria 3053, Australia
Kurfürstendamm 57, 10707 Berlin, Germany

The right of Philip Alperson to be identified as the Author of the Editorial Material
in this Work has been asserted in accordance with the UK Copyright, Designs, and
Patents Act 1988.

First published 2002 by Blackwell Publishers Ltd

Library of Congress Cataloging-in-Publication Data

Diversity and community : an interdisciplinary reader / Philip Alperson [editor].
    p. cm.
   Includes bibliographical references and index.
   ISBN 0-631-21946-3 (alk. paper) – ISBN 0-631-21947-1 (pbk. : alk.
paper)
    1. Community – Philosophy.   2. Multiculturalism.   3. Identity (Psychology)
4. Social structure.   I. Alperson, Philip, 1946–

   B105.C46 D58 2002
   307 – dc21

                          2002066431

A catalogue record for this title is available from the British Library.

Set in 10 on 12 pt Photina
by Ace Filmsetting Ltd, Frome, Somerset
Printed and bound in the United Kingdom
by TJ International, Padstow, Cornwall

For further information on
Blackwell Publishing, visit our website:
http://www.blackwellpublishing.com

Contents

List of Contributors

Philip Alperson is Professor of Philosophy at Temple University. He is the author of articles on aesthetics, the philosophy of education, creativity, and value theory. He has edited three books on aesthetics: *What is Music: An Introduction to the Philosophy of Music* (Haven Publications, 1987; Penn State Press, 1994), *The Philosophy of the Visual Arts* (Oxford University Press, 1992), and *Musical Worlds: New Directions in the Philosophy of Music* (Penn State Press, 1998). He was also editor of *The Journal of Aesthetics and Art Criticism* for many years.

Christopher Beem is Program Officer for Democracy and Community at the Johnson Foundation in Racine, Wisconsin. He is the author of *The Necessity of Politics: Reclaiming American Public Life* (University of Chicago Press, 1999).

Duane Champagne is a member of the Department of Sociology and Director of the American Indian Studies Center at the University of California at Los Angeles. His main research interests are in social change among American Indians, change in macro institutions, historical comparative sociology, contemporary American Indian issues, and theory. He is editor of the *American Indian Culture and Research Journal*, and the author of *Political Change and Social Order: Constitutional Governments Among the Cherokee, Choctaw, Chickasaw and Creek* (Stanford University Press, 1992) and *American Indian Societies: Strategies and Conditions of Political and Cultural Survival* (Cultural Survival, 1989). He has edited several volumes, including *The Native North American Almanac* (Gale Research Inc., 1994).

Frank Cunningham is a Professor in the Department of Philosophy and Political Science, and Principal of Innis College, at the University of Toronto. His principal research interests are democratic theory, environmental philosophy, and socialist theory. His publications include articles in these areas as well as five books: *Objectivity in Social Science* (University of Toronto Press,

1973), *Understanding Marxism* (Progress Books, 1978), *Democratic Theory and Socialism* (Cambridge University Press, 1987), *The Real World of Democracy Revisited* (Humanities Press, 1994), and *Theories of Democracy: A Critical Introduction* (Routledge, 2002). Professor Cunningham is Past President of the Canadian Philosophical Association and is a Fellow of the Royal Society of Canada.

Carl Dyke is Assistant Professor of History at Methodist College, Fayetteville, North Carolina. He did his doctoral work on identity and rationality in early twentieth-century Marxism and "bourgeois" social theory. He is currently doing work on the Italian political philosopher Antonio Gramsci and on the prehistory of postmodernism.

Chuck Dyke is Associate Professor of Philosophy at Temple University. He is the author of numerous essays in the areas of the philosophy of the social sciences, social and political philosophy, the philosophy of biology, and complex dynamical systems.

Marcia Muelder Eaton is Professor and Chair of the Department of Philosophy at the University of Minnesota. She is the author of many articles and books on ethics and aesthetics, including *Art and Non-Art* (Fairleigh Dickinson, 1983), *Basic Issues in Aesthetics* (Wadsworth, 1988), and *Aesthetics and the Good Life* (Fairleigh Dickinson, 1989). She is Past President of The American Society for Aesthetics and has lectured widely in North America, Europe, and the People's Republic of China.

Jean Bethke Elshtain is Laura Spelman Rockefeller Professor of Social and Political Ethics at the University of Chicago. She is especially interested to show the connections between political and ethical convictions. Her many books include *Public Man, Private Woman: Women in Social and Political Thought* (Princeton University Press, 1981), *Meditations on Modern Political Thought* (Praeger, 1986; Penn State Press, 1992), *Women and War* (Basic Books, 1987), *Augustine and the Limits of Politics* (Notre Dame Press, 1996), and *Real Politics: At the Center of Everyday Life* (Johns Hopkins University Press, 1997). Her 1993 Massey Lectures for the Canadian Broadcasting Corporation form the basis for her book, *Democracy on Trial* (Basic Books, 1995), which was named a *New York Times* notable book for 1995.

Lewis Gordon is Professor of Afro-American Studies and Religious Studies at Brown University, where he is also an affiliate of the Department of Modern Culture and Media, a member of the Center for the Study of Race and Ethnicity in America, and a Presidential Faculty Fellow of the Pembroke Center for the Study and Teaching of Women. His areas of interest are

Africana philosophy and religious thought, phenomenology, philosophy of existence, social and political philosophy, and philosophy in literature, film, and music. Among his many publications are *Her Majesty's Other Children: Sketches of Racism from a Neocolonial Age* (Rowman and Littlefield, 1997), *Fanon and the Crisis of European Man: An Essay on Philosophy and the Human Sciences* (Routledge, 1995) and *Bad Faith and Antiblack Racism* (Humanities Press, 1995). He is also the editor of *Existence in Black: An Anthology of Black Existential Philosophy* (Routledge, 1997) and co-editor of *Franz Fanon: A Critical Reader* (Blackwell, 1996).

Mary E. Hawkesworth is Professor of Political Science and Women's Studies and a Senior Scholar at the Center for American Women and Politics at Rutgers University. Her research interests include contemporary political philosophy, feminist theory, and social policy. She is the author of *Beyond Oppression: Feminist Theory and Political Strategy* (Continuum Press, 1990), *Theoretical Issues in Policy Analysis* (State University of New York Press, 1988), and editor of *The Encyclopedia of Government and Politics* (Routledge, 1992) and *Feminism and Public Policy* (*Policy Sciences* 27(2–3), 1994).

J. Blaine Hudson is Associate Professor and Chair of the Department of Pan-African Studies at the University of Louisville. His research and teaching interests include African-American, African Diaspora, and African history, the history and social science of race, and inter-cultural education. His recent publications in *The Black Scholar*, *The Journal of Negro Education*, *The Journal of Negro History*, and *The Journal of Black Studies* reflect these interests.

Samuel Oluoch Imbo is Associate Professor of Philosophy at Hamline University. His research and teaching interests are in social and political philosophy, value theory, modern philosophy, contemporary African philosophy, and the philosophy of religion. He has written articles on African philosophy and has given papers on the politics of race, communitarianism, and community and cyberspace. He is author of *An Introduction to African Philosophy* (Rowman and Littlefield, 1998) and *Oral Traditions as Philosophy: Okot p'Bitek's Legacy for African Philosophy* (Rowman and Littlefield, forthcoming).

Eileen John is Associate Professor of Philosophy at the University of Louisville. Her research interests are in philosophy and literature, aesthetics, and philosophical psychology. She has written on issues of moral and conceptual knowledge in fiction. Her recent publications include "Subtlety and Moral Vision" (*Philosophy and Literature*) and "Reading Fiction and Conceptual Knowledge: Philosophical Thought in Literary Context" (*The Journal of Aesthetics and Art Criticism*).

Maria Lugones is Associate Professor of Comparative Literature and Director of the Program in Latin American and Caribbean Area Studies at Binghamton University of the State University of New York, and also teaches at the Escuela Popular Norteña in New Mexico. Her interests are in feminist theory, lesbian theory, US Latino studies, and social and political theory. Her published essays include "Enticements and Dangers of Community for a Radical Politics," "Purity, Impurity, and Separation," "On the Logic of Pluralist Feminism," "Playfulness, 'World'-Traveling, and Loving Perception," and "Have We Got a Theory for You! Feminist Theory, Cultural Imperialism, and the Demand for the Women's Voice" (with Elizabeth Spelman).

D. A. Masolo is Justus Bier Professor of the Humanities and a member of the Department of Philosophy at the University of Louisville. He is the author of many articles and books on the philosophy of culture and on African thought and culture in particular, including *African Philosophy in Search of Identity* (Indiana University Press, 1994). He is also co-editor of *African Philosophy as Cultural Inquiry* (Indiana University Press, 2000).

Martha Nussbaum is Ernst Freund Professor of Law and Ethics at the University of Chicago. She has received numerous awards for her work in ancient philosophy and culture, ethics and political philosophy, the theory of the emotions, and current controversies in higher education. Among her books are *The Fragility of Goodness: Luck and Ethics in Greek Tragedy and Philosophy* (Cambridge University Press: 1986), *Love's Knowledge* (Oxford University Press, 1990), *The Therapy of Desire* (Princeton University Press, 1994), *Poetic Justice* (Beacon Press, 1996), *For Love of Country: Debating the Limits of Patriotism* (Beacon Press, 1996), *Cultivating Humanity: A Classical Defense of Reform in Liberal Education* (Harvard University Press, 1997), and *Upheavals of Thought: The Intelligence of Emotions* (Cambridge University Press, 2001).

Gary Y. Okihiro is Professor of International and Public Affairs, Director of the Center for the Study of Ethnicity and Race, and Director of the Asian-American Program at Columbia University. His research interests include Asian American history and southern Africa. He is the author, most recently, of *Margins and Mainstreams: Asians in American History and Culture* (1994), *Whispered Silences: Japanese Americans and World War II* (University of Washington Press, 1996), *Storied Lives: Japanese American Students and World War II* (University of Washington Press, 1999), and *The Columbia Guide to Asian American History* (Columbia University Press, 2001). Professor Okihiro is Past President of the Association for Asian American Studies.

Nancy Potter is Associate Professor of Philosophy at the University of Louisville. Her areas of interest are in ethics, feminist philosophy, and social and political philosophy. She is especially interested in the philosophical analysis of trust. Her recent publications include "The Severed Head and Existential Dread: The Classroom as Epistemic Community" (*Hypatia*), "Loopholes, Gaps, and What is Held Fast: Democratic Epistemology and Claims to Recovered Memories" (*Philosophy, Psychiatry, and Psychology*), and "Discretionary Power, Lies, and Broken Trust: Justification and Discomfort" (*Theoretical Medicine*).

Crispin Sartwell is Chair of the Department of Humanities at the Maryland Institute College of Art. His research interests include multiculturalism, addiction, body decoration and mutilation, communication and narratology, and epistemology and metaphysics in Western and non-Western philosophical traditions. His publications include *The Art of Living: Aesthetics of the Ordinary in World Spiritual Traditions* (State University of New York Press, 1995), *Obscenity, Anarchy, Reality* (State University of New York Press, 1996), *Act Like You Know: African-American Autobiography and White Identity* (University of Chicago Press, 1998), and *End of Story: Toward an Annihilation of Language and History* (State University of New York Press, 2000).

Michael A. Schwartz, M.D., is Clinical Professor of Psychiatry at Case Western Reserve University and a Lecturer in the Department of Psychiatry at Johns Hopkins University School of Medicine. He is the Founding President of the Association for the Advancement of Philosophy and Psychiatry and associate editor of *Philosophy, Psychiatry, and Psychology*. In 1998, he and Osborne Wiggins received the University of Zurich Margrite Égner Award for research in philosophical psychiatry. Dr. Schwartz was designated an "Exemplary Psychiatrist for 2000" by the National Alliance for the Mentally Ill.

Arlene Stein is Associate Professor of Sociology at Rutgers University. Her research focuses on the social construction of sexualities and the relationship between culture and power. She is also interested in processes of group identity formation and change. Professor Stein is the author of *Sex and Sensibility: Stories of a Lesbian Generation* (University of California Press, 1997) and *The Stranger Next Door: The Story of a Small Town's Battle Over Sex, Faith, and Civil Rights* (Beacon Press, 2001).

Osborne Wiggins is Professor of Philosophy at the University of Louisville. He has published numerous essays on phenomenology, existentialism, ethics, political philosophy, and philosophy of medicine and psychiatry. He is one of the editors of *Philosophical Perspectives on Psychiatric Diagnostic Classification* (The Johns Hopkins Press, 1994) and he is the co-winner, with Michael Schwartz, of the 1998 University of Zurich Margrite Égner Award for research in philosophical psychiatry.

Preface

This book grew from a rather local concern, aired among friends around a dinner table – that a university, on the occasion of its bicentennial celebrations, make an appropriate and meaningful academic contribution to the communities it serves – to a much larger project involving many people quite removed from the original site. One goal was shared by all who contributed to the project as it grew from the original idea to the present volume – a commitment to understanding the meaning of diversity and community in the twenty-first century.

There are many people who deserve thanks for helping the project come to fruition and I would like to thank them here. Provost Wallace Mann at the University of Louisville provided crucial encouragement at the beginning. Without his help in supporting the bicentennial conference at the University of Louisville on "Understanding Communities" this book would not have come into being. I also wish to thank President John Shumaker and Professor Dale Billingsley at the University of Louisville for their encouragement and support of the conference. Many people contributed to the substantive and intellectual core of this book as it developed well beyond the parameters of the original conference. These people are Mary Hawkesworth, Nancy Theriot, Cass Sunstein, Robert Hariman, Arnold Berleant, Martha Nussbaum, Jean Bethke Elshtain, J. Blaine Hudson, D. A. Masolo, Samuel Imbo, Eileen John, Nancy Potter, Maria Lugones, Lewis Gordon, Christopher Beem, Chuck Dyke, Carl Dyke, Crispin Sartwell, Duane Champagne, Frank Cunningham, Marcia Eaton, Arlene Stein, Gary Y. Okihiro, Osborne Wiggins, and Michael Schwartz. I am grateful for their advice. I am also indebted to Jean Marlowe at the Commonwealth Center for the Humanities and Society and Cindy Saling in the Department of Philosophy at the University of Louisville, Peter Morrin at the J. B. Speed Museum, and Melanie McQuitty and Caroline Meline at the Department of Philosophy at Temple University for their conscientious and dedicated help at various stages of the project. I would also like to thank my colleagues at Temple who supported me while completing the final version of the manuscript. Finally, I am grateful to the people at Blackwell who supported the publication of this book, in particular Stephan Chambers, Steve Smith, Nirit Simon, and Sarah Dancy, all of whom exhibited a depth of patience that meant more to me than they will ever know.

P. A.

Introduction: Diversity and Community

Philip Alperson

The idea of belonging to a community seems to most people something so basic as to constitute part of what it means to be a human being. The familiar meanings of the word "community" – fellowship, what is held in common with others, a body of people organized into a political or social unity, and so on – seem to appeal to the sort of ideals that ought to capture near universal and virtually automatic assent. Who, except in perversity, would deny that human beings ought to strive to live in cooperative, harmonious association with others with whom they have common interests and identities, that is, in community with them? Who would deny or at least want to deny having some sense of community?

But what exactly *is* a community? In its most general form, the concept of "community" refers to a state of being held in common, so that in the most general sense and from an ontological and structural point of view, community refers to a relation between things. As such, the idea of community can have application to an indefinitely large range of relationships. In ecological terms, for example, a community refers to any population grouping found living together in a particular environment or habitat. Within the realm of specifically human relations, however, we generally think of communities as groups of people living together bound by some set of reciprocal relationships. The kinds of relationships that may bind human communities are various. We may think of communities, for example, as constituted in geographical terms, or by adherence to certain social structures, with respect to beliefs, kinship relations, economic similarities, notions of identity or self-consciousness, religious, artistic, or cultural affiliations, and much more.

And, as we have already intimated, commonsense ideas of community generally involve another important dimension: we typically think of community as having a *normative* component, as involving both individual and common goods. In particular, we usually take it for granted that being a member of a community is good thing and that, ideally, communities serve to foster cohesion and harmonious relations among its members. That is one of the reasons why tradition is valued so highly in so many cultures.

But it does not take much reflection to move past this rough and ready notion of community to ask more difficult questions about the nature of human communities and the generally positive normative value commonly attributed to the idea, especially when we consider that communities are rarely homogeneous entities. How far, we might ask, do communities actually conform to the ideal of cooperative, harmonious associations? How are communities constituted? How are they preserved? How much change or assimilation can a community tolerate before it ceases to remain the self-same group? We may say that a community is a society linked by a common set of beliefs and values, but is it the case that communities must have shared norms, values, and interests? If so, what degree of synchronic and diachronic fluidity or individual autonomy, idiosyncrasy, privacy, and disassociation can or should communities tolerate in the context of their collective goals and ideals?

And if it is true, as many believe, that we are living in an age when there exist especially deep divisions and controversies concerning race, class, gender, sexual, ethnic, religious, and national identities, how do we define the meaning of community? How do we comprehend the conflicting norms, values, and modes of identification and allegiance of individual communities or particular microcommunities constitutive of larger communities, especially in the cases of communities whose affiliations may be as much a matter of voluntary association as, say, membership through kinship or family relationships? What specific challenges arise in the attempt to forge communities that are inclusive but that respect the distinctiveness and differences of particular groups that constitute the larger whole? Just how far can we understand the relationship between the apparently competing demands of community and diversity?

Diversity and Community: An Interdisciplinary Reader seeks to investigate the complexities of the idea, ideals, and dangers of community in contemporary society. The book examines general questions about the nature of community, the relation of individual and group identity to community norms and values, and the possibilities for cross-cultural understanding. It inquires into the self-understandings of diverse communities, including African, American, African American, Asian American, Native American, Latin American, Anglo- and Franco-Canadian, Canadian Aboriginal, Japanese, gay and lesbian, computer-mediated, and "counter-culture" communities. The book examines the influence of rhetoric, political style, and aesthetic and cultural production and values on communities. It probes the power relations constituted by and constitutive of race, ethnicity, class, gender, sexuality, nationalism, within and across communities. The book also explores the relations between community and certain forms of mental illness. In addition, it considers universities as communities as well as their role in community-making. It inquires into the possibility and challenges of creating and sustaining inclusive communities that respect individual and group differences. The book also takes seriously discontinuities, dislocations, and fissures in contemporary society and communities. The aim of the book is to increase understanding of the nature, value, complexity, and problems of communities in contemporary society in North American, global, and transnational contexts.

The essays in this book manifest a variety of disciplinary approaches, methodologies, and analytical styles of writing. Most of them can be read, however, against the backdrop of debates in political theory that pit proponents of liberal individualism against various versions of communitarianism. Liberalism emerged in the seventeenth and eighteenth centuries in reaction to notions of "organic community" associated with the ancient and feudal worlds. "Organic communities" were organized hierarchically, stratified by gender, class, and caste, and depicted as part of the natural order of the universe or divinely ordained. Within such "ascriptive" communities, the individual's place in the social order was fixed by birth, replete with specific familial duties, economic responsibilities, and political obligations. Prospects for social change were drastically constrained.

Liberalism took issue with notions of natural hierarchy, fixity of social relations, and preordained political obligations central to feudal conceptions of organic community. Liberal political theorists such as Thomas Hobbes[1] and Jean Jacques Rousseau[2] crafted radical accounts of a "state of nature" in which individuals pre-existed communal relations. On this view, individuals exist alone, as autonomous beings capable of providing for their own subsistence needs long before they enter into "social contracts" to create communal relations. In contrast to feudal claims about a natural hierarchy among human beings, liberal theorists posited equality among self-interested individuals, as well as natural rights to the earth's resources. The individual could combine energy, talent, and hard work with the world's resources to transform the conditions of existence. Thus the individual's social role and life prospects depended on individual achievements independent of society, rather than on some ascriptive status prescribed by an existing social order. Indeed, even the social order was a product of the individual's making. According to liberal theorists, the mechanism by which rights-bearing individuals enter into binding social relations – marriage, economic partnerships, employment agreements, geographic communities, or modes of political organization – is the covenant or contract. Since rational and equal individuals would only enter into voluntary agreements designed to foster their self-interest and improve their conditions, the social relations created by contracts are necessarily limited in scope. Political communities constituted by social contract must respect pre-existing rights of individuals and recognize the individual's right to consent to any proposed changes in the fundamental rules of the game. By conflating community with voluntary associations, liberalism created a very "thin" theory of community in which membership, responsibilities, and obligations were matters of individual choice. While majority rule was introduced as the decision rule, each individual retained the right to "exit" if the majority's decision violated the individual's sense of the permissible.

Since the 1970s, liberalism has been frequently criticized on the grounds that it rests on a flawed conception of human beings as autonomous, self-interested, competitive, atomistic individuals, an account underwritten tacitly or explicitly by adherence to a capitalist view of social and economic order. What is missing from the liberal view, its critics argue, is an understanding of the fundamental social dimension of human existence and the role that communities play in the constitution of individual identity and in contributing to the conditions under which freedom can be exercised. Communitarians, on the other hand, stress the importance of various forms of social life including the family, religious organizations, schools, and the manifold institutions of society on which the preservation of individual liberty depends. Communitarian theorists such as Alasdair MacIntyre, Michael Sandel, Charles Taylor, Jean Bethke Elsthain, and Amitai Etzioni generally argue that values constitutive of individual identity are rooted and embedded in the practices of communities.[3] Communitarians stress the importance of a sense of social responsibilities and duties within and across generations, community attachments, collective values, and public goods – some of the features of social organizations that often come under fire by liberals for their potential to constrain individual freedom.

Beyond the debates between liberals and communitarians, contemporary discussions concerning the nature of community have been enriched by feminist theorists, critical race theorists, postcolonial theorists, and queer theorists, who take issue with both liberal and communitarian accounts. Feminist theorists have argued that liberalism suffers from pervasive "masculinism." Although social contract theories posit an original equality among individuals, the abstract individuals who are party to the social contract are exclusively male, and the terms of political membership they construct through their social contract are restricted to men of a particular race and class. The autonomous individuals posited in the state of nature appear to be mature adults, who have never experienced the prolonged periods of dependency associated with infancy and childhood.[4] Not only are women's contributions to the creation of life and the sustenance of social relations omitted from social contract origin stories, but the grounds for consent to social relations such as sexual intercourse and marriage appear to be markedly gendered. Thus Carole Pateman has argued that the liberal social contract presupposed an oppressive sexual contract.[5] Feminist theorists have also pointed out that within contemporary liberal theories of community, rights of participation, privacy protections, individual freedoms, social welfare provisions, legal processes, institutional practices, and conceptions of public goods seem to be drawn disproportionately from affluent, white men's experiences.[6]

For feminist theorists who are committed to the political struggle to create gender-inclusive communities, the systemic defects of liberal accounts of community are inadequately addressed by communitarians. Although communitarians recognize the profound importance of intimacy, dependency, and interdependency to the constitution of the self and to the functioning of community, communitarians are accused of a failure to grapple with gender inequities that pervade intimate and communal relations. While families are valorized in communitarian discourses, feminist theorists have suggested that the rhetoric of familialism often romanticizes oppressive heterosexual relationships, calls for self-sacrifice on the part of mothers, blames working mothers for a range of social ills, and marginalizes single mothers and lesbian and gay parents. Communitarian claims that individual rights must be overridden for the social good far too frequently impose disproportionate burdens on women.[7]

Critical race theorists have also questioned romanticized conceptions of community that mask racial stratification and discrimination, as well as the pervasive role of racism in constituting dominant communities' self-understandings. Rather than treating slavery and racial segregation and oppression as "aberrations" from the dominant ideal of liberal equality, critical race theorists have argued that racism is constitutive of American liberalism, pervading the Constitution, legal statutes, court proceedings, definitions of community membership, distribution of rights and responsibilities, educational, employment, and economic opportunities, sexual relations, and popular culture.[8]

Postcolonial theorists have raised critical questions about the relationship between self-proclaimed liberal democratic communities and the colonization and continuing economic exploitation of the peoples of Africa, Asia, and Latin America. Notions of global community, such as the "Free World," the "American Alliance," or the "Commonwealth of Nations," suggest relations of equality and mutual respect as well as national rights of self-determination. But postcolonial critics have argued that these benign self-representations mask relations of economic, political, and, occasionally, military domination. As globalization increases social and economic connections across North and South and sustains movements across national boundaries, postcolonial theorists have subjected ongoing processes of incorporation and assimilation within increasingly multicultural communities to intensive scrutiny.[9]

Queer theorists have pointed out the "heteronormativity" of virtually all discussions of community. Whether the basic unit of community is taken to be the individual, as in liberal theories, or the family, as in communitarian theories, the basic unit of community is assumed to be heterosexual. Lesbians, gay men, bisexuals, and transsexuals have been written out of community theory in much the same way that they have been rendered invisible in contemporary communities. Rather than fostering inclusive communities, community discourses and contemporary laws tend to marginalize and exclude those who refuse the terms of the heterosexual social contract. To eliminate such systemic exclusion, queer theorists suggest, would require radical transformation of social institutions such as marriage and the family.[10]

These are only capsule accounts of very complex and often subtly presented theories, but even these brief accounts illuminate fundamental questions confronting contemporary communities. Thorny theoretical and practical issues arise concerning the domains and degrees of autonomy, dignity, and respect accorded to individuals in community, the range of governmental control to be exerted over community, the tensions between drives for ethnic and subgroup identity and the pressures for cultural homogenization from dominant groups within communities, the roles of social and religious groups, ethnic, national, and heritage groups, non-profit organizations, the press, schools, and colleges in community-making, and efforts to acknowledge and redress inequities in social and political opportunity and power related to race, gender, class, ethnicity, sexuality, geographical origin, aboriginal status, nationality, age, language, and ability. How can inclusive communities restructure access to education, health, welfare, voting rights, and participation across all levels of governance? How do divisions and differences within and across communities manifest themselves in the symbolic and cultural domain? How do such complicated questions about life in communities play out in the face of twenty-first-century developments in technology and mass media communications that coexist with increasing consumerism and urbanization and the growing inequality within and across nations?

Any viable conception of community in the twenty-first century must address these theoretical and practical concerns. In a global age can community still be understood as a grouping of people affiliating on the basis of shared goals? What weight does "affiliating" carry in this conception? What processes and boundaries does affiliation imply for the ground of belonging? Is community better understood as a social formation that respects the diversity of backgrounds, origins, interests, values, and beliefs of its diverse members in a transnational age? How are disputes to be resolved in ways that allow for the flourishing of the individual and the community simultaneously? What space is created for participation, democracy, creativity, innovation, and social change? How are non-members' demands for inclusion to be met in a world of radical inequality and shrinking natural resources? Questions such as these serve as the point of departure as contemporary thinkers interrogate ideal and idealized conceptions of community and diversity.

Community and its Contestations

However familiar and comforting the ideal of community is, it has come under scrutiny in recent years. In the opening essay of Part I, "Communities and Community: Critique and Retrieval," Jean Bethke Elshtain and Christopher Beem capture many of the basic elements of the idea of community in twenty-first-century America and spotlight several issues and tensions surrounding that conception. They begin with a familiar image from World War II films: the picture of the wartime crew composed of Americans from different ethnic, religious, or national backgrounds – LaRosa, O'Brien, Goldberg, Chavez, Olafsen, Mickweicz – united, fighting a common enemy. Elshtain and Beem are quick to point out the absent members from the grouping – African Americans and Japanese Americans – but, they argue, the dream of American community that lay behind the filmic cliché is clear enough: "America was different because it enabled people who were 'different' to nevertheless hold something in common: their identity as citizens, their aspirations as free men and women, their determination to make life better for their children."

And yet to many people nowadays, scenes such as the above seem quaint, naive, or worse. Weren't these men from different ethnic groups really pawns, co-opted in the service of an American, male, Waspish, racist, and imperialist hegemony – a reading that also explains the absence of African Americans and Japanese Americans? What has happened in the last sixty years such that we can look upon pictures like this with such cynicism?

Elshtain and Beem tell two stories which, taken together, help account for the current malaise. First, there is the story of the drive for homogeneity, sparked by the waves of immigration at the turn of the last century, which prompted such notables as John R. Commons, Walter Lippmann, and Woodrow Wilson to decry the increasingly diverse make-up of American society as dangerous. The driving force of the view was an unbridled universalism, a move toward "Americanization": one community, one nation indivisible. The second story is the current rise of what Elshtain and Beem refer to variously as localism, particularism, identity politics, and the excesses of the multicultural movement, and which they brand as reductive: "[W]e reduce ourselves (hence, our communities) to ethnic, racial, or gender categories that are dismissive of the possibility of reaching outside our own group. Oddly, in the name of diversity and multiculturalism, this rigidifying of difference types people by racial, ethnic, gender, or sexual orientation categories and says, in effect, that *these* are the differences that matter – not the quality of a person's intellect, the depth of a person's commitment to community, the scope of a person's understanding of the human condition, the dignity of a person's life, or the ill-dignity heaped on a person by an unjust social circumstance." The concatenation of these stories yields the particular brand of cynicism that Elshtain and Beem condemn, a "hermeneutics of suspicion" according to which "the entire thrust of American history has been to destroy our particular identities, even our dignity, in order to create some common identity."

Elshtain and Beem make no bones about what they take to be the corrosive effects of such cynicism on the fabric of American society. The public world increasingly becomes construed as a world of ulterior, particular, and competing interests. Along with that world-view comes a distrust of the governmental, educational, and familial institutions of civil society, a corresponding sense of isolation, and a decline in the participation in community life, especially with respect to involvement with political parties and social and civic associations. With this politics of resentment comes a general weakening of democratic civil society and a decline in social trust reflected in a range of evils: increased levels of drug abuse, crime, truancy, youth suicide, family breakdowns, and declining levels of education.[11]

What is to be done? Elshtain and Beem argue for a return to an ideal of community espoused in various ways by Martin Luther King, Jr., the social critic Randolph Bourne, and the philosopher Charles Taylor. The view seeks to strike a balance between the two poles of homogeneity and particularism. Elshtain and Beem write, "A political body that brings people together, creating a 'we,' but that enables these same persons to separate themselves and to recognize one another in and through their differences as well as in what they share in common – that was, and is, the great challenge."

How is this challenge to be met? Elshtain and Beem advance a local, "backyard" approach that stresses the importance of strengthening what they call the "mediating" and "virtue-building" institutions that sustain civil society: the informal and formal civic associations, family, neighborhood, and religious institutions. Elshtain and Beem acknowledge the importance of national action but, just as legal desegregation did not and could not in itself effect true integration – what King referred to as a change of the heart – what is needed is a strategy that will deal with the spiritual dimension of community.

Have Elshtain and Beem adequately characterized the apparently competing demands of community and diversity in our age? And if so, what exactly are the prospects for achieving a community that is not imposed from above but which emerges, in their words, "through the vibrant interplay of cultures, communities, and individuals under a capacious constitutional formula"?

The idea that communities can be understood as constituted primarily in terms of shared norms and values receives a sharply critical examination by Crispin Sartwell in his essay, "Community at the Margin." Sartwell begins by relating the unlikely but true story of the arrest of members of the Pagan motorcycle gang and members of a local Amish community who were cooperating in the purchase of cocaine for sale to Amish youth. We normally think of these two groups as quite distinct, but, Sartwell points out, they have much in common, not the least that they each reject central aspects of mainstream American culture.

This leads us to an important observation. Communities, Sartwell says, "are made by exclusions: by excluding others or by being excluded by others." Sartwell makes the point in connection with the formation of many kinds of community and group identities, from students gathering together on school grounds to taunt a classmate, to the distinction between "white" and "black" people or between hetero- and homosexuality, to the determination of which group is dominant and which is not. Communities are not based on the abstractions of shared beliefs, Sartwell argues, but on something more basic and more difficult to articulate, a deep level of communication that Sartwell calls "emitting noise in the right shape." That is true with respect to the dominant culture as well as communities at the margins, such as bikers, the Amish, devotees of S&M, and fans of Marilyn Manson. To the extent that conceptions of community miss the crucial formative role of exclusion and the non- or quasi-conceptual communicative aspects of community, they misconstrue how and why communities form and perpetuate themselves.

The modes of exclusion and communication are often quite complicated, Sartwell notes. The self-mutilations, Goth clothing, and gathering together of Marilyn Manson fans in mosh pits are ways in which the group invites the exclusion from what Sartwell calls "the dominant pseudo-community" – white, consumerist, middle-class America. But the exclusions do not stop there, for there can be exclusionary practices within the excluded group. In addition, the figure of Marilyn Manson himself arises out of a relation with the dominant culture's mass media and commercial distribution system, just as the Amish community identifies itself to a significant degree in terms of its rejection of features of contemporary mainstream life. So there exists, in effect, a reciprocity of exclusion between dominant and marginal communities. For its part, the dominant culture requires exclusion not only in order to construct itself but also because it requires the constructions of the marginal communities to keep itself alive. Sartwell draws the parallel with language: "The major language depends on its minor languages or slangs for life, even as it seeks in that same process to appropriate the satellite or colonized tongue. . . . The zones where the English language is alive, the zones that the English language depends on to stay alive, are the slangs of black America, of Jamaicans in London, of rednecks in the deep south, of sex workers, of Marilyn Manson fanatics, and so on." Furthermore, the reciprocity of exclusion between communities is always something of a moving target, since communities are constantly transforming themselves. For all these reasons, Sartwell is less than sanguine about the project of conceiving of communities as being established or as persevering in terms of a stable set of shared beliefs.

In "Impure Communities," Maria Lugones adopts a different perspective on the basis of which to critically examine the notion that communities need be – or ought to be – understood as requiring a clearly defined sense of commonality, shared values and norms, and convergent needs and desires, especially as they are institutionalized by such powerful entities and structures as the state, the family, the church, and the neighborhood. Such a view, she argues, runs the danger of crude dichotomizing as between the subjected and the non-subjected, the dominant and the subaltern, the pure and the impure. "Impure," Lugones argues, is a double-edged word. First, it impugns the integrity of those who fall under its rubric in that the term carries connotations of pollution, the perverted, the subordinate, the outcast, the tamed – in short everything one associates with the subaltern. In addition, it is used in a way that implies that the impure poses a threat to the common good insofar as the community embraces an ideal of homogeneity and unity (i.e., purity) and it puts pressure, often in an institutionalized way, on the "impure" to conform to the image of the pure.

Perhaps now is the time, Lugones argues, to advance a rehabilitated notion of impure communities. The idea that communities need to be pure (in the sense of homogeneous and fixed) is at odds with the concrete nature of human subjectivity in daily life: its incompleteness, its fragility, its evanescence, in general the notion that people exist more as projects than as fixed entities, as persons with a complicated "fleshy and problematic interrelationality," as "possible beings whose possibility lies in the uncertain creation of a loosely concerted intersubjectivity." Further, from a social point of view, there is much to be valued in the idea of impurity insofar as it carries with it the idea of resistance and liberatory behavior, what Lugones calls an "against the grain sociality." Community, on Lugones's view, should "be sensitive like a spider web is sensitive to communicative motives in different spatialities, tonalities, and expressive means."

Another perspective on the dynamic nature of identities is taken by Chuck Dyke and Carl Dyke in their essay, "Identities: The Dynamical Dimensions of Diversity." Dyke and Dyke seek to sketch out a general theoretical model, which they see as aligned with certain trends in feminist theory, on which the concepts of diversity and individual and group identity can be understood. On their view, the larger categories of race, gender, ethnicity, nationality, and sexuality, are best understood as dimensions within a dynamic system – a system of histories. Individuals are dimensionally variable, social systems are variably diverse, and in social settings, the variabilities of individuals and groups are dynamically interactive.

Dyke and Dyke acknowledge that in human affairs there is no a priori way of determining what will be a significant dynamic dimension. Self-identity, they argue, is a consequence of the interaction of one's self-conception and one's conception of others, which is to say that self-identity is an emergent phenomenon, understandable in the context of its dynamic history and situation. For these reasons, human affairs do not always seem to develop in linear, law-like ways.

But neither is society bereft of recognizable patterns and families of patterns. Dyke and Dyke suggest that a fractal, dynamic, and nonlinear model, illustrated by the structure and dynamics of the Mandelbrot set in mathematics, can shed light on the dynamics of identities, community, and diversity. The dimensions of social space, they argue, are not static "types" or the additive results of "independent variables" but, rather, "more or less stable, more or less abiding occupations of bio-social space." Furthermore, social dynamics are embodied – involving senses of the self, good and bad, distinction, and so on – which results in a nonlinear system of pushes and pulls: "Better by far for dealing with this situation than the traditional image of static classes is an image of multiple dimensioned space through which people are pulled by a web of allegiances, belongings, and identities that are now more, now less important to the patterns of their lives." Indeed, one of the familiar strategies for the control of social boundaries is precisely to "squeeze" the interactive field of identities into a single dimension: "We are told 'You're only a child; a woman; a savage; an old fart; a peasant.'" Herein lies one of the dangers of too easy a notion of identity politics and of the idea that diversity can be construed as a simple matter of accommodating Platonically fixed identities.

D. A. Masolo also contributes to the examination of the ways in which people, especially in the early twenty-first century, can be members of different communities simultaneously. In his essay, "From Village to Global Contexts: Ideas, Types, and the Making of Communities," Masolo starts by identifying a traditional way of thinking about community according to which the identities of persons are "determined, biologically and socially, by some assumed characteristics which they share with other members of the group to which they belong." He illustrates the traditional idea of community with an account of the community in which he grew up, the Luo of Kenya. The Luo, Masolo says, have shared a unified set of beliefs and behavior patterns rooted in kinship relations that more or less fixed the individual's sense of identity within the community and provided the basis for norms of behavior, socio-political and economic relations, central notions of justice, and other regulative principles.

However, Masolo points out, owing largely to changes in the political economy, changes in immigration patterns, and technological developments since World War II, this "fixed" notion of community has been supplemented in Luo society – as it has been elsewhere in the world – by a more fluid and "expressive" notion of community and changes in the ways in which communities are constituted within and across cultures.[12] We have seen, for example, the rise of communities bound together by such interests as environmental protection, animal rights protection, and human rights interests, as well as concerns for issues regarding sexism, race, gender, disability, and age. Contemporary communities, on Masolo's view, are best conceived as dialogically, not ontologically constituted. They are invented, dynamic, frequently transnational embodiments grounded in the movement of discourses that frame common global, political, and ethical interests. The older forms of community are not supplanted by the newer forms but they are significantly affected by the forms that coexist with them. The result is a changing array of new political roles of community and of communities, a changing landscape that, as Masolo illustrates, carries the potential for both liberatory and oppressive policies, institutions, and behaviors. Individuals can belong to multiple communities simultaneously by moving between different people and forms of discourse commensurate with their interests and participative roles in institutional formations. In the face of these complications, Masolo holds out the hope that one can participate in and carry out responsibilities in simultaneous communities in a compatible way – that one can be both a patriot and a cosmopolitan.

Lewis R. Gordon rounds out the contributions to Part I with further reflections on the concrete nature of social relations with a consideration of an ethical and social issue that he believes to have received inadequate attention in contemporary debates: the matter of obligation across generations. In "Obligations Across Generations: A Consideration in the Understanding of Community Formation," Gordon takes contemporary ethical thought to task for what he sees as its abstractions and oversimplifications concerning the relation between the self and the community. Following the French philosopher Maurice Merleau-Ponty, Gordon chides contemporary Western accounts of social and ethical life for valuing logical rigor over the contradictions and paradoxes of life. Modern philosophical approaches have been especially bedeviled by what Gordon calls the "valorization of an independent, self-contained 'I'" and by the radical eclipse of the importance of past and future relations. As a result, contemporary accounts have dropped out of the equation what Gordon calls the "binding" force of moral relations among human beings in community, a force that he associates with the religious dimension of human experience.

In this connection, Gordon draws attention to the central role that the notion of obligation plays in the formation of communities, pointing out that the notion of obligation has both backward and forward dimensions. Generations connect over time, Gordon argues. The presence of one's ancestors makes itself felt in the traditions that are passed on to current generations, helping to frame what counts as rightful and wrongful conduct. "Community does not stop simply at those who stand around us, but also through those who have preceded us," Gordon writes. He illustrates the force of these observations with reference to philosophical views of the Akan and the Manianga, who have an especially rich account of the network of relations between the world of ancestors and the present. The Akanian and Maniangan world-views capture the realities of social existence with greater clarity than their Western counterparts perhaps in part just because of their recognition of particularity, as opposed to what Gordon sees as the universalist tendencies of Western philosophical thought. But in the end, Gordon is less concerned to stress the differences between African and European philosophical views than to argue for what the African views bring to light, the applicability of the notion of obligation across generations to human social existence generally. Obligations across generations bind our ancestors to us just as we are bound to our descendants, a point that must be borne in mind when considering the depth of the notion of community as it manifests itself in human affairs.

Community, Constitutive Identities, and Resisting Subjects

As we have seen, the manner in which individual and group identities are constituted in the context of the diversity of contemporary communities is a matter of great theoretical and practical importance. The essays in Part II explore these issues from the perspective of several identifiable voices, including representations from gays and lesbians, African Americans, Native Americans, Anglo-Canadians, French Canadians, Aboriginal Canadians, women, the family, and people suffering from two sorts of socio-psychological afflictions: melancholia and sociopathy. These essays examine a wide variety of factors that come into play when individuals and groups develop and assert their self-identities and endeavor to establish their positions within the larger societies of which they are constitutive parts.

In "Citizenship or Transgression?: Dilemmas of the US Movement for Lesbian/Gay Rights," Arlene Stein examines the intricate relationship between different conceptions of lesbian and gay identity and their political consequences. Stein begins by noting Michel Foucault's argument that the idea of understanding homosexuals as a distinct, definable, and recognizable category of people is itself a construction, emerging with the development of socio-sexual medical categories. Three decades ago, Stein says, gay liberationists adopted a "transgressive" stance against the rigid distinction between heterosexuality – presumed to be normal and natural – and homosexuality, hoping thereby to gain a measure of sexual freedom. Gradually, however, the American gay rights movement adopted a "politics of citizenship," reasserting the categorical distinction, becoming more visible as a distinct interest group, seeking, and in some measure achieving, civil rights on a strong analogy with civil rights demands on the basis of race.

It is now the conservative movement in the United States that has taken up the transgressive position, arguing that the distinction between homosexuality and heterosexuality is indeed mutable insofar as membership in one or the other category is a matter of choice, "a behavior, not a way of being," as Stein puts it. But on the conservative reading, the lesson to be taken from this state of affairs is quite different from what the gay liberationists had been envisioning. If homosexuality is conceived *as* a matter of choice, as a "lifestyle," the homosexual claim for civil rights is undermined. On the conservative view, gay demands for civil rights just *are* the claims of a special interest group, a ploy for "special rights." Moreover, the conservatives claim, the lifestyle being put on offer by homosexuals is aberrant, perverse, and dangerous to society especially when private behavior is brought into the public arena for display. So, the conservatives argue, while the boundaries of homosexuality and heterosexuality are not fixed in nature, so to speak, they can – and should – be asserted politically and patrolled.

Stein traces the way in which these theoretical positions were played out in a small logging town ("Timbertown") in Oregon when a Christian conservative organization, The Oregon Citizens Alliance, sought to change the town's charter in an effort to prohibit the dangerous "special rights" which, they said, gays were seeking. Interestingly, organized opposition to the charter proposal did not seek to undermine the conservative position that homosexuality is unnatural, abnormal, and a perversion. Opponents instead adopted an "ethnic" model of homosexuality, preserving the idea of rigid boundaries, arguing that homosexuality is a natural disposition (i.e., one is born gay) rather than a choice, and promoting the idea that the offending behavior was, as a matter of fact and practice, private behavior, posing no threat to the townsfolk. The ethnic defense proved politically ineffectual. The measure was enacted into law by the voters of Timbertown, as were similar measures in other communities throughout the state (though they were later declared unconstitutional by the courts).

The "ethnic" line of opposition, Stein argues, is not only bound to be political ineffectual. It fails, on her view, to face squarely the fact that the borders are, after all, messy and unstable, and in that sense homosexuality *does* pose a threat to heterosexuality conceived as a fixed category. If gay, lesbian, bisexual, and transgendered people are to come to grips with their sense of communal identity and their place in the context of other communities, they must adopt a more radicalized way of thinking and talking about socio-sexual categories, a way that does justice to the ideals of both the politics of citizenship and the politics of transgression. That view, Stein argues, embraces a deeper vision of equality and is more in accord with the position of members of sexual minorities who are, she argues, simultaneously insiders and outsiders.

In "Diversity, Inequality, and Community: African Americans and People of Color in the United States," J. Blaine Hudson presents a frank and disturbing account of the origins, development, and maintenance of an American racial state that stands in stark contrast to commonly held views of the American "melting pot" or the American "mosaic." "The American 'racial state,'" Hudson argues, "was created neither entirely by accident nor entirely by conscious design – but was the inevitable, although perhaps unforeseen, consequence of the origins of the United States as a European 'settler colony.'" Hudson offers a capsule story of the forcible colonization and near extinction of Native Americans and the slavery of African Americans by means of which the interests of primarily white, male, Christian, propertied, Northern Europeans were secured and protected. The racial state manifested its values and controls in many arenas, including but not limited to the sphere of defined rights, strictures on who could be born a citizen and who could become a citizen, and educational and economic opportunities.

In this context, the "marker" of skin color has been of signal importance. As Hudson points out, a generation after the end of slavery in the "north," free people of color still suffered an anomalous and degraded status, especially with respect to political rights and economic opportunities. Segregation insured that even as African Americans were able to build communities with their own institutions, infrastructure, social systems and social relations, those communities were kept in a subordinated and distanced position relative to the dominant white society – a prototype that would serve to define relations with other people of color, especially Mexican Americans and Asians. In this way, Hudson writes, the United States, "having invented itself as a 'racial state,' chose to remain a 'racial state' even after the virtual extinction of the Native Americans and the end of slavery."

This history has had a telling effect on the meaning of community for people of color and for African Americans in particular. "Fourth world" people – non-European people living within the geographical confines of former white settler colonies – are both visible and invisible: visible to the extent that they can be identified with respect to the marker of skin color, they remain invisible to the dominant group in terms of social, political, and economic status. To be sure, the removal of legal barriers has had beneficial results for some people of color in certain respects, but, Hudson argues, when the data regarding social and economic opportunity are examined closely, it is clear that a deep level of racial inequality, exclusivity, and disparity of opportunity remains for the disproportionate number of African Americans and people of color in the United States. In some respects, the situation seems even worse: many young African Americans, Hudson points out, experience the same limiting conditions of their parents and grandparents who grew up in "old" segregated communities, but they lack the cultural rootedness that the older society provided. There is a very deep "culture of poverty" abroad in the land that is characterized by anger, bitterness, and frustration.

This background informs debates among African Americans about the relative merits of assimilation, integration, and voluntary segregation. The implicit "racial covenant" – a silent but broad consensus of white Americans to defend white privilege and maintain racial inequality and discrimination in favor of whites – remains the single most formidable barrier to the creation of community in America, Hudson argues. In the face of this admittedly dismal account, however, Hudson still manages to hold out hope for the creation of a pluralistic, color-blind, and race-neutral social order, one that makes room for cultural particularity within the context of a suitably broadened sense of what it means to be an American. The ideal is difficult, but not impossible, Hudson says.

As Hudson observes, colonial domination had crucial consequences for all people of color in the United States. In his essay, "Renewing American Indian Nations: Cosmic Communities and Spiritual Autonomy," Duane Champagne explores the impact that the colonial order has had on the senses of self and community and the fundamental organizing structures of Native American communities.

Champagne points out that early European accounts of North American Indian life had characterized Native American communities as egalitarian and consensual, an image that had considerable influence among the French *philosophes* and other political and social thinkers, from the framers of the Bill of Rights to Marx and Engels. The view carried some important insights about Native American society, though the picture that was promulgated was crude and was typically presented in the context of evolutionary models that relegated Native American societies to early or "primitive" status, thus making way for another familiar story, that of the "vanishing Indian." The truth of the matter, however, is that indigenous communities have not gone away. Indeed, in some countries, such as Canada, New Zealand, and Australia, Native communities have strongly reasserted their presence, especially in connection with land rights claims and political recognition.

At the same time, it is undeniable that traditional ways of life of Native American communities continue to undergo tremendous pressure from within and without. To understand the vitality and the fissues within Native American communities and the relations between Native communities and non-Native communities, one must first come to grips with the overarching world-view within which notions of Native American culture, community, and institutional structures are situated. Acknowledging differences among various Native American communities, Champagne characterizes the basic view as encompassing a vision of a universe of people living in deep continuity with both natural and sacred domains. Social relations and groupings are ordained by the organizing force of the universe, the Great Spirit, through the intermediary of tricksters, seers, and spirit beings in nature. Human beings situate themselves in the orderly context of the myriad forms of spirit beings in the universe, including plants, animals, and earthly and heavenly spirits.

That is to say, the idea of community among American Indians extends not only to relations with other human beings but to all the spirit beings in the universe; and proper action is understood in terms of the preservation of harmony and order within the cosmic community. To take an important example, animals give themselves up as food for human beings on the implicit understanding that human beings treat them with respect, honor them with rituals, and take no more than is necessary for survival. Within the Native view, human beings are accorded a considerable degree of autonomy within the cosmic order. As Champagne puts it: "An individual has a sacred right as an autonomous power being to fulfill his or her sacred life tasks as long as his or her actions conform to the rules of social and cosmic order, which, if violated, would bring retribution from angry power beings upon the social community and the transgressor." In accordance with the respect given to individual autonomy and cosmic order, group decisions are arrived at through discussion and consensus among individual community members, including women and elders who, in many Native lineages and clans, hold special sway in facilitating consensus. The result is a community in which decision-making is decentralized, egalitarian, and processual. (Champagne points out that the word "caucus" was originally an Algonkian expression.) Local groups and lineages similarly have degrees of autonomy and decisions among social groups are generally arrived at by consensus.

The colonial era put many of these traditional features of Native community under extreme stress. The fur trade, for example, undermined the covenant relation with animals insofar as hunting and trapping were put increasingly in the nexus of market demand. Moreover, as the fur trade expanded and stocks were depleted, American Indians were forced to become more specialized, spending more time hunting and curing. When the fur and buffalo trades collapsed toward the end of the nineteenth century, American Indian communities were left largely impoverished, being forced to sell their worldly goods and settle on reservations. Other relations between colonizers and Native Americans left their marks on American Indian communities. Colonial officials found the decentralized decision-making structures frustrating, preferring to conduct trade relations with young men rather than deal with women and elders. At the same time reservation life has diminished the political and economic influence of young men. The introduction of Christianity and American assimilatory education introduced beliefs and codes of behavior that are at odds with the traditional world-view. The secular and centralized forms of political governance urged by the Bureau of Indian affairs often conflict with the consensually and spiritually oriented social and political traditions of Native communities. In addition, in part out of political necessity, new forms of pan-Indian identification have spread in Native communities. Out of such conditions arise the complex of identities and dislocations among reservation and urban Native American communities in the twenty-first century. The continuing challenge for Native communities, Champagne argues, is to renew cultural and institutional relations in the face of global economic and social pressures and to do this in a way that will preserve Native values that have traditionally formed the basis of Native community and autonomy.

The essays by J. Blaine Hudson and Duane Champagne underscore the role that nationalism has played in the formation and nature of communities in the United States. Canada presents another, and an unusually rich, example of the intersection of cultural, constitutional, political, and national matters in the construction of communities. The current situation in Canada is discussed by Frank Cunningham in his essay, "Nations and Nationalism: The Case of Canada/Quebec."

Central to the Canadian conundrum is the ongoing conflict between Canadian federalists and Quebec nationalists. In a 1995 referendum held in Quebec, the Parti Québecois (PQ) nearly won a mandate to begin sovereignty negotiations with the Canadian Federal government. The P.Q. lost by a narrow 49 percent to 51 percent margin, with 93 percent of those eligible voting. As Cunningham observes, it remains as unclear now as it was in 1995 what a PQ victory in the referendum would have meant. Among other things, there is no provision in the Canadian Constitution for secession, Aboriginal peoples who claim a large portion of Quebec territory declared before the referendum that they would not leave the Canadian federation – raising the question of how secession would have been enforced against the wishes of the Aboriginal peoples in Quebec – and a sizable number of non-English/non-French speaking Quebeckers had voted against sovereignty. The Federal Parliament introduced legislation designating Quebec as a "distinct society," giving it, along with other Canadian regions, certain constitutional veto powers; but this move has hardly repaired the fractures that persist within and across Canada and Quebec.

Cunningham traces the dizzying overlay of actors and factors at play: the various entities or groups that might lay claim to being regarded as nations, the array of provinces and regional associations in the country, the ethnic diversity of Canada and the Federal policy of multiculturalism, the Canadian Charter of Rights, the interests and activities of business and labor organiza tions, political parties, social movements, the press, Aboriginal communities and spokespersons, the efforts of "ordinary" citizens throughout the coun- try, and the failure of two attempts (the 1987 Meech Lake Accord and the 1992 Charlottetown Accord) by Federal and Provincial leaders to negotiate a solution to the impasse, both of which were brought down in part as a result of the concerted action of Aboriginal people.

In the face of this daunting backdrop, one might easily despair of conceiv- ing a mode of community that could accommodate the history and com- plexities of the Canadian situation. Cunningham defends the view, however, that, with certain qualifications, the land of Canada can be understood from a "tri-nationalist" orientation as being composed of three national group- ings – a Franco nation, an Anglo nation, and an ensemble of Aboriginal na- tions – rather than from the more usual bi-national Franco/Anglo divide. The tri-national approach is both descriptive and political. From a descrip- tive point of view, Cunningham in effect construes Canada as a nation of national communities. From a political point of view, the national approach offers promise in framing a solution to the deep problems facing the country. The tri-national perspective, Cunningham writes, "would tap popular sym- pathy for Native peoples, attempt to reinforce it by highlighting the way that Aboriginal peoples have legitimate, if largely thwarted, national aspirations, and try to effect a union of Quebeckers and Canadians from the rest of the country to address with First Nation and Inuit peoples the moral and territo- rial problems they face in common."

In "Love, Care, and Women's Dignity: The Family as a Privileged Commu- nity," Martha Nussbaum draws attention to the nexus between women and families and, in particular, the roles that the family constructs for women. As Nussbaum points out, the family is itself a form of community. In that context, women are traditionally givers of love and care. As such, they are seen to embody moral virtues such as concern and responsiveness to others' needs and they are associated with moral abilities such as the ability to rea- son resourcefully about ways to meet needs in particular situations. At the same time, Nussbaum points out, the family has been an arena for the op- pression of women, where women have been the object of domestic violence, marital rape, and many other degradations and violations of human dig- nity, and in which women have not been treated as equals in full personhood but rather as instruments to the desires and needs of others. The family, there- fore, reflects and perpetuates the values and conditions of society at large and it merits public scrutiny.

How is one best to understand, then, the nature of the family as a form of community, valuing on the one hand the distinctive virtues and abilities of women, while, on the other, providing critical scrutiny that will enable all who are a part of it to flourish? On Nussbaum's view, the family is not a "natural" unit whose form is invariant in all cultures. It is, rather, a creation of laws and institutions and the state has a stake in monitoring how it functions. Nussbaum notes the criticism, advanced by some, that analyses based on liberal theories of justice wrongly characterize the family as an assemblage of self-interested individuals and do not provide room for the traditional female virtues of love and care and their associated moral abilities. She argues, however, that a liberal approach that focuses on the needs of individuals is best suited to provide a framework in which to understand the structures, dangers, and positive potential of the family.

Instead of adopting a proceduralist liberal account, however, Nussbaum advances what she calls a "human capability" approach to the family. On Nussbaum's view, it is reasonable to think that a society ought to promote central human capabilities. The family is concerned in particular with several of these: life, health, bodily integrity, dignity and non-humiliation, associational liberties, emotional health, the opportunity to form meaningful relationships with other people, the ability to participate in politics, the ability to hold property and work outside the home, the ability to think for oneself and form a plan of life. Public policy should be oriented toward the institution of the family in such a way as to ensure that the family can promote these capabilities. And Nussbaum is insistent that the capabilities that must be examined are the capabilities of individuals. The family as such has no moral standing. Nussbaum writes, "It is not enough to ask whether the family promotes a diffuse and general kind of affection and solidarity. We must ask in detail what it does for the capabilities of each of its members." This is an especially important matter for women, Nussbaum argues, who have often been deprived of the basic goods of life on the grounds that they are parts of a supposedly "organic" entity rather than existing as political subjects in their own right. Nussbaum deals at length with several theoretical and practical applications and consequences of her view.

Osborne Wiggins and Michael A. Schwartz draw the essays of Part II to a close by drawing attention to the intensely personal dimensions of relating to other human beings in community. In their contribution, "Community and Society, Melancholy and Sociopathy," they offer a stark reminder that at the level of everyday life there are some people for whom the experience of the social bonds of community is more a threat than a means of sustenance and affirmation.

Wiggins and Schwartz begin with a particular distinction between "community" and "society." On their rendering, a "community" is a relatively small, non-voluntary form of human association into which one is born and expected to remain for one's entire life, and in which one shares a "nomos" or common set of values and beliefs with other members. Families and traditional churches are examples of communal organizations. It is an important feature of such organizations that one's roles and actions are transparent in the sense that they recognizable and consistent with the nomos of the group and that if one performs several roles, these, too, should be seen to be consistent with the nomos. The sense of belonging one may feel in a community is a direct result of a pervasive, if unspoken, agreement about the kinds of behavior that are expected and understood within the group.

A "society," on the other hand, is a relatively large assemblage of different groups that serve individual interests. Membership in constitutive groups is voluntary, the individual always being free to leave a group when, for example, the group no longer serves his or her needs. There is no single nomos that holds the groups of a society together, with the exception perhaps of the principle of non-interference among groups. Because it is understood that members join groups for particular interests, there is no demand that one's "whole person" be involved with the group: one is free to "compartmentalize" one's life with respect to the group. If one seeks integration of oneself, one does it on one's own. Finally, because the groups in a society are based on individual interests rather than overarching values or beliefs, societies tend toward the toleration of nomic pluralism.

What does it take to live well in communities and societies? Wiggins and Schwartz answer the question by focusing on the direct experience of people participating in these socialities and, even more particularly, on ways in which the self may be related to the social roles it performs as people engage in action. On Wiggins's and Schwartz's view, an individual may identify with states of perceiving, valuing, and willing that are prescribed by a given role along a continuum that goes from full role-identification on the one hand to full role-distance on the other. Living well in communities and societies normally calls upon people's abilities to live flexibly in this regard: appreciating both the stability and the sense of belonging afforded by communities and the freedom, anonymity, and variety offered by societies, and being able to find satisfaction in performing various roles while maintaining a sense of distance from them and having the ability to move from role to role as required. Such an individual, they write, "would therefore need an inner flexibility in his or her personality so that he or she could be 'different selves' in different situations while still maintaining a sufficiently coherent sense of personal identity."

There are, however, individuals who lack this kind of flexibility. One type – the *typus melancholicus* – exhibits excessive dedication to (overidentification with) particular norms and roles, is firmly rooted in an idealized past, has an intolerance of ambiguity, a strong need for structure, and is easily agitated. Such a person requires for his or her well-being familiarity, manageability, and predictability. He or she might flourish in a community but is at great risk in society with its pluralism of values, beliefs, and roles. The *sociopathic* personality, on the other hand, has little attachment for (underidentifies with, has extreme distance from) the roles he or she performs; they may be performed well but they are done purely out of self-interest. Such a person typically has a high threshold for emotional stimulation, little capacity for emotional attachment to others, and prefers to move from one role to another. These traits make living in a society easier for the sociopath at least insofar as the sociopath can pretend to conform to changing norms and roles. Life in a community, however, becomes difficult to the extent that communities call upon stable behavior.

These personality "types" are, of course, indicative of the far ends of a continuum. Most people will fall in between the two poles. But Wiggins's and Schwartz's essay serves as a cautionary tale as against romanticized notions of community or diversity and against idealized conceptions of the benefits they may be said to provide for people "in general." For some people, living in communities or in societies can become unbearable. As Wiggins and Schwartz say, "community is no unalloyed good, just as life in society can prove to be destructive."

Community, Culture, and Education

The bonds that link us in community and the differences that divide us do not come to us, nor do they exert their sway, *ex nihilo*. They are the product of concrete existences and particular histories. They are also deeply embedded in the culture by means of which we make sense of ourselves and of others. As commentators from Homer, Plato, and Aristotle, to Hegel, Marx, Foucault, and Bourdieu have noted, the arts and other forms of cultural production play an important role in reflecting and affecting the ways in which human beings understand themselves and relate to one another. The essays in Part III address the question of the relationship between diversity and community and human activity in the symbolic and cultural domain.

In "The Role of Art in Sustaining Communities," Marcia Muelder Eaton asks whether the arts can reasonably be thought to sustain communities. As Eaton observes, there is a lot of loose talk on the subject, especially from arts advocates who, understandably enough, try to explain why artistic and cultural institutions, including arts education programs, should be defended and supported, especially in times of limited financial resources or when particular artists or institutions come under attack for what is perceived as vapid, malicious, cynical, immoral, pornographic, subversive, or otherwise harmful performances or works. What is one to make of the familiar claims that the arts express fundamental values of a society, that they encourage virtu-

ous or ethically valuable behavior, or that they promote sympathetic understanding and respect for others? And even if a positive claim can be made out
for the arts, is the good work they do in any way distinctive? Or do we simply
say that art – like any other form of activity – can be put to good or ill purposes?

Eaton frames her answer in terms of a particular theory of the nature of
art according to which something is a work of art if and only if the thing
(typically an object or an event) presents intrinsic properties available to in-
spection that reward aesthetic experience as understood within a particular
culture. On the basis of this view, Eaton argues that art can indeed contribute to the maintenance (the sustainability) of a community. The distinctive
kind of contribution that art makes in this regard consists in the way that art
supports one necessary feature of sustainable communities, namely that "in
a sustainable community, individual members are aware of other members
and take some responsibility for their well-being." Art is able to contribute to
this aspect of sustainable communitiy in virtue of two activities that are essential to the practice of art: creation and contemplation. Artists generally
create for audiences. Similarly, audiences engage in appreciation and descriptive and evaluative commentary that assumes an implicit relationship
with others. In these ways, the fundamental activities of art contribute to
the creation and sustenance of community, a shared sense of responsibility,
and "the good of the commons."

These are features of art that may be predicated at a very general level.
Eaton goes on to say that some works of art are likely to be more successful
than others in the creation of sustainable communities. In particular, good
art – by which Eaton means art that sustains attention – is likely to provide
deeper benefits because it can sustain more than mere pleasure. She writes,
"Group contemplation and discussion requires that members enter into relationship with the objects and with each other. When this is combined with
the ways in which artworks present the shared ideas, values, myths, metaphors, and feelings that characterize flourishing communities, sustainability
is enhanced." Of course, it is true that art can also be put to harmful and
oppressive purpose. Further, the works that carry particular meaning in one
culture may not carry the same meaning in others. But, at its best and under
the right conditions, art can function in the manner that Leo Tolstoy had
put so forcefully, as a means by which artists and members of audiences who
experience a work can come to feel the same way and be united thereby in
community. This is no small thing. As Eaton puts it, "If communities cannot
stand in the face of too much cynicism, neither can they stand in the face of
too little hope."

Marcia Eaton's analysis is concerned with specifically artistic aspects of
culture, by which she understands artworks with the capacity to reward
a particular sort of contemplation: contemplation of intrinsic aesthetic

properties. She is careful to include mass art in her analysis. But it is also true, of course, that cultural products can convey meaning and figure into the construction of community quite apart from their status as art objects. In "Images of Community in American Popular Culture, " Eileen John and Nancy Potter take up the question of the meaning of images in popular culture considered more generally as bearers of meaning. John and Potter are concerned with the way that images in television, radio, film, and so on, display the life of communities, either by actually creating communities (as when, say, an audience arises for *Prairie Home Companion*) or by referring to or symbolizing the features of communities (as for example when a television sitcom represents a particular fictionalized or real community). Images in popular culture are especially effective ways to display the life of communities in part because of their ability to engage our desires and emotions by means of both simple and complex images. On John's and Potter's view, images of popular culture "function as mnemonic devices for complex ideological structures – as abstract reminders of our attempts to organize and evaluate our fundamentally messy social existence."

A second point to note is that John and Potter are concerned to examine the display of the life of communities in popular culture from a particular normative position. They are critical of both liberal and communitarian accounts of community. They are more sympathetic to a position articulated by the political theorist, Chantal Mouffe, and others, which involves a pluralist recognition of different conceptions of the public good and a radical democratic attention to the power relations that play across different social positions and contexts. John and Potter write: "Our approach to specific images of community will reflect the concerns of pluralism and radical democracy through our examination of the boundaries, exclusions, hierarchies, and visions of normality held within these images. Do these images help us find some interesting middle ground between the extremes of celebrating the benefits of communities and exposing their oppressive potential? Do these images open up spaces for us to play with and, perhaps, flaunt the power of the dichotomous subjectivities and oppositional world-views that we encounter?"

When John and Potter turn to the images, they make a number of interesting discoveries. They examine several varieties of popular culture: two network television serial shows (*Seinfeld* and *Ellen*), two films (*Waiting to Exhale* and *Boyz N the Hood*), a special news broadcast (on Princess Diana's funeral), a radio and MTV call-in show (*Loveline*), and a public radio serial show (*Prairie Home Companion*). They identify various kinds of community represented or created in these shows: communities of ideas, of crisis, of memory, of home, of transience, and outlaw communities. They also find that these shows can have destabilizing effects on audiences, opening up some possibilities for community-building, closing down others, and introducing an element of affective ambiguity into the consciousness of audiences. In these and other ways, John and Potter argue, images of community in popular culture can support the ideals of a radical pluralist society.

Yet another way in which culture can contribute to the construction of communities is by means of narratives that seek to introduce people to peoples at distant geographical or cultural removes. Duane Champagne, in his essay, discussed the role that colonial narratives played in the imagination of Native American community for Europeans and American colonists. Gary Y. Okihiro provides an examination of narrative accounts of San Francisco and New York Chinatowns in his essay, "Virtual Communities: Chinatowns Made in America."

Okihiro examines two accounts that are emblematic of the way in which the idea of Chinatown has been represented in America. The first of these is Will Irwin's text that accompanied Arnold Genthe's book of photographs of San Francisco's Chinatown prior to the great earthquake that virtually destroyed the district in 1906. The account characterizes the residents and community of Chinatown as at once alien and all too human, but in both cases a "racialized other." The Chinese man is represented as both woman (the courteous, "shy," and "feminine" domestic) and man (the gambling, opium-smoking criminal). The Chinese woman is described both as both a "lily woman" and a "soiled" prostitute. The community of Chinatown itself is portrayed as clannish and inscrutable, except insofar as one detects, beneath the veneer of courtesy, a hellish maze of tunnels, a "network of deviance" and crime. In Gwen Kinkead's description of New York's Chinatown, written nearly a century later, the streets are crooked, the smells off-putting, and the community is characterized by an "oyster-like impenetrability" by the lights of which white people are dismissed as barbarians. Beyond that, what is remarkable about the community to the outsider is the fanatical devotion to making and hoarding money, often by means of the drug trade, and the inhumane treatment of captive migrants and workers.

Okihiro notes several things about these "textual" and "virtual" Chinatowns. There is, of course, the regressive, formulaic, orientalist core of these accounts, the main features of which will sound familiar to many white outsiders. Okihiro writes: "Chinatowns and their residents are racialized, gendered, and sexualized simultaneously in their prominence and isolation, transcendence and immanence, surfaces and interiors, attractions and repulsions, passion and materialism, familiarity and distance. Those apparent polar positions are collapsed and confused in this impenetrable, contradictory, anomalous place and people."

At the same time, however, the social construction of Chinatowns has been deployed by a range of interested parties both outside and inside Chinatown for material gain. Okihiro notes the prostitution, gambling, and opium-smoking rings run by Chinese gangs in partnership with whites in late nineteenth-/early twentieth-century Chinatowns in San Francisco and New York City as well as the influx of tourist dollars that continues to flow into Chinatowns across the country. Okihiro points out that after the San Francisco earthquake, whites and Chinese merchants alike supported the rebuilding of Chinatown with American caricatures of Chinese architecture consciously designed to create a clearly recognizable "oriental" city whose future as a nationally recognized tourist destination would be assured. These people, it seems, were well aware of Okihiro's general observation that "social constructions have material reality."

The notion that communities can be constructed "virtually" takes on deepened meaning in the age of the computer, which, by most accounts, has resulted not only in new forms of communication but also new forms of social organization. This point is explored by Samuel Oluoch Imbo in his essay, "Villages, Local and Global: Observations on Computer-Mediated and Geographically Situated Communities." Imbo begins his essay with some general remarks on liberal and communitarian theories in the context of twenty-first-century realities. Considering these theories in light of what he sees as the increased interdependence of people in the global village, Imbo casts a suspicious eye on both approaches. Liberal theories, with their emphasis on an excessively individualistic conception of the person, presume that persons ought to pursue their autonomy by being wary of interdependent relationships that compromise personal independence. Communitarian theories, on the other hand, while valuing the embeddedness of individuals in community, run the risk of placing the concepts of autonomy and moral agency in jeopardy by insisting on a single substantive idea of the common good.

Imbo offers the possibility that certain features of computer-mediated communities provide insight into new conceptualizations of the idea of community. Imbo builds his case by first looking at two geographically situated communities, the Luo of Kenya and the Japanese, that offer some promising leads for understanding the possibilities of community in contemporary life. The Luo, a traditional and non-industrialized society, place a high premium on what has been called "African socialism" and "African humanism" and which Imbo calls "communalism." The view endorses a very strong notion that the community – as opposed to an abstract quality such as rationality, will, or memory – defines the person. Two features of social organization are central to this view of community: that people "find themselves" in communities (as opposed to being members of a community on the basis of a voluntary, contractual agreement) and that members are not thought to be able to opt out of the community. The Japanese are also group-oriented, the commitment to the social being visible in many areas of Japanese society, so much so that the entire society takes on the appearance of a family. It is especially significant that this ideal of a "collective conscience" can exist in the context of a flourishing modern industrialized society. The Luo and the Japanese thus offer strong views of communal life. They are societies, however, that are defined essentially by ethnic and national boundaries; they are communities structured around specific geographical spaces.

Computer-mediated communities, on the other hand, transcend the limitations of time, place, and physical attributes. It is in virtue of these features that computer-mediated communities recommend themselves as models for new ways of thinking about communities. Imbo writes: "Computer communication focuses attention on precisely those questions about how we experience both ourselves and other persons in real and virtual environments. The transphysical 'places' of cyberspace can have a role in extending the range of authentic social relations because such electronic interactions focus attention on the relations between virtual worlds and traditional communities." Participants in virtual communities share membership in the community not necessarily because they share interests or a single idea of the common good but, rather, because they are engaged in a shared activity. In Imbo's words, "The diversity of gender, class, race, ethnicity, and sexual orientation in cyberspace evokes a community (with ever increasing subcommunities) held together not by a common good but by a common bond." And, with the potential for transcending limitations of time and place in communication, computer-mediated communities offer the means for what Maria Lugones has called "world traveling." The computer, Imbo says, can help one to "find one's place in a community with no national boundaries but in which all members are rooted in specific cultures, countries, and traditional communities." These are ways, then, in which people can come to share their world-views and cultures with one another.

The final word in this collection is given to Mary Hawkesworth, who critically examines the university – an institution that has traditionally played a pivotal role in the creation and transmission of culture and that has often been regarded as exemplifying one ideal of community life, that of "the ancient and honorable community of scholars." In "The University as a Universe of Communities," Hawkesworth investigates possible ways in which a university could be construed as a community.

Hawkesworth argues that the historical warrant for considering university faculties as homogeneous communities has been largely eroded. Ancient and medieval conceptions of the university as a community of scholars who share fundamental beliefs and values about religion, politics, the nature of truth, the order of the universe, and the intrinsic values of the life of the mind have been displaced by the complexity of twenty-first-century research institutions that encompass diverse and often conflicting modes of organization, social ontologies, cosmological commitments, and understandings about the nature and purposes of university education. The proliferation and narrowing of academic specializations, accompanied by increasing divisions of labor within and across departments, disciplines, and employment categories, make universities appear more akin to "multiple solitudes" than cooperative communities united by educational objectives.

As "inclusive communities," universities also fall short of the mark. In contrast to the suggestion of inclusivity exuded by the term "university," which subtly envisions a space for all to learn and research "the whole of existing or created things," Hawkesworth argues that universities are sites of exclusion far more than inclusion. The grounds for exclusion have included caste, class, sex, religion, race, ethnicity, nationality, age, intellectual ability, as well as disciplinary approach and methodological commitment. The mechanisms of exclusion – decisions by current members of the academic community to police their borders through hiring and tenure decisions, as well as admissions policies – establish clear limits to the range of diversity tolerated within higher education.

The notion of the university as an "intentional community" suggests that the communal bonds among scholars are forged by their intellectual labor manifested in the tripartite mission of teaching, research, and service. But Hawkesworth argues that such a benign image of the university community is purchased at high cost. For it conflates the university with the faculty, which consists of a small minority of workers, and occludes the hierarchical and exploitive relations structuring the work life of support staff, custodial workers, service workers, as well as graduate, part-time, seasonal instructors and fixed-term faculty appointments, without whom the university could not function.

If the complexity, hierarchy, and bounded diversity of universities are taken seriously, then they can be considered communities only if notions of unity, homogeneity, and harmony of interest are jettisoned from the assumptions about the nature of community. When that move is made, universities – as sites of exclusion, stratification, contestation, and conflict – have much in common with the larger communities in which they are situated. Yet universities also make a unique contribution to those larger (local, national, and international) communities. Hawkesworth suggests that the distinctive work of universities lies in "community-making." By creating and accrediting ways of knowing and bodies of knowledge, universities help produce understandings about past, present, and future that make particular modes of life possible. Community-making, as the intellectual production of a shared world replete with assumptions about what is taken as natural, normal, given, and unalterable, is intensely political. What is at stake is not only what kinds of people and communities we are, but what kinds of people and communities we will become. In that regard, Hawkesworth's reflections on the university serve as a mirror and as a fitting conclusion to the myriad problems and contestations that have been at issue throughout this book.

Notes

1   Thomas Hobbes, *Leviathan* [1651], C. B. Macpherson, ed.(London: Penguin Books, 1968).

2   Jean-Jacques Rousseau, *Discourse on the Origin and Foundations of Inequality Among Men* [1755], Roger Masters, ed. *The First and Second Discourses* (New York: St Martin's Press, 1964); Jean-Jacques Rousseau, *The Social Contract* [1762], ed. Charles Frankel (New York: Hafner Publishing Company, 1947).

3   Alasdair MacIntyre, *After Virtue: A Study in Moral Theory* (Notre Dame: University of Notre Dame Press, 1981) and *Whose Justice? Which Rationality?* (Notre Dame: University of Notre Dame Press, 1988); Michael J. Sandel, *Liberalism and the Limits of Justice* (Cambridge, Mass.: Cambridge University Press, 1982), *Liberalism and Its Critics* (New York: New York University Press, 1984), and *Democracy's Discontent* (Cambridge: Harvard University Press, 1996); Charles Taylor, *Sources of the Self: The Making of the Modern Identity* (Cambridge, Mass.: Harvard University Press, 1989) and *The Malaise of Modernity* (Cambridge, Mass.: Harvard University Press, 1991); Jean Bethke Elshtain, *Democracy on Trial* (New York: BasicBooks, 1995) and *Real Politics: At the Center of Everyday Life* (Baltimore: Johns Hopkins University Press, 1997); and Amitai Etzioni, *The Spirit of Community: The Reinvention of American Society* (New York: Touchstone, 1993).

4   Christine Di Stefano, *Configurations of Masculinity: A Feminist Perspective on Modern Political Theory* (Ithaca: Cornell University Press, 1991).

5   Carole Pateman, *The Sexual Contract* (Cambridge: Polity, 1988).

6   Anita Allen, *Uneasy Access: Privacy for Women in a Free Society* (Totowa, N.J.: Rowman & Littlefield, 1988); Martha Fineman, *The Neutered Mother, The Sexual Family, and Other Twentieth -Century Tragedies* (New York : Routledge, 1995); Deborah Rhode, *Justice and Gender: Sex Discrimination and the Law* (Cambridge, Mass.: Harvard University Press, 1989); Zillah Eisenstein, *The Female Body and the Law* (Berkeley : University of California Press, 1988); Rita M. Kelly and Georgia Duerst Lahti, eds., *Gender Power, Leadership, and Governance* (Ann Arbor : University of Michigan Press, 1995).

7   Elaine Stavro, "Communitarian Discourse and New Labour: Privileging the Nuclear Family," paper presented at the Annual Meeting of the American Political Science Association, San Francisco, August 29, 2001. Uma Narayan and Julia J. Bartkowiak, eds., *Having and Raising Children: Unconventional Families, Hard Choices, and the Social Good.* (University Park, Pa.: Pennsylvania State University Press, 1999).

8   Toni Morrison, *Playing in the Dark: Whiteness and the Literary Imagination* (New York: Vintage Books, 1993); Patricia J. Williams, *The Alchemy of Race and Rights* (Cambridge, Mass.: Harvard University Press, 1991); Charles W. Mills, *The Racial Contract* (Ithaca: Cornell University Press, 1997); Tommy Lott, *The Invention of Race : Black Culture and the Politics of Representation* (Oxford: Blackwell, 1999).

9   Gayatri Spivak, *The Postcolonial Critic: Interviews, Strategies, Dialogues* (London: Routledge, 1990); Grewel Interpal, *Home and Harem: Nation, Gender, Empire, and the Cultures of Travel* (Durham, N.C.: Duke University Press, 1996); Chela

Sandoval, *Methodology of the Oppressed* (Minneapolis: University of Minnesota Press, 2000)

10   Valerie, Lehr, *Queer Family Values: Debunking the Myth of the Nuclear Family* (Philadelphia: Temple University Press, 1999); Shane Phelan, *Sexual Strangers: Gays, Lesbians, and Dilemmas of Citizenship* (Philadelphia: Temple University Press, 2001); Shane Phelan, ed., *Playing with Fire: Queer Politics, Queer Theories* (New York: Routledge, 1997); Mark Blasius, *Sexual Identities, Queer Politics* (Princeton: Princeton University Press, 2001).

11   For other accounts alleging the decline of civil society and community values, see Robert Bellah, Richard Madsen, et al., *Habits of the Heart: Individualism and Commitment in American Life* (Berkeley and Los Angeles: University of California Press, 1985) and Robert D. Putnam, *Bowling Alone: The Collapse and Revival of American Community* (New York: Simon and Schuster, 2000).

12   For an influential work on this theme, see Benedict Anderson, *Imagined Communities* (London: Verso, 1983).

PART I

Community and Its Contestations

1

Communities and Community: Critique and Retrieval

Jean Bethke Elshtain and Christopher Beem

We've all seen them – the World War II films in which the airplane crew or the platoon lectures a group of guys – all GIs and proud of it – with names like LaRosa, O'Brien, Goldberg, Chavez, Olafsen, Mickweicz. They're Americans to the man, and they are making a point – we're different from the people we are fighting.[1] America is open to all comers. You don't have to be of a particular race, or adhere to a given religion, or bear an identifiable ethnic name from one of a handful of accepted groups to be one of us. But the picture is by no means perfect. You don't see an African American or a Japanese American in the group.[2] The Armed Services were segregated until after World War II, and Japanese Americans fought in a separate Nisei regiment. But the point could be taken nonetheless: America was different because it enabled people who were "different" to nevertheless hold something in common: their identity as citizens, their aspirations as free men and women, their determination to make life better for their children. That seems rather a long time ago – a frozen tableau from another time and place; a time when we were innocent, perhaps, or naive, or just "didn't get it."

A "reading" of the "text" of a World War II war film, in today's "lit-crit" jargon, would probably go something like this: men from various ethnic groups were co-opted to conform to the model of the hegemonic Anglo-Saxon Protestant male, save for those the society implacably refused to normalize – namely, blacks and, in this era, Japanese Americans. Having encoded this dominance more generally, such men, already oppressors in their own households by virtue of their superior standing in patriarchal society, became even more eager embodiments of the normative standards of a racist, sexist, imperialist society.

We exaggerate a bit – for comedic effect or shock value, depending on how familiar the reader is with the coinage of one pervasive trend in academe – but not by much, for we are all now enjoined to see the past only through a "hermeneutics of suspicion": Christianity is nothing but the violent re-encoding in new guise of the violent Jewish God; the US Constitution is nothing but the writing into law of the privileges of a dominant, male class; community is a nice word marking repressive, exclusionary practices. The relentless drumbeat goes on. Harsh criticism seems to have become an end in itself. But we worry about this willful contempt for the past. A free society cannot long survive widespread cynicism among its citizens. Cynicism, the assumption that a person's words and deeds always mask an ulterior and crassly self-interested motivation, breeds a politics of resentment. And resentment drains our normative institutions, including education and politics, even families, of their ethical legitimacy and deters them from doing the tasks they are there to do. The sad thing is that much of what we here decry is undertaken in the name of putting things right, of correcting wrongs, of celebrating what is called "multiculturalism" and creating some sort of new and better order of things.

We, too, want to "put these things right." But that involves both critique and retrieval. The prism of community is our focus. We propose to examine alternative models of community as these have emerged historically, paying particular attention to themes of race and ethnicity. Our aim is twofold: first, to display "the good, the bad, and the ugly" manifesting in American struggles around community; and, secondly, to retrieve a vision of a fair, complex political community that does justice to our multiple loyalties as citizens and as members of less inclusive communities.

We begin with this salvo: there are two false and dangerous stories about ethnic and racial diversity, American identity, and political community. The first is drawn from a historical era, now past; the second, from the present moment. We shall rehearse these two tales that pose or posed particular threats to a more generous dream of a democratic community as the way free citizens come to know a good in common that they cannot know alone.

Our first cautionary tale is the story of a quest for unity and homogeneity that assaulted diversity in the process: a too strong and too overreaching homogeneous identity was deemed necessary as a prerequisite for citizenship and responsibility. We want to take the reader back to the World War I era, when the allure of an overreaching, collective civic purpose took a statist turn that seemed to be a cure for what ailed the republic, at least in the view of those who lamented our excessive diversity. Nationalizing progressives often found themselves disheartened at the cultural impact of both the rampant, unbridled industrialism of the Gilded Age and the messy, cacophonous sprawl brought on by wave after wave of immigration. Desirous of finding some way to forge a unified national will and civic philosophy, these progressives saw the coming of World War I as a way to attain at long last a homogeneous, ordered, and rational society, and political community.[3]

Evincing the spirit of the times, John R. Commons, a progressive labor economist, maintained that national greatness required a singularity of purpose and identity – one nation, one mind. Walter Lippmann assailed the evils of localism and fretted that American diversity was too great and had become a block in the way of order, purpose, and discipline. Progressives like these saw World War I as the great engine of social progress. Conscription would serve, in historian David Kennedy's words, as an "effective homogenizing agent in what many regarded as a dangerously diverse society. Shared military service, one advocate colorfully argued, was the only way to 'yank the hyphen' out of Italian-Americans or Polish-Americans or other such imperfectly assimilated immigrants."[4]

President Woodrow Wilson, who had already proclaimed that "any man who carries a hyphen about him carries a dagger that he is ready to plunge into the vitals of the Republic,"[5] thundered, in words of unifying excess:

> There are citizens of the United States, I blush to admit, under our generous naturalization laws born under other flags but welcome to the full freedom and opportunity of America, who have poured the poison of disloyalty into the very arteries of our national life. . . . Such creatures of passion, disloyalty, and anarchy must be crushed out. . . The hand of our power should close over them at once.[6]

"Americanization" became the goal, the watchword – for some, the threat: one community, one nation indivisible. To be sure, genuine regard for the welfare of immigrant groups lay at the base of much of this progressive sentiment, the fear that separatism and heterogeneity were synonymous with inequality and marginality. One must also acknowledge that this drive for national unity was born of pressing political demands. There was, after all, a war going on. For all this, progressive opinion proved particularly susceptible to the cry for unity because of its emphasis on the notion that the voice of the American community must speak as one. The temptation to forge a unity that is indistinguishable in practice from conformity is evidently great; it invited figures from Woodrow Wilson down to trim the sails of free speech on the grounds that the war against dissent was a war against civic dismemberment, a war for great national aspirations, and an opportunity to forge a community that might encompass the entire continent. The coming of the First World War offered this particular mind-set an optimistic set of "social possibilities."

Perhaps, then, the current practitioners of the "hermeneutics of suspicion" are right. Perhaps the entire thrust of American history has been to destroy our particular identities, even our dignity, in order to create some common identity. There is a kernel of truth to such claims, but it is not the truth unadorned, for even in the midst of the rush to yank out the hyphens there were strong dissenting voices. One was that of Randolph Bourne, himself a member of the progressive crowd and a regular correspondent for *The New Republic* until he fell out with the publishers over their newfound war fervor. Bourne wrote a wonderful piece at the height of war suspicion, fanaticism, and attacks on aliens and immigrants. Against the effort to cement a homogenized, decidedly Waspish American community, he called for a politics of commonalties that cherished the bracing tonic of perspicuous contrasts. Bourne celebrated a social world within which many voices were heard:

> America is coming to be, not a nationality but a trans-nationality, a weaving back and forth, with other lands, of many threads of all sizes and colors. Any movement which attempts to thwart this weaving or to dye the fabric any one color, or disentangle the threads of the strands, is false to this cosmopolitan vision.[7]

No "tight and jealous" nationalism for Bourne; he called for an experimental ideal in which each of us is left free to fashion our own ways of living. Yet Bourne also believed in the possibility of politics of the sort expressed in Josiah Royce's idea of a "beloved community." While politics requires a common set of terms, Bourne believed those terms could not and should not be wholly imposed from above. They must, rather, emerge through the vibrant interplay of cultures, communities, and individuals under a capacious constitutional umbrella.

This Bournian ideal (or, perhaps, Bournian mean) is hostile, then, to any overly robust proclamation of American community that demands a single, overarching collective identity under the aegis of the state to attain or to sustain its purpose. But his ideal also alerts us to a second false and debilitating story: the harsh particularism, current in both American civic and scholarly life and political argumentation, in which we reduce ourselves (hence, our communities) to ethnic, racial, or gender categories that are dismissive of the possibility of reaching outside our own group. Oddly, in the name of diversity and multiculturalism, this rigidifying of difference types people by racial, ethnic, gender, or sexual orientation categories and says, in effect, that *these* are the differences that matter – not the quality of a person's intellect, the depth or a person's commitment to community, the scope of a person's understanding of the human condition, the dignity of a person's life, or the ill-dignity heaped on a person by an unjust social circumstance. Bourne's rich tapestry contrasts with this identity-absolutist quilt, a collection of solid patches representing this color, this gender, and this or that identity, all kept separate and each threatening at any moment to detach itself. This second story is also a distortion of the dream of democratic community and the civic life constitutive of it.

Rather than negotiating the complexity of public and private identities and embracing the notion of the "citizen" as the way we have to sustain a public identity, more and more we are told by so many voices that we must gain recognition exclusively along race, gender, or sexual preference lines.

The public world becomes a world of many "I's" who form a "we" only with others like themselves in these prefixed categories. Of course, democrats recognize in the demand for recognition a powerful concern. Forms of equal recognition are not only possible in a democracy but form its very lifeblood. But one must ask: What sort of recognition? Recognition of what? For what? To claim "I am different. You must recognize me and honor my difference" tells us nothing that is interesting.

Indeed, one could even argue that it is incorporation within a single civic body – not, remember, a homogeneous community – that makes meaningful diversity possible. Our difference must be recognized if they are to exist substantively at all. As political philosopher Charles Taylor writes, "My discovering my own identity doesn't mean that I work it out in isolation, but that I negotiate it through dialogue, partly overt, partly internal, with others. . . . My own identity crucially depends on my dialogical relations with others."[8] What this means is that we cannot be different all by ourselves. A political body that brings people together, creating a "we," but which enables these same persons to separate themselves and to recognize one another in and through their differences as well as in what they share in common – that was, and is, the great challenge. Bourne's call for transnationality was thus a call for balance that is the core of democratic community. The worst excesses of the multicultural movement are just as destructive to this balance as an unbridled call for unity. Thus, in our time and place, the great challenge remains.

A survey of the landscape of *fin de siècle* America makes it apparent that the drive for identity politics is merely one manifestation of many current troubles. Although a dwindling band of pundits and apologists insist that Americans are suffering the pangs of dislocation en route to salutary change, even progress, such reassurances ring increasingly hollow. Experts and ordinary citizens lament the growth of a culture of mistrust, cynicism, and scandal. Our suspicion is that this broader cultural crisis is also properly characterized as a problem of imbalance. If this is so, then exploring this crisis affords us an opportunity to connect a discussion about race with these basic questions about American politics' community, communities, and culture. We therefore want to focus for a moment on another source for, and manifestation of, our cultural malaise – namely, the overall weakening of democratic civil society.

By any standard of objective evidence, our society has experienced a serious growth of corrosive forms of isolation and depolitization reflected in declining levels of involvement in politics and community life – from simple acts such as voting and exchanging pleasantries with a neighbor, to more demanding participation in political parties and in local and other civic associations. Collectively, these myriad opportunities for social interaction and civic engagement constitute a democratic community, for that is where

Americans forge the bonds of social and political trusts and competence. Yet in our contemporary social world, these opportunities are increasingly passed over, and American society manifests the unhappy results. Social scientists who have researched the matter argue for a causal relationship: The sharp decline in participation has led to a notable decline in social trust. Ultimately, the evaporation of American civil society points, they tell us, to a crisis in "social capital formation." Just like identity politics, the decline of civil society at once manifests and reinforces the increasing inability of American society to pursue a good that is common.

Historically, democratic theorists either took for granted the web of mediating institutions, vibrant informal and formal civic associations, or they have pointed specifically to those institutions as the means by which a society maintains the relationship between democracy and the everyday actions and spirit of a people. In the latter group, the most famous thinker is Alexis de Tocqueville. Democracy requires laws, constitutions, and authoritative institutions, but Tocqueville also insisted that it depends on democratic dispositions. These include the preparedness to work with others for shared ends; a combination of often strong convictions coupled with a readiness to compromise in the recognition that one cannot always get everything one wants; a sense of individuality, and a commitment to civic goods that are not the possession of one person or of one small group alone. The world that nourishes and sustains such democratic dispositions is a thickly interwoven social fabric, the web of mediating institutions already noted.[9] The tale here gestured toward is a story of the weakening of the institutions of civil society, and hence the dramatic upsurge in social mistrust and generalized cynicism.

The effects of mistrust, privatization, and anomie are many. For example, there is strong empirical support for the view that where neighborhoods are intact – that is, where there is a strong sense of common interest and a fairly strong moral consensus and community – drug, alcohol abuse, crime, and truancy among the young diminish. Because neighborhoods are now less likely to be intact, socially and self-destructive behavior is either on the rise or at unacceptably high levels. Children have borne the brunt of these negative social trends. The unraveling of neighborhoods and communities leads to strain on families and child-rearing. Family breakdown generates unparented children who attend schools that increasingly resemble detention homes rather than centers of enduring training and discipline. Declining levels of education and training contribute to out-of-wedlock births, violence, and youth suicide at shocking levels.

This cultural transformation and its various effects, taken together with the fact that too many are hunkered down into "identity" groups expecting the worst from each other, help to explain the quaint, faraway feeling that is likely to be evoked by the platoon of GIs. But perhaps there is still something to be learned from the World War II images. Consider the social world that the GIs are supposed to symbolize. If those men with their strong ethnic identities are indeed representative, then it is clear that the efforts of Wilson, Croly, Lippmann, and others to yank out the hyphens and erode "localisms" were at best only partially successful. Twenty years or so after strict immigration quotas were imposed, the men portrayed in World War II movies likely lived in neighborhoods where theirs was the dominant ethnic group. Strong lines of demarcation separated these communities, and they were often crossed only with impunity. They likely went to church, and that church probably would have reflected a strong ethnic and cultural heritage. They were not members of the Lutheran church, they went to the Norwegian Lutheran Church; they didn't belong to a Catholic parish, they belonged to Santa Lucia's or Saint Patrick's. Some of these men came to know members of other ethnic groups through the public school, or later, through the workplace; for many World War II veterans their cultural experience was a singularly "hyphenated" one, and their first and most significant exposure to other sub-cultures, other ideas about what it meant to be an American, took place during the war itself. In other words, war movies celebrated a shared sense of identity and national community for which the war itself was largely responsible.

This does not mean that the message of war films was pure propaganda. Indeed, social scientists concerned about civil society argue that experiences within very cohesive neighborhoods facilitated commonality. The mediating institutions of civil society – such as family, neighborhood, and church – bridged the gap between particular communities and the nation. At their best, these institutions inculcated a shared sense of national identity and solidarity even as they expressed and reinforced a specific and unique particular identity. If this is so, then it is precisely strong community identities and neighborhoods that enabled or at least facilitated their coming together in a wider community. People had a robust sense of what it meant to be a member of a community. It also means that, willy-nilly, something like Bourne's vision triumphed in World War II America. Americans maintained their separate identities even as they were able to come together in pursuit of a common cause.

But let's not forget that the movie scene is notable for what is left out – most relevant here – African Americans. To be sure, the war had a remarkable impact in this respect as well. The shameful reality of segregation, in light of the heroism and sacrifice of Negro units, helped accelerate the black migration to the North as well as Truman's first fitful steps toward civil rights. Yet the exclusion of African Americans in war films is representative of society at large. All the ethnic communities of the 1940s were notable in their ability to inculcate a strong sense of ethnic identity and civic virtue; thereafter, they often became united in their desire to keep blacks out.

As the civil rights movement came alive, the idea of segregation – whether manifested at drinking fountains, in movie houses, or in neighborhoods – was rejected as an inherently illegitimate structural impediment to full citizenship and full humanity. A new ideal of a color-blind society was put forward, and desegregation was championed as the indispensable means for achieving this end. In his famous speech at Howard University in 1965, President Lyndon Johnson noted that the "deep, corrosive, obstinate differences" between "Negro poverty" and "white poverty" were "simply and solely the consequence of ancient brutality, past injustice, and present prejudice." He therefore "dedicated the expanding efforts of the Johnson administration" to addressing the differences, so that the nation might some day "reach the time when the only differences between Negroes and whites is the color or their skin."[10]

Surveying the state of race relations and civil society at the end of the century, we can see that Johnson's hopeful exhortations seem like a long time ago too. To be sure, it is easy to forget or belittle the remarkable achievements of the civil rights era, but it is nevertheless the case that 40 years after these words were spoken, 60 years after World War II, most interaction between whites and blacks takes place where it always has: in the schools, in the workplace, and in the military. Integrated communities are more common, but they remain a rare commodity, and even when they exist in fact, it is more unlikely that they manifest the kind of ethical cohesion that characterized neighborhoods past. As for the idea that our commonality might some day be limited only by our pigmentation, that goal, too, seems a far-off memory.

Historical hindsight allows us to suspect that our faraway feeling is born of the fact that while President Johnson's intentions might have been wholly benign, his policies are open to critique from the standpoint of communities versus "one Big Community." In the end, the goal of desegregation as Johnson outlines it bears a striking similarity to the World War I era of national community. Johnson, too, sought to yank the hyphen out of the American experience, and he wanted to use the power of the national government to further that end. To be sure, both movements were hopeful and noble ideals, born of the best intentions, seeking to address serious problems. Wilson and Johnson might have put forward a different understanding of the evils of localism, but both described it as evil. And, at least in the latter case, one must be clear about the successes. The civil rights movement brought down the social ethos of Jim Crow. In some large measure, it achieved the goals outlined by Croly and Lippmann. Scenes of fire hoses, attack dogs, and blown-up churches instigated a national moral consensus that crushed the localism of the old South. But, in common with the homogenizing urge of the Progressive movement, desegregation sought community at an unsustainable level – the nation. It also sought to redress the wrongs of prejudice by slowly extinguishing ethnic identity and cultural difference. From a contemporary perspective, it appears that for all their noble intentions, both movements failed in their ultimate objectives because both goals were skewed from the start.

There is a similar connection on the reverse side as well. Notice that a kind of ethnic insulation attaches both to identity politics and to the neighborhoods of World War II America. Whatever goods this insularity might make possible within a particular community – a point that is surely debatable – there is an intolerant and isolated quality manifest here that undermines a commitment to a common, transethnic good. The America of the 1940s was, for the most part, able to achieve a common good, but it was a racially constricted conception. The identity politics associated with contemporary America seeks to identify and reject that conception, but, in doing so, it makes the search for a common good not more possible but more distant, and even tends, disastrously, to see "culture" as an outgrowth of race or gender. In both cases, commitment to the particular community undermines and invalidates the search for a common good that is truly common without pushing for homogeneity.

This long and often unhappy jaunt through twentieth-century American history reveals that there is, finally, a shared dimension to the problem of race and the problem of community. Living in the aftermath of Wilson and Johnson has shown us that real, sustainable community is local and that a national community is at best a temporary reality. Desegregation can address serious historical injustices, and a strong national government may be able to ameliorate the inequities of unbridled capitalism, but neither can create community and neither can legitimately or profitably seek to homogenize the American experience.

Nevertheless, in both instances, a serious problem remains. On the one hand, we want to reinvigorate the institutions of civic culture, the virtue-building neighborhoods of two generations ago, and we guardedly question whether such neighborhoods do not depend on, or at least thrive on, a kind of ethnic identity that sustains long-standing prejudices. On the other hand, we want to ameliorate, and finally eliminate, the remaining vestiges of a racist culture, and that requires a commitment to a specific conception of fairness and justice that is almost universal and that transcends the insulary ethos of an ethnic community. There are, of course, always voices that represent either the overly strenuous vision of a unified (if not homogenized) single national community, or alternatively, that preach a version of separatism. One well-known work that cautions blacks against nearly any form of association or, community-building with white Americans is James Cone's *Black Theology and Black Power*.[11] Cone's rough language sets blacks apart from whites. The possibilities for dialogue, for Cone, are simply not present or are present in the most tenuous and anemic ways. He has a "word to Whitey," and that word is that the structures of what he calls "white society" are a nigh demonic force.

Of course, Cone's anger is all too understandable. But Christianity and, it must be said, the liberalism that Cone spends a good bit of time berating, all turn on the possibility that we might move beyond resentment even in situations of oppression. This is, to say the least, an extraordinarily challenging and demanding regimen and Cone really doesn't want any part of it. Politics, for him, is war by other means – or possibly other means, as he leaves the door open to the use of violence *if* blacks deem it necessary. "There is no neutral position in war," he claims.[12] Now the problem with such a stance is its absolutism: its demand for absolute surrender or total victory. That is not the way of democratic politics, which is always a frustrating business, a series of half-advances, half-retreats because one is obliged ongoingly to deal with people who differ and who dissent from whatever it is one is oneself endorsing. In this recognition lies the basic challenge of creating and sustaining communities and trans-ethnic and trans-racial community.

The difficulty with Cone's position is that it leaves "whitey" very little room in which to make gestures of friendship and solidarity with black Americans. One is, so to speak, condemned for doing nothing or condemned for doing something. Cone approaches Martin Luther King condescendingly, claiming that most whites "loved" him because his "approach was the least threatening to the white power structure," not because of his attempt to free his people.[13] H. Richard Niebuhr is taken to task for praising the historic example of blacks and whites worshiping together. For Cone this form of integration was a way to prevent blacks from controlling their own churches; integration, so to speak, was a way to keep track of blacks.[14] But this runs counter to our experience and that of thousands of others. Elshtain, for example recalls her sisters returning from a Lutheran Youth Leadership Conference in Chicago in 1956 declaiming about Martin Luther King, who had addressed the group, and about the plight of African Americans in America's southland. For those of us living in small towns in northern Colorado this was a startling and troubling revelation. We began to agitate about it in our school and our church. Elshtain and one of her sisters were part of the first protest ever (at least according to the local paper) in front of the federal post office in Fort Collins, Colorado, at the time of the Birmingham sit-ins. It seemed as if there *was* something we could do and we were obliged to do it.

Now this is no doubt small potatoes. But, you can't be universal anywhere save in your own backyard. It is vital to take the decent actions one can and to be able to see oneself as a citizen contributing to a wider sense of what a fair, just, and free community could look like. Cone undermines this possibility for "whitey," and that is consistent with his counsel of division, if not outright separatism. If white society is a "racist Antichrist," why should black Americans want anything to do with it?[15] If "black theology counsels all black people to be suspicious of all white people," the upshot is that we stand and bleat at one another across a vast distance rather than engaging, sometimes angrily and militantly but engaging nonetheless, as free citizens or would-be free citizens.[16] Suggesting that burning down seminaries with Molotov cocktails cannot be ruled out doesn't seem a way to build the necessary political bridges to achieve enduring political ends.[17] This, then, leads us to endorse Martin Luther King's vision, not because it is easy but precisely because it is hard. It demands a generosity of spirit (rather than inviting bitter withdrawal) that is difficult for people to muster consistently. But muster this spirit we must, King insists, embracing as we go a complex notion of freedom composed of a number of critical registers.

A modulated politics whose practitioners open their hands in gestures of anticipated fellowship to all persons of goodwill, white or black, rich or poor, offends those who want a totalistic politics. But hate is easy; arousing the regressive urges of one's fellow men and women requires little more than a capacity for spite. What is difficult is to fight the allure of hate, particularly when it comes to us in the name of revolution. Martin Luther King knew well what an experience of "the political" was and how it rested uneasily within the confines of a politics of mere proceduralism, yet stood as an alternative to a politics of revolutionary violence each of which either erodes or destroys community. The historian Richard King talks of the "repertory of freedom" embraced by the civil rights movement. He observed that freedom in Western political thinking involves at least four basic meanings: legal freedom, freedom as autonomy, participatory freedom, and freedom as collective deliverance from a subjugated condition. The tens of thousands of ordinary folks who found within themselves the courage to act on behalf of each "I" and in so doing help to create a "we" are the result of a generous vision of democratic community. Rooted in hope, the action of a free citizen marks new beginnings and generates possibilities that once seemed foreclosed. To see the goals of the civil rights movement, namely, the "liquidation of racial segregation and black disenfranchisement" and the solidaristic vision of freedom and self-transformation constitutive of it, as peripheral or even a kind of sell-out is to lose the ethical power and historic complexity of this movement.[18] In a culture brimming with cynicism it no doubt sounds as if we want to have our cake and eat it too, but what we want is a Bournian ideal for American community. Fortunately, that ideal has already found an able advocate, and we therefore close by turning to the words of Martin Luther King Jr.

King championed much of Johnson's program – indeed, he repeatedly noted that desegregation and the dismantling of Jim Crow laws was a good in and of itself. King acknowledged that while these changes "may not change the heart," they could "restrain the heartless."[19] Nevertheless, King was equally adamant that desegregation was not enough. "Our ultimate goal," he said, "is integration." King argued that desegregation was merely a physical description and "only a first step on the road to a good society."[20] True integration was a spiritual reality that got embodied in transformed communities. It reflected the belief in the sacredness of all persons and required nothing less than a change of heart.

It is true that King's rhetoric reflected the tone of the time. His writings sometimes echo Johnson's strategy of bringing all races together only by eliminating cultural differences. King also used terms that are reminiscent of the Progressives, even talking about "a national community." But these words are not the whole story. Because integration is a complex transformation, and because it respected the status of all persons, King did not demand that race or ethnicity could or should be yanked out of a person's identity. In short, true integration did not constitute homogenization. His words are worth quoting at length:

> The Negro is the child of two cultures – Africa and America. The problem is that in the search for wholeness all too many Negroes seek to embrace only one side of their natures. Some, seeking to reject their heritage, are ashamed of their color, ashamed of black art and music, and determine what is beautiful and good by the standards of white society. They end up frustrated and without cultural roots. Others seek to reject everything American and to identify totally with Africa, even to the point of wearing African clothes. But this approach also leads to frustration because the American Negro is not an African. . . . The American Negro is neither totally African nor totally Western. He is Afro-American, a true hybrid, a combination of two cultures.[21]

Martin Luther King Jr. believed that the spiritual ideal of integration requires that equality and commonality coexist with racial and ethnic pride, cultural diversity, and spirited, challenging exchange. So understood, King's objectives for race relations echo Randolph Bourne's objectives for American culture. They independently appeal to the phrase "the beloved community" to describe what a truly integrated American community composed of diverse communities would be like. King's use of the term "community" has a more deeply spiritual dimension. But in both cases, their entreaties reveal that what is required is an uneasy yet charitable and deeply principled balancing act – between unity and diversity, between pluralism and consensus.

We know that in our jaded age, King's exhortations are cloying to many. And we have made no effort to connect these exhortations to specific policy suggestions. Many who are concerned with these issues may well fear that questions about neighborhood cohesion are nothing more than yet another elaborate strategy for maintaining segregation. These are formidable matters, and we do not want to minimize their importance. But race relations in the United States seem to have reached an impasse in recent years and, at times, to have soured gravely. There is new and recurrent talk of a gigantic and insoluble fissure in the American body politic. If this is so, then perhaps it is enough to suggest that we take another look at exactly what we want to achieve for our communities and in the name of our polity. If such a reinvestigation allows us to integrate our hopes for racial justice with our more general concerns about American culture and community, so much the better.

Notes

1   We draw here on a lecture delivered by Jean Bethke Elshtain in 1992 at the University of Dallas.
2   Exclusion of African Americans in this depiction of the military melting pot was common but not complete. The movie *Bataan* (1943) is probably the most important counterexample. See Larry May, "Making the American Consensus: The Narrative of Conversion and Subversion in World War II Films," in Lewis A. Erenberg and Susan E. Hirsch, eds., *The War in American Culture: Society and Consciousness During World War II* (Chicago: University of Chicago Press, 1996), pp. 76–77.
3   The longer story can be found in Jean Bethke Elshtain, *Women and War* (New York: Basic Books, 1987).
4   David M. Kennedy, *Over Here: The First World War and American Society* (New York: Oxford University Press, 1980), p. 17.
5   Quoted in ibid., p. 87.
6   Quoted in ibid., p. 24.
7   Randolph Bourne, "Trans-national America," in Christopher Lasch, ed., *The Radical Will: Randolph Bourne, Selected Writings, 1911–1918* (New York: Urizen Books, 1977), p. 262.
8   Charles Taylor, *Multiculturalism and the Politics of Recognition* (Princeton: Princeton University Press, 1992), p. 34.
9   Alexis de Tocqueville, *Democracy in America*, trans. George Lawrence, ed. J. P. Mayer (New York: Anchor Books, 1969), esp. vol. 2.
10   Lyndon B. Johnson, "The Howard University Address," in Diane Ravitch, ed., *The American Reader* (New York: HarperCollins, 1990), pp. 341–2.
11   James H. Cone, *Black Theology and Black Power* (New York: Orbis Books, 1997; published originally in 1969).
12   Ibid., p. 67. Here it must be noted that Cone draws Albert Camus in as support for an "all or nothing" position when this is a view Camus explicitly *denies*. Camus associates this view with the metaphysical rebellion and he rejects most Marxist-inspired forms of historical rebellion. Camus insists that the rebel, by contrast tot he revolutionary, always affirms solidarity with others even in revolt. The point of the rebel is that he or she must recognize a limit. The rebel aspires only to the relative, for Camus; and the rebel affirms ongoingly that there are limits in rebellion itself. See Camus, *The Rebel* (New York: Knopf, 1956), pp. 14 and 290, and contrast with Cone's comments about Camus, especially on p. 7.
13   Cone, *Black Theology and Black Power*, p. 56.
14   Ibid., p. 77.

15 Ibid., p. 135.
16 Ibid., p. 145.
17 Ibid., p. 131. Another problem is Cone's insistence on speaking of "white culture." But we have no idea what "white culture" is. White isn't a coherent category. Is "white culture" the plays of Eugene O'Neill? The films of John Ford? The writing of Herman Melville? The pragmatism of William James? The social activism of Jane Addams? The pacifist militancy of Dorothy Day? There is so much variation and disagreement and fundamental difference in ordering visions, that to speak of a monolith called "white culture" is really incoherent. There is an American culture, and that culture is unthinkable without the contributions of African Americans.
18 Richard H. King, *Civil Rights and the Idea of Freedom* (Oxford: Oxford University Press, 1992), p. 28.
19 Martin Luther King, Jr., "An Address Before the National Press Club," in James M. Washington, ed., *A Testament of Hope: The Essential Writings and Speeches of Martin Luther King, Jr.* (San Francisco: HarperCollins, 1986), p. 100.
20 Martin Luther King, Jr. "A Public Address Before a Nashville Church Conference" (December 27, 1962), in *A Testament of Hope*, p. 18.
21 Martin Luther King, Jr., *Where Do We Go from Here: Chaos or Community?* (New York: Harper and Row, 1963), cited in *A Testament of Hope*, p. 588.

2

Community at the Margin

Crispin Sartwell

Close to where I live there was a drug arrest recently. This one was unusual because two of the people who were busted were Amish. And they were arrested along with members of the Pagans motorcycle gang, for buying cocaine in the Philadelphia area and selling it to members of Amish youth groups. The clash of worlds seemed almost too extreme to be believed: Old Order meets road warrior. Buggy meets Harley. Christian meets blasphemer. Abner and Abner meet Twisted and Trog (I'm not kidding about the names). But the Amish and the Pagans have a lot in common.

The Amish tourist strip in Lancaster County is a commercialization of the anti-commercial, an up-to-date marketing of the supposed innocence and simplicity of people who seem committed to living in the past. But no one lives in the past, as the Amish are the first to admit, and the relentless marketing of the Amish is not even ironic. It's just one example of the relentless marketing of everything. What is marketed here is a community that rejects marketing; Lancaster County businesses peddle an illusion of innocence. The Pagans are not innocent by anyone's standards. But they too constitute a community that in many ways rejects the mainstream form of life. The Pagans, like the Amish, form an insular community devoted to nurturing selves that are defined by their opposition to the dominant culture: to suits and ties, gleaming skyscrapers, climate-controlled luxury cars. Like the Amish, the Pagans represent for the rest of us a life outside the mainstream, a life that escapes some of the pressures and pains and prefab pleasures of postmodernity. Perhaps we fear the Pagans, but we also romanticize them, as we do the Amish. And like the Amish, one of the things that makes the Pagans romantic, that we yearn toward in them, is their cohesion as a community.

More and more, our "community" is national or even global. Or at least, so runs the familiar yammering. More and more, what lends us the semblance of a collective identity is what the Amish and Pagans reject: corporate culture, the culture of franchises and logos, advertising, mass media. The Amish and the Pagans want to check out of the global economy and into a highly local, cohesive community.

In this chapter I am going to explore the consequences of a few bald assertions. First, there are no communities that consist of a million or 270 million or 6 billion people. Talk of a national or world community should be read as some sort of trope or metaphor, and it's a good thing, too, because any community on that scale would be a horror. There can be no American or world community. The unity of groups that large is really just a sad joke, a myth perpetuated in empty political or commercial rhetoric. Communities exist where people can come face to face, where people can actually know each other and find a way of life together. Second, communities are made by exclusions: by excluding others or by being excluded by others: usually both. This could not be more obvious than in the case of the Amish or the Pagans. If there are still any genuine communities in the United States, they are communities like that. Third, the places where community happens in our culture are at the margins: among skinheads, religious cultists, street gangs, sexual minorities, addicts and recovering addicts, skaters, militias, farm communes left over from the 1960s. You have got to be ejected from or eject yourself from the mainstream culture to find anything like a genuine community. Your suburban subdivision isn't going to do the job. The scale of our collective culture is huge; it is inhuman. Our institutions, governments, and corporations no longer have anything really to do with community. It is only at the margins and interstices, in the little spaces where people conceal themselves from or confront these institutions, that the possibility of community exists.

Exclusions

Communities are formed by exclusion and by violence, both internal and external. What is normal is articulated by a process of scapegoating, wherein a person is selected at random, or not, and is treated as being weird. That's how you end up being a normal person: you're one of those who torture weird people. If you want to see this process in operation, you can look carefully at almost any schoolyard or perhaps consult your memory. And what is essential is not that the person selected for exclusion actually be weird, even in whatever vague sense the term "weird" might be used in a given context, but simply that someone be excluded on some grounds or even on no grounds at all. It is such exclusions that make a community of children possible, because the exclusions define an "identity" for the children to share: we are the people who are not like her, that; we are the people that aren't weird, queer, retarded. When I was in elementary school, we picked out a girl named Shelley for no reason at all that I can fathom from here and spent all of fifth grade torturing her psychically for her supposed weirdness. I suppose that is something that she remembers pretty vividly.

Now people who get excluded this way or who exclude themselves from their own groups of origin sometimes form satellite communities, or maybe communities for celebrating a certain kind of weirdness (and of course such communities also practice analogous scapegoatings) – communities of violence, S&M communities, biker communities, gangs, and so on. To say that communities like that aren't real communities or aren't communities in the truest sense or are pseudo-communities is just wishful thinking; probably those communities are closer to the communitarian ideal than is "American society" or whatever amorphous abstraction you may have in mind. And of course to say these aren't real communities is just saying again "You're weird." That is, condemning the street gang community as unreal or defective is just another way of saying you wish you had an actual community or in which you actually go about trying to make one. The street gang is as genuine a community as can be found: it is paradigmatic and in many ways desirable. You should see what I mean by that as soon as you compare the cohesion and communication in a street gang with "the American community" or the "global village" or for that matter with a meticulously planned suburb.

You don't have to be Jacques Derrida or Georg Wilhelm Friedrich Hegel to understand that dominant identities are formed almost solely by exclusions. Think, for example, about what it means to be a white person. Intrinsically, it means nothing: whiteness for white people is a kind of empty space in the racial taxonomy, the norm from which all other races are deviations. That is because it was white people who made the taxonomic grid, white people who were the anthropologists. Writing *The Sexual Life of Savages*[1] or measuring the cranial capacity of Africans is a pseudo-scientific exercise in what we did on the playground to Shelley; they are ways of delineating the normal, or defining what it means to be human as what it means to be ourselves. They are forms of ejection that make community possible.   To repeat, being white seems to be to inhabit an empty space, but it is a specific empty space, a space that has been emptied of certain specific qualities or aspects of human personality. The ejections that create whiteness have very specific content. Roughly, whiteness is constructed out of the basic series of dualisms that constitute Western metaphysics: mind/body, culture/nature, master/slave, reason/emotion. To be black in the cultural imagination of white folks is to be highly embodied, or even to be pure body; all the stereotypes of black people are about embodiment: that black folks have rhythm, that they are highly sexualized, violent, and so on. These hallucinations are ways we exclude people and they are occasions or excuses to dominate and exploit people, but they are also ways by which we pretend to make ourselves who we think we ought to be: to be white means to be a mind, not a monkey; it means to have a culture and hence to be free of nature; it also means, perhaps, to yearn romantically toward what has in hallucination been excluded from the self. And with some variations of detail, the same could be said for other dominant identities: being a man, being heterosexual, and so on.

"Mind," "culture," and so on are empty abstractions, or perhaps we could say that they are abstraction itself. Mind is what floats free of the particular into the realm of concepts. "Body" too is an empty abstraction; but "body" is not abstraction itself: it is, rather, an abstract sign of particularity. That is why whiteness in a sense has no content: it is an abstract sign of abstraction, and the only content the sign has arises in its exclusion of the sign of particularity, an exclusion which devolves in imagination to every particular thing.

A central point of the philosophy of Alasdair MacIntyre and others is that community and identity are bound up with one another, that your community bequeaths you an identity: it articulates a range of possible or acceptable roles, for example.[2] Now if that's true, then I think something interesting follows about folks in the dominant positions: they have no real community. Think about whether there is a community, in any rich sense, of heterosexuals. The only time I can think of having a sense of hetero-sexual community was once when I was in Greenwich Village, on Christopher Street – an epicenter of gay America. A pretty girl walked by (at least I think it was a girl), and I noticed that another guy was staring at her too. This guy and I looked at each other and smiled in mutual recogni-tion: we were both breeders. Really, we should at this point have gone to a strip joint and had a beer together and talked about pussy, but all the bars were drag bars.

The "white community" or "the community of men" (and think of how odd these phrases actually sound) are odd or defective in this sense. First, they have no awareness of themselves as communities, because they have no awareness of the identities their communities construct. Those identities are made by something close to a pure exclusion, and they think of them-selves as the normal neutral examples of the universal human condition: in imagination these identities have no content, though in reality their con-tent is perfectly specific and is delineated in a series of exclusions from the self and oppressions of parts of the self. So folks in the dominant groups do not in awareness bind themselves to one another through a recognition of a shared identity, nor are they forced to cohere in order to survive: their iden-tity is precisely their lack of awareness of their own identity.

Second, and here I put some realist cards on the table, there is something defective in these communities because the identities they con-struct are false or fictional or, as I put it before, hallucinatory. Really, there could not be, for example, a community of minds, because you need bodies to communicate. The whiteness that constructs itself from the ejection of the devalued bit of each dualism is impossible in reality, and the demand for an appearance of ejection is an invitation to hypocrisy. Whiteness is a pathological fear and exclusion of the body, which in a creature that is a body can only finally consist in a deep self-loathing and self-betrayal. One might call this self-loathing and self-betrayal "metaphysics."

Community and Meaning

Which brings me to another aspect of dominant groups: their communication is semiotic. That is, they communicate various "meanings" to one another with noises and scribbles that "signify" things. Throughout the history of the West, the privileged bits of the dualisms (mind, culture, master, reason) have been associated with language in its semiotic function, language conceived as something that conveys a distinct series of meanings. Language is the mind's medium, the repository of concepts, the abstraction into which whiteness abstracts itself. Whiteness is writing. The "savage," the "primitive," and so on are conceived to be linguistically defective in that they lack a system of writing. Dominant groups wield language like a transparent medium and use it to carve up and control the world. Call that "science." But my view is that language is degenerate when it is used as a transparent medium and that communication that is conceived that way is impossible in a pure sense and defective to the extent that it is possible.

By extension, the communities that form themselves around "truths"–for example around documents such as the Bible or the Constitution or the works of Nietzsche – are defective communities. A community that coheres in virtue of shared recognition of certain "principles" or "values" is an artificial creation, a simulation. Such a pseudo-community lacks the intensity and directness of communication that originates and consists in the reality of shared experiences. It is a nostalgia or a fantasy and always also a potential horror, because if the fantasy is vivid enough one attempts to impose it on reality: our "shared beliefs" are the ideology with which or for which we will kill or imprison each other in a furious attempt to compensate for their and our lack of reality, a furious attempt to make real what is by definition nothing at all: the abstraction.

Language at its best is noise with shape. I wonder whether you talk while you are making love. It is important "what you say," but it is more important that you say something, that you make some noise, and that the noise have, as it were, the right contour and the right intonation. When there are words, they are part of the general moaning; they are expressions of desire not primarily in virtue of their semantics but in their participation in a pure syntax of pleasure. That is a very intense and important form of communication: it is central. Most human communication is more or less like that. I say, "How ya doin'?" and you respond "I'll probably survive. You?" The point obviously is not whatever propositions our utterances may represent, much less the truth value of those propositions; the point is just to be in proximity to one another making the right kind of noise. It is a kind of touching. When I'm listening to country music on the radio, I am not usually decoding a series of assertions; I am just bathing in human-made noise.

Human communication reaches its most intense and beautiful and typical moments where all the semantics slips away and we are just emitting organized noise in the right shape. And that is key to community. Communities (just stick a little "in my opinion" in each of these sentences for me) are not about "shared beliefs." They are about bathing in the same noise: like gang colors or a neighborhood slang or rap music or Marilyn Manson. Beliefs that we allegedly share turn out, for the most part, to be the completely empty ideology we are all capable of mouthing when our minds have gone blank or when our minds are being scripted by advertising agencies and campaign consultants. This emptiness is the empty space in which dominant identities consist; this emptiness is the abstraction that demonstrates our transcendence of particularity; we reside in the empty space of concepts, of general ideas that we can all come to "share," that "hold us together as a people." This is where our civic documents and institutions reside: in a sphere from which all traces of the non-conceptual have been immolated. That is, these documents and beliefs are also noise, or perhaps we should say that they can only actually occur to anyone through a particular visual or aural interchange. But here we attribute to the noise the power of expressing truth, a power gained by a bit of syntax when it has detached itself from particular contexts of use and floated free like a blimp onto the plane of the eternal. The identity of these truths is like white identity: the blank neutral place where the communication is no one's communication in particular, where truths are self-evident, unchanging, and empty.

And of course these things are related to one another. Dominant identities, conceived through the dualistic ejections, are the identities that possess and wield the truth. The people who inhabit dominant identities, in conceiving themselves through this particular set of exclusions, arrogate to themselves the power abstractly to wield the abstract truth: we are mind, culture, essentially textual items. That is, "mind" is the language in your head, the semantics or the hectoring lecturer within you. "Culture" consists of literacy, science, discourse, technique. But in claiming to float free of the world into these abstractions, we also lose ourselves. We lose ourselves, first of all, as bodies. And we lose ourselves as communities, because we live in "structures" or texts: corporate flow charts, governments, universities. Then we have institutions but we can have no communities.

Beyond Semiotics

Contemplate two fans of Marilyn Manson. Let us say that they mutilate themselves together, that they harm themselves, pierce themselves, cut themselves. That is an extremely intense form of communication: they are literally opening their bodies to one another and the world. Maybe it is "pathological," too. That's what we say in our little institutionalized discourse for purposes of inflicting truth on these people and community on ourselves. But it is an extraordinary process of communication and mutual identification: these kids are marking their bodies with the syntax of community membership or in a resolution or hope of joining a community. Notice, of course, that these might be white male kids from the suburbs; in fact, that's most likely; they are part of the dominant pseudo-community. But what they are trying to do, or one thing they are trying to do, is remove themselves from that pseudo-community in a way that will be immediately visible to anyone, and in particular to the members of that pseudo-community. This may be a form of play that will end soon enough, and these boys will perhaps restart their training as stockbrokers. But what I am asserting is that if they have any chance of finding a community, it is going to have to be by a conscious process of self-exclusion, as well as by joining others. And there can be a snowball effect: they exclude themselves by self-mutilation, then are excluded further because they are mutilated.

Up to now I have been talking as though there are dominant psuedo-communities and subalternate communities, where the dominant pseudo-communities are constructed by ejection, the subalternate communities through being ejected. But even this little Marilyn Manson example shows that to be far too simple. First of all, the Marilyn Manson subculture emerges out of the dominant culture by self-exclusion. Second, it also requires exclusions to exist: we are not stockbrokers. And probably it practices internal exclusions as well, policing its goth borders: you are not weird enough, committed enough, suicidal enough, pierced enough. No doubt there is even a series of "truths" that the Marilyn Manson community might acknowledge, some of which we might find in Marilyn's bestselling autobiography.[3] Furthermore, Marilyn Manson the figure flows through the dominant culture and the dominant culture's media and commercial distribution systems. Even as he attacks the pseudo-community, he depends upon it, and even as it condemns him it embraces him, markets him, provides him, circulates him through all the channels of image and commodity. His location with regard to the grid or flow of communities is extremely complex: he is multiply located, contradictorily located, impossibly profuse in his presence and effects. No community can be purely dominant or subalternate, and all communities have processes of ejection at the heart of their self-construction. Think again of the Amish, who form up through a rejection of "the English", as they call the rest of us, as much as through any positive religious or social commitment, but who also obviously interact with the English continually and in vexed or contradictory ways, as when they get caught up in the co-caine-distribution system.

As the interchange of Amish and Pagan shows, communities are fluid into one another in indefinitely many directions at once. Marilyn Manson is him-self a corporate entity, whether he likes it or not. And he probably likes it, at least at some moments, because he is getting rich. Marilyn Manson is not only an individual who named himself with a beautiful pop culture flair: he is a set of products (t-shirts, compact disks, books, stickers); he is a fashion model, commercial musician, professional weirdo. He is a marketing machine and like all pop culture icons in this era he is perfectly accessible to anybody in all media simultaneously. So Marilyn Manson's relation to the dominant pseudo-community is extraordinarily complicated: he emerged from it; he is a symbol of resistance to it; he is exploiting it toward a suggestion of its own disintegration or destruction; he is exploited by it and producing fortunes for publishers and record companies and concert promoters; he is showing peo-ple a way out of it; he is cashing in on his nihilism; and so on

Deleuze and Guattari have an excellent way of describing these sorts of phenomena: they talk about "major" and "minor" languages,[4] but the very same things can be said about communities. On their account, "major" lan-guages such as "standard English" – which is housed in dictionaries, grammar handbooks, books of quotations, and so forth – are dead. Insofar as they are indeed standard, major, set in stone, they have no life. They have lost the ability to become. They sit there in haughty detemporalized grammatical grandeur, like Latin. Minor languages, slangs, dialects, vernaculars are, on the other hand, alive, in constant flux; they are always becoming. Black American slang, for example, is one of the truly vital linguistic zones in the world. However, this simplistic opposition breaks down, because of course black slang is part of English; it is a slang of English. That in turn makes it appear that black slang is parasitic on standard English: a variation of it. The differing temporal status of major and minor languages follows from their imaginary character and implicates the communities that speak them. The major language, which is the repository of eternal concepts and the medium of the minds that wield such concepts, partakes in a release from the filth of becoming, and promises that release to the people who wield it. The minor languages, on the other hand, are noise: they are thoroughly polluted by particularity and temporality.

One might, again, conceive of the minor language as a dialect or distor-tion of the major language, but that would be a serious misinterpretation. In fact the dependence runs more clearly the other way: the major language depends on its minor languages or slangs for life, even as it seeks in that same process to appropriate the satellite or colonized tongue. Black slang is one of the zones where English becomes: what is black slang today will be in the dictionaries tomorrow. The zones where the English language is alive, the zones that the English language depends on to stay alive, are the slangs of black America, of Jamaicans in London, of rednecks in the deep South, of sex workers, of Marilyn Manson fanatics, and so on. That is, the places where the language is alive are the subalternate communities. This shows that such communities are not distinct from the dominant pseudo-community, but it also shows which way the dependence really runs: the dominant pseudo-community absolutely requires the subalternate communities in order to keep itself alive. The dominant culture, as the culture of eternality and abstraction, is dead. And the dominant culture is entirely false, because its truths purport to float free of the particular in its becoming: the only sphere in which things live. Think again of Marilyn Manson: Marilyn looks to be dependent on the record companies, the press, and so on, in order to be a pop culture "phenomenon." But the record companies and the press need Marilyn, or someone analogous, both to make money and to give them the sense or illusion that they are alive, that they are hip, that they are actually able to become. Issuing the next reunion album by the Eagles or Fleetwood Mac is not going to do the job. The dominant pseudo-community lives vampirically on the blood of the communities it dominates: it needs to exclude them in order to construct itself, and it needs to incorporate them in order to keep itself alive.

One thing this means is that the subalternate communities are always in danger of being destroyed through appropriation, of losing their characteristic weirdness or kinkiness because their language and even their activities are being sucked into the death machine. We can see this in the "slumming" of the dominant culture, or in the romanticization to which the Amish and the Pagans are subject. But the subalternate communities also depend on that for their own life. What pushes gangsta rappers to get ever more extreme, what pushes the leather sex world to get kinkier and devise new pleasures and new pains, what pushes rednecks to stay red or get redder, is precisely the use of their inventions by the dominant community to keep itself alive. Marilyn Manson needs to violate taboos, needs to be right on the edge of what could possibly be done in a public concert. But when his followers have all grown up and there are twenty Marilyn clones out there, someone will have to push beyond that and start something new that will be alive for awhile. People will warm themselves at its life as at a fire.

We folks in the dominant culture romanticize the subalternate communities, we yearn toward them because of their aliveness and because of their cohesion as communities. We encounter them on slumming safaris or through mass media products: rap CDs, Easy Rider, Witness. We require these communities to be in proximity to ourselves as well as to be ejected. We define ourselves as distinct from them, but that means that we must maintain a constant awareness or illusion of who and what these people are. We require ourselves to be what they are not, and that requires us to know or pretend to know who they are. But we also require them in order to become who we will be: they constitute lines of escape from the intolerable and finally impossible Parmenidean stasis of our normality. We need the fear and the desire that the Pagans, for example, or the very idea of the Pagans, arouse, in order to constitute ourselves and in order to keep ourselves from being so fully constituted that we freeze into death and immortality like Platonic Forms.

Limits of Communitarianism

It may seem as though the dream of community is a dream of stability, if not of stasis. Sometimes it seems that communitarian philosophers are reactionaries in the sense that they would like to slow time down or stop it: they like to imagine the Greek polis. Communitarian philosophers also like to contrast their approach with the abstract ideology of liberalism or libertarianism, preferring to start with the concrete situation of people actually trying to get on together. One of the implications of the points I have been developing, however, is that communitarianism is as abstract as the views it rejects. For example, the "Responsive Communitarian Platform" says that "communities that glorify their own members by vilifying those who do not belong are at best imperfect." From which, of course, it follows that there are no perfect communities, which of course was obvious to begin with. Or this: "For a community to be truly responsive . . . it will have to develop moral values which meet the following criteria . . ."[5] That simply drops us out of the possibility of any community at all and lands us in the never-never land of concepts and empty fantasy identities. As a Marilyn Manson fan might say, "Shut up and thrash."

It is perhaps ironic, given these dreams of stasis, that the actual communities that we can point to are the zones of our culture that are most in flux, in which identities are most liquid or most volatile, in which the language shifts with lightning rapidity, in which there is no telling what might happen on any given night. This is not surprising, though, because such communities consist without remainder of their members: they change as quickly as the people that are in them. And those people change quickly because they are constantly engaged in the processes of being excluded and of excluding others. Subalternate communities do not, by and large, worship texts or worry much about whether they have a system of shared beliefs: they just engage in a constantly fluctuating process of real communication. They bathe in each other's noise. That's what a community is, and it's not something that you make happen; it's something that just happens, and happens by an incredibly elaborate process of nested exclusions that is different in each case. So here's my advice: stop pretending to make communities happen or specifying how they can happen and simply allow them to continue to emerge. Anything else is an abstraction and a delusion.

Notes

1   Bronislaw Malinowski, *The Sexual Life of Savages in North-Western Melanesia; An Ethnographic Account of Courtship, Marriage and Family Life Among the Natives of the Trobriand Islands, British New Guinea* (New York: H. Liveright, 1929).

2   See, e.g., Alasdair MacIntyre, *After Virtue* (Notre Dame: University of Notre Dame Press, 1984), chs 14 and 15.

3   Marilyn Manson with Neil Strauss, *The Long Hard Road Out of Hell* (New York: HarperCollins, 1998). An example of a truth articulated by Manson and no doubt recognized by his community as central to membership: "You're gay if you get hard while sucking another guy's dick. If you don't, you're straight" (p. 134).

4   Gilles Deleuze and Felix Guattari, *A Thousand Plateaus*, trans. Brian Massumi (Minneapolis: University of Minnesota Press, 1987), pp. 104–5.

5   This platform is posted at *www.communitariannetwork.org/platformtext.htm* . It is endorsed by such figures as Jean Bethke Elshtain, Amitai Etzioni, Francis Fukuyama, and Orlando Patterson.

3

Impure Communities

Maria Lugones

"Impure" is a word I began to work with to capture the disruption of dichotomies from a threatening location. It is from a threatening location that I address the need for impure community, the need for an against-the-grain sociality. The ambition of construing oneself among others as a non-subjected subject, when one is marked as outside that possibility, gives a sense of movement and activity to the location. The location is actively inhabited by a multitude of interrelated beings harboring this ambition. To understand the location is to understand that their/our subjectivity cannot be presupposed to be marked by agency. Self-determination, autonomy, in the modern sense, has been left out of our profile. But then agency and self-determination do not exhaust the possibilities of active subjectivity. The ambition to metamorphose into non-subjected subjects is marked as outside institutionalized sociality, institutionalized sense. Our intentionality as non-subjected subjects is thus in need and in search of sociality, a sociality that cannot be found within the confines of "articulate structures." There are no sanctioned, public rhetorical spaces where we can make sense as non-subjected subjects, where our intentions as non-subjected subjects have full credibility, full "choral support," full sense.[1] Everywhere we turn we are incited to make a sense and to inhabit intentions that turn us away from this ambition.

"Impurity" is a double-edged word that marks the location as one that threatens both the "integrity" of those who occupy it – the subaltern – and one that threatens the grounds and practices of domination. Impurity's threat lies in its very constitution in disruption of dichotomies, in its being out of place or order in a dichotomous order. To understand the threat, we can turn to Mary Douglas, who in *Purity and Danger* relates pollution behavior – behavior to control pollution, impurity – as a guarding of structure from the threat of impurity.[2] Douglas sees power in impurity, a threatening-to-order power. She understands what is impure as anomalous and ambiguous relative to some order. The order is normed and *constitutes* the impure as a threat, since, within it, what is impure is not definable, it is outside the order. So separation from it is a manner of containing it. Douglas makes the important claim that "Where the social system is well articulated, I look for articulate powers vested in the points of authority; where the social system is ill-articulated, I look for inarticulate powers vested in those who are a source of disorder."[3] I myself have become interested in inarticulate powers that disrupt well-articulated social systems through impure connections.

The impure contain an ambiguity that is consistently concealed from view. On the one hand the operation that constitutes the subaltern – the subordinate, the pervert, the outcast – takes the form of polluting behavior. The subaltern is imagined, constructed, treated as the bad side of a multiplicity of dichotomies that constitute subjectivity, and constitute the subjectivity of the subaltern as in need of subjection. The subaltern is understood as body in need of control, unbridled passion, undirected energy. So with dichotomies as central in the conceptual framework, some of us are simultaneously conceived as impure and tamed. Taming is justified by "our" very "own" "natures." The subaltern are turned from their out-of-control constitution – produced by the dichotomizing operation – into subjected, controlled, under-control, beings.

I want to recapture and reconceive the impure, but not as those who constituted themselves as whites might have recaptured their own "dark" side, their own "unbridled passions," through the ritual of black face. Rather, I want to reconceive the impure while dwelling in the ambiguity of us when understood as outside, in transgression of, in disruption of, the impulse to dichotomize. We are then not just thoroughly in the middle of "either/or," but incomprehensible, inconceivable, as impure—neither this nor that – from the position of order. We are comprehensible, conceivable, from within an unruly relationality that is both resistant and inarticulate, a relationality that finds its ground to be unstable, ephemeral, one that is as evanescent as the non-subjected subjectivity of its terms.

My interest in the phenomenon of community, then, is an interest in the possibility a more articulate, more tightly connected, less ephemeral, resistant collectivity. Thus I am not perched in the relative safety of what we have in common, of ossified tradition, or the common good. That is, I am not interested in the relative safety that excludes the impure in an impulse to control it, to control pollution. I seek to disrupt dichotomies from within impurity. To understand the impulse to reject dichotomies is to understand it as crucially related to the impulse toward collectivity. But indeed this is a reconceived collectivity. This sense of collectivity stands in contrast, and in tension with community understood by those communitarian theorists for whom community is identified with social structures that are intelligible from within a logic of dichotomies and are thus hostile to the impure. So it is the impulse to reject dichotomies and to live and embody that rejection that gives us some hope of standing together as people who recognize each other in our complexity.

"I" – the *possible* being—formulate "my" stance – both my ground and direction—in the midst of a concrete plurality, a multitude of interrelated subjects: concrete, complex, non-reducible, cantankerous, fleshy, interrelated, positioned subjects non-containable within any hard-edged, simple, classification. This relationality stands conceptually outside the order of dominance and subjection, but also stands at a tense angle with the multitude classified, broken up, segregated, categorially conceived, fragmented, looking for our bread and butter, our pride, and our ground in hard-edged, smooth inside, prickly outside, nations. I take fragmentation to be of a piece with the logic and politics of dichotomizing. So, it is also from within and in tense relations with the nations and the politics of identity that I want to reconsider the ambition to create a non-subjected subjectivity. It is from this reconceived sense of the multitude of interrelated subjects that I am considering the relation between impurity and community.

It is helpful in understanding the project to unveil the difference between this multitude as a possible community and community as understood by communitarian moral theorists. In doing so, I also want to mark the way that the communitarians' sense of community backs up, gives sense to, makes possible the agency and intentionality of particular subjects who are within and benefit from the order of communities so conceived. I want also to mark the contrast between the solidity of this backing and the sense of *possibility* that might be created from within the fleshy, complex, and fragile relationality of subjects harboring the ambition toward non-subjected subjectivity. The former makes for the illusion of individualism, individual authorship, individual achievement and creation, and the illusion of intentionality as an affair that resides in individuals.

The collective backing for the individual, or, better put, the collective guise of the individual's doings, the set of institutionalized practices, norms, structures, the collectivity backing-up, affording credibility, authorizing the individual's sense, achievement, authorship, intentionality, determination, becomes obscured, invisible in the illusion of individualism, it becomes a backdrop. And this obscuring as a matter of course conveniently includes the obscuring of those relations of exploitation and subordination that partly weave the monument of individual sense. There is an oddity in communitarian theory, that the fleshy collectivity, the concrete relationality that builds and maintains the community understood carefully in all its ugly oppressive dimensions, is not what is constitutive of community. In communitarian theory, community is unburdened of its concreteness, of its fleshiness, and taken to be the monument itself, standing alone, unmanned as it were, a collection of institutions ascribing roles and subtracting, "disappearing" responsibility in a maybe forced, maybe unreflective, but surely supportive relationality.

I want to pay close attention to that concrete relationality and look for the traces, clues, inarticulate powers, evanescent intentions, fragile connections, disguised disruptions of and by non-subjected subjects as we feel our way toward a non-public (or perhaps a counterpublic) sociality.

Contemporary communitarians have conceived of communities as constituted by shared norms, values, practices, and by particularly powerful institutions such as the family, neighborhood, school, church, and nation. The logic of community in this understanding is one of homogeneity, of simplicity, of purity. Not only Alasdair MacIntyre and Michael Sandel, but also Marilyn Friedman adopt this view of community.[4] They understand the strength of community as an ethical starting point to reside precisely in commonality, though Friedman is wary of the institutions that she takes to be definitive of what she calls "communities of place." She understands communitarian philosophy to be "a perilous ally" for feminist theory precisely because of its invocation of family, church, neighborhood, and nation: "These sorts of communities have harbored numerous social roles and structures that lead to the subordination of women."[5] So, Sandel and MacIntyre understand communities and Friedman understands communities of place as sets of institutionalized, stable, given, relationships that leave all deviations from traditional institutional prescriptions, all resistant connections and relations outside their limits.

Because Friedman understands communities of place as this set of institutionalized, stable, given, relationships, she conceives of all deviations from traditional institutional prescriptions, all resistant connections and relations, as communities of choice, as matters of choice that are pitted conceptually and spatially in tension with communities of place. But communities of choice are conceived also in terms of commonality, of shared values, of convergent needs and desires. And most importantly the use of the word "choice" makes clear that the need, the desire, the value, is understood as residing whole and clear in the individual rather than collectively made. The impulse, the intentionality, toward others is more articulate than I think possible in isolation. As I think of the intentionality of the resistant subject, it strikes me as unclear, barely formed, not quite articulable, or articulable but whose meaning and direction are not quite congealed. I think of it as transferred carefully and daringly from hand to hand, from mouth to mouth, body to body in the absence of trust and assured reciprocity, a thoroughly dangerous and necessary gesture that comes from a blurriness in who we are, even if we have been taught to trust our very "own" sense of ourselves. This is a circulation moved by both active subjectivity and uncertainty.

In an essay entitled, "Persons and Others," Lorraine Code moves us forward in the epistemology of an ethics of relationality as she points out that "treating a person as a person involves recognizing the pertinence of her self-conception to the person that she is, working to understand the interplay of correctness and incorrectness that goes on when that self-conception is wholly at odds with other people's perceptions of her."[6] Code recalls Elizabeth Spelman's distinction between "treating someone merely as a bearer of rights, and treating someone as the person that she is."[7] In doing so, both Spelman and Code take us rightly away from the illusion of altruism captured by Thomas Nagel in his characterization of seeing an other as a person, a person among others, where the multitude of others are depersonalized away from their fleshy and problematic interrelationality, from the complications of their locations.

I bring Code and Spelman into my text because as they depart from the logic of depersonalization and from disconnected, non-intersubjectively negotiated altruism, they bring to us this phrase, "the person she is," and the injunction "to treat her as the person she is," taking into account her own sense of who she is, a sense which may fly in the face of others' understandings of her. This is a troubling expression and a very problematic injuction when considered from the point of view of subjected subjects seeking to unravel, give direction, form, and sociality to their possibilities. It is problematic because the emphasis lies on the person who one is rather than on the person one can become. Treating her as such is very different from treating her in ways that support and further the project of becoming.

I earlier used the expression "possible being" with respect to myself when I said "I – the possible being – formulate my stance—both my ground and direction – in the midst of a concrete plurality." I want to end by giving greater fullness to this phrase and its place in the relation between the ambition towards non-subjected subjectivity and impure community. I understand subjected subjects inclined, leaning towards, non-subjection as possible beings whose possibility lies in the uncertain creation of a loosely concerted intersubjectivity. I choose to converse with Code on this because she seems to have similar preoccupations without giving full sail to the consequences of her epistemic framework. Code herself is preoccupied by rhetorical spaces that rob certain statements of the very possibility of counting as true or false.[8] These rhetorical spaces also rob particular speakers of cognitive authority, of credibility.[9] She recommends testimony to us as a source of knowledge for its dialogic, intersubjective qualities: "a testimonial report looks to its listener(s) for evidence of comprehension, acknowledgement. For testimony is, inherently, a form of address in which epistemic interaction, intersubjectivity are explicitly invoked. Hence it would appear to be a place where epistemic individualism could no longer hold."[10] She questions monologic understandings of knowledge production that pose knowledge claims and don't take interlocutors as necessary to their completion.[11]

I myself take subjects, claims, intentions, as all being partly products of knowledge-needing-interlocutions, some form of reception and response, needing a carrying of one's incipient meaning[12] to other hands and ears and tongues toward praxical completion in the liberating project. So when it comes to subjects with an ambition to create ourselves historically and socially as non-subjected, I don't think of us as we are, but as possible, in formation, as projects, collective, communal projects who construct an unruly collectivity in the process, a collectivity they are dependent on for sense and reality. Or perhaps I would rephrase the injunction, and would talk of knowing others as the persons they are plotting to become, something that requires that they be known relationally as they barely exist in isolation. I think my rephrasing of the injunction may be faithful to Code's own framework and preoccupations in ways that the possibility of completed/made/understandable-apart-from-interaction subjects who have much of a chance to know themselves is not. The subjectivity of the impure seems to me more incomplete, fragile, evanescent than the subjectivity of Code's central characters. And indeed hers are depicted as less than on solid ground.

So, why speak of community instead of collectivity or sociality in this project? It is because I understand the impulse toward sociality connected to the ambition to become non-subjected subjects as one that makes one ready for a different disposition to communicate in complex ways. A disposition to communicate in ways that can bring about a complex oppositional community, organized relationally in ways that we can merely adumbrate. The disposition includes an awareness of the fragility and incompleteness of one's sense and authority and creativity as one passes meaning on. One is clear that one does not have mastery over "one's own" sense, over one's own intentions. Uncertainty is one of the modifiers of the tonality of the circulation of meaning. It is an active wait and see, delicately, carefully, carrying the expressive sign from person to person in a listening for what they are concocting mood. We can adumbrate that the community, this complex relationality, would be sensitive, as a spider's web is sensitive to communicative moves in different spatialities, tonalities, and expressive means.

Notes

1   There are of course infrapolitical rhetorical spaces where we can make sense as non-subjected subjects, where our intentions as non-subjected have full credibility. Bernice Johnson Reagon tells us in *The Songs are Free* (New York: Mystic Fire Video, 1991) how she experienced Black churches in this way, though she does not use the word "infrapolitical." In thinking about impure communities, I am thinking of socialities that transgress racial dualisms, among others. See Lorraine Code, *Rhetorical Spaces* (London: Routledge, 1995), p. 95.
2   Mary Douglas, *Purity and Danger* (London: Ark Paperbacks), 1989.
3   Ibid., p. 99.

4   Alasdair MacIntyre, *After Virtue* (Notre Dame: University of Notre Dame Press, 1981); Michael Sandel, *Liberalism and the Limits of Justice* (Cambridge: Cambridge University Press, 1982); Marilyn Friedman, "Feminism and Modern Friendship: Dislocating the Community," *Ethics* 99 (1989): 275–90.
5   Friedman, "Feminism and Modern Friendship," p. 288.
6   Code, *Rhetorical Spaces*, p. 96.
7   Ibid., p. 94.
8   Ibid., p. x.
9   Ibid., p. 64.
10   Ibid., p. 65.
11   Ibid.
12   In "By Bread Alone," Homi Bhabha offers a complex interpretation of the circulation of traditional signs "in-between the colonizer and the colonized" from which I have profited. He understands the "indeterminacy of meaning" differently than I do, yet the sense of "rhetorical uncertainty" is common to both projects. Homi Bhabha, *The Location of Culture* (London, New York: Routledge, 1991), p. 202.

4

Identities: The Dynamical Dimensions of Diversity

Chuck Dyke and Carl Dyke

Diversity of every sort, including social and biological diversity, is a matter of stably coexisting differences.[1] To examine the relationship between diversity and community we are going to have to see how various differences arise, and the conditions under which they can persist. But to say this is already to have made a commitment to thinking of diversity as a feature of one or another dynamic, historical process, not a matter of a priori typology. This commitment informs everything that follows. In fact, the overall task of this essay is to spell out the overall merits of a dynamical approach. After all, this volume is examining a range of possibilities. It seeks to find out what sorts of diversity can coexist with what sorts of communities, what combinations might reasonably be expected, and what combinations can be expected not to occur. To be serious about such questions is to seek the best possible models.[2]

Though more familiar than they were a few years ago, the language and modeling techniques of nonlinear dynamics are not yet trilling melodiously from the mouths of the multitude. This means that this chapter will have to deal with more theoretical background than most of the other contributions. But the work is worth it. In our own process of learning from and thinking with nonlinear dynamics, we have noticed a pleasing increase in our ability to make sense of things that previously were mysterious and inexplicable. We are also sustained by the rapidity with which the insights of nonlinear dynamics have settled into many sub-fields of both the natural and the social sciences.

Identity and Dynamical Space

We need a nontrivial conception of diversity. The differences we settle on as those that "measure" diversity have to matter. Any bunch of things that can be distinguished from each other is trivially diverse. So we shall follow the lead of those who have been thinking about diversity in the contexts of race, class, gender, and sexuality, and proceed on the premise that the kinds of difference that make a difference are those that contribute to self-identity and social identity. This immediately circumscribes a problematic space. In the terms of an analysis we build on, "If what matters about me is my individual authentic self, why is so much contemporary talk of identity about large categories – race, gender, ethnicity, nationality, and sexuality – that seem so far from individual?"[3] A good question: we shall reply that the apparent categories are, when looked at in the most useful way, dimensions within a dynamical system, a system of histories.

Similarly, women, since de Beauvoir, have been thinking of these matters in terms of the dynamical structuring of alterities, ways in which they are "the other," and have gone beyond de Beauvoir in trying to integrate class and other factors with gender in a complex interactive dynamical picture.[4] In fact, something very like our theoretical viewpoint is articulated by Rosi Braidotti in the following:

> The theorists emerging in the 1990s are consequently working along the lines of a multiplicity of variables of definition of female subjectivity: race, class, age, sexual preference and lifestyles count as major axes of identity. They therefore innovate on the classical notion of materialism, in that they are bent on redefining female subjectivity in terms of a network of simultaneous power formations. We shall argue next that a trend seems to be emerging that emphasizes the situated, specific, embodied nature of the feminist subject, while rejecting biological or psychic essentialism. This is a new kind of female embodied materialism.[5]

There are actually two kinds of diversity we shall have to deal with, even given the decision to focus on identities as the dynamically relevant ways in which people can be different. Both are historical matters. First, people are multidimensional. We shall have to pay attention both to the multiplicity of dimensions and to the depth of entrenchment of any of the dimensions of potential difference (not to speak, yet, of the defining feature of dynamical systems, the interactions among dimensions). Some things about us are more abiding than others. "Philandering" may be an odd old word for woman-chasing, when you think about it, but if philandering were very important to us, that would have enormous consequences for our chances of living in community with women, and, in any case, constrain the kinds of community possible. Alternatively, if certain kinds of community became important for us, we might well mend our ways. To become a woman, on the other hand, would be a longer and more difficult process. Most abidingly, if we are anything essentially, it is human animals.[6]

It is probably more accurate to call people multifarious than diverse, but notice that any pattern of diversity will be constituted by the dimensions of individuals. So, second, diversity proper is a matter of the number and distribution of dynamically relevant dimensions within a population or social whole. It is conceivable that individuals be stolidly low dimensional yet different from one another, and it is possible that people are richly multidimensional, but in the same ways. Of course the other permutations might occur as well.[7] For instance, when people talk about biodiversity, they are generally talking about a wide variety of species in which individuals are assumed to be pretty much the same. In fact, chauvinists that we are, we seldom pay much attention to the dimensionality of individuals of other species – except maybe for our pets. But even that is interesting in the present context, for there is a strong sense in which people are in community with their pets.

So we can say that in any typical social setting individuals will tend to be dimensionally variable and that social (as well as ecological) systems are variably diverse. The fun comes when we see that dimensional variability and variable diversity are dynamically interactive. Or, to put it in a sentence a bit more readable, the kinds of ways in which individuals will tend to characterize or ally themselves change, and the kinds of people there are around them will be sensitive to each other.

While it is a little hard to say, the last point is not big news to any of us.[8] At one end of the spectrum it is as unremarkable as the fact that genetic variability in individuals and the range of phenotypes in the population are mutually dependent. At the other end of the spectrum it comes to the truism that if everyone around you conforms to the same way of life, the chances of your deviating from the pattern are far less than they would be if you had "role models" of many different kinds. Historical contingencies have made the Balkans uncomfortably plural, and Japan uncomfortably singular.

There is no a priori way of deciding what will be a significant dynamical dimension. These dimensions are diagnosed, and their relevance tested with experience of the system in question. Of course this is not just a part of research heuristics. It is also part of making friends, deciding what organizations to join, and probably also deciding whom to marry. The surprising number of personality differences we encounter are a tribute to the nonlinear combinatorial possibilities of a plurality of dimensions. But in deciding what really matters to the people we encounter, we are doing the same thing we would be doing if we were trying to specify a dynamical dimensional space for them.

Because we are interested in humans, we are obviously going to find that imagination and conceptualization are going to figure strongly in the dynamics of both their individuality and their community formation. In fact, this is the issue that has taken the worst beating from the tradition of atomism and linearity in Western thought. All the traditions that ended up in the twentieth century with logical atomism are traditions of linear additivity. As such, they are utterly inconsistent with the nonlinear model being developed here.

But from the opposite point of view, with nonlinearity as the norm, exclusive reliance on the language of "and" and "not" is a bit bizarre in any case. Indicatively, the nearest brush with interactive nonlinearity that the atomist traditions had was with "intentionality" and "intensionality," the first a nest of perplexities about the "subject/object" interaction; and the second having to do with the "failure of substitutability" of apparent synonyms, in other words the location of a major nonlinearity in language attempting to cope with our multidimensional interaction with the world. There is really no need to vex this any more these days, save for the fact that, for some, recalling these controversies will be a way of orienting themselves to the consequences of nonlinearity in a realm other than mathematics. But we can also note that identity is a consequence of the interaction of self-conception and the perceptions of others.[9] In solipsistic splendor we can think of ourselves any way we please. Without the affirmations (and denial) of others, this simply defines a site of illusion and delusion.

So, in our view identity is emergent. That is to say, it is to be understood in terms of its history and situation. There are strong spatial and temporal limits to the degree to which self and identity are fixed. They change with time and ambiance. Thus, selves and identities are not primordial, given in an irrevocable act of special creation. No one is born with either a self or an identity; they emerge interactively in a real "here and now."

A fractal, dynamical approach recognizes these sites of interaction.[10] It welcomes active interlaced indeterminacies as important indications of the dimensions and strengths of disagreement and difference producing an array of actual and possible identities. We might reflect that classical Marxism claimed precisely that class boundaries would harden, class identity would totalize the dynamical space, and violent attempts at readjustment would result. But we can also reflect that class boundaries did not harden in the developed economies. Ways (the welfare state and consumerism, among others) were found to soften these boundaries – at least for a century.

The conditions of their emergence calls for a rather radical revision of the common sense of self and identity. Insofar as the interactive fields in which selves and identities are formed are differentiated, those selves and identities will also be emergently differentiated. Selves and identities change not only over time, but over everything that changes around them. From this we can expect that selves and identities will be distributed in what we will see presently to be a fractal pattern. Apparently identical combinations of identity dimensions at one moment will result in radically different social selves at a next moment. Alliances and allegiances will be chosen in surprisingly different ways. No one who is a man, or a woman, or black, or white is simply such. Every "good" family has its black sheep, and every "bad" neighborhood has its guy who made something of herself.

As any good disciple of linear rationalism would point out at this juncture, there appear to be no "law-like" connections determining the outcomes of these various circumstances. The exact outcomes of any given configuration of dimensional variability and diversity appear to be intrinsically unpredictable. And indeed they are, in any exact sense.[11] But that, after all, is an expectable situation for nonlinear phenomena, even phenomena that are rigidly deterministic. So it is into these realms that we have to make a theoretical excursion to understand the dynamics of diversity. The way of thinking involved is new enough to justify a moment's pause.

The Mandelbrot Set

By now everyone has seen the standard picture of the Mandelbrot set, an exemplar of which is appended (see figure 4.1). The story it tells may not be as familiar as the picture, but it has to be told if we are to be clear about the job the picture can do for us. The compressed form of the Mandelbrot set story is an equation. All equations are highly compressed narratives, after all, and quite often pretty boring narratives even when decompressed. In this case we shall decompress the story in terms of the construction of the picture as follows: A set of points makes up a surface – the monitor screen, a piece of paper, or whatever. In this case, the surface is laid out as the complex plane.[12] Every point on the plane has a complex number as its address. The equation describes trips from any given point on the surface to an ultimate destination. All points are eventually to be identified in terms of the sort of destination the trips beginning at them have. There are two sorts of ultimate destination. A trip may end at a determinate finite point (or points),[13] or it may end up in the never-never land of mathematical infinity. So, to generate the Mandelbrot set you, in effect, insert the address of a particular point on the surface into the equation-thought-of-as-a-machine and turn the crank. After many (often really many) turns of the crank, the machine coughs up either the address of the ultimate destination, or the laconic and enigmatic news that the trip from the entered address ends up in never-never land. The starting points that do not begin trips to never-never land will be called insiders. The starting points that begin trips to never-never land will be called outsiders.

So far the narrative is a banal story of simple alterity, but the plot thickens. The machine cannot always tell insiders from outsiders – at least in time to let us know which we are dealing with. In such doubtful cases it has to cough up an apology and a guess instead of a destination. It has a rule, called the escape algorithm, for guessing.

The familiar picture of the Mandelbrot set is the result of burdening the machine with the task of telling us about all the insiders and the outsiders. However, the machine is preoccupied with its limitations, so when it detects a clear insider or a clear outsider it simply leaves the starting point blank and moves on. But often it has to guess. When it guesses that it has an insider on its hands, it again leaves the starting point blank and moves on, but when it guesses that it is dealing with an outsider it blackens the starting point. So what we see when we look at the Mandelbrot set is a pattern of guess results – rigorously justified guesses to be sure, but guesses nonetheless. The confident story of insiders and outsiders is a story told in what an artist would call negative space.

One more point has to be made about the Mandelbrot set before we can use it. Every time we are given a picture of it, the picture is at a particular magnification. At that magnification the boundaries of indecision look pretty sharply drawn, as if we could draw a nice thin line around the clear white inside and the clear white outside, leaving the multicolored area neatly walled off. But this is an illusion created by the limitations of the representation. Any line we drew around the area of indecision would have to be infinitely long, weaving around infinitely complex twists and turns. In fact, there are edges everywhere. As close as you please to any insider,

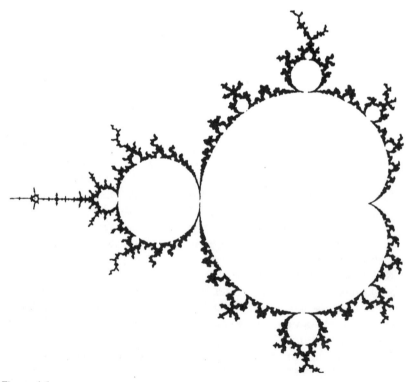

Figure 4.1

there is an outsider, and as close to them as you please there is a doubtful case.[14] The pattern we see when we look at the Mandelbrot set is the pattern in which the insiders, outsiders, and doubtful cases are mingled together. No matter how finely and closely we looked at the mingling, it would always exhibit the same pattern. There is no level at which doubtful cases disappear. There is no level at which the characteristic pattern would fail to be identifiable. This is expressed by saying that the Mandelbrot set is a true fractal.

As we would expect in a mathematical context, the definition of the difference between insiders and outsiders is more precise than any that could ever be cooked up for, say, a particular sort of social dichotomy. Greek/barbarian, man/woman, believer/unbeliever: you name it, the distinction can be no more precise than that between the Mandelbrot set and its other. Still, despite the rigor and precision with which the Mandelbrot set is characterized (and, as a matter of fact, because of them) the definition cannot put us in the position of being able to decide between insiders and outsiders in all cases in any finite time no matter how large. Of course, in some infinitely long run, a big enough machine could crank out a decision about every point in the space. But that wouldn't do a bit of good if you need an answer in, say, a lifetime, or the lifetime of our universe. More to the point, what good would such a definition do you if your political or social policy depends on a clean distinction between insiders and outsiders?

The Mandelbrot set is only one among indefinitely many cases now well studied in which a space is divided into apparent dichotomy, an unmarked "category" and its marked "other," but in such a way that clean lines cannot be drawn. The availability of such cases, super-rigorous as they are, does two things for us. First, on the positive side, it gives us an extensive and fertile fund of highly flexible easily manipulable models for use in examining phenomena with complex edges, as we will in a moment. Second, on the way to the real pay-off, it holds a certain sort of rationalist criticism of social theory at bay. Social theorists and historians do not need to duck away from a dialogue with the natural sciences because they study phenomena that aren't as regular as clockwork; nor need they feel pressure to pretend to reduce what they study to clockwork. Only a tiny fraction of dynamical systems run like clockwork in any realm, physical, chemical, biological, or social.

Notice that we have been careful to say that the fuzzy visible area of the set is an area of indecision rather than, say, an area of indeterminacy. There is nothing mathematically indeterminate about any of the iterations producing the Mandelbrot set. What is well defined (either mathematically or socially, we might say) can have infinitely complex edges.

Dynamic Diversity

On this view, what we have become used to thinking of as social or psychological categories are not static "types," but more or less stable, more or less abiding occupations of bio-social space. Any of these "categories" is to be thought of as a dimension of social space. But the dimensions are not orthogonal, not independent contributors to trajectories through the space of identities. There are vectors, pushes and pulls, in each dimension, but the space is folded and stretched. In the course of multiple interactions, the system operates on its own previous states, producing results that cannot be considered as (approximated by) the additive results of two or more "independent variables." We are complex, not simple loci of our socially relevant characteristics. Any attempt to draw boundaries around people in any given dimension will threaten futility. At best, the boundary lines will all be very, very long. At the conceptual level there will be instability also. For as the space of available options changes shape, the decisions about marginal cases will shift; also as part of and as a result of the dynamics. Questions of diversity and community are questions of possible sizes for state spaces, attainable compossibilities for spaces of various sizes variously dimensioned, and the stability conditions for any state attained.

Further, a lot of the dynamics involves embodied conceptualizations – senses of self, good and bad, distinction, and so forth, involving differential pulls toward various states. These pulls create the dynamical field; and their interaction creates the nonlinear, stretched, and folded manifold upon which the social system lives. The story of complexity is built on interactions resulting in nonlinearity. Nonlinear phenomena are not additive results of their components, but novel and often surprising reorganizations of them. Linear phenomena, historically the most studied phenomena because of their simplicity, can be "taken apart," and the individual components "traced" in their trajectories thought of as independent trajectories. It is relatively straightforward to say of them "what would have happened" had some component been absent. It is possible to assess the relative (additive) effect of each of the components, and say with reasonable precision, for example, what "part of the variance" is due to this or that component. All this is, in general, impossible with nonlinear phenomena. In consequence, new research heuristics and methods of evaluating data have to come into play when we look at social and other systems and, indeed, ourselves as genuinely complex. [15]

This may sound pretty abstract and arcane when put in more or less "technical" terms, but it is our view that this sort of formulation merely articulates from a theoretical point of view what others, such as feminist theorists, have been able to see far more concretely from theirs. Their viewpoint has been well represented and has proved illuminating. But seeing matters from the abstract point of view shows how central the feminist theorizing really is. The conceptualization they have developed turns out to be far more generally accurate and useful than the one they replaced. Complexity and nonlinearity deeply affect the way we understand definitions; and, we would say, especially self-definitions. Interactive plurality does not produce essences and categories; it produces a complex play of edges – some of which wend their fractal way to our core.

The feminists have been able to see concretely at the root what we frame abstractly while hovering above the branches. They have also been able to feel the disciplinary power of rationalist definition. One of the more prominent moves of traditional Western rationalism is to try to force us into the acceptance of a hard dichotomy between that which is explicable (read "rigidly determined") and that which is inexplicable (read "indeterminate or random"). Thus was underwritten the chronic agonizing over the (self-generated) problem of the freedom of the will, and, more crucially, a series of reductive transformations of human life based on the particular version of mechanistic theory of a given moment. But we now could know better. Anything characterized by interactive plurality can be expected to have a complex behavior that is irreducible to added simplicities. Yet it is not indeterminate. It turns out that essentialism is tied not to determinism, but only to a particular sort of determinism conceived through and through in essentialist terms. There is no reason whatsoever to base any fundamental account of the goings on of the world on such a theory. For example, being a Muslim woman is not a matter of adding two static class inclusions. Neither, of course, is being a member of the middle class a matter of statics. To be any of these is to be on a complex dynamical trajectory. Better by far for dealing with this situation than the traditional image of static classes is an image of a multiple dimensioned space through which people are pulled by a web of allegiances, belongings, and identities that are now more, now less important to the patterns of their lives.

Despite the momentary irony we produce, we have to think of "woman," "middle class," "Muslim," and undoubtedly a number of other identity characteristics in the example as "degrees of freedom," that is, dynamically relevant things that can vary. To find out what is dynamically relevant, we have to observe for a while and find out what differences are associated with differential trajectories. There is nothing a priori about degrees of freedom. Sometimes we actually perform social experiments that help us see the dynamical relevance of this or that fact or factor. For instance, enforced principles of equality are always, among other things, attempts to render characteristics – potential alterities – dynamically irrelevant. Trajectories of blacks, for example, are expected to be the same as those of whites; the patterns of women's lives, in relevant respects, identical to the pattern of men's lives. Then we assess the success of egalitarian social policy by examining lots of trajectories for signs of difference.

Of course, finding a way to manipulate a social system along a preordained trajectory will be tricky, and this is a disconcerting prospect for the positivist social sciences. They descended from Comptean roots with the dream of manipulation and control as their ideal. Reliable techniques of manipulation and control are available (in general) only for systems operating in linear regimes, and there are very few of these outside textbooks. We should not forget, however, that attempts at manipulation and control are being made all the time at many social scales. These attempts are a real part of social dynamics even when the hopes for their reliable success are misplaced.

Diversity and Community

We can now try to confront the major issue of diversity and community in terms of the model sketch we have. In dynamical terms, the key issue is that diversity implies the ample exploration of a large dimensional state space, and community implies constraints both on space dimension and allowable exploration. This means that the stability conditions for a community embodying diversity will require a delicate poise between interactive dimensions: a harmony. This is not late breaking news, since it characterizes what has been called (justly or not) the "Rousseauean community," and in the Western tradition it has its roots in the ancient classics. The news, on the other hand, is that our ability to evaluate possibilities and assess prospects is better than it was. We can get where we want to go fastest if we set up a contrast.

In *Discipline and Punish*, Foucault claims that one of the main agendas of developed modern states is the production of docile bodies: conforming, reliable, dull, malleable candidates for the workforce.[16] Whether right or not, this conception can serve us as a paradigm of the installation of constraints. We can also reflect that Foucault's account of the self-installation of the constraints as the gaze circulates among us is also a paradigm of nonlinearly self-organized structure. The result is a radical contraction of the degrees of freedom (dimensions, remember) of individuals, and the loss of diversity of the population as well. There is every attempt in this to promote stability, but certainly no attempt to create community. But we can move on from the docile bodies Foucault imagines as a reliable labor force to another phenomenon characteristic of advanced capitalism, that is, Fordism, K-martyrdom, or, as it is sometimes called, consumerism. As is often pointed out, consumerism involves a high degree of discipline at one level, with the promise of individual distinction in what we can now call for short "lifestyle."[17] Can community be built on lifestyle? The yuppies think it can. But more important than the opportunities afforded by the market simply in terms of consumption is the often tacit belief that with the market as the overall organizing structure, room will also be made available within which "deeper" grounds for community can survive and thrive. For, the story goes, the market is naturally as blind as justice itself to historical differences such as race, religion, and ethnic origin. Hence there is no reason to suppress these traditional loci of unity. In effect, the market is thought to partition the state space of possible identities, decoupling economic life from life in other terms.

In contrast to the "Rousseauean" strategy, this can be called the "American" strategy, for, as a nation of immigrants and imports, we have constantly called upon economic well-being to manage overall discipline as ethnic, racial, and religious groups have sought to maintain separate communities in traditional terms. This has been Americans' most common conception of themselves, at least since the definitive dismissal of the image of the melting pot by Glazer and Moynihan half a century ago,[18] and it is arguably the way we have, in fact, thought of ourselves from the very beginning.

But as we know, the market really is not orthogonal to the rest of life – that is, an independent dimension not subject to modification by other dimensions. Because of the contingencies of our history here in the United States, the market comes closest to the ideal of independence with us. Elsewhere in the world no such claim is plausible. Furthermore, it could be argued that we are hostages to the market and a constant policy of military dominance precisely because of the intractability of building community in the face of the fragmentation of our origins. From a dynamical view the following can be said. It is tempting to think of the market, police, and military as exogenous disciplinary forces imposed on an underlying chronic instability. But that assumes the orthogonality that's subject to question. All those "exogenous" institutions interact with our self-conceptions in a way that modifies the institutions and alters our own sense of self as well. These modifications are quiescent in fat peaceful times, but show themselves by producing strong gradients in the tougher times. The 1960s were virtually a laboratory demonstration of this. Our view would be that the stance of the United States vis-à-vis the rest of the world on ecological issues is a similar demonstration. World opinion laments our recalcitrance, but we might reply that we are not internally stable enough to relax the pressure for plenty.

About 150 years ago, in one of the most famous of all works on diversity and community, Marx questioned the possibility of achieving communitarian sociality in the presence of religious differences.[19] The question is still open. Furthermore, the terms of the problem have changed radically since his time, as nations have gotten bigger, communication faster, and our awareness of the global arena more acute. It is in this light that tolerance has to be discussed.

Control of Boundaries

Strategies such as the production of docile bodies can be seen as attempts to control boundary conditions, either the dimensions of the social state space or its extent. Religious and moral systems are the most common devices to this end, but, in fact, the institutional arrangements that do the job are almost always legal or legalistic in nature. Kosher laws and observation of the Sabbath come to mind as the easiest examples. This sort of boundary policing has been discussed extensively in terms congenial to our analysis by Foucault and others, so we won't dwell on the obvious. Somewhat less obvious, but essential to a discussion of diversity and community, is another locus of boundary policing, so-called "identity politics." It is largely in this context that issues of diversity and community are being worked out at present.

Identity politics is the recent descendant of the class politics of the Marxist era. It depends on the view that solidarity and unity in one dimension are the key to empowerment of those defined in that one dimension. Hence, energy and rhetoric are turned to the service of totalizing (in this case linearizing) the dynamical space of politics and the space of self-identity in terms of that dimension. If we are only ballistic objects, then ballistics is our life. If we are only workers, we are the proletariat.

Thus, we would agree with Judith Butler, who is "permanently troubled by identity categories," that one-dimensional identity ascriptions *and* assertions are signs of disciplinary regimes at work.[20] We recognize explicit attempts to rule out the interaction of dimensions, hence fractal edges. However, we disagree with Butler's reliance on a subversive identity flexibility implied by its performativity. Identities have a nasty tendency to harden into place under, say, agonistic pressure. They become the active symbolic content of performances of hate, exclusion, and violence. Their performativity makes them no less real.[21]

Accordingly, we can find situations that squeeze the normally complex interactive field of identities to a single dimension, but in political situations this is simply the signature of domination. We are told, "You're only a child; a woman; a savage; an old fart; a peasant." But from a dynamical point of view the implied constraints of those reductions to a single dimension are very like the implied constraints of the self-reductions performed by revolutionaries and reformers themselves. If identities compressed by opposition are the problem, then they are also a problematic solution. There is no romance in the identity forged by struggle, only the play and counterplay of power.[22]

Ironically, by and large the solidarity sought by those seeking change in the name of one dimension is more internally unstable than externally destabilizing. A symptom of this is the utter failure of the Marxists to produce the "class consciousness" they had posited as the essential condition for the formation of a revolutionary class. Very simply, the working class turned out to value their lives as consumers, and modern states have been able to satisfy that dimension, thwarting the reduction to "working class" or "proletarian" that was required. Marx had thought that the exigencies of capitalism would force the single identification. They did not.[23]

More complexly, and in a form that sheds a lot of light on the formation condition for communities, we can say that a complex interactive process was miscast as linear and inevitable. The following is the "sequence" in question.

1 Identifiability, the mere mark, the possession of traits (e.g. gender, color, laboring) potentially connected with social or political identity, but latent, not yet dynamically active.
2 Identification, the self-recognition that the mark constitutes membership in a category, perhaps among others, but still not yet a dynamical dimension.
3 Identity, when the mark dominates all other potential dimensions and is activated as the term in which social and political activity is undertaken. Typically this is an exclusionary phase, in which the only attainable community is the community of the mark: us vis-à-vis all others.
4 Plurality, as the recognitions of identity distributed in the society multiply, alliances are considered, commonalities of interest are assessed, coalitions are proposed.
5 Pluralism, as compatible identities settle down together in recognizable movements, perhaps defined in terms of some generic identification created to reestablish identity across a plurality, e.g. "the oppressed."
6 Freedom, the liberal ideal, where justice is blind and particular identities again become decoupled from the social and political dynamics.

We need to see just how linearity is imposed on this sequence to produce what, after all, is a sort of classic modernist Bildungsroman. The first place this happens is right off the bat, when identifiability is considered as the mark of a category. When this mark is indelibly pigmental, or, less obviously, primary and secondary sex characteristics, the tendency to think categorially is nearly overwhelming. The biology seems to underwrite it. But you have to reflect that there are ultimately no categories in the living world. We summarize in cladograms a long history of reproductive interactions. The only known workable concept of species, for example, is based on failure of reproductive interaction – between individuals whose ancestors were, in contrast, successful. So color and the visible marks of gender are historical bookmarks, not metaphysical marks of destiny: just as women and blacks have insisted.

But just as the linearization of interdynamics fails as a ground of racism or sexism, it also fails, in the same way, as a ground of political solidarity. This is a typical result of taking the nonlinearity of social dynamics seriously. The most conspicuous analogue is that the very same conditions that make equilibrium and optimization claims for the market unreasonable would infect the abilities of would-be socialist planners.

The second attempt to force linear causation is in the claim that consciousness galvanizes to categorial solidarity. We have mentioned the frustrations that beset the political Marxists in this regard, where we see once again the importance of moving toward respect for nonlinearity. Class consciousness could be expected to develop only if class and the awareness of class could be made to totalize the dynamical space: that is, only if social dynamics could be reduced to the dynamics of class. There is no reason to expect any other dimension of identity to fare better.

Third, at the stage of coalition formation very interesting opportunities to see nonlinear dynamics in action appear. Typically, some alliances will produce positive returns. That is, they will not simply be the additive result of the strengths of the constituencies in alliance, but will generate new grounds and new spaces for possible action. Everybody has their favorite example of some apparently serendipitous juxtaposition that has "taken off" in a way that could never have been predicted. The most conspicuous recent case is Microsoft's conversion of DOS into a flying carpet with the unwitting aid of IBM. But there are many examples outside economic life as well.

The image of positive returns is intriguing in the realm of identity and diversity just insofar as it involves amplification. Most views of coalition formation foresee the identity state space contracting as compromise and accommodation smooth the edges of the identities that come into alliance. The major expectation from a positive returns scenario is that while something of initial identities will surely be lost, new more comprehensive identities will be enabled and will emerge.

The upshot of this process (a couple of centuries ago we would have said "this dialectic") is that an opening does appear to exist within which community formation and diversity go hand in hand. But this is not much comfort to those who want a present array of variation to persist into a more communal future. For the normal course of positive returns processes is for new persistent structures and patterns to emerge. In this way such processes resemble biological evolution more than any eternal persistence of types. Because these new structures constitute the conditions enabling a continued evolution along determinately constrained lines, Pierre Bourdieu calls them "structured structuring structures." The awkward phrase at least has the advantage of reminding us that the process does not (in general) stop at one stage.

If diversity depends on the preservation of old identities, or if an identity politics depends on a solidarity built on a hardening of identifying marks, then the dynamics of amplification is another argument against them both. But, almost incidentally, why should our interactions with one another leave our identities untouched? Do not we matter to each other? Do not identities grow with the important relationships we engage in? The two of us writing this paper are mutually respecting intellectual colleagues adjusting to each other paragraph by paragraph; but we certainly didn't start out that way.

But, then, no dynamics is context independent, and the ample opportunity we had certainly is not shared by all. This brings us to the tensions of the politics of the oppressed. For what shows up here is the difference between a statics of identity and diversity, constrained to a linear regime by the narrow boundaries of oppression, poverty, or some other exogenously structuring conditions, and a nonlinear dynamics of identity and diversity within the luxury of an ample state space to be explored mutually and interactively by numbers of people in growth and development. From this perspective it looks like what it is, a politics insistent upon frozen and abiding identities because it finds that, by stereotype and by institutions, identities are in fact frozen, and for some the dynamics of growth and development are barred. We do not find this to be a promising path to freedom.

Thus, when the ladder of identity is considered with respect to the possibility of a nonlinear dynamics, it seems expectable that the very conditions that prompt the articulation of the ladder in its nonlinear form are the conditions under which the hopes embedded in the ladder are most forlorn. But the converse seems more constructive. When the hopes are real, there is every reason to think that identities will thaw and change, making the politics of identity obsolete. Where space for growth and development exist, the diversity of fixed identities gives way to the emergence of new identities. Hegel was so far right.

The twentieth century was not kind to linear narratives of freedom. Access to the workplace, active citizenship, discursive legitimacy in the classroom and the academy, and, in general, access to the "public sphere" continues demonstrably to be structured by narrow sets of procedures, standards, and values over which the appearance of diversity is draped, and to which its reality is sacrificed. Without attention to this monocultural resistance to multiculturalism, good intentions and classical liberal approaches are unlikely to produce an effectively diverse public culture, or so our experience strongly argues.

We may dream of equivalent diversities interacting on a level playing field, but at this moment in history, diversity is generally measured against a historically entrenched privileged center, a position of power from which the rules of the game have been and can be dictated. We know what the institution of such games means for accessible dimensions of diversity. In the United States, this center is still defined by people at the intersection of national, class, race, gender, and sexuality privileges, that is, by native "middle class" white heterosexual men. [24] These primary privileges, it is virtually a cliché to point out, elaborate themselves into a variety of secondary advantages with psychological, motivational, educational, and social network dimensions. They also produce and reproduce, as any process of social formation does, a complex of shared values, assumptions, standards, and practices to which all others become entrained, resulting in the dominant culture of public space in this country. Thus, in the United States diversity tends to be not a source of interaction between or among equals, but, at best, an added feature of no dynamical consequence.

With respect to any given center, another way to talk about diversity is in terms of margins. Nationality, culture, ethnicity, race, and gender as dimensions are only weakly determinative of social trajectories (in general; in particular, they may range toward the totally determinative – think again of points in the Mandelbrot set). They define the attractive center as they move into contact with it. As a rule, individual goal orientation, self-interest-based economic rationality, aggressive competition, a problem-solving orientation, mastery of nature and the environment, the patriarchal division of labor, interpersonal heterosexuality, and short-term tastes and preferences are the dominant dimensions in shaping the course of lives. As such, far from promoting genuine diversity, they function as screens to identify, marginalize, and filter it away, in the process reaffirming the dominant terms of identity and discipline of the center.

This, of course, brings us back to the use of the market to manage the number of significant dimensions in the social space. When diversity is a matter of individual access and advancement, there is little or no chance that the public sphere will be substantively transformed by diversity. Individuals do not have this power, even in the aggregate. The formation of power is not a matter of adding bits of weakness together; it is a matter of the self-organization of new constellations of constraints and enablements that transform the possibilities (and probabilities) of trajectories within the social space. For example, university faculties do not get their power from their numerousness on campus. (When it comes to numbers, they routinely get outvoted 12 to 79 by the board of trustees.) A faculty gets whatever power it has by virtue of its control of accreditation and gatekeeping.

Only within the last ten or fifteen years has a focused conceptual awareness of cultural diversity as an inevitable and desirable feature of world systems begun to emerge within the mainstream in this country. Inevitably, it has tended to take the classical liberal form: assertion of rights of access, and proclamations of the enrichment to be expected from diversity. This makes American responses to global multiculturalism directly analogous to the historical civil rights and feminist movements. Unfortunately, those are the cases that have shown most clearly how an abstract affirmation of diversity can be part of the strategy for the maintenance of uniformity. Genuine cultural difference is inefficient from the points of view we looked at earlier, so if the appearance of diversity is enough to satisfy the demand for it, then the appearance is created at the expense of the reality.

Not surprisingly, we find that egalitarian and other social experiments have ambiguous outcomes, complexly patterned and often unpredictable in individual cases. This is largely because removing one "factor" from social interaction does not simply leave all the other "factors" as they were. They typically all readjust in a new interactive constellation. A sort of empirical confirmation of the likelihood of such rearrangement is gained by noticing how attempts are constantly being made to rigidify the dynamics of multiple character in the service of various social agenda. A major political strategy is to force polarities, binary decisions, on us by reminding us that we are women, or middle class, or, especially, Muslims. As with Marxism, these appeals try to stop the interactive dynamics for a time, to get us to define ourselves in a single dimension, and act canonically in accord with the (now made-static) definition.

The Prospects

A discussion of this sort does not get a conclusion, but, rather, a few relatively robust resting places. The first is the observation that the contributions to this volume range wide, and collect a family of phenomena about which it seems hopeless to generalize. To this we say "Right." This is what we should expect from any candid and intelligent discussion of community. (He say: "That data set looks like a mess." She say: "So far so good; what kind of a mess?") Dedication, like-mindedness, shared ways of life, and shared meaning-giving experiences are the usual conspicuous features of communities we would be likely to identify as such historically. But there are all sorts (and all sorts of ground) of dedication, like-mindedness, and so forth. And there are all sorts of trajectories to get to them, informed by all sorts of interactive contingencies, many of which have been exhibited and explored in this volume. It is no accident that the word "community" floats around even more than most politically freighted words. Less than almost any other concept is it detachable from the conditions of common existence of people in a worldwide historical whirl.

Attempted formal definitions of community grasp at some of the multiplicity at the expense of the rest. For example, one of the few fairly well-bounded concepts of community is *Gemeinschaft* as it was contrasted with *Gesellschaft*. However, this contrast is both historically and geographically local: an artifact of the growth of market society of the course of the modernization of Europe. For Europeans sensitive to their history, the contrast produces a certain nostalgia. A very different nostalgia was produced by Nyerere when he invoked *ujamaa*, the tradition of communal cooperation, as the foundation of a post-colonial Tanzania. Both are deeply connected to identities. The former was an atavistic gesture by German romantics, the latter an essential structural piece of a hard-won liberation and stability.[25] Neither is "the" concept of community.

So we have to be intelligent about such matters as the compossibility of diversity and community without benefit of the traditional rationalist crutch of a definitional major premise. The chief intellectual victim of nonlinearity is the subjunctive mood – so beloved of modern Western theorists. But the development of new heuristics and strategies in field after field has shown is that we indeed *can* be intelligent about such matters. We are dealing with recognizable patterns and families of patterns, not an incomprehensible random walk. So it is as a comprehensible family of patterns that the contributions of this volume help us to be intelligent about community. They aren't to be, couldn't be, and should not be thought of as a vain search for generalizations and laws.

Second, it is possible to make some judgments about prospects for our own time. To do this we think back to the fundamental tension: that between the tendency to expand the state space of possible identities, and the tendency to minimize it. But now we can add another characteristic concept central to nonlinear dynamics, the concept of scale. Sometimes size matters. Very often rate matters. In general, the size of the substructures in any whole, the way they are connected or sealed off (phase separated) from one another, and the rates at which processes occur relative to various substructures give rise to processes at characteristic scales. This is often called scalar hierarchy, but this suggests far too static a situation, and further suggests a dominance of "higher" over "lower," so some of us prefer to call them heterarchies. Biology is full of the most conspicuous cases of them, but so are phenomena more proper to physics and chemistry – under the current division of labor. We think that social systems are heterarchical as well.

Heterarchies are typically characterized by two kinds of phenomena: structures and processes at one scale stabilize structures and processes at another; and structures and processes at one scale *regulate* processes at another. These are features of the model we can explore here. In fact they've been discussed for a long time: at least since Aristotle's speculations on the optimum and maximum size of the polis. The rule of thumb developed was, in dynamical terms, that there was a natural scale for the size of a polity, and this had to do with the possibility of citizens knowing each other. This has come down to us in the concept of the "face-to-face" society. In dynamical terms, you'd say that there is a natural correlation length in human communities. That is, in terms of a chosen quality of relatedness (probably involving the capacity to have significant impact on one another) there is a limit to the size of the community within which that quality can be maintained. Characteristically, beyond that length restructuring would occur.

Of course, different demands on the quality of relationship would be expected to yield different natural sizes. You could ask, for example, how many people care what you do insofar as it is precisely you who are doing it, how many care insofar as someone is doing it, and how many do not care at all. (Especially narcissistic people seem to think that the correlation length for sensitivity to bad hair days is infinite.) The degree to which others will want to constrain what you do will depend on these correlation lengths, hence the nature of the disciplinary apparatus that tends to be utilized. In terms of identity again, what are people going to let you be, and how are they going to try to get you to be that way? The market, for example, once a system of property is defined, has no theoretical limits on correlation length. In a fully flowing world economy, everybody would have a (marginal) impact on everybody else. Concomitantly, the market correlates us only as the goods we bring to market, the offers we make, the offers we accept. No other features of our identity are intrinsically relevant to the market, though, of course, they may be relevant to decisions about what to bring to the market. The disciplines required will be those that secure property, and consist of the justice system and the gaze. We well know how both can differentiate us from one another, but the lore of the market is that to do so is illicit and inefficient. The point here, though, is that correlation through the market is supposed to have the least possible impact on our capacity to be what we want to be. Of course that's the trouble with purified ideals like the market. For once it is in place it can be used to establish constraints at other scales.

In addition, the market constrains our behavior in other dimensions of our identities. Suppose, for example, we are a vegetarian community. In the market, we are a consumer group, whatever may be our reasons for vegetarianism. These are the rules of correlation. Our impact as people committed to principle and so on can link us to others only through other institutions at other scales. Well, how about the electoral politics, another institution at another scale, and, in fact several scales as the polities are nested. Well, here we become a special interest group. In both cases our identity is redefined to fit the conditions of correlation. Identity politics is *intrinsically* frustrating, given our dominant institutions, not just a result of ill will, evil intent, or whatever. To succeed, an identity politics would have to expand the correlation length in its own terms of correlation. It is not enough to be tolerated and allowed to participate in the dominant institutions, as any congressional lobbyist knows.[26]

It is easy to get cynical at this point, for it will inevitably occur to everyone that "rich guy" is an identity whose scope can be expanded successfully. But that's interesting in the present context only as a confirmation of the capacity of the economic sphere to dominate social dynamics. The question is how, if at all, a community with a clear identity can increase its ability to correlate a significant part of the social state space. Or, in terms of our earlier formulation, what is the nonlinear analogue of the linear ladder of identity?

Our present diagnosis is that as the "information age" has emerged as a dominant feature of mature capitalism, and modern military technology has foreclosed on the old opportunities for serious revolutionary activity, identities, causes, or movements can be expanded only at the expense of eventual trivialization and impotence. Insofar as traditional religion still establishes the boundary conditions for any social dynamics, it can avoid this fate so long as it respects any current state of the truce at the fractal edge between "church and state." When there is no such truce, as with the abortion issue, then opinion petrifies into rigid factionalism. This is to say that for historical reasons the traditional religions retain some control over what they can mean, some control over the conditions of their own legitimacy, hence stability. No other putative community is so fortunate.

In the United States, the correlation length required for even fleeting power is enormous, and the only access anyone has to this scale is through the media. The media then assume the lion's share of the control of meaning. But here the lessons of nonlinear systems are most important. The dialectical interaction between the media and every other possible segment of society is intense. It is safe to say that no one gets it right in their own terms; and that's exactly what you'd expect in a system so intensely interactive. Ephemeral accidental alliances abound – until surprise at the strangeness of bedfellows leads to their dissolution. All the interdependencies of self and surround exhibit their creative capacities, to no one's satisfaction. So, in the end, many if not most opt out or retreat into bickering about local minutiae. They can be as diverse as they please so long as they are impotent; they can form any community they please so long as it remains docile.

Notes

1   The line of thought worked out here was originally thought through in the context of feminist, postcolonial, critical race, and queer studies critiques of essentialism. It would have been as natural to think it out in the context of the issues central to this volume, and that's what we shall do. But we shall try to retain some of the connections with feminist anti-essentialism especially for two reasons: to pay the intellectual debt, and to suggest that the issues addressed by the anti-essentialists are absolutely crucial for our assessment of the possibilities of diversity in community.

2   We seek dynamical models, not static ones. Readers may decide if this allows us to escape the usual critiques of models as procrustean beds, such as those commonly directed against Weber's "ideal types." Of course, no model dynamical or static captures every case in its most glorious detail. To do so, the model (theory)

would have to be identical to the world it seeks to describe, hence, redundant. The value of modeling is reduction of information to manageability; but which information remains? If the model is dynamic, the answer is, "that depends."

3 From K. Anthony Appiah, "Race, Culture, Identity: Misunderstood Connections," in K. Anthony Appiah and Amy Gutmann, eds., *Color Consciousness: The Political Morality of Race* (Princeton: Princeton University Press, 1996).

4 De Beauvoir, in turn, was inspired by W. E. B. DuBois' theory of double consciousness, itself a theory of situated alterities. The contemporary feminist debate is anchored in the now classic *Innessential Woman: Problems of Exclusion in Feminist Thought*, by Elizabeth V. Spelman (Boston: Beacon, 1988). See also the critical responses "White Philosophy," by Avery Gordon and Christopher Newfield, and "The No-drop Rule," by Walter Benn Michaels, *Critical Inquiry* 20 (Summer 1994). References to additional earlier contributions to the debates can be found there.

5 In Rosi Braidotti, Ewa Charkiewicz, Sabine Hausler, and Saskia Wieringa, *Women, The Environment, and Sustainable Development: Towards a Theoretical Synthesis* (London, Atlantic Highlands: Zed Books (INSTRAW) 1994), p. 49.

6 We should all be able to agree on this abiding essence even if we cannot agree whether these kinds of animals have souls, or will later be reincarnated as higher or lower forms, etc.

7 Familiar primitive attempts to typologize such possibilities for social systems are Toennies' "*Gemeinschaft*" and "*Gesellschaft*" and Durkheim's "mechanical solidarity" and "organic solidarity." From the first, everyone could tell that these typologies really captured something, yet no one could ever make them fit any particular case. This is a characteristic conundrum with static models of dynamical systems.

8 None of this discussion is even theoretically very novel. Interactionists, at least since George Herbert Mead (DuBois and Beauvoir have already been mentioned), have argued that selves are both ordinarily and extraordinarily formed in dynamically interactive fields of (significant) "others." Some interactionists have attempted to stabilize the dynamics of interaction in terms of "roles," which is certainly one way that interactions can settle into more or less durable patterns. In comparison, Freudian and Jungian depth psychology is hopelessly static. The partial exception is the object relations theorists, whose prodigious struggles to whack their way through the tangled primordial jungle of the unconscious to emerge into the clearing where the interactionists are native is to be admired, but perhaps not emulated.

9 For many, the most familiar statement of this is Cooley's notion of the "looking-glass self," although in adapting Cooley to the present discussion it is important to note that since this mirroring is a dynamical process, not a just-so story, there is no original or "core" self or self-conception that is not itself an emergent product of prior interactions with others and their perceptions.

10 We note Dewey's suggestion that a distinction be made between interaction and transaction: interaction can simply mean "between," like billiard balls colliding, while transaction requires mutuality. As long as no fussy attempt definitionally to foreclose the range of possible interaction dynamics is made, however, we think that the one term will do just fine.

11   In "Expectations and Strategies in a Nonlinear World," *Systems Research* 7 (1990), Chuck Dyke makes the distinction between prediction and reasonable expectations. He argues that you can have reasonable expectations about the distributions involved here, and it is the nature of these expectations that will be worked out as we go along.

12   Every point on the plane has a complex number as its address, that is, a number with a real and an imaginary part. The real part is represented on the horizontal axis, the imaginary part on the vertical axis. Thus (0,ni) is on the vertical axis, (n,0) on the horizontal axis. The usual operations for complex numbers hold, and the equation $y = z^2 + c$ (where z and c are both complex numbers) is being iterated from an initial choice of z and c. No point I make requires any more of the details than this – in fact, no more than is in the text.

13   A few minutes with any of the good software for iterating $y = z^2 + c$ will show you the range of point and periodic attractors present, as well as the range of indecision, of course. Especially good is ORDER by M. Casco Associates, 1993, available through Cedar Software, RR1 Box 5140, Morrisville, VT 05661.

14   Trinh T. Minh-ha notes in *When the Moon Waxes Red : Representation, Gender, and Cultural Politics* (New York: Routledge, 1991) that in the play of centers and margins "we are often them as well," and Walt Kelly has Pogo discover that "we have met the enemy and he is us."

15   Accordingly, initially complexifying "intersections" studies have now themselves been challenged on the grounds that intersectionality presupposes the a priori existence of multiple dimensions which then intersect (race, class, gender, sexuality, etc.), an approach that yields serial linearity rather than dynamical complexity. The keywords for nonlinear intersectionality are "hybridity" and "network." See Braidotti, quoted above (and note 5), and Bruno Latour, *We Have Never Been Modern*, trans. Catherine Porter (Cambridge, Mass.: Harvard University Press, 1993 [1991]). Latour also usefully criticizes the hitherto closest approximation to dynamically complex modeling of social systems, dialectics: see pp. 55, 57.

16   Michel Foucault, *Discipline and Punish: The Birth of the Prison*, trans. Alan Sheridan (New York: Pantheon Books, 1977).

17   A lucid yet satisfyingly complex analysis of the structuring dynamics of consumption identity formation can be found in the first half of Juliet B. Schor, *The Overspent American: Why We Want What We Do Not Need* (New York: Harper Perennial, 1998). Strangely, Schor's analytic breaks down in the second half, where all of a sudden she writes as if people have complete autonomy to opt out of these structuring dynamics within which their selves, and wills, were constructed.

18   Nathan Glazer and Daniel Patrick Moynihan, *Beyond the Melting Pot* (Cambridge, Mass.: MIT Press, 1963).

19   "On the Jewish Question." Not an unambiguously successful work, but one that should be studied. The antisemitism some find in the work is probably real, but irrelevant.

20   For the quote and a characteristic discussion, see "Imitation and Gender Insubordination," in Diana Fuss, ed., *Inside/Out: Lesbian Theories, Gay Theories* (New York: Routledge, 1991), pp. 13–31. Also in Henry Abelove, Michèle Aina Barale,

and David M. Halperin, eds., *The Lesbian and Gay Studies Reader* (New York and London: Routledge, 1993), pp. 307–20.

21 In fact, once we give up the notion of platonic essences (such as real identities, core selves, or gender per se) lurking behind the surface of appearances or performances, exposing any particular appearance or performance as such does no critical work whatsoever.

22 And when the struggle ends, perhaps even is won, where does that identity go? Will the identity wither away, or must a new struggle be found?

23 From a century-long scramble to adapt Marxism to this grim reality, already central in Gramsci's theory, an iconic recent text is Ernesto Laclau and Chantal Mouffe, *Hegemony and Socialist Strategy: Towards a Radical Democratic Politics* (London and New York: Verso, 1985).

24 The canonic inventory of this center, never actually accomplished in every particular by any particular person, is taken by Erving Goffman in *Stigma: Notes on the Management of Spoiled Identity* (New York: Simon and Schuster, 1963), p. 128.

25 How hard the victories can come and how some dimensions of identity can be sacrificed to others in the drive for effective community has been grimly demonstrated on the bodies of Kenyan women and in the literature about the revival of cliteridectomy as part of the strategy of Kenyan nationalist opposition to British imperialism.

26 For a diagnostic exemplar of exactly this point, see Lani Guinier's essays in *The Tyranny of the Majority: Fundamental Fairness in Representative Democracy* (New York: The Free Press, 1995). In effect, she argues that the tyranny of the majority is just such an expansion of correlation length, at the expense of radical shortenings everywhere else. She proposes a solution by vote weighting that remains linear by forcing minorities to aggregate and focus their political identities through rigid correlations that are "their own" only by virtue of being "other" than the majority's.

5

From Village to Global Contexts: Ideas, Types, and the Making of Communities

D. A. Masolo

Each of us seeks to know our personal identity and where and how we fit into the scheme of things so that we can make sense of our lives and plan for the future. . . . Whereas we are Kenyan South Asians, we are not a monolithic community with an organized leadership. We are a conglomeration of many diverse communities, languages, religions and customs. Occupationally, though predominantly business-oriented, we also are professional, artisans and service workers.

Zarina Patel, a young Kenyan ("Who am I?," *Daily Nation*, Nairobi, March 28, 2000)

Community: From Tradition and Modernity

If we take some time to think of our social genealogy it is likely that we will either discover or at least imagine and correctly assume, as Zarina Patel points out in the epigraph above, a complex network of social histories from which we come. In addition, our complex lives of multiple choices and interests, ranging from occupation to friendships and amusements, and to participation in public policy-oriented activities, all bring us into bonds with others in yet more complex ways. Playing roles within each of these segments of our social lives brings us into union with others; we become a comm-unity.

Patel's appeal for recognition of a new and more complex sense of community is based on the premise that identities of persons are shaped by the social worlds in which they play various roles, and are susceptible to change as such social worlds mutate through time and space. This view is clearly a break from the one that regards identities of persons to be determined, biologically and socially, by some assumed homogeneous characteristics which they share with other members of the group to which they belong. In many cultures of the world people continue to regard identity in this older way.

Because such a view of identity plays a crucial role in the management of the social system, good knowledge of one's kinship network is honored. The growing and increasingly reliable genetic methods, in addition to oral and written historical ones now made much easier to access by computerized databases and networks, have made the recovery and reconstruction of the past a matter of a few finger strokes. What is not yet widespread or obvious is the value of such knowledge. Valuation of knowledge, including knowledge of personal and shared histories, sometimes differs significantly between cultures, and also between individuals within and across cultural boundaries.

When and where I grew up among the Luo of Kenya, genealogical knowledge was important both in itself and for social reasons. Knowledge of the larger social system of which one was part, and of one's exact location within it, was crucial for determining rights and duties as well as general comportment toward others. Individual and community were related in a constant mutual dependency: the specific behavior of individuals in various contexts gave the community its cultural boundaries and identity just as much as the normative standards of the community regulated the practices of individuals and groups within it. As one grows up and attains the age of adulthood in this cultural environment, this knowledge and the derivable behavioral expectations become more demanding. An adult Luo man or woman is always expected to behaviorally relate to others – by speech and deeds – within the limitations provided for (or expected of) the kinship relations between them. One knew or could know her or his relatives and calculate or adjust their behavior toward them accordingly. Also, because the socio-economic distributive system was based on such relations, knowledge thereof provided a critical source of socio-political hierarchy, justice, and other regulative principles. Put simply, the fairly well-known boundaries of the autonomous cultural system, its sub-systems of kinship relations and permanence of neighborliness, placed restrictions on possible adventurous thoughts and practices of members of the group. They provided the ultimate reference for social and moral control. Knowing and practicing culture within these bounded domains have for a long time signaled the close relation between consciousness and society, and it satisfies both theoretical and practical purposes. By constantly evaluating and adjusting one's conduct in accordance with known or assumed expectations of other members within any relational circuit, one shifts the focus of their conduct from self to the group where the maintenance of shared values takes precedence. Relatedly, however, people also paid keen attention to others' comportment toward them, and felt grieved if such was deemed unbecoming.

The Luo model of maintaining social order is only one among multiple schemes of other peoples and cultures. But it represents a typically traditional model where most actors either know or can easily determine the nature of kinship relations between them. Together, members of such a community commit to the beliefs and behavioral norms which they share; relations with those recognized as strangers – that is *mwa*, those who inhabit different schemes – are carefully handled and negotiated in search of middle-ground norms. When these people talk of "community," they refer to this schematic unity of beliefs and behavior as well as to the people who inhabit the scheme; they think of this community as a separate and independent entity which is permanent and enduring because it outlives its individual members. They feel they belong to it and are obliged by its laws which they have the duty and responsibility to protect and pass on to later generations.

However, for many Luo people in the traditional setting, like for people from many other societies, time has exacted its toll on the traditional values. The demands of modern economy have made it possible for people to migrate to places far away from those locations once considered "home" and from the ways once considered to be larger than life, thus making people once regardable as "strangers" to be our closest neighbors, friends, and associates. As a result, not just our senses of neighborhood have changed; our interests also have shifted or expanded. The shifting horizons of social and cultural maps have revolutionized the traditional senses of community into those in which neither the homogeneity of practice nor embodied genealogies are necessary constituting requirements. Also, it has become more evident that sharing embodied genealogies does not always include or imply the sharing of cultural or moral beliefs and practices like it was once assumed to be in the traditional society. Social mobility has revealed the categorial separation between socio-somatic and psycho-intellectual genealogies. In this chapter I wish to outline some of the characteristics of such changes in the idea and constitution of community. Also, I want to argue that while these new senses and constitutions of community have been liberating in certain senses, especially from the traditional ones like that of the Luo, or like the ones Patel alludes to, their political uses do not always guarantee liberty for all.

The above-mentioned changes in the idea and constitution of community, occurring speedily since World War II, do not necessarily blur our ideas of and feelings about our social histories, but they certainly have awakened the world to an awareness of new questions regarding previous assumptions about the "fixed" nature of community. In both the academy and public arena, the shift from thinking of community as entity to expression has transformed not only how we think of academic disciplines and their claims, but also, and even more importantly, how we regard the various socio-cultural systems of the world and their values and attitudes. Post-World War II immigrations significantly modified the faces, colors, languages, as well as beliefs and practices of old communities and enabled the formation of new social and cultural constituencies within and across nations and cultures. As a result, even in older liberal democracies, both the indigenous and the immigrant have found new comradeship and alliance. Where shared values were originally vague, they received robust redefinition to forge new forms of unity, thus, in the process and in some cases, significantly redrawing original cultural maps to connect groups of people who share beliefs and practical preferences. Sometimes religion is the leading rallying factor, sometimes it is shared ethical principles about persons, animals, or the environment. Across national boundaries, such groups usually refer to themselves as communities because they share common global political and ethical interests defined on new terms and with varying goals and degrees of power and ability to influence public policy and action. Members of groups such as the Greenbelt Movement for environmental protection, animal rights protection groups and the Human Rights Watch fit into this type of community. They differ from the traditional community and from others we shall mention later in that membership in them is governed almost solely by the ethical principle of sympathetic impartiality. In other words, commitment to their principles is based purely on their rational appeal.

These examples show how the idea of community has changed alongside the political and economic mutations of the post-World War II period, without totally replacing its older configurations. Patel is therefore right in suggesting the multiple identities for East African peoples originated in South-East Asia, a view equally true for communities indigenous to Africa itself. That the acceleration of these changes is owed largely to the political economy of the post-World War II period is, of course, not surprising.

What is significantly new is that the moral and social-political consequences of these changes have prompted new commensurate theories, in both the academy and the public arena, all aiming, it is assumed, at outlining the best of principles and values which can and should universally improve and protect the rights of all individuals and groups both within and across the borders of the various socio-cultural and political orders. However, these new and multiple theoretical orientations leave no doubt that much discord and controversy have erupted around the meanings, value, and relevance of a variety of descriptive and normative concepts thereby generated for the creation of a new, peaceful, and orderly world. Blessed is she who can develop the dual virtue of being linguistically and morally consistent and correct in her political discourse and practice in the new world culture. In the post-communist world, terms such as "sexism," "diversity," and "minority," "race," "gender," "age," "disability," and "culture" have all become the new search terms for probing and identifying "the enemies of the people." They are the new indicators of the political stands (correctness or insensitiveness) of individuals, groups, or institutions. To show commitment to adapt to these "new times" as addressed by these terms and concepts, academic institutions as well as social-political movements across the globe scramble to incorporate various mixtures from this lexicon into the language of their curricula and behavioral ideals of their respective spaces.

The message is often quite clear, despite the definitional controversies around the concepts themselves: strive to show conceptual and structural acceptance and enhancement of pluralism. The application of the message to the everyday practical world is not always clear-cut, hence the avalanche of lawsuits, countersuits, and other types of charges and accusations resulting from related ambiguities of precise classification.

Inside or alongside these neologisms and the accompanying debates lies a crucial transformation in the idea of community itself, a major shift from the custom-based traditional type we started with. The world-view represented by these new terms and concepts suggests that people can form cultural, political, economic, and moral communities as separate interest groups in which individuals can participate, simultaneously or in sequence with different other people in each case, without abandoning any. In other words, communities are no longer viewed as fixed entities, but rather as open-ended and amorphous groupings definable more by the organizing beliefs, principles, and practices than by the bodies which inhabit them.

It lies beyond our scope and goals here to examine adequately the diverse and rival versions of political and moral implications of the changes we have mentioned above. We will, however, create room, even if only in a limited fashion, to mention some views, often appearing to be in opposition, about the new political roles of community as discussed in the work of Michael L. Gross on the one hand and, on the other, the moral (and political) threat which claims to specific group-membership pose to the idea and practical cultivation of universal humanity as argued by Martha Nussbaum.[1] Both positions underscore the significance of community to the idea and practice of democratic values and to the enriching reflections and enjoyments of the cultural diversity of the human phenomenon. As the sociologist Jeffrey C. Alexander observes, "Social movements that ignore these [new] structures encourage the domination and violence that has characterized the degenerate line of twentieth-century life."[2]

I argue first, against both Gross and Nussbaum, that although much power has shifted to groups – that is, to communities of various kinds – as the location of both the check on political power and the influence of public policy, this arrangement is bereft of the capacity to engender equality; instead, it has several ingredients for social polarization, antagonism, and conflict. In urban settings, for example, neighborhoods demarcated on the basis of communities of sorts can also serve, advertently or otherwise, as a way of keeping apart such groups, whether they are defined on the basis of racial, ethnic, or socio-economic factors. In this sense, communities are those political pockets or constituencies which are constantly steeped in competition with each other for government distribution of power and influence, goods and services. In the so-called Third World, traditional communities transformed into these roles against each other and against the state or government system are always considered a threat to the formation, integrity, and stability of the nation-state. Second, against Nussbaum's claim that the most potent way to stem the oppression of disadvantaged groups and to increase equality and mutual respect among all humans is to establish education reforms which stress the universality of humanity rather than cultural or national patriotism, I argue that localized identity is not inherently bad, nor does it become bad only because over-zealous people throughout history have used it to carry out atrocities against those they regard as different from themselves. Instead, at least sometimes, as the history and project of colonization have shown, it is those who see their own values as solely deserving to be universally good rather than as historically and anthropologically particular who have been the carriers of global oppression and imperialism. I add my support to the voices of those who have argued in response to this debate that it is not incompatible to be both a cosmopolitan and a patriot.

Communities, Nations, and Nation-states

It could be objected that I started with a highly controversial view of community when I characterized "the Luo" as one. An objection might be raised that mine was a colonially informed view of community, a fabrication of the colonial archive in which the old-type cultural anthropological texts played crucial, albeit at times inadvertent, part. To that anthropological view, African peoples were deemed to be distinct from each other in physical, customary, and moral terms. I hope to show later that African peoples themselves hardly ascribe to these essentializing characteristics as separating them from each other. Rather, at least to the Luo, communal identity is acquired, and can be shed or abandoned by choice of practice. The variations in the norms defining belief and practice of culture attest to the view that being Luo is itself not uniform. It is a continuously negotiated process in legal and cultural domains.

Together, however, and in very general senses, various populations of the non-Western world, especially in Africa, Asia, and Latin America, present yet another variant of the meaning of community and the way it is expressed through political power. With the growth of the disciplines of social and cultural anthropology, differences between communities were to be found in their organizational patterns driven by the dominant mode of production. Thus the difference between Western and non-Western communities, it was thought, were due to the respective differences in the economic dynamics that molded them. While Western communities were the function of the dynamics of advanced industrial economies, those of Africa, Latin America, and vast portions of Asia were held together by kinship systems put in place by primitive nature-dependent economies. They were simple or primitive societies structured into fairly homogeneous communal groups or tribes. Chief among the factors that appeared to inform social anthropologists in their classification of, say, African societies into separate "communities" was common language. It was the single major invariant that connected what were sometimes widely dispersed and loosely politically organized social systems. Yet even social anthropologists are by no means consistent or agreed amongst themselves about their usage of the term "community" in this sense. Other factors became clear to them regarding the boundaries separating different communities. Not only did each one have its own language, they also had separate types of socio-political organization, and had separate and sovereign authorities irrespective of how these were defined and symbolized.[3]

But because social anthropology flourished in close relationship with and within the framework of the political economy of colonialism, it produced a structural political planning system that bears interesting analogies with the communal layout of the racially multipolar urban American society. In the colonial system, the so-called tribal "communities" were thought of as self-sustaining socio-political and cultural units with (semi-)autonomous local power systems capable of working more effectively on their own because of the already existing (traditional) power hierarchies. The colonial system entrenched itself partly by claiming that it would protect these communal interests and bonds by observing their semi-autonomy, and also by protecting the separate "community" systems from mutual threats within its sphere. The assumption was that societies and communities bear sharp contrasts. In the latter, people were viewed primarily as individuals, related to others only through a complex of laws which bind them into a society of independent agents. Economically, social relations in advanced capitalist economies were assumed predominantly to be driven by relations connecting participant individuals to groups based on the nature of their labor and levels of income. Together they formed a society (*Gesellschaft*). By contrast, communities (*Gemeinschaft*) were thought of as being held together by world-views defined by metaphysical values and ritual which tie people into a common bond. They thought of themselves as needing and belonging to each other. The idea of the ritual self-regulation of communities was particularly important for colonial administrations. For the British colonial system quickly formed the basis of indirect rule which allowed it to retain some of its traditional systems of social order and control. The difference was that under this new arrangement, the traditional authorities gave up their former powers in exchange for ceremonial space. The traditional leaders became the shock absorbers for the tensions that were soon to arise. Where there was no local system of centralized authority to absorb the rising local pressure against colonial administration, the colonial system created and imposed one. This latter way is how, for example, the Luo reinvented themselves under a single leader, Ker, a system they had lost for a period of more than a century as they migrated southward from today's Southern Sudan to today's Kenya. Through this colonially enhanced reinvention, they became a community, either for the first time, or once again. Either way, their make-up became more complex. The newly formed political power base became an influencing factor around which different peoples, formerly Luo-speaking and non-Luo-speaking alike, forged their new identity.

The colonial objectives for creating semi-autonomous communities in the above manner was quite clear. Some of them survived well into the 1990s. For example, in the last decade of apartheid, the minority white regime in South Africa attempted, but failed, to institute a system of federated racial and tribal states by urging local African leaders to accept a "homeland" system which would give them a measure of limited political autonomy over their tribal territories. The goal was mainly to lure the powerful Zulu leaders to take the offer as an opportunity, for them and their faithful followers, apparently to continue to practice their traditional monarchical system with minimal interference. The real reason and opportunity, however, was to create multiple competing forces whose rivalry would help to deflect pressure from the apartheid system mainly by setting the Inkatha Freedom Party into a head-on collision with Nelson Mandela's ANC. The prospect of preserving the traditional monarchy in which he would continue to play a visible role of chief and prince easily lured Mongusuthu Buthelezi into wildly and blindly supporting the apartheid regime against the radical liberation movements spearheaded by the ANC.

Elsewhere, in Kenya in 1904 and 1911, Maasai Laibons (ritual and political leaders) were conned into thumbing their consent on treaties with the representatives of the British government; these supposed agreements were quickly and immediately used to expunge indigenous communities not only from the vicinity of Nairobi but from the entire highland plateau area which soon became the "White Highlands." The original indigenous owners of these lands were transformed into either squatter-laborers or criminal trespassers in the only lands they had known as their homes for centuries. By these political fiats in the form of treaties, people were herded into groups and other forms of alliances in unprecedented ways. Administrative boundaries were drawn to keep each group together and to separate it from others. By these political acts the British colonial system created, for its convenience and interests, new communities with the support of their social anthropologists whose work purportedly confirmed each group to be linguistically and culturally autonomous and homogeneous.

In analogous ways, fragmentation of society into communities has become a key strategy in urban social planning and control. The United States in particular finds it an effective tool in the management and sustenance of the de facto racial divide. As groups defined in terms ranging from ethnicity to race and to social class, neighborhood communities have become a trendy notion of urban, regional, and global policing and delivery systems. The official justification is that such groupings provide ways to "[maximize] participation and political efficacy, particularly at the local level [allowing] individuals and local organizations to develop a clear idea of their interests as well as the means necessary to realize them. [But], as needs are developed locally, [wider and] global criteria for distribution collapse."[4] In reality, by giving neighborhoods some measure of autonomy – often only fictitious – through their participation in the keeping of law and order at the local level in exchange for social amenities and services, neighborhood communities can be more effectively contained and better supervised; their confrontational capacity is considered minimized and therefore less threatening to the overarching power system. Above all, their desire and capacity to infiltrate other parts of the society are thus blunted and reduced to ineffective minimums. The result, then, are mosaic urban maps composed of racialized and ethnicized blocks making up the urban setting. The dominant economic and social characteristics of these neighborhoods are clearly highlighted in the judicial records of the urban governments. They range from drugs to alcoholism, to murder, to rapes, and to theft. Those of us who speak from the colonial context know for sure the flaws of this British-type divide-and-rule or indirect-rule style of control and domination. It is flawed because it is based on the mono-optical view, developed first by social anthropologists for the liberal colonial capitalists, but today also strongly present in the American urban settings, that communities are systems in which the reproduction of power structures is the primary concern. It assumes that when communities make demands they do so for a place in an accepted scheme rather than for the revision of the scheme itself. But because the distribution of power is often an autonomous issue in politics, it has been easy for entrenched and dominant power systems like the colonial and apartheid systems in Africa, and the white power system in America, to sell off the idea of political autonomy to groups targeted for marginalization as a way of keeping them off limits from those goods with which political power is crucially associated. In its desires, not so much to give autonomy to native South African ethnic groups as to protect the privileges of the minority white population, the apartheid system struggled for decades to institute the homeland system for indigenous South Africans in order both to separate the communities from each other and to keep all of them out of the minority white enclaves. According to Manning Marable, a similar situation is rapidly emerging in the United States with regard to the changing meanings and political uses of the concepts of race and ethnicity.

The idea of community as a homogeneous social unit of sorts has been an important aspect of American urbanization since the 1930s. The racism and impoverishment that pushed blacks out of the rural South entrapped them into ghettos in the industrial cities of the North. Segregation and inability to afford better housing forced black populations into a squalor in which they lived together in run-down sections of the cities like people herded together by nature. Jews have had similar racially discriminatory treatment in the United States, especially between 1880 and the late 1960s. But while Jewish people have benefited greatly from the anti-discrimination laws of the 1960s and '79s, African-descended Americans and other so-called "people of color" have continued to be subjected to subtle yet prevalent racially discriminatory practices. Ironically, while struggle to success amid adversity has kept Jewish Americans connected around the nation through strong community commitment, continued struggles of African-Americans against persistent discrimination bind only some of them into a commitment to a sense of community; others try to tear away in attempt to escape the inferior stereotyping that accompanies anti-black and anti-colored racism. Oftentimes, African-Americans are visibly at a loss regarding where to throw their efforts, or what to emphasize in order to garner a solid sense of direction in the ranks. The result is the sense of vulnerability and constant position-changing that characterizes African-American politics. According to Marable, "The Irish [also] experience severe discrimination upon their arrival. But within several generations, they had become 'white.' They had assimilated the values of privilege and the language and behavior of white domination that permitted them to claim status within the hierarchy."[5] This assimilation, he notes, has not happened to "racialized" immigrants from Latin America and Asia.

Either America has refused or it has utterly failed to move from mere desegregation to integration where African-Americans are concerned. Racial discrimination still defines the attitudes and practices with which policies for the provision of such public amenities and services as education, housing, and employment are implemented. The resultant demarcations of the American social world almost unstoppably engenders the impression that racial communities are natural entities, into which people are born and embedded. Where the colonial governments naturalized "tribal communities," the West naturalizes racial ones.

How, one might ask, have so-created communities affected the evolution of civil society, of nation-states as a cohesive body politic? Indeed, the creation of new states over the fragmented communities served the colonial state. What was not clear was how these communities would position themselves vis-à-vis the postcolonial state. The outcome betrays no theoretical uniformity. In some cases, like Botswana, the new universalistic state appears to have succeeded in sidestepping the community approach. By sidestepping the chiefs, elders, and other community leaders, the president has succeeded in defining the presidency as the sole "chieftainship" over the whole of Botswana. It might be argued that Botswana presents a unique picture with its small national population (of 1.2 million) divided into only two (Sotho and

Tswana) communities. That these factors do not necessarily account for Botswana's success becomes clear from the contrasting quagmires in Burundi and Rwanda which share similarities with Botswana. On the other hand, ethnic pluralism, which has reigned havoc in Nigeria, Uganda, and Kenya, for example, has not produced any comparable problems in, say, Tanzania. Even mono-ethnic states like Somalia have hardly fared better than plural ones. The better approach, then, is to observe each case in terms of how each case of the colonial apparati influenced the outcome of their replacements by their respective strategies. Commenting on the Botswana case, John Holm and Patrick Molutsi point out that "[t]he problem with all these community-based approaches is that they have an impact only on policy implementation in individual communities, while top national leaders remain unaffected."[6] The Botswana case is further helped by its proximity to South Africa, whose labor market left no other option for Botswana's leaders than the universalistic approach to keep its labor force at home for nation-building. In several African cases, the colonial positioning, by design or by default, of specific communities to make greater national claims relative to others has clearly impeded the onset of democracy and good governance rooted in the rift and/or competition between state and society.[7]

Social and Political Activism: The Role of Modern Communities

Let me return now to that type of community that emerges as the location of adequate and efficient agency for influencing changes and enactment of public policy in liberal society. This category of community is the result of a critical review of the Lockean theory of the mass society as a moral political body; its theorizers argue that in view of recent social and political transformations, the Lockean model has become weak and therefore incapable of overseeing and safeguarding public policy. Its exponents argue that small organized social groups, formed as either rights-based communities or other forms of compact interest groups, have replaced Locke's political society as the most effective bodies for negotiating or pressing for the enactment of laws in recognition of the rights of groups where they are denied or absent. As recently argued by Gross,[8] this development is a shift away from the strong political morality — partly derived from Locke but accentuated by Mill and recently rearticulated by Rawls — which charges individuals with the moral duty to oversee public policy and take appropriate action when it violates certain moral limits. It contends that the democratic welfare depends for its survival on the rational actions of the individual such as autonomous judgment and concerted political action, whether these are manifested through her vote, the right to political participation, or the duty of civil disobedience.

However, today, owing to the ever-growing complexity of interests as well as the cognitively complex feature of political cognition itself, even this vaunted individuality has needed the tempering of a "moral community," the pre-political social entity that forms the basis for civil society and perseveres on the dissolution of government. In other words, political action is collective. It is not taken at the instigation of isolated individuals but only on the basis of consensus and general agreement. This, Gross observes, suggests a weak model of political morality that severely constrains the moral demands of the strong model.

The reason this model represents the weak political morality is that in them, according to Gross, moral principles are not pursued so much for their hedonistic value as for their protective role; as soon as they are codified and enshrined in positive law they are left to slide into the backdrop against which self-interest is played out. Political stability is not found in moral competence but in informed self-interest and institutional regulation. Weak political morality has become the phenomenon of the growing pluralist and often also conflictual world in which the perceived threat of Otherness has identified "protection" as the primary duty of government – to protect individuals and groups from the perceived harsh realities of political life such as corrupt leaders, unjust majorities, crime-proned and/or ill-tempered neighbors.

This is certainly another level of social evolution, an attractive model of liberal democratic values at work. But it doesn't work equally for all interest groups. It is not guaranteed that people will give equal support, on the basis of reason and moral conviction alone, to the causes of all those social categories to which they themselves do not belong as they do to their own. The example I have in mind is the relations between racial or ethnic rights and the rights of, say, gay people. Will a gay black woman receive equal support of non-black gay people in race-related issues as she gives to gay-related ones? There are no guaranteed answers to this kind of question, simply because people may respond differently to questions of what I will call "choosable identity" (such as sexual orientation) than they would to "non-choosable" ones (like being black, white, or yellow). This would mean that although a yellow gay person may believe that denying black people certain rights only on the basis of race alone is morally just as wrong as denying a gay person certain rights given to others only because of their sexual orientation, they might not feel pulled strongly enough, on those moral grounds, to march on the streets, or to donate money toward a legal defense for a race issue as they do or would for gay issues in which their interests are directly addressed. A slightly more complicated case arose, *exempli gratia*, from what is now widely regarded as a race-driven reluctance or only quarter-hearted willingness by America to help resolve the Rwanda genocide which stands in sharp contrast to how it later mobilized massive resources to intervene in the Balkan genocide.

Another factor that may influence the degree of effectiveness of interest group communities in influencing policy may well be their ability to muster financial backing, a matter which, sometimes, gets closely related to the race factor. The point is that in situations where separate communities do not share equal access to the same channels of self-representation and argumentation, or do not or are not likely to have the same effect on the institutions to be lobbied and controled, the pluralist structure of the weak political morality can be an avenue to even greater social and civil inequities. The protective democracy of the weak political morality is more likely to benefit already privileged and politically and economically strong (influential) communities which wield recognized and not easily compromisable power bases than it is to have any effect on less advantaged groups. Such a situation is more likely to preserve, if not to enhance, the status quo than it is to generate substantive social and political changes. Those who have cared to watch South Africa's push to a post-apartheid state of social cohesion and integration will wonder why the Commission for Truth and Reconciliation was so seriously hampered in its endeavors. The government of South Africa has openly admitted that it cannot effectively carry out justice against those guilty of apartheid crimes for fear of the possible economic and political backlash from the reactions of the overly privileged white minority, despite the criminal nature of their political path to such privilege.

In the context of international aggression, weak political morality makes provisions for political and moral justifications for rescuing and/or protecting disadvantaged nations and societies from invasions by its neighbors, as happened in the aftermath of the German invasion of her neighbors during World War II, or in recent Euro-American unified forces' involvement in the Kuwaiti and the Balkan region conflicts. It also justifies involvement by powerful nations in peace negotiations or in the prevention of the escalation of potential conflict between bickering neighbors, as is happening in the United States' protection of South Korea, or in her brokering of peace between Israel and her Arab neighbors.

To claim that protective democracy is the way to the stabilization of the world order is to ignore its capacities to engender conflict. Gross would agree with this view because he remarks that protective democracy has sometimes been characterized as a system that "glorifies individualism and self-interest, seeks to control the insidious effects of partisan politics by encouraging more factions, abjures any moral transformation of political consciousness, and encourages competitive rather than cooperative political relationships motivated by a rather dim, if realistic, view of human nature. "[9] This kind of competitive partisan politics shows up frequently almost everywhere in the world where there are multiple social formations. In some cases it creates acrimonies between ethnic groups or clans, in others between racial groups.

In Gross's view, for weak political morality to work, it must be guided by moral reasoning which will incorporate political activism with specific accounts of normative first principles, democratic character, and moral learning. Contrary to Locke's view Gross argues that, as a general principle, mass society can no longer be relied upon as the subject of collective action for checking the excesses and shortcomings of government. And he rightly recognizes that the rational model of collective action might work only if its incentives already assume the existence of a context which determines their efficacy. As he says, "Altruism, normative duty, and fairness are operative relative to a particular set of 'significant others' whose interests are weighed with one's own, whose leaders and norms are authoritative, and among whom mutual feelings of fidelity and fairness run high."[10] In other words, for the rational model of collective action to work, there must be another form of "communal feeling" of common belonging among the participants of the group. Although small groups united solely by shared interests of moral nature, by intellectual convictions, are for Gross the ideal (perfect) communities, they emerge only at that ideal stage when individuals are able to "ignore calculations of expected utility." I have tried to point out above that this ideal moral principle appears to serve those who already enjoy privilege or are more likely to get it rather than the less privileged and weaker segments of society.

Gross's communitarian view is purely methodological. While it emphasizes the psycho-social and ethical importance of belonging to communities for specific ends, the interests and beliefs which are conceived of and valued as common ends by members of the group are actually private, although congruent with those of other people. Based on the central role of congruency rather than commonality of interests of members, this view of society affirms that the betterment of society is guaranteed by the conflictual and competitive relations between its constituent parts. It does not aim to achieve a common humanity.

Gross's theory, like Locke's, is evolutionistic. It claims that weak political morality is the function of an increase in social complexity – such as the rise of once unknown or tabooed claims of moral and legal rights for individuals and groups – and of a higher epistemological sophistication in political cognition. This complexity of the nature and knowledge of society has rendered the Lockean mass political body ineffective as an agent of political moral control. Locke's single political community has now been replaced by a multiplicity of political communities defined by varieties of moral claims and beliefs which are only shared by relatively small groups. Also, in the place of mass protests available to Locke's political community as the effective means for bringing change, the effectiveness of small interest group communities depends first on the logical and epistemological strength of moral and legal arguments and only later reverts to active protests.

Ethnic, National, or Global Community?

The reality of ethnic communities enables many African people to experience their world and to identify themselves in multiple ways. "They think of themselves as one people in some settings and as a different people in others."[11] One may identify himself as a member of one ethnic community or only a section of it when the nature of political discourse so demands, and firmly as a Kenyan at another time under a different setting of discourse. As Appiah tells us in a moving story about his father's death and funeral, in Africa communities appear to continue to claim high stakes in the control of individuals' experiences of their identity.[12] But it has been suggested by supporters of moral globalization that nationalism and ethnocentrism are hindrances to the development of universal human moral values.

While socio-cultural pluralism raises interesting political questions about nation-building, the impact of inter-ethnic rivalries on the stability of the state raises pertinent moral issues regarding how members of different groups treat each other in settings of divided loyalty. Nepotism, tribalism, and other forms of discriminatory behavior are bad and wrong any time or anywhere they are practiced. They are founded on the commitment, on occasions of distributing goods or apportioning claims, to favor those who share kinship ties with us against those unrelated to us, regardless of whether or not they are justly qualified or deserving. Such forms of behavior are the antitheses of distributive justice. Akin to them are those feelings that we develop and frequently exhibit to express our committed love for our group, whether this is family, clan, ethnic group, or nation. In the present world of international corporations and common political bodies requiring service from citizens of member-states, even patriotism can lead to the kind of injustices we have identified with nepotism and tribalism.

Besides distributive considerations, love of one's group can lead to morally questionable expressions, such as a show of rejection and hostility toward those of other groups for no reason other than that they are from groups different from one's own. Indeed, history is replete with accounts of wars and other forms of atrocity carried out against people of other identities. On this account, it has been argued, all expressions of love of one's own identity over others have at least the potential to lead to immoral behavior toward others and should therefore be replaced with a more cosmopolitan view of equality among all humans. Let us call this view the pan-humanist moral theory and quickly endorse its chief moral objective: the cultivation of a world in which all humans can enjoy equal rights and respect regardless of their racial, national, ethnic, religious, gender, or any other form of affiliation.

Pan-humanist or universalist moral theorists argue that any form of emphasis on one or more social identity over others, such as ethnocentrism or patriotism, hinders the development of true moral and cognitive values because it makes only the members of one's own identity group one's moral equals, to the perilous exclusion of those who stand outside it. According to this view, cultural pluralism is a notion that can lead to moral and cognitive relativism which, it argues, is often invoked in defense of atrocities played out by one group against another.

While pluralism and relativism remain distinct, they both equally worry pan-humanists. Current debates[13] that define as mutually opposed the categories of ethnicity and nation, nation and the globe are sort of reformulations of the same old problem of the opposition between the particular and the universal. The strength of these debates lies in their ability to situate moral discourse within the wider context of the sociality of humans which has been made even more complex by recent and ongoing technological advancement and economic growth, especially in the West and Japan. These gains have made it possible to interrogate old moral and other society-related theories which now appear to have depended for their strength on the idea of social closures such as ethnically or nationally defined systems. Among such questions one can formulate the following: how do we define people culturally today in the face of widespread immigration, by individuals and groups, across geographical, social, religious, and other forms of cultural boundaries? Should people continue to compartmentalize themselves when technology is making it possible to unify in once unimagined modes? What have been, are, and will be the moral consequences of ideas, theories, and ideologies which encourage the compartmentalization of people through the theories of identity and difference? But counter-questions come to mind quickly too. Does cultural self-identification entail the negation of cosmopolitanism? Or, does it entail hostility toward others? Can we be both simultaneously? These are difficult questions, and they do not suggest easy answers. But people who are mindful enough of the future of humanity must ask and confront them.

While keeping in mind the injustices and other evils against humanity resulting from calls by the dark world's political leaders as a result of unwarranted ethnocentrism at the expense of greater social values, I worry also about other assumptions underlying the claim that feelings associated with identities based on community or nation-state, such as patriotism or those based on religion, are incompatible with cosmopolitanism and a universal moral order. It is hard to imagine an argument that would successfully defend the claim that one cannot give allegiance to being, for instance, a Zande and a Sudanese at the same time, or that doing so inexorably limits one's ability to develop truly human values that are universal. It is worrying, because for such a claim to succeed it would have also to argue successfully that social identities, such as being Zande or Sudanese, are inalienable, and are ontologically and cognitively determining and mutually exclusive conditions which no one person can possess together at the same time.

Martha Nussbaum argues that nationalism – and, by extension, other bounding identities – limits our ability to develop true moral values.[14] While commenting on Rabindranath Tagore's novel, *The Home and the World*, she writes:

> I believe that Tagore sees deeply when he observes that, at bottom, nationalism and ethnocentric particularism are not alien to one another, but akin – that to give support to nationalist sentiments subverts, ultimately, even the values that hold a nation together, because it substitutes a colorful idol for the substantive universal values of justice and right. Once someone has said, I am an Indian first, a citizen of the world second, once he or she has made that morally questionable move of self-definition by a morally irrelevant characteristic, then what, indeed, will stop that person from saying, as Tagore's characters so quickly learn to say, I am a Hindu first, and an Indian second, or I am an upper-caste landlord first, and a Hindu second? Only the cosmopolitan stance of the landlord Nikhil – so boringly flat in the eyes of his young wife Bimala and his passionate nationalist friend Sandip – has the promise of transcending these divisions, because only this stance asks us to give our first allegiance to what is morally good – and that which, being good, I can recommend to all human beings.[15]

Like most of those (universalists) who argue that any principle of social action is wrong and must be rejected if it bears the capacity to produce results contrary to the ideal aspirations of the dominant theory, Nussbaum too argues that in a world geared toward bridging at least most differences between peoples across political, social, and cultural borders, all types of bounded identities should at best take a secondary place to the value of a universal boundless society.

While its objective is undeniably a good one, the universalist demand is, however, an expression of fears based on some historical facts rather than on an assessment of a logical relation between claims of identity and violence. From a historical viewpoint, it is unquestionably legitimate to raise awareness about the capacity of people, generally speaking, to move from a mere recognition of diverse ethnicities to believing, to paraphrase Appiah, that members of different ethnicities differ in respects that warrant their differential treatment.[16] In Africa, such a move spells the onset of tribalism, one of that continent's public moral problems. Given the amount of evil committed in remote and recent history by people in the names of the groups within which they claim identity, Nussbaum's point hardly requires emphasis or elaboration. But it is wrong to infer from this that anyone who identifies herself as, say, Zande first and Sudanese second will thereby be a tribalist in this moral sense. Nussbaum does well to place the blame on ideology, an important aspect of which is the packaging of education and its role in creating and instilling in the minds of young generations the false connotations of the sentiments about our identities as local and global citizens. Such education can create awareness of universal human values, one of which is the important cultural diversity among human groups.

Needless to say, educational systems provide us with the ideological lenses through which we view ourselves in relation to others. And if Nussbaum is right that "[t]hrough cosmopolitan education, we learn more about ourselves,"[17] then, ironically, colonial education, with its emphasis on the colonizer, produced the unintended product in the colonized by making him more humane and more universally oriented than the colonizer was. In other words, forced to focus on the colonizer and his world as the sole content of his (the colonized's) education, the colonized was able to cast his gaze away from himself without casting out his self-image. Aimé Césaire has a powerful description of this irony of colonization in his *Discourse on Colonialism*.[18] There is no doubt that Nussbaum's concerns are both justified and timely; they address wrong uses of identity – for cultic differences rather than for the riches of cultural diversity which the human phenomenon makes possible. But, it is not hard to see that they are concerns with what she identifies to be wrong education policies, and not with identity as such. To put this in the idioms of her portrait of the Aristophanic tragedy, it is not true that all who learn about difference will be father-killers. There may always be bad pupils who erroneously make tragic inferences from ideas about difference. Also, while Socrates was not among them, there may always be bad teachers who might lead their pupils to be father-killers. But should we therefore denounce the teaching profession altogether just because there is a persistent likelihood of there being both bad pupils and bad teachers? Nussbaum's proposal is, of course, that we should reform education to stress universality rather than eliminate it altogether. In her view, reference to the classics will instruct us on the original importance of the universal as the true object of knowledge.

Communities: Can We Transcend Them?

Recent debates on the nature of communities were popularized and made current by – and continue to draw from – Benedict Anderson's *Imagined Communities*.[19] Since then, birds of all feathers have learned to feed on Anderson's grains. But before he made current the idea of community as a product of post-Word War II ideological campaigns aided by the media, there was Pierre Felix Bourdieu's idea that the worlds we inhabit are networks of carefully negotiated schematic rules in which individual and society are mutually dependent and produce each other.[20] There is no society without the practical and improvising skills of the individual, just as there is no self-sufficient individual whose practical skills are primarily in response to the regulations of society within given structures. Several other thinkers too, including Kuhn and Polanyi in the recent past, and Charles Wade Mills among many others today, have addressed the role of communities, both professional and everyday ones, in the epistemic shaping of our world.[21] They examine the social mechanisms by which the construction and validation of theory and norms are done. Mills is far more deterministic in ways that Bourdieu is not. It is Bourdieu whose work directly addresses the individual–society co-relation in the production of culture in general in manners relevant to the issues raised by Nussbaum. His general social theory in particular aims at transcending the opposition between individual and society that he sees to be mutually conditioning. His thesis is that the cultural worlds that we assume to be common for the actors within them are constituted by the effects of the actors' own actions within society as an influencing and conditioning (also self-preserving) institution. On the one hand, people exhibit practical skills that are adjusted to the constraints of the (social) environment. On the other hand, society does not determine people's actions: the same practical skills allow them to act with some measure of freedom and even to improvise in the process of dealing with an infinite number of situations, thus influencing and reshaping the practical appearance of society itself. Together, in reciprocity, they produce these cultural communities by a systemic action-response behavioral scheme. For Bourdieu, cultural knowledge, such as knowledge of ritual, is a kind of practical knowledge based on the same schemes of *habitus* as daily life in which the patterns of ritual and daily activities interpenetrate and interact to create the cultural significance of the *Lebenswelt*. In Bourdieu's social world or *habitus*, ritual, language, actors, and agency all play specific and open-ended roles in the creation of the worlds that structure the social world into units of specific modes of rationality, legitimation, power, and social action.

The key notion in Bourdieu's practical logic, *habitus*, leads to his emphasis of cross-contextual links.[22] As a set of generative schemes of perception, action, and appreciation that are learned and reinforced by actions and discourses produced according to the same schemes, *habitus* is applied equally in agricultural labor and calendrical rites, in daily interaction and in ceremonial action. This wide-ranging application of a small set of schemes gives practical logic its approximate cohesion, its "fuzzy" regularity. Social phenomena exist and can only be understood relationally, that is, as they occur in diachronic and synchronic relation to other sociological phenomena. Notions of good taste in clothes, for example, are a product of the social position of the person who holds the beliefs or, more exactly, who practices a certain way of dressing. He holds such beliefs in relation to other beliefs and practices that are consciously or unconsciously aspired to or rejected as strategies in a struggle for recognition and acceptance in a particular place and role in society; these notions and practices can only be understood if all such relations are taken into account. One can relate this example to the current phenomenon of teenage fashion in the United States. Similar sub-cultural phenomena sweep through many societies all the time.

Bourdieu's analysis of the socio-cultural world of the Kabyle of Morocco is often meticulously described with rich accounts of ritual, language, and agency through which the systemic structure of practice is produced.[23] But due precisely to the emphasis on the synchronic structure and logic of the production of this social world, the *habitus* appears to lose focus on the process of the production. As a result, Kratz observes, "his relational understanding [of interpenetration of cultural contexts] tends to displace other associations that rely less extensively on interreferencing, positive meanings that do not rely on oppositions to other schemes or objects."[22] Secondly, Bourdieu's theory assumes a single linguistic marketplace and a single set of values that are recognized and shared by all concerned. It ignores the multidimensional world in which people inhabit diverse social relations contemporaneously, or frequently migrate between them. In other words, Bourdieu does not take into consideration the real and figurative multilinguistic capacity of individuals to engage in discourses across diverse cultural fields. The Marxist framework which makes it possible for Bourdieu to lose focus on the process through which social worlds are open-endedly produced – because it shifts attention to power structure within limited contexts – also leads him to a deterministic view of cultural institutions as windows through which classifications and definitions of peoples and societies can be observed. He defines cultural institutions as units of power, the power to represent and to sustain the status quo: to reproduce structures of belief and experience through which cultural differences are understood. An overview of Bourdieu's system would then produce an image of communities as collectible, exhibitable, and manageable social units – because they have fixed structures – juxtaposed but unconnected one to the other. For Bourdieu, then, communities are self-generating and tend to be mutually exclusive. A race-based variety of this view feeds the American conservative political discourse, especially in the southern states.

By comparison, Gross's theory of weak political morality has one major advantage over Bourdieu's *habitus*. The sense of moral communities that Gross works with need not be taken to refer only to geographically situated social units. Rather, they are characterized only by shared beliefs and actions in ways that bring personal identity into a stereotyped connection and solidarity with other moral reasoners "firmly anchored in tight social networks."[25] He writes:

While solidarity benefits and, in particular, personal identity incentives are enhanced by conventional moral development, close friendship networks, and social interdependence, none of these factors affects the strength of post-material incentives. Instead, these incentives, characterized by norms of citizenship and universal moral duty, are closely tied to post-conventional moral preferences and a firm rejection of pre-conventional norms. They address autonomy and motivate individuals to act regardless of the actions and opinions of others.[26]

One of the things that the above statement implies is that one does not have to share all the beliefs of the other members of a moral community to become one of them in a specific regard. This characteristic sets Gross's liberal community significantly aside from the traditional model. It uses community only as a strategic alliance for the achievement of deeply individual interests. Thus its morality is definitely not communitarian in the substantive sense. Its fortress lies not in the actuality but in the rationality of the (common) beliefs about a good life. As Will Kymlicka says,

Some people say that our essential interest is in living our life in accordance with the ends that we, as individuals or as a community, currently hold and share. But that seems a mistake: for our deliberations are not just predictions about how to maximize the achievement of current ends and projects. They are also judgements about the value of those ends and projects, and we recognize that our current and past judgements are fallible.[27]

Because membership to such community depends on the deliberative (i.e. rational) tenability of its claims, Gross argues that responsiveness to selective incentives would be sufficient to constitute one type of such community. Also, this makes it possible for one individual to become a member of multiple communities characterized by a diverse array of interests that are coordinated through different relevant groups. A crucial difference lies, of course, in how different schools of liberalism define the origin and type of moral reason.

It is not within the scope of this chapter to discuss how Gross resembles or differs from Kymlicka on the issue. It is enough to note that Kymlicka shares the liberal position of John Rawls and, back in history, that of J. S. Mill.[28] Like Rawls, Kymlicka believes that some communitarian ideas could be repressive, possibly because they might want to define our ends for us. Gross, on the other hand, plays down the significance of the "objectivist" status of the shared beliefs of a political morality. It is sufficient that an individual actor sympathizes with them sufficiently to warrant her/his action. While he shares with Kymlicka the liberal individualist commitment to the role of individual responsibility and self-direction, his interest in the work cited here is chiefly with the role of advocacy in influencing public policy rather than with the ontological issues of political morality. Thus for him, like for Kymlicka, if individuals see value in a particular group membership, they should have the right to pursue that membership. But they should preserve their fundamental freedom even while they maintain their membership therein and believe and act in agreement with other members thereof.

In real life, at least in the kind of setting presupposed by Gross, and which is in several ways similar to that inhabited by most of those who debate these issues in the academy, individuals cross boundaries to participate in as many actions of different activist interest groups as may be related to or urge their moral stands and demands for change. Gross's historical observation is correct that such cases are many and may keep multiplying with the course of social evolution. Much of this may be dependent on the growth of knowledge and its impact on economies that then result in continuous reconfigurations of social roles, connections, and relations. The result is that an increasing number of people find themselves performing increasingly variant roles in the course of their active lives without renouncing any. For example, many of us inhabit, by day, communities defined by our professionally specific and institutionally connected and coordinated interests. And while giving our full dedication to these profession-based communities, we at the same time carry awareness of and responsibilities to other communities which we return to by evening without retiring from the former. And, as immigrants know well, the complexity does not stop there: it extends beyond household and neighborhood to cultural reconnections over long geographical distances through a variety of symbolic and ritualistic means such as language, dress, music, religion, and other forms of both spontaneous and organized activities. I believe that these layers and transfers of personal alliances do not negate each other, at least not significantly enough to make it impossible for individuals and groups to participate in a number of them either simultaneously or alternately.

I sit in my university office and rotate in my chair to admire the rich multiplicity of what the room brings in between the walls without overburdening them with the contradiction between the particular and the universal, the patriotic and the cosmopolitan. The ability to play a CD of my Luo music while working on a philosophy paper, one that even cites references to a work by some British philosopher I don't care about except for his or her ideas that reach me in their abstracted and symbol-based medium of a book, makes no conditional demand upon me that to participate in one I must first abandon the other. I can be both Luo and a member of the academic community of the University of Louisville at the same time without a burden. I can be, and in fact I am, a patriot and cosmopolitan, a nationalist and ethnocentric at the same time, obsessed with the pride of being a Kenyan and, above all, a Luo. Where is the universal dress, and who shall be its universal tailor? Where is its universal pattern? Each of these identities occurs within and is sustained by a series of mental acts with which I transfer from one set of memorable symbols to another. It is a way in which I construct my multiple histories which share and compete for embodiment in the same self. Remember that oftentimes even the music I play may vary from being Luo to Congolese, and occasionally even to Bach, Beethoven, or Mozart. Yes, I love my youth too, and I often celebrate it by listening to the Italian popular music of the early to mid-1970s. Usually my children cannot connect with these, but they appreciate the complexity of real life when they say, "Now Dad has just traveled back to his days that we will never really know." Those behaviors, like the act of listening, the claim of involvement and enjoyment of the musical pieces, an occasional fall into a trance of dance in response to some *Kwasa Kwasa* beat, or the regular transfer of resources to take care of distantly located kin, are all ways in which I am drawn into and from one or the other of the multiple worlds of my everyday experience.

Yet, whoever passes by my door and catches a glimpse of me in my office most probably situates me within one or several aspects of the institutional constructs at that time, with their idea of who I am closely related to a set of character dispositions, acts, roles, and behaviors which to them are what make sense of who and what kind of person they imagine me to be, and why I am there at all in the first place. If I speak, an additional factor of this social imagination is quickly prompted by my accent, which frequently solicits the question "Where do you come from?" The fact that I might be seated there immersed in a world where being Luo might be the primary experience going through my mental processes would be completely hidden to those who in advance did not know of this aspect of my identity. And experiencing being Luo is not consistently my primary experience at all times. But at will I may invoke it as my primary root. Each encounter requires a leap from one to other modes of self-experiencing. Assuming that *actual* mutually responsive behavior, acting and getting responses, like in dialogical speech, is crucial but not necessary for making part of Bourdieu's *habitus* – because, for example, we still claim and get claimed as belonging to some group even when removed from the scrutiny and glare of others – then we can make part of any and many groups by means, not only of shifting our participatory behavior from one set of the conventional behavior patterns by which belonging to such a group is recognized, but also by believing that we continue to be disposed to comply with the conventions which we share with other people with whom we belong to other groups. Hence individual identities and experiences never derive entirely from single segments of society. An individual can in the space of a short time move back and forth between emphasizing one or other part of their identity that comes from membership of either a national, professional, ethnic, or social community. Those who travel far to relocate home or frequently change jobs as participants in the modern aggressive economies know first hand the toils of readjustments at professional and social levels. Children's pains of readjustments into school and neighborhood age-groups are well known to parents and children who are company in these crossings and transitions.

We can infer two things from the above: first, that communities are dialogically rather than ontologically constituted. With the practical skills of Bourdieu, we weave and negotiate our ways in and out of several communities everyday. It is for survival, as a way of life. Second, that one can be part of multiple communities simultaneously – such as being both patriotic and cosmopolitan, or Luo and Kenyan, and others, all at one and the same time. Appiah puts it aptly thus:

> The cosmopolitan patriot can entertain the possibility of a world in which everyone is a rooted cosmopolitan, attached to a home of his or her own, with its own cultural particularities, but taking pleasure from the presence of other, different, places that are home to other, different, people.
>
> In a world of cosmopolitan patriots, people would accept the citizen's responsibility to nurture the culture and politics of their homes. Many would, no doubt, spend their lives in the places that shaped them; and that is one of the reasons local cultural practices would be sustained and transmitted. But many would move, and that would mean that cultural practices would travel also (as they have always traveled). The result would be a world in which each local form of human life was the result of long term and persistent processes of cultural hybridization: a world, in that respect, much like the world we live in now.[29]

Our own example – of sitting in a university office in the United States reading from a British philosopher and practicing being Luo all at the same time – testifies to the cosmopolitanism that Appiah's father had so wisely spoken of. It typifies the ever and increasingly changing socio-cultural character of the *kosmou* in which we represent the migratory roots of the change. Those who remain in their respective home country experience identity shifts of a briefer order. According to Karp:

> We experience these identities not as all-encompassing entities but through specific social events: encounters and social settings where identities are made relevant by the people participating in them. Communities are often thought of as things and given thinglike names such as "the Irish", "the blacks", "the Jews", "the WASPs." But they are actually experienced as encounters in which cultures, identities, and skills are acquired and used. These settings can involve communal groups as small and intimate as the nuclear family or as large and institutional as the convention of a professional society. People form their primary attachments and learn to be members of society in these settings, which can be referred to collectively as the institutions of *civil society*.[30]

There are many examples that can further amplify the flexibility of the idea of communal belonging as based on Bourdieu's action-response model; and such examples also might amplify the idea that one person can identify with multiple action-response communities at the same time. In the domain of religion, several families are made up of members who belong to or are related to people who profess Islam, Christianity, and perhaps other modes of religious expression. Members of such households learn to relate to each other according to each person's or group's religious requirements in belief and conduct while breachlessly keeping their own. They learn to perform in the common place, but also when and how to retreat to their own respective domains of belief and behavior. Because they live in a shared space, they constantly engage in mutual critique without condemnation.

Although drawn from real life examples, this may be an over-idealization of religious conviviance. Indeed much of our history is inherited from the effects of religious intolerance — wars, persecutions, and other forms of domination of those that either profess different things or none at all. And there could not be a better time to directly point at religious intolerance in the world than now, with the resurgence of religious extremist and fundamentalist movements which span the globe from Timor to Nigeria, and from the Balkans to Sudan. As Nussbaum points out, religion has been made a source of acts which from different theoretical or cultural value perspectives may seem to be great injustices committed against various groups of people, especially women and children.[31] And it is indeed a wonderful idea to point out, not only that some things in other cultures are radically different from our own, but also that they might not be right from our own positions. Critical comparisons between cultures are at least partly how cultural evolutions start and occur in history. The point, however, is not to mete out quick condemnations in such cases, as is frequently done in imperialistic rhetoric disguised as universal moral duty. These, we have seen, are often the best avenues for propping hard-line conservative nationalist sentiments among those who are attacked. Nationalism is often born in response to real or perceived external threat of cultural, political, or military invasion. The problem with Nussbaum's otherwise worthy prescriptions – and this may also apply to Gross's idea of strong political morality – is that small groups of activists from distant lands often attempt to carry out revolutions in distant societies with little or no regard at all for the complex social and historical circumstances surrounding such problems.

The same agency with which people shift between different group identities provides the capacity with which they transform the cultures of those groups just as much as the beliefs and practices already existing in them contain the individuals and groups who so move by forcing them to readjust. The reader can take their pick from, among others, Chinua Achebe (in *Things Fall Apart* and *No Longer at Ease*) or the late renowned Ugandan poet Okot p'Bitek (in *Song of Lawino* and *Song of Ocol*).[32] They both set side by side, in dramatic opposition, conservatism and change. They foreshadow the debate rekindled by Martha Nussbaum's well-noted essay and subsequent debate on "Patriotism and Cosmopolitanism."[33] Her reference, as we noted above, is an Indian variety of the postcolonial text.

Nussbaum's essay raises as many questions as it answers others, both old and new. First, it evokes the old question, part of which we already made reference to above in regard to the claim that patriotic sentiments limit people's ability to develop universally applicable moral values such as justice and respect for humanity. Those who defend this view – and I do not separate myself from them by use of the distancing expression "those" – can cite the gross abuses to humanity such as the holocaust, the Somalias, the Rwandas, the Balkans, East Timor, and so on, as horrors that can emerge out of emphasis on the primacy of the particular when applied to fragmented socio-political orders. But I want to put emphasis on "can emerge" rather than "do emerge." One of the questions that arises here is whether or not epistemological categories can and/or should be applied with wholeness to how we evaluate the moral worth or quality of social, political, and cultural processes with strict regard to their capacity to generate desirable moral goods. Another question is whether, based on historical evidence to the effect that emphasis on social fragmentations have caused calamities in the cases cited, it follows that patriotic sentiments are therefore bad, or whether the only way to prevent a repetition of such calamities is to recommend the eradication altogether of the bounded social groups which give rise to patriotic rather than cosmopolitan sentiments.

A response is not hard to get: celebrations of own culture need not lead to conflict with others merely on the basis of difference. While it is true that abuses of the reality of cultural differences have led to calamities, it is also true that abuse and violence against those unlike us is neither a necessary nor a desirable part of the idea of difference. We must not lose track of the possibility that the kind of calamities we so readily cite have in some of these cases been caused by the desire for universality, by a drive to create a homogeneous and universal sense of belonging where those who are different have no place. At the same time, passive difference also can lead to calamity. Difference is not a value in and of itself. What if, for example, all different opinions on an issue were false? There certainly cannot be any pleasure derivable from having a multiplicity of false opinions to a problem. This would be pluralism at its epistemological worst. We all have the need to protect ourselves from those who say "My country [or community], right or wrong."[34]

In conclusion, there are two sayings in the Luo language: "*piny luore* (the universe is steeped in unending change)" and "*wuoth eka ine* (travel, and you shall witness its diversity)." Local people know far too well that they live in a cosmos and confront it everyday. As the celebrated Martiniquan man of letters Aimé Césaire has said, "There are two sure ways to lose oneself: either by bounding oneself in the windowless particular, or by throwing oneself into the unidentifiable universal."[35] He surely realized and wisely hinted at the compatibility between the local and global, the patriotic and cosmopolitan.

Notes

1   See Michael L. Gross, *Ethics and Activism: The Theory and Practice of Public Morality* (Cambridge: Cambridge University Press, 1997); Martha Nussbaum, "Patriotism and Cosmopolitanism," in M. Nussbaum and J. Cohen, eds., *For Love of Country: Debating the Limits of Patriotism* (Boston: Beacon Press, 1996).

2   Jeffrey C. Alexander, *Fin de Siècle Social Theory: Relativism, Reduction, and the Problem of Reason* (London: Verso Books, 1995), p. 79.

3   See Meyer Fortes and E. E. Evans-Pritchard, *African Political Systems* (Oxford: Oxford University Press, 1940).

4   Gross, *Ethics and Activism*, p. 239.

5   Manning Marable, "We Need New and Critical Study of Race and Ethnicity," in *The Chronicle of Higher Education* XLVI, 25 (February 25, 2000): B4–7.

6   John D. Holm and Patrick P. Molutsi, "State-Society Relations in Botswana: Beginning Liberalization," in Goran Hyden and Michael Bratton, eds., *Governance and Politics in Africa* (Boulder, CO: Lynne Rienner, 1992), p. 85.

7   See, for example, Donald Rothchild and N. Chazan, eds., *The Precarious Balance: State and Society in Africa* (Boulder, CO: Westview, 1988).

8   See Gross *Ethics and Activism*.

9   Ibid., p. 24.

10   Ibid., p. 108.

11   Ivan C. Karp, Mullen Kreamer, and S. D. Lavine, eds., *Museums and Communities: The Politics of Public Culture* (Washington, DC: Smithsonian Institution, 1992), p. 221.

12   Kwame A. Appiah, *In My Father's House: Africa in the Philosophies of Culture* (Oxford: Oxford University Press, 1992), pp. 181–92.

13   As appear, for example, in Nussbaum and Cohen, eds., *For Love of Country*, and in Pheng Cheah and B. Robbins, eds., *Cosmopolitics: Thinking and Feeling Beyond the Nation* (Minneapolis: University of Minnesota Press, 1998).

14   See Martha C. Nussbaum, "Patriotism and Cosmopolitanism," in Nussbaum and Cohen, eds., *For Love of Country*, pp. 2–17.

15   Ibid., p. 5.

16   Kwame A. Appiah, "Racisms," in David Theo Goldberg, ed., *Anatomy of Race* (Minneapolis: University of Minnesota Press, 1990), pp. 3–17.

17   Nussbaum, "Patriotism and Cosmopolitanism," p. 11.

18   Aimé Césaire, *Discourse on Colonialism*, trans. Joan Pinkham (New York: Monthly Review Press, 1972), pp. 15–19.

19   *Imagined Communities: Reflections on the Origin and Spread of Nationalism* (London: Verso, 1983).

20   Three of Bourdieu's major works, *Outline of a Theory of Practice*, *The Logic of Practice* (Stanford: Stanford University Press, 1990), and *The Field of Cultural Production* (New York: Columbia University Press, 1993), are dedicated to the analysis of the dialectics by which social formations reproduce themselves by means of a practical logic to incorporate structures and objectify the habitus.

21   Charles Wade Mills, *The Racial Contract* (Ithaca: Cornell University Press, 1997); and *Blackness Visible: Essays on Philosophy and Race* (Ithaca: Cornell University Press, 1998).

22   For a general discussion of the structure and dialectics of the habitus, see Bourdieu, *Outline of a Theory of Practice*, chs 2, 3, and 4; and *The Logic of Practice*, Book 1.

23   See *The Logic of Practice*, Book II, p. 20.

24   Corrine A. Kratz, *Affecting Performance: Meaning, Movement, and Experience in Okiek Women's Initiation* (Washington, DC: Smithsonian Institution, 1994), p. 31.

25   Gross, *Ethics and Activism*, p. 218.

26   Ibid., p. 218.

27   Will Kymlicka, *Liberalism, Community and Culture* (Oxford: Clarendon Press, 1989), p. 11.

28   Two works of J. S. Mill, *On Liberty* (1859) and *Ulitarianism* (1863), and John Rawls's classic *A Theory of Justice* (Cambridge, Mass.: Harvard University Press, 1971) have been enormously influential to the central positions of liberalism.

29   Kwame A. Appiah, "Cosmopolitan Patriots," in Nussbaum and Cohen, eds., *For Love of Country*, pp. 22–3. (An expanded version is printed in Pheng Cheah and Bruce Robbins eds., *Cosmopolitics: Thinking and Feeling beyond the Nation* (Minneapolis: University of Minnesota Press, 1998, pp. 91–114.

30   Ivan Karp, "Introduction: Museums and Communities: The Politics of Public Culture," in Karp et al., eds., *Museums and Communities*, pp. 3–4.

31   See Martha C. Nussbaum, "Feminist Internationalism" (The Seeley Lectures in Political Theory, Cambridge University): Lecture 3 – "The Role of Religion" (unpublished at the time of citation), 1998.

32   Chinua Achebe, *Things Fall Apart* (London: Heinemann Educational Books, 1997); Chinua Achebe, *No Longer at Ease* (London: Heinemann Educational Books, 1983); Okot p'Bitek, *Song of Lawino and Song of Ocol* (London: Heinemann Educational Books, 1984).

33   See Nussbaum, "Patriotism and Cosmopolitanism.".

34   Appiah, "Cosmopolitan Patriots," p. 24.

35   Césaire, *Discourse on Colonialism*.

6

Obligations Across Generations:
A Consideration in the Understanding
of Community Formation

Lewis R. Gordon

Obligation has suffered the fate of narrow foci in its modern and contemporary philosophical treatments. The tropes are familiar to the point of cliché: duty versus consequence versus virtue.[1] It is as if the moral philosophical universe, save for Friedrich Nietzsche's metaethical reflections and critique, is an ontological tripartite pretty much as the age of Christianity signaled the primacy of threes. Primacy of duty subordinated consequence, which meant that rightful action was the order of the day. Should one aim for the good, the result was a subordination of rightful action. In a liberal age, however, agreement on the good is difficult to substantiate; hence, as the great John Rawls has shown, agreement on reasonably reflected ways of organizing the social and political world is such that the differing conceptions of the good could be tolerated.[2] In defense of a virtue approach, however, objection could be made to a world of horrible human beings who aim at no good beyond making sure that their actions were fair or just, even though their own characters may be quite vicious. What's more, in narrow approaches that simply look at rightful noncontextualized actions, there is a loss of the common good beyond the concession that justice is a good thing for all.[3] Aiming for the good of all raises the familiar objections as well of possible sacrificed innocence. And so these debates go on, fine tuned, with what William Barrett once described as illusions of technique.[4]

Are these accurate portraits of ethical life?

A problem I have always found with academic treatments of ethics is that they are clearly written by people who lack an understanding of mature ethical life. In many ways, they cannot be entirely blamed. Ethics are, after all, taught in a social milieu that prizes inexperience and pure analytical rigor. It is a world that, for the most part, extols what Maurice Merleau-Ponty has criticized as the desire for validity without existence.[5] The sloppiness of ethical life, its contradictions and paradoxes, are often pushed to the wayside. Unlike ancient Mediterranean communities, where tragedies portrayed the complex moral world in which innocence and virtue often suffer, or ancient African communities, where there is always a larger, cosmological consideration for ethical life, or the paradoxical world of Søren Kierkegaard, where the search for universality encounters struggles of faith and the demonic standing *above* universal dictates – academic ethics struggle through a moral universe whose neatness befits, at best, adolescents.[6] It is no wonder that the world of standardized tests and naive argumentation churn out generations of say-nothings. What else can we expect from a world that invests its hope for moral reasoning in the hands of whiz kids?

Here is a classic example of the kind of reasoning one encounters with such approaches. There are two children drowning. You can only save one. One is your child. Which is it morally correct to save? I have seen this example broached in professional philosophical settings, and I have seen professional philosophers actually argue their case with the fervor of teams in a forensic competition. That there *are* issues to argue through at all here is a function of something lost in the valuational life of such philosophical thinkers. No doubt, they are well armed with Kant's condemnation of philosophical anthropology and his plea for a genuine metaphysics (that is, philosophy) of morals, and since the kingdom of ends require absolute – that is, "categorical" – equality, otherwise there would be no *law* of morality that stands counter to the inclinations of nature, how in the world is the moral agent to decide between two equally drowning moral agents? A problem, however, lies in the intentionally over-abstract, reductive concepts of "moral agents," which here often means "rational being." Once one of the drowning moral agents is "your child," it should be obvious that you are a parent, and, as a parent, you are in a different relation to your child than you are to other people's children if only for the fact that *you* brought your child into the world. Bringing someone into the world places one in a different set of moral relations than not having anything to do with bringing someone into the world. It becomes your duty to do what you can for that person's survival, as is evident from feeding to diapers to clothes to education, and so on. That being so, there is a peculiar *relation* one has to such a being, and it should be obvious that other such beings – that is, family – carry special obligations by virtue of how we are related to them and how they are related to us.

The famed moralist and philosopher of religion Josiah Royce wrote quite a bit on fleshing out ethics.[7] Informed by Hegel's insights into social morality, Royce took seriously such moral acts as "loyalty" and "reverence" – acts that no doubt turn the stomachs of more egotistic moderns grown on a rich diet of secular, ahistorical individualism. At the heart of Royce's explorations is an understanding that philosophy loses much when it fails to see its religious aspects. Put differently, no moral theory is worth anything if it lacks "binding" force, and to be bound is, after all, a fundamentally religious phenomenon.

My aim here is to advance the importance of looking at obligations across generations in any project of understanding communities. The obvious argument in this regard is that obligations that bind only one generation to itself fail to carry features of that generation that may constitute tradition and other important features of identity formation, particularly membership. For communities to exist, membership must be possible, but for membership to be possible, there must be something already available for admission or something constituted as available for future admission. That being so, the very notion of community entails demands that may go counter to the demands we have placed upon how teleological concerns comport with the dictates of modern life. Modern life is, after all, as Max Weber and Jürgen Habermas have argued, guided by the final arbitration of laws legitimated by secular reasoning over all other normative claims. The possibility of an empty positivism lurks in every crevice of such a view of social life.[8] Although Habermas has attempted to rationalize this reality through the legitimating resources of communication (dialogue), such an attempt clearly reasserts this situation instead of addressing it, for the communicative action of which he speaks is clearly a function of the Kantian reality already criticized. Again, the formalism establishes at best valid relations, but not necessarily cogent ones. They lack the complexity of ethical life, what we could as well call *adult sensibilities*.

A problem I find with modern Western ethics is that it works on the level of the subjunctive and the conditional with regard to social phenomena; it works in a world in which past and future are suspended, which makes the object of moral reflection an *everpresence*.[9] Obligation, even those in the consequentialist vein that appeal to "the greatest number," cannot address the past – save as some trite rule-utilitarianism of the importance of, say, trying to keep promises – as a site of moral obligation and, consequently, always faces a sacrificed generation. In other approaches to the critical study of morality, the concerns seem at first to be much different. I say "at first" because it has become evident to me, after several years of teaching courses on African philosophy and religion, that the people who now comprise "Western civilization" have been put on by the people who theorize their morality. The story is familiar: a special class emerged that needed a morality that suited their political assent. In a world in which one has to get rid of aristocrats, heredity had to go, and arguments that placed obligations on abstract moral subjects helped pave the way for people whose pursuit of wealth and political capital depended upon principles of noninterference. The problem has been that no one is ever really *moved* by an abstraction, so the values of special obligation continued to assert themselves.[10] Think of the contradiction of a group of people like the bourgeoisie, who reject divine heredity (the values of the aristocracy) but who have developed naturalistic explanations of superior lineage – first through "race" and now through "genes." One rarely meets an accomplished couple in contemporary society who do not pray that their genes will confirm their special worth through repetition of accomplishments – namely, their children.[11]

Most Westerners don't believe that moral life is as taught in many philosophy classes. I see much philosophical work on ethics stand to moral life pretty much as Zeno's demonstrations stood in relation to motion and distance. Recall that Zeno argued that since there is an infinitesimal number of spaces between each step, motion is in fact not possible. After accepting the validity of his argument, one simply gets up and goes home. Aristotle's insight on ethical life rings true here. As a function of practical reason, it requires more than definition for the purposes of assessment.[12]

I should like to add here that although I have been using the term "Western" thus far, it has only been to work through the general geo-epistemic conditions that have become colloquial. I don't, however, subscribe to ascriptions of the contemporary world as "Western" versus "non-Western." Such ascriptions go counter to both history and the charges of globalism today. We cannot have both – that Western civilization is everywhere but there are enclaves of non-Westernization here and there. Such views presuppose a "pure" west instead of the highly hybridized reality that emerged when some people on a small northern continent began to travel, conquer, and expand. It is that reality that created "Europe" and "the West," which means modern western civilization has always been intimately tied to places that were supposedly non-Western. How in the world did those places come into being as non-Western when there was no reason to regard themselves as "East" or "South" prior to the collision of communities that made them begin to look "up" at Europe?

The divide between things Western and things non-Western is often a Western phenomenon. Looking at the Mediterranean on a contemporary map, it is easy to forget that that sea was not always there and that Europe and Africa were on many occasions a single land mass, and one of those occasions was during the last ice age. That is why there are caves with human artifacts beneath those waters. That being so, the links between Europe and Africa may be stronger than separatists would hope them to be.

All this is to say that values that a moral anthropologist may call European may well be African with superficial differences. If that is so, then African and Western values may seem different, but their referents are the same. Here are, for example, some familiar sayings among the Akan religion among the Asante in Ghana:

1   At the start of any undertaking the Akan would say: "Onyame [God], help me!" (*Onyame boa me*).
2   The expression "If it is the will of Onyame" (s_ *Onyame p_ a*) is constantly on people's lips at the start, or in the course, of a pursuit.

3   If one inquired about another's health, the latter would almost invari-
     ably say, "By the grace of Onyame, I am all right" (*Onyame adom me ho
     y_*).
4   Salutations and words of farewell are couched in the form of prayer to
     Onyame. For instance, "may you go in the company of Onyame" (*wo ne
     'Nyame nk_*); "I leave you in the hands of Onyame" (*me de 'Nyame gya
     wo*).
5   If one narrowly escapes a disaster one would say, "If Onyame had not
     intervened . . ." (*Se Onyame ampata a . . .*); "Onyame alone" (*Onyame nko
     ara*).
6   The priest at the shrine of a deity, when consulted in case of illness, would
     always say: "If Onyame permits, I shall cure you."[13]

There is nothing here that has not manifested itself in the idioms of most
European and Middle Eastern religions. I'm certain every one of these sayings is familiar to all theistic communities and those with theistic foundations.

The "alien" quality of the African has been more a *project* of European
modernity than a reality, and for good reason: most European religions are,
after all, a function of deliberate amnesia. Having acquired religions that
evolved in hot climates, European "domestication" took the form of a returned
gaze into a white mirror. Thus, instead of looking through at brown people
in the historic past (as most Semites in fact are, not like the Slavs who now
dominate the meaning of the term), there is a normative-cum-reality picture
of an ancient Middle East and Eastern Africa populated by Europeans. Brown
people in this narrative would suggest a link that no doubt would make Africa a little too close for comfort, geographically close as the two continents
are. I have often found it amusing to watch European-projected whiteness
on East African and Middle Eastern religions. What often struck me as amusing is their *sincerity*. For such worshippers the past is truly *theirs* – not humanity's – but *white* humanity's past. It is a displacement of cultural reality
to match racial ideology. That it would be folly for Southern Africans to begin thinking, say, of their ancestry in Odin and pray to enter Valhalla is an
indication of how such absurdity has achieved all the seriousness of reality
in the history of European communities seeking to claim a non-European
past. The whitening process made the Semitic religions that swept through
Europe, albeit through a creolization process with European paganism, less
alien. A version of this emerged in philosophical literature as well. That late
eighteenth- and early nineteenth-century philosophers like Hegel and
Schopenhauer devoted considerable energy to exploring connections between Europe and Asia, and in Hegel's case explicitly arguing for a distance
from Africa (no march of history there), was an effort to bring close civiliza-
tions that were in fact at a distance, and push to a distance those that were in

fact close. Put differently, if the black was racially distant from the white, then the black must also be culturally distant. The Asian, as a racial mediation of that distance must also be a point of cultural mediation as well. Such effort is made even though there are Asian religions without deities, but no European or African religions that are not theistic. In all my studies, I have yet to encounter the genuinely alien between anything African and European. Some objectors to this claim might bring up the example of animal sacrifice in some African religions, but such a claim is part of the continued failure to look closely at European communities and correlative African communities. Most Europeans and European-Americans do sacrifice animals – the Thanksgiving turkey and the Christmas goose are but two examples – but the spilling of blood, among the urbane, is often left to the butcher. In *rural* Europe, America, and Australia, however, farmers still slaughter animals for special rituals – weddings, religious celebrations, etc. In the case of Africa, animal sacrifice is a predominantly rural activity for the same reason: rural people are often farmers. That is why urban Africans don't engage in such activities except when they go to visit relatives in rural regions. The difference is that fewer urban whites maintain connections to rural white communities, which leads to increased invisibility of the realities of rural white life. The distinctions between European and African religiosity are, in the end, superficial. Nevertheless, scholarship guided by the presumption of that distance continues.[14]

Edward Blyden, the famed anticolonialist from the Caribbean, had studied African religions closely. In his investigations, he came upon a useful observation in this regard: it is easier to change a people's theology than their religion. The theology of modern European man has been liberal secularism whose values are, as Nietzsche has shown in such works as *The Genealogy of Morals*, *Beyond Good and Evil*, and *The Will to Power*, Christian.[15] We can call this theology modern Western philosophical ethics. But the religion, the spirit that binds members of the social world, manifests dances to a different reality. It is that dimension of ethical life that has enabled generations to connect over time. What is carried on is not simply information but something normatively vital, something precious. In this regard, contemporary Western ethics can learn much from contemporary African philosophy. Because Western philosophy has deemed itself universal, it has a tendency to treat the social world as a settled matter that enables the philosopher to float toward pure forms as the unanchored kingdom in the clouds. Because of that severance from reality, there is a cadre of questions never broached because of their supposed non-philosophical significance. There is irony here. For it is because of the presumption of its universality that many Western philosophers fail to see their particularity. Conversely, it is because of their recognition of their particularity that African philosophers often articulate universal dimensions of the human condition. They tend to articulate how and what people really are. In effect, a European may learn more about *his* or *her* morality through studying African philosophy than Western philosophy because on the level of moral agent he or she may live more of the moral questions broached there than in European and American universities. Moral life doesn't mean to be obligated to rational beings in the abstract but to people of flesh and blood, people who are alive and people who have lived.

The part about the people who are alive is something that modern deontic ethics can at least account for, since, in principle, members of, say, the kingdom of ends must at least be present, if only on the subsistent level of an idea. But how about the part about people who have lived? There, context reveals much. It is possible to study Western philosophical ethics without a single mention of predecessors. In fact, the two most ambitious discussions emerge in texts whose aims were not normative but phenomenological description. Alfred Schutz's phenomenology is rich with describing relations to predecessors. Elias Canetti examined this community under the rubric of "crowds," "the dead," and the present generation as "survivors." The linkage with death betrays what is unavoidable in the African context: ancestors.

In African societies, there are complex networks of beings to whom one is obligated. Particularly striking are ancestors. One pours libations for them; one maintains contracts for them; one maintains property for them; and on and on. Observe:

> Supreme God, who is alone great, upon whom men lean and do not fall, receive this wine and drink. Earth goddess, whose day of worship is Thursday, receive this wine and drink. Spirits of our ancestors, receive this wine and drink.[16]

This libation prayer among the Akan reveals a cosmological hierarchy from God to ancestors, below which are human beings and the rest of the world. Since degrees of power follow the hierarchy, ancestors stand above human beings on the plane of spiritual power (*sunsum*). What this means is that ancestors are in touch with a wider field of knowledge and can affect the outcome of human affairs, but the relationship cannot work in the reverse. Thus, it becomes vital to show ancestors respect. It is a position shared by other African communities as well, as Benjamin C. Ray relates about the Manianga:

> The Manianga say that "at Mpemba [world of the ancestors] is one of yours who will assist you in time of trouble." In funeral speeches, people wish the deceased well in the world of the ancestors and remind them of their obligations to help the living, "Do not forget us in your new world. As we are thinking of you / Please do the same for us." A good member of the family is called upon to visit the living community from time to time in visions and dreams. If family members find they need help, they visit the grave and tell their troubles to the deceased, who is expected to respond.[17]

Among both the Akan and the Manianga, consequences are severe if such obligations are violated. Here is a story that illustrates this view well:

[Simon] Bokie tells the story of his two cousins who, upon the death of their father, were abruptly thrown out of their house with their mother by their paternal uncle. The two boys lost all their money and property in addition to the inheritance promised by their father. Finding themselves abandoned by their mother's kinsmen, they went in secret to their father's grave to ask for help. They fell down upon the grave weeping and explained their plight. Then they departed, telling no one. Later, one of the boys began to dream of his father and received encouragement and advice from his father's spirit. He quit school, following the father's advice, and traveled to a distant city. He found a well-paying job that later led to a successful career and great wealth, which he shared with his maternal kinsmen. The paternal uncle, meanwhile became incapable of conducting his affairs and eventually left his deceased brother's house, after all the fruit trees, planted by his brother, had died. All of these events were attributed to the power of the deceased father's spirit.[18]

A key feature of ancestral intervention is that even where suffering is caused, it is always temporary and meant to call attention to wrongful action. Thus, although there is a deontological structure, the number of forces involved in maintaining the norms of the society are many. It is not enough to say that this is a deontological system, however, since there is always consequence involved. Wrongful actions, as in classical tragedies, are always to be made right. But a consequential system this is not, as well, since the action's moral values are not a function of the consequences. In the case of the two sons, for instance, the uncle's actions were simply wrong. But they weren't wrong in isolation. They were connected to a long chain of related wrongs that hold the society together. Thus, in violating the sons, the uncle also violated their father, and in violating their father, he also violated the order of things.

The order of things here is a community wrapped in a complex understanding of what it means to be in community. Community does not stop simply at those who stand around us, but also through those who have preceded us. The message from this is that we, too, precede others, and in that regard, we are linked to them if but in the fact that our actions set the conditions for their lives. Implicit in "us," then, is a broader "we." This "we" is a motif that has become a dictum of contemporary African philosophy: "I am because we are."[19]

The dictum of an inextricable link between the self and the community is not solely African. I am sure it is a position shared by a typical Chinese, Italian, Swede, Cherokee, Choctaw, or Native Hawaiian. It signals a link between identity claims and teleological claims, that who we are makes no sense unless we see ourselves as part of a larger community, and that larger community is understood in terms of binding projects. That is why communities tend to have origin myths. These myths attempt to tell them why they are here. They are myths that function with as much legitimation as the rationalistic myths we find in the modern era, as Paget Henry has argued in his critique of Habermas's conception of mythic rationality.[20] It is a view shared, as well, by Karl Jaspers in his famous debate with Rudolf Bultmann.[21] The upshot is that ethical life requires organizing narratives that "emplace" (i.e., transform spaces into places, into homes, into communities) its members into relations that may be, at times, unique.

Now, there is an obvious area of contemporary ethics to which such considerations pertain: environmental ethics. Can environmental ethics be justified with the approaches to ethics offered by the conceptual options available in contemporary, professional ethics? Kantianism argues for respecting rational beings, but how do future beings, whose rationality may not be recognizable to us, configure here? What's more, even if future beings will be like us, what is their status when they have not only not yet been born, but also not yet been conceived or even imagined? How about a utilitarian perspective – are the future numbers of people greater than the present? Does not this argument face both the problem of counting those who do not yet exist as well as an epistemic problem of determining greater proportion of harm? After all, if population control is effective, there might be fewer people in the future, which means that rules of restraint only really affect the happiness or fulfillment of people in the present. And in both cases, the people in the past are already dead, so there is not environmental suffering for them. And how about virtue ethics? Here, the argument requires demonstrating that it is virtuous to take care of the environment, especially for subsequent generations. But it must first be demonstrated that doing so for subsequent generations is a good or a rightful action through which the excellent character manifested by doing so could emerge.

Any serious defense of the environment requires taking seriously the well-being of subsequent generations and requires those generations re-enacting the present generation's value of having taken them seriously. In effect, it requires an ethos through which one becomes an ancestor through a commitment to making descendants. Since one is a descendant by virtue of having ancestors, such an ethos binds one as well. Thus, in binding the subsequent generations, the present one is also bound by the past. It is this insight that undergirds ancestral obligations. In honoring such obligations, we bind generations. It this is correct, then a deterioration of such obligations has a necessary consequence of environmental decay. Given our age, advancing evidence of such decay is not necessary here.

It should be clear at this point that our age requires different approaches through which to address its unique problems. I am not here offering a nostalgic return to pre-modern values. Such returns are always silly since, in truth, "we" were never there to begin with. Where we have been, and continue to be, is connected to each other through relations that continue to affect our understanding of such terms as "tradition" and "community." The values that undergird those terms have been repressed, however, through valorization of an independent, self-contained "I." The world we now face is one in which we need to bring to the surface that "we" that undergirds that "I" if any of the projects that speak to subsequent generations can flourish. Such a project involves discarding much of Western civilization *as we have come to know it*, but not in terms of what it could become.

Notes

1   These categories have become ontological tropes in the philosophical study of ethics. Those in doubt should consult the many anthologies on ethics in the Western academy. A particularly influential recent example is *A Companion to Ethics*, Peter Singer, ed. (Oxford: Blackwell, 1993).

2   See, of course, Rawls's introduction to *A Theory of Justice* (Cambridge, Mass.: Harvard University Press, 1971).

3   Discussion here is manifold. Perhaps the most influential is Alisdair MacIntyre's *After Virtue* (Notre Dame: Notre Dame University Press, 1984). For a particularly insightful recent discussion, see Agnes Heller's *A Theory of Modernity* (Malden, MA: Blackwell, 1999), ch. 13, "Law, Ethos, and Ethics: *The Question of Values*," pp. 200–20. For an example of a particularly noxious example of formal consistency with a vicious ethos, see Lewis R. Gordon, *Bad Faith and Antiblack Racism* (Amherst, NY: Humanity Books (formerly Humanities Press), 1995), Part II.

4   See William Barrett, *The Illusion of Technique: Searching for Meaning in a Technological Civilization* (Garden City, NY: Anchor Books/Doubleday, 1979). Of course, the illusion of technique is a dimension of modern obsessions with method, which Nietzsche identified as a function of the egalitarian efforts of Christianity secularized; see Friedrich Nietzsche, *The Will to Power*, tr. Walter Kaufmann and R. J. Hollingdale, ed. Walter Kaufman (New York: Vintage, 1968).

5   Maurice Merleau-Ponty, *The Primacy of Perception*, tr. Colin Smith (New York: Routledge, 1962), p. vii.

6   The complexity of tragedy emerges in MacIntyre's discussion, but see also Lewis R. Gordon, *Fanon and the Crisis of European Man: An Essay on Philosophy and the Human Sciences* (New York: Routledge, 1995), ch. 4. For ethics in African communities, see Fred Lee Hord (Mzee Lasana Okpara) and Jonathan Scott Lee, eds., *I Am Because We Are: Readings in Black Philosophy* (Amherst: University of Massachusetts Press, 1995), Part I, "Africa," and the list of texts in note 14, below. Kierkegaard's classic treatment is "Fear and Trembling" and "Repetition," tr. and ed. Howard V. Hong and Edna H. Hong (Princeton: Princeton University Press, 1983).

7   See Josiah Royce, *The Philosophy of Josiah Royce*, ed. John K. Roth (New York: Thomas Y. Crowell, 1972); see also *The Philosophy of Loyalty* (New York:

Macmillan, 1908) and *The Religious Aspects of Philosophy: A Critique of the Bases of Conduct and of Faith* (New York: Harper Torchbooks, 1958).

8   For discussion of this outcome, see Heller, *A Theory of Modernity*, pp. 200–7.

9   The difficulties here have been spelled out well by Hannah Arendt in *The Human Condition*, 2nd edn. (Chicago: University of Chicago Press, 1998), pp. 17–21, where eternity and immortality are distinguished. The eternal does not come into being since it always was, is, and will be. The immortal comes into being and continues. That laws of action are to be constructed carries a paradox, since, to be binding, they are understood as being greater than the act of constructing them. They are treated, in other words, as eternal realities rather than constituted ones, realities that could as well disappear in another epoch.

 An objection might be made that Hegel's ethics in *The Philosophy of Right*, well focused on social morality and well attuned to the march and impact of history, is an exception to this critique (see Hegel's *Philosophy of Right*, tr. T. M. Knox (Oxford: Clarendon, 1967)). But even there, Hegel faces the difficulty of an eventual isomorphism between law and morals and his linear progresssivism suggests a point of historic erasure. Put differently, Hegel defers the problem instead of overcoming it.

10   See, e.g., Heller, *A Theory of Modernity*, pp. 217–20.

11   The motion picture *Gattaca* (1998) is a haunting allegory of this dimension of the present age. There, "genoism" emerges in a world where there is a narcissistic striving for genetic perfection.

12   See Aristotle's *Nicomachean Ethics*.

13   Kwame Gyekye, *An Essay on African Philosophical Thought: The Akan Conceptual Scheme*, rev. edn. (Philadelphia: Temple University Press, 1995), pp. 71–2.

14   The main influence in this regard is Hegel's *Philosophy of History*, tr. J. Sibree (New York: Dover, 1956), introduction. Schopenhauer was more concerned with the pessimistic dimensions of Buddhism. See *The World as Will and Idea*, tr. R. B. Haldane and J. Kemp (London: Kegan Paul, Trench, Trubner, 1883). The influence of Hegel's telling of history has been such that it is difficult for many scholars to imagine history otherwise. Think of the uproar that emerged against recent "revised" histories – in other words, histories that reveal that accounts that have become normative simply do not add up. See, e.g., Martin Bernal's *Black Athena: the Afroasiatic Roots of Classical Civilization* (New Brunswick, NJ: Rutgers University Press, 1987).

 There is a version of the racist eugenics argument that makes its way into cultural production, i.e. a kind of cultural eugenics. In the biological sphere, Europeans and Asians are endowed with the most rationality. The same mentality continues to affect philosophical literature, where only Europeans and Asians are regarded as properly philosophical people. Thus, whereas philosophical reflections on ethics from Asia, the Middle East, and Europe emerge as "Great traditions" in Singer's *A Companion to Ethics*, Africa is almost absent over the 565 pages save for a brief discussion of ancient Egypt (Gerald A. Larue's "Ancient Ethics," pp. 33–5) through the continued tendency to locate it in relation to Mesopotamia and ancient Israel, as though Egyptians had no relation to people both West and South (in the ancient world, upward) of the Nile, and there is an earlier discussion of the Bushmen of the Kalahari Desert (George Silberbauer,

"Ethics in Small-Scale Societies," pp. 14–28) to illuminate, of course, ethical values from humanity's neolithic past. An even more egregious exclusion emerges in Randall Collins's *The Sociology of Philosophies: A Global Theory of Intellectual Change* (Cambridge, Mass.: Harvard University Press, 1998), where even Egypt doesn't emerge among the 1,098 pages.

It is a distinctive feature of racist occlusion of Africa as a place of ideas and reason to engage the people of that continent primarily through the lens of anthropology. Thus, even where philosophy is at times considered, it is often under the rubric of "ethnophilosophy," which entertained unanimistic fallacies and the obvious homage to ethnography (i.e., having the scientific validation of "field research"). I don't know whether the *Companion to Ethics* and *The Sociology of Philosophies* were guided by such prejudices, but interested readers are encouraged to consider problems of ethics in the African context through the following volumes: Emmanuel Eze, ed., *African Philosophy* (Oxford: Blackwell, 1998) and Kwame Gyekye's *An Essay on African Philosophical Thought*. For examinations and criticisms of how philosophers (African, European, and Asian) look at Africa, see V. Y. Mudimbe, *The Invention of Africa* (Bloomington: Indiana University Press, 1988), D. A. Masolo, *African Philosophy in Search of Identity* (Bloomington: Indiana University Press, 1994), and Tsenay Serequeberhan, ed., *African Philosophy: The Essential Writings* (New York: Paragon, 1991). For a critique of the evasion of reason in Africa, see Lewis R. Gordon, *Existentia Africana: Understanding Africana Existential Thought* (New York: Routledge, 2000), ch. 2; see also Paget Henry, *Caliban's Reason: Introducing Afro-Caribbean Philosophy* (New York: Routledge, 2000), pp. 1–46.

15   *On the Geneaology of Morals*, tr. Walter Kaufmann (New York: Vintage, 1969) and *Beyond Good and Evil*, tr. Walter Kaufmann (New York: Vintage, 1989). In *The Will to Power*, see especially Books I and II.

16   Typical libation prayer, quoted in Gyekye, *An Essay on African Philosophical Thought*, p. 68.

17   Benjamin C. Ray, *African Religions: Symbol, Ritual, and Community*, 2nd edn. (Upper Saddle River, NJ: Prentice Hall, 2000), p. 106.

18   Ibid., pp. 106–7.

19   See Hord and Lee, *I Am Because We Are*, "Introduction." See also Ray, *African Religions*, p. 92, and John Mbiti, *African Religions and Philosophy* (New York: Doubleday, 1970), p. 282.

20   See Paget Henry, *Caliban's Reason*, pp. 167–196. See also Henry's critique of Habermas in the forthcoming Open Court Library of Living Philosophers volume on Habermas.

21   The debate can be found in Karl Jaspers and Rudolf Bultmann, *Myth and Christianity: An Inquiry into the Possibility of Religion without Myth*, tr. Norbert Guterman (New York: Noonday, 1958).

PART II

Community, Constitutive
Identies, and Resisting Subjects

7

Citizenship or Transgression?: Dilemmas of the US Movement for Lesbian/Gay Rights

Arlene Stein

For many centuries, Michel Foucault tells us, the boundaries separating the homosexual and heterosexual worlds were either weak or nonexistent; homosexual and heterosexual behavior existed side by side. There was not yet an understanding of homosexuals as a recognizable, definable category of people. With the emergence of socio-sexual medical categories, this changed: homosexuals became understood as a distinct group of individuals, radically different from heterosexuals, and the boundaries separating the homo and hetero world imagined as virtually impenetrable. The construction of a "homosexual role," Mary McIntosh argued, "kept the bulk of society pure."[1]

For several decades there have been a number of efforts to dismantle the homosexual role, tear down the boundaries separating homosexuals and heterosexuals, and envision sexual freedom in transgressive terms, as a threat to the assumption of heterosexual normality and naturalness. In the 1970s, for example, gay liberationists suggested that the boundary separating heterosexuality and homosexuality was a social illusion. Their hope was that eventually sexual and gender roles of all sorts would become meaningless. For a brief moment, these ideas caught fire. Many people, influenced by the movement, were faced with a choice about whether to be with women or with men. Those who had never entertained the idea of homosexuality were forced to scrutinize the nature of their attractions. The heterosexual imperative was profoundly shaken.

Over time, gays openly intermingled with the heterosexual world and began to see themselves as the moral equivalent of heterosexuals and demanded rights on that basis. By the 1980s, the American gay rights movement had become professionalized, sophisticated, mainstreamed, and largely wedded to a model of gay "ethnicity." In an effort to strengthen the analogy between homosexuality and race, civil rights advocates presented scientific evidence of the immutability of sexual orientation.[2] Lesbians and gay men emerged as a distinct interest group, wielding political action committees, political clubs, and human rights organizations seeking greater social and political integration – sexual citizenship – rather than lodging a profound critique of sociosexual categories.

The process of normalization has been steady, though incomplete. By 1997, eleven states and dozens of cities and counties in the USA had passed laws protecting lesbians and gay men (and sometimes bisexuals and transgendered people) from various forms of discrimination based on sexual orientation, and elsewhere gubernatorial executive orders and mayoral proclamations officially banned discrimination. By the end of the decade, more than one fifth of Americans lived in cities or counties providing some legal protections. Five states, including New York, offered domestic partner benefits to gay and lesbian state employees.[3]

Today, paradoxically, as the lesbian/gay movement has all but abandoned its commitment to a politics of transgression in favor of a politics of citizenship, the conservative movement has taken up many of its ideas. Like gay liberationists, conservatives argue that the homo–hetero divide is highly permeable, and that homosexuality can pose a radical critique of hegemonic heterosexuality. But they draw very different conclusions from this insight. If sexuality is a matter of choice, and if homosexuality is dangerous, heterosexuality must be protected from the homosexual threat, they assert. Sexual boundaries must be reinforced and made stronger rather than weaker.

The Conservative Challenge

In the 1990s, as national rightwing organizations shied away from sexual politics, fearing it would divide their constituencies, organized homophobia moved to the grassroots, and the right busily mobilized at the local level to influence school boards, city councils and local public bodies.[4] Conservatives attacked the appearance of homosexuality in multicultural curricula, such as New York City's Rainbow Curriculum, insisting that homosexuals pose a threat to children, and that lesbians and gay men, rather than constituting a legitimate cultural identity, live an aberrant lifestyle.[5] Central to conservative rhetoric was the belief that gay activists had taken a private behavior and politicized it, using it as a springboard for gaining unjust protections. Gays were, the right suggested, following the model of other minority groups in American society, including blacks and women. But being gay wasn't like being a woman, or a member of an ethnic group, they claimed. Anyone could choose to be a homosexual. Therefore, efforts to gain homosexual civil rights were a sham. Homosexuality is a behavior, not a way of being.

A new modernized purity campaign distinguished between the public and the private realms – publicly, at least – echoing the US military's "don't ask, don't tell" policy. It suggested that what goes on between consenting adults is nobody's business – we won't tell you how to live your private life. Rather than attacking individuals as perverse, it attacked the status of homosexuals as a group that deserves legal protections. Enacting a more aggressive political strategy, Christian Right organizations began to sponsor ballot initiatives to deny civil rights protections to lesbians and gay men, prepared voter guides that were distributed to millions of churchgoers nationwide, influenced local politics, running for school boards, city councils and packing PTA meetings, and took advantage of the citizen initiative process.

Most US state constitutions provide for some form of direct democracy, or citizen lawmaking, usually through an initiative or referendum process. In 1992, the rightwing group Coloradoans for Family Values sponsored an amendment to Colorado's state constitution to ban civil rights protections for lesbians, gays, and bisexuals, which passed. The following year, the Oregon Citizens Alliance followed suit, running Ballot Measure 9, which lost statewide, but won in rural Oregon, and spawned a series of local charter amendment campaigns which sought to amend local by-laws to prevent anti-discrimination protections for gays and lesbians and prohibit government spending to promote homosexuality.[6]

The right had found the movement's Achilles heel. It fashioned a homophobic rhetoric which attacks the status of lesbians and gays as a "minority" group deserving equal rights under the law. Conservative rhetoric claimed lesbians and gay men are an undeserving "special interest group" which has won "special rights" by manipulating the system. Against the deployment of the ethnic model, conservatives suggested that homosexuality is a behavior, not a way of being. It is tolerable if it is kept private. But once homosexuals make claims for public space and power, they are asking for too much. Once we give into the gays, who knows who'll be knocking down our doors for privileges and handouts of all sorts? If everyone just kept their private vices to themselves, we'd all be much better off.

In small communities across Oregon, and in several other states, the intimate acts of individuals became the subject of raucous public debates which pitted neighbor against neighbor. Should the community recognize lesbians and gay men as a legitimate minority group, and accord them equal protection under the law? Since towns possess little power to create such protections, the question was, above all, a symbolic one. Nonetheless, it created a storm of controversy that few will forget. Families stopped their children from playing with those whose parents stood on the opposing side of the issue. Newspapers covered little else for months. Practically overnight, the question of lesbian/gay civil rights became a matter of public debate and acrimony.

Why did small town folks find homosexuality, seemingly a non-issue, so confusing and troubling? And why bother organizing against lesbian/gay rights in places where lesbians and gay men were barely visible?

Trouble in Timbertown

Timbertown, Oregon (a pseudonym) is home to about 8,000 people, nearly all of them white. It began as a logging town, and lumber mills are still the largest employer. It is perhaps a typical small Oregon community, even a typical small American town in many respects. The early 1990s was a period of unsettling change for Timbertown. As the lumber industry in Oregon declined, the town lost more than 1,000 jobs. At the same time, a growing number of people from cities, particularly from California, were moving to the area, drawn by its natural beauty and relatively cheap land. A number of lesbians, who were probably invisible to all but the most savvy residents, were among this influx.

The Oregon Citizens Alliance, a Christian conservative organization, arrived in town and put a political spin on the sense of uncertainty that many people were facing. The problem was homosexuals, they said, who were demanding "special rights." They tried to change the town's charter to prohibit civil rights protections for homosexuals. The rhetoric of "special rights" was a brilliant tactical move, one that spoke to the sense of economic and cultural dispossession many people were feeling. If people's pocketbooks were hurting, it was because undeserving minorities, such as gays, were getting unfair handouts and protections from the government. If people's families were falling apart, it was because homosexuals were undermining the moral foundations of the family.

During the campaign, the right circulated a number of stories to make their case. A former mayor of the town, the owner of the local café, told a story about two lesbians who were kissing in his café, assaulting public decency. Others claimed that gay people possessed a vast amount of power and visibility. In the public schools, conservative activists roundly condemned sex education efforts for challenging the essential innocence of children. For about a year, homosexuality was lurking everywhere in Timbertown, a town where few people had ever even met an openly queer person.

This campaign, and many others like it, was an attempt to police the boundaries of heterosexuality, whose normative foundations had been shaken. Conservatives simultaneously acknowledged that the boundaries separating the homosexual and heterosexual worlds were highly permeable, and argued that it was important for us to reinforce these boundaries. Citizens of this small town wanted to maintain a sense of identity, solidarity, and intimacy with one another, in the face of threats to the community. Homosexuals created noise, posing a threat to what Zygmunt Bauman calls "uncontentious social space."[7] The right exploited the fear that if homosexuals became full members of the community, this would upset the town's sense of itself.

Sociologists tell us that in order to create a sense of social order, which all societies must establish, deviants are created and punished. "Whenever a boundary line becomes blurred," writes Kai Erikson, "the group members may single out and label as deviant someone whose behavior had previously gone unnoticed."[8] The act of naming as dangerous demonstrates to those in the community "just how awesome its powers really are."[9] It clarifies what is acceptable and what is not, who belongs in the community and who does not. It seems that boundaries become more important during periods of rapid social change – as geo-social boundaries become less central.[10] In this country, during the past few decades, an unprecedented number of women entered the workforce; the globalization of the economy has made us less and less dependent upon a sense of place, economically and culturally. Residents of small town Oregon, who consume media beamed from satellite dishes and work for companies whose manufacturing operations are located in far flung parts of the world, are subject to these and other modernizing processes. "A symbolically contrived sense of local similarity," writes Richard Jenkins, is sometimes "the only available defense."[11]

How better to construct a sense of identity, the we, than by articulating a clear sense of what one abhors? How better to affirm one's purity than by getting rid of the dirt? Homosexuals seemed to be the perfect foil; whether supporters of the ballot measure personally knew any gay people, or even whether they were a real threat to their community, were of little relevance. When asked whether homosexuals had ever pushed their agenda in small towns such as his, an activist in a neighboring town whose campaign against "special rights" was already under way, replied that they had not. "Let's get it done," he said, "so that we know we're not going to have any problem in the future."[12]

The Progressive Response

These campaigns did not go unopposed. In Timbertown, as in many small communities throughout Oregon, concerned citizens, who were predominantly heterosexual, organized to try to defeat the measure. The left used the language of interest group liberalism. It spoke of the importance of inclusion, of "tolerance," and of the evils of "discrimination." Homosexuals deserve civil rights, they argued. We all deserve civil rights.

Countering rightwing claims that homosexuality is a choice, a potential that exists in all of us, liberal gay rights supporters suggested that lesbians and gay men are a fixed group of individuals, who are born gay, who keep sexuality out of the public sphere, and who therefore pose no threat to the good people of Timbertown. In short, they used the "ethnic model" of homosexuality, a model that imagines sexual boundaries as solid and unchanging, but fails to challenge the notion that heterosexuality alone is natural, normal, and beautiful. Hence, the well-meaning but misguided effort to defeat the measure proved unsuccessful. When it finally appeared on the ballot, the citizens of Timbertown supported the measure by a narrow margin. In 35 other communities across Oregon, similar measures passed. Though these measures were later declared unconstitutional, they gave homophobia a new public legitimacy.

In the 1970s, the lesbian/gay liberation movement created an enormously powerful way of seeing the world, and attempted, with mixed success, to remake patriarchal, heterosexual society. In the 1990s, it took an outside enemy to reignite a sense of immediacy and reconnect the lesbian/gay movement to its early project of liberation. That enemy came in the form of the Christian Right, which targeted the homosexual population and sought to roll back its meager legal protections, and spawned a lively movement to resist such campaigns. While these efforts diverted the attention of many lesbian and gay activists from more pressing concerns, such as the AIDS crisis, it also permitted them to move beyond the "identity politics" model that had dominated lesbian/gay organizing at least since the mid-1970s, and to enter wider conversations about justice, power, and citizenship. Yet the example of a small Oregon town suggests that there has been a failure of imagination. When vilified for being transgressive, the supporters of lesbian/gay rights chose to portray themselves as normal, law-abiding citizens. They failed to address the pervasive fear of the erosion of sexual boundaries, to challenge the belief that heterosexuality alone is normal, natural, and good, or make links between homosexuality and other groups under attack.

On the national level, a similar pattern is repeated. In the summer of 1998, several rightwing organizations placed a full page ad in several national newspapers. Pictured in the ad was a picture of a woman who, they claimed, had once been gay, and was now straight, suggesting that through prayer and self-control lesbians and gay men can go straight. Homosexuality is not born, it is a choice. Shortly after the ad appeared, a consortium of gay rights groups, including the Human Rights Campaign Fund, the largest gay lobbying group, placed a full-page ad in the *New York Times* which featured a smiling American family: Dave and Ruth Waterbury and their 20-something lesbian daughter Margie, pictured above the caption "We're living proof that families with lesbians and gay kids can be whole, happy, and worthy of all that this great country promises." It said the following:

> Our lesbian daughter is the apple of our eye. . . . We now understand with all our heart and soul that Margie is as complete and dynamic a human being as our other wonderful daughter who happens to be heterosexua.l . . . We are a typical American family, with old roots in the heart of America. We love our church, our community, and the beautiful Minnesota countryside. We bike. We cross-country ski. We're Republican. . . . Gay people and their families are people of faith. . . . All leading medical experts agree. . . gay people are just as likely to be healthy and happy as the rest of us.[13]

This image, which emphasizes the notion that lesbians and gays are hardworking, family people, plays into the rhetoric of the Christian Right. It reinforces an "ethnic" understanding of gay identity – the belief that "we can't help it – we were born that way" – and in so doing fails to problematize normative heterosexuality and challenge the hetero–homo binary. In the long run, these citizenship strategies work against lesbians, gay men, bisexuals, transgendered people and their allies. It is no wonder that campaigns against gay rights won't go away. In 1998, voters in the state of Maine repealed a statewide ordinance which prohibits discrimination against lesbians and gay men. And the "Defense of Marriage Act," which decrees that only heterosexual marriages will be recognized by law, received nearly unanimous approval in Congress, and in several states. These and other developments are legally as well as symbolically significant, as they shape the course of public discussion of sexuality in a society where such discussions are few and far between.

Christian conservatives, it seems, are beating the lesbian/gay movement at its own game. They have taken the gay liberation insight that the homo–hetero divide is permeable and are using it to argue against homosexual rights. They reject the minoritizing model of gay ethnicity in favor of a more diffuse notion of sexual possibility. But they substitute for gay liberation's profoundly humanistic view the belief that homosexuality poses a threat. The left's defense, to defend homosexuals as a squeaky clean minority group that has little to do with heterosexuality, is unsatisfactory. It fails to address the pervasive fear that "they" might well be "us." And it fails to connect the defense of gay rights to a broader vision of equality.

In other words, homosexuality does pose a challenge to normative heterosexuality. It challenges the notion that sexual boundaries are fixed for all time. As the case of Oregon shows, the right cannot be successfully fought by playing their own game, by shoring up the boundaries. Such strategies fail to challenge the fundamental truth that sexuality is inherently messy, unstable, and boundary-defying.

Toward a New Language of Sexual Difference

It is clear that we need a new language, a new way of talking about sexuality, that captures its messy complexity. We need a different way of talking about our lesbian/gay/bisexual and transgendered selves, and their relationship to the dominant culture, in a fashion that moves beyond the ethnic model. The most daring attempt to do this has emerged under the rubric "queer," a grouping which includes all sexual dissidents, including bisexuals, transsexuals, and even some heterosexuals in the fight to enlarge our definition of what counts as "normal." Rather than submerge their sexuality in exchange for the hollow promise of social acceptance, queer theorists and activists call into question binary, bounded notions of sexuality.[14] But queer theory, because of its dense vocabulary, has been difficult to translate for non-elite audiences. Queer theory won't go very far in helping me engage with my mother, who lacks a college education, and who still thinks my lesbianism is somehow her fault. It certainly wouldn't move the people I'm talking with in small town Oregon, who for the most part don't hate queers but still can't figure out why homosexualities should be protected by law.

Hence, what we have in the United States is a lesbian/gay movement that is divided between two impulses: the desire for citizenship and the desire for transgression, as Jeffrey Weeks once put it so well.[15] We have a citizenship movement which seeks civil rights protections, utilizing an ethnic understanding of homosexuality that imagines gay people as a fixed category who pose no challenge to heteronormativity. And we have another, much smaller movement on the margins of this movement, which possesses a far more nuanced understanding of sexuality, but has trouble representing itself to the public. A politics of citizenship seeks inclusion in the social order; the politics of queer transgression fundamentally challenges the very basis upon which citizenship rights are imagined. The former emphasizes the fight for equality ("We're just like you and we want the same rights"); the latter emphasizes difference ("We're here, we're queer, get used to it"). The first treats the homo–hetero divide as a given and goes on with the business of equalizing the sides. The second seeks to attack the divide itself.

These two impulses, citizenship and transgression, have existed within the lesbian/gay movement since its inception. They may in fact characterize all identity-based movements. But as we near the close of the century, the lesbian/gay movement in the USA seems more divided than ever between these two camps. Increasingly, they seem to be working at cross purposes. In the public eye, queer efforts to challenge heteronormativity seem most often to reinforce the widespread belief that lesbians and gay men are different in some essential, irrevocable way – rather than undermine the very basis of this difference. But thanks to the greater financial clout of mainstream gay organizations, a rather conservative vision of homosexuality has become ascendant in the public sphere.

In 1997, the Universal Fellowship of Metropolitan Community Churches – the United States' largest gay Christian denomination – and the Human Rights Campaign – the nation's largest gay rights lobby – announced joint plans to produce the "Millennium March for Equality" in April 2000 in Washington, DC. They proposed a very different event from the three previous gay marches on Washington, in 1979, 1987, and 1993: one that would showcase gay statements of "faith and family." As one of the organizers explained: "We want to show middle America that we're mature people who work, just like them. This is our country and we pay our taxes."[16] Certainly, most lesbians and gay men do pay their taxes. But the fight is much more than simply about the right to be a carbon copy of heterosexual normality. It is about much more than the right to achieve integration into family structures which privilege married, monogamous couples at the expense of the diverse array of actually existing family forms. Many lesbians and gay men wish to be citizens, to be a part of the social order, but they want to enter it on their own terms. And while they're inside of that social order, they want to tweak it, subvert it, and challenge received notions of who and what it means to be normal and natural.

Neither of the two dominant images of lesbian/gay/queer existence visible in the United States today – citizens versus transgressors – captures the way that most lesbians and gay men think about our sexual identities – as simultaneously traditional and transgressive. Queer people will never be of one mind on the meaning of sexuality, and how it translates into a political movement. But it is time to construct a movement that is committed to the knowledge that sexual minorities are simultaneously insiders and outsiders – neither the same as straight people nor radically different from them. Rather than simply seek integration, or stand outside of the wretched system, we should challenge the assumptions by which that system defines family, intimacy, community, and equality. We should seek inclusion in the social order at the same time as we fundamentally challenge it.

Notes

1 Michel Foucault, *The History of Sexuality*, vol. 1 (New York: Random House, 1980); Mary McIntosh, "The Homosexual Role," *Social Problems* 16 (1968): 262–70.

2 Steven Epstein, "Gay Politics, Ethnic Identity: The Limits of Social Constructionism," *Socialist Review* 17 (1987): 9–50; Lisa Keen and Suzanne Goldberg, *Strangers to the Law: Gay People on Trial* (Ann Arbor: University of Michigan Press, 1998).

3 Steven Epstein, "Gay and Lesbian Movements in the US," in Barry Adam, Jan Willem Duyvendak, and Andre Krouwel, eds., *Gay and Lesbian Movements Since the 1960s* (Philadelphia: Temple University Press, 1999).

4 Sara Diamond, *Not By Politics Alone: The Enduring Influence of the Christian Right* (New York: Guilford, 1998).

5 Janice Irvine, "A Place in the Rainbow: Theorizing Lesbian and Gay Culture," in Steven Seidman, ed., *Queer Theory/Sociology* (Cambridge, Mass.: Blackwell, 1996).

6 Lisa Duggan, "Queering the State," *Socialtext* 39 (1994): 1–14; Didi Herman, *The Antigay Agenda: Orthodox Vision and the Christian Right* (Chicago: University of Chicago Press, 1997).

7   Zygmunt Bauman, *Postmodern Ethics* (Oxford: Blackwell, 1993), p. 63.
8   Kai Erikson, *Wayward Puritans: A Study in the Sociology of Deviance* (New York: John Wiley and Sons, 1966), pp. 8–19.
9   Robert Scott, "A Proposed Framework for Analyzing Deviance as a Property of Social Order," in Robert Scott and Jack Douglas, *Theoretical Perspectives on Deviance* (New York: Basic Books, 1972), p. 29.
10   Kai Erikson, *Wayward Puritans*.
11   Richard Jenkins, *Social Identity* (New York and London: Routledge, 1996), p. 107.
12   Joe Mosley, "Charter Measure Makes Battlefield of Junction City," *Eugene Register-Guard*, June 12, 1993.
13   *New York Times*, July 19, 1998, p. 19.
14   See, for example, Diana Fuss, ed., *Inside/Out: Lesbian Theories, Gay Theories* (New York: Routledge, 1991); Eve Kosofsky Sedgwick, *Epistemology of the Closet* (Berkeley: University of California Press), 1990.
15   Jeffrey Weeks, *Invented Moralities: Sexual Values in an Age of Uncertainty* (New York: Columbia University Press, 1995).
16   Alisa Solomon, *Village Voice*, June 29, 1998, p. 63.

8

Diversity, Inequality, and Community: African Americans and People of Color in the United States

J. Blaine Hudson

In 1835, Alexis de Tocqueville described the United States as a nation of "three races" – Native Americans, and persons of either European or African ancestry.[1] While these three races inhabited the same territory, Native Americans and African Americans were neither viewed nor treated as equals of the European colonists and their descendants. Stated somewhat differently, racial diversity was not synonymous with racial equality, and this inequality was institutionalized early in American colonial history. On this foundation, the United States was established as a "racial state" nation of colonizers (and their ethnic immigrant "cousins"), the colonized and dispossessed (Native Americans), and the enslaved (Africans) – with those not fitting neatly into one racial status category (e.g., free people of color) occupying a marginal or "intermediate" status. In such a state, intra-racial class, ethnic, and gender cleavages among those deemed "white" were far less significant than inter-racial differences in status, conditions, and life chances.[2]

Thus, from its colonial origins to the present, the United States was not intended to be and has not become a racially inclusive national community. But what this nation is and has been set no preordained imits on what this nation might become. In this respect, the questions regarding the meaning of American citizenship for African Americans and other people of color posed by Frederick Douglass in his 1852 "Fifth of July" speech remained valid when he delivered his last great speech, "The Lessons of the Hour," in 1894 and remain cogent and urgent today.[3] Can a "racial state" be just? Can true community exist without justice and equality? Is community possible in a "racial state"? What does community "mean" in a society divided structurally, historically, and culturally by race?

Ironically, not only do these questions remain unanswered, but a broad social consensus regarding even their legitimacy as questions remains elusive at the dawn of a new millennium. Unfortunately, the power to impose political, economic, and cultural domination is also the power to universalize the values and world-view(s) of the dominant group and to rationalize its privileged status, i.e., to create a distorting interpretive lens. For this reason, the conceptualization of and ostensibly objective answers to these fundamental questions are often filtered through this lens of racial myths that permeate both American academic and popular culture. Thus, theories of race and community in the post-industrial "West" tend, in effect, to ignore or trivialize diversity or avoid these questions altogether by assuming that the life-ways of one racial group can serve as the legitimate standard for all others. For this reason, several widely accepted views with respect to race and community are inadequate.

First, that race has no "biological significance" is a simple truth of modern empirical science. However, the standard notion of race as a "social construct," as an alternative to the old biological determinism, warrants revision and clarification. As Berlin notes:

> While the belief that race is socially constructed has gained a privileged place in contemporary scholarly debates it has won few practical battles. Few people believe it; fewer act on it. The new understanding of race has changed behavior little if at all. Perhaps this is because the theory is not quite right. Race is not simply a social construction; it is a particular kind of social construction, a historical construction. Indeed, like other historical constructions – the most famous of course being class – it cannot exist outside of time and place.[4]

Second, it is crucial not to equate racial differences, so constructed and based on the visible and heritable "marker" of skin color, with ethnic differences based on cultural and national variations within the major racial groups. Stated simply, ethnic differences within the same racial group fade as acculturation leads to assimilation over one or more generations. However, acculturation cannot change one's color and, thus, in a multi-racial society with a "color line," acculturation is possible but assimilation is blocked – leaving people of color "all dressed up with nowhere to go."[5]

Third, perhaps most pernicious of all, is the assumption that the "testimony" of people of color – on their own behalf and as a means of establishing the validity of their own experience – is "inadmissible" in the political and/or scholarly discourse on race and community. From this follows the presumptuous notion that only persons of European ancestry are capable of an objective and balanced perspective regarding the lives of people of non-European ancestry, an assumption that resonates with centuries-old stereotypes concerning the mental acuity of people of color. Yet, those who have been both the victims and the builders of the "modern" world are not likely to view that world, or its more privileged inhabitants, as those inhabitants would view themselves.[6] The records of their lives, past and present, are a crucial body of authentic evidence that illuminates how the

American "racial state" was established, how it has been perpetuated, and how it might be transformed.

Community in Early America: The Colonizers, the Colonized, the Marginalized, and the Enslaved

The American "racial state" was created neither entirely by accident nor entirely by conscious design, but was the inevitable, although perhaps unforeseen, consequence of the origins of the United States as a European "settler colony." Between 1607 and 1840, British colonists and later United States citizens acquired and settled the millions of square miles between the Atlantic coast and the Mississippi River. This vast territory was already inhabited and, from the Native American perspective, European settlement was a process of invasion and colonization, with several distinct and fateful phases.

The "first contact" phase was inaugurated by European explorations, followed by the establishment of small and usually vulnerable settlements. If the exploration phase was peaceful, relations between Native Americans and Europeans were often characterized by acceptance, mutual aid, trade, and treaty-making. Europeans were allowed to occupy Native American lands and depended on Native American assistance for their early survival while forests were cleared and land brought under cultivation, i.e., during the typical "starving time" of early colonies. The experiences of the early English colonists at Jamestown and Plymouth illustrate this phenomenon quite graphically. If the exploration phase was violent (as with the Spanish in Florida, the southeast and the southwest), European settlement became possible only after Native American societies had been weakened by military defeat and disease.

In the second phase, as European settlements stabilized and expanded, the swelling white population encroached inevitably into Native American territory – there being no other available territory into which they could possibly expand. Earlier agreements were abrogated, which prompted protests and eventually violent reprisals from Native Americans against white settlers and settlements. These reprisals, in turn, were used by whites as evidence of "Indian perfidy" and as a justification for removing the "savage Indian presence" from the frontier.

The third phase was characterized by conflict that led to military conquest. Small- or large-scale military encounters between colonists and Native Americans commenced. Native American villages and crops were destroyed; Native Americans were sometimes massacred or captured – and even sold at times into slavery in the Caribbean (and even in Africa). At other times, "biological warfare" tactics were employed by the Europeans – for example, blankets infected with smallpox were sent to Native Americans. Also, in prosecuting these "wars," Europeans often built frontier forts and outposts that later developed into substantial settlements – e.g., Pittsburgh, Cincinnati, Louisville – and facilitated further European penetration of the interior of North America.

The final phase brought displacement and dispossession. Native Americans were eventually overwhelmed by superior numbers and sometimes by hunger and disease. In suing for peace, if they survived the wars, Native Americans were pressed to agree to further territorial concessions. The survivors then withdrew deeper into the "wilderness" or, in later years, were forced onto reservations.[7]

In this way, British settlers, the British colonial governments and, later, the United States government all recognized or ignored Native American claims to the land, depending on which stance was most advantageous at the time. In other words, these claims were recognized as legitimate when Native American lands were ceded to whites through treaty or outright purchase agreements, i.e., the right to cede or sell assumed prior ownership and the legal right to dispose of property. Otherwise, these claims were most often disregarded when they interfered with the inexorable westward movement of white settlement – i.e., when the Native Americans were "uncooperative." Beyond the myths, legalisms, and historical revisionism, North America was colonized by force and its original inhabitants were driven to the brink of extinction by force.

This process, as part of the European colonization of the New World, was not without its justification in both religion and an evolving ideology of race, as exemplified in the chilling words Christopher Columbus wrote in his journal on October 12, 1492, after making landfall in the Caribbean. Regarding the "ideal" relationship between the Taino (Arawak) people of the Caribbean and the Spanish, Columbus stated without reservation: "They ought to be good servants and of good intelligence. . . . I believe that they would easily be made Christians, because it seemed to me that they had no religion. Our Lord pleasing, I will carry off six of them at my departure to Your Highnesses."[8]

Since the Native Americans of the Great Plains and Far West were less numerous, the most effective Native American resistance to the expansion of white settlement in North America ended in the "east" with the death of the great Shawnee leader and visionary, Tecumseh, in 1813. The full import of their history is often denied through underestimation of their numbers and/or misrepresentation of the complexity of their societies; that is, colonization was "alright" if only a few primitives were "in the way" of the advance of a superior civilization. What remains unstated, however, is that, by its very nature, colonization did not and perhaps could not produce a "community" that included – or could include – both the colonizers and the colonized.

Much as European colonization brought death and dispossession to the indigenous people of the Americas, the new colonies were built and made profitable by the labor of millions of Africans brought involuntarily to the New World. The first Africans entered British North America in August 1619 (at Jamestown). Their numbers were small and their status ambiguous. Because the labor needs of the early colonies were met principally by white indentured servants, the legal structure of American slavery was "invented" slowly and incrementally between 1640 and 1680 – in contrast to the Caribbean, Spanish America and Brazil, all of which were settled in the 1500s and had become thriving slave societies by the mid-1600s. In its fully developed form, slavery in the "New World" had three key characteristics, each of which was unprecedented in human history:

- those enslaved became chattel, i.e., property;
- their enslavement was perpetual – i.e., enslavement was life-long and slave status was inherited from one's parents and bequeathed to one's children;
- and, most unusual of all, slavery was racial – i.e., by the 1700s a status deemed suitable only for Africans and persons of African descent.

Within this institutional framework, heavy slave trade and high birth rates in the 1700s combined to produce both the rapid growth and rapid "Creolization" of the black population – i.e, Africans soon became African Americans. For example, the African American population increased from 30,000 in 1700, most of whom were African-born, to 757,000, only 20 percent of whom were African-born, by the time of the first federal census in 1790. Driven by the expansion of the "Cotton Kingdom" in the 1800s, and despite the end of (legal) international slave trade in 1808, there were 4.4 million African Americans in the nation by 1860, only a fraction of 1 percent of whom were African-born.[9]

In seeking to justify human bondage as a "positive good," the European colonists drew on both the European and the American past to create the social and cultural foundation of the American "racial state." The colonists who became the first citizens of the United States derived primarily from the British Isles: roughly 60 percent of white Americans in the late eighteenth century were of British birth or ancestry. Thus, American "nationality" was not a blending of all the peoples that populated the United States, or even an amalgam of the white Europeans inhabiting the country. An "American" was a modified Englishman.[10] In addition, these early colonists were also predominantly Protestant in their religious leanings and identified strongly with a folk myth of Anglo-Saxon racial superiority. Many of the founders of American democracy were dedicated proponents of this Anglo-Saxon myth. Thomas Jefferson, for example, held the conviction that US independence would allow for the full and unencumbered expression of the Anglo-Saxon gift for sound, democratic government.[11]

The institutionalization of this myth excluded a significant minority of the American population from the possibility of membership in the national community – from the beginning. This was accomplished, first, by ensuring that only *two* types of rights were defined and protected by the letter of American law: *individual* rights and *majority* rights. In theory, the US Constitution created a government based on the rule of the "majority" with protection for the rights of individuals added through the "Bill of Rights." However, "majority" rule was, in fact, the rule of affluent white males under a body of laws designed (by them) to protect their property and privilege.

Second, the appearance of democracy was created by a strict racial construction of US citizenship and the denial of rights to those defined as noncitizens. For example, until the ratification of the Fourteenth Amendment (1868), there was no definition of US citizenship in the US Constitution. It was simply assumed that those who were citizens of the several states when the Constitution was ratified would "automatically" become citizens of the United States – a status that would be inherited by their American-born children. Under the resulting body of laws, most African Americans (more than 90 percent) were enslaved and were considered property; those who were not enslaved, i.e., free persons of color, occupied a nebulous and degraded status in which they were subjects, not citizens. Native Americans were placed "outside" the body politic and were considered subjects of a government that considered Native American lands to be US territory. White women and the white poor were citizens, but citizens whose rights were limited – for example, they could not vote. In other words, the US Constitution empowered those who wrote and ratified it – whites, males, and property owners of Northern European heritage who, if religiously affiliated at all, were predominantly Protestant.[12]

Third, the founders of the country understood that it served no purpose to restrict who could *be* a citizen if a similar restriction was not imposed on who could *become* a citizen. Consequently, the first US Immigration and Naturalization Act (1790) limited eligibility for US citizenship to "free white persons."[13] Thus, not only were persons of color within US territory excluded from citizenship, but persons of color throughout the world were excluded from eligibility to become US citizens.

In this context, the United States was intended to be ethnically, not racially, diverse; that is, the possibility of citizenship was open only to other "European Christians." However, the farther even Europeans departed from "English" or "Christian" norms, the less welcome they were and the more social conflict their presence provoked. Still, these immigrants, once acculturated over a generation or two, could assimilate because the visible marker of color identified them as "white" – i.e., indistinguishable, in theory, from other whites. There was one American mainstream and only certain groups were allowed to "swim" in that mainstream.

As the nineteenth century unfolded, increasingly radical views of race and national identity were advanced. "Manifest Destiny," which presumed the right of white Americans to rule "from sea to shining sea," was used to justify the Mexican War and the conquest of the "Plains Indians." In Europe, similar attitudes fixed on the Indo-European roots of Caucasian peoples and on the superiority of the Germanic, now deemed the Aryan, branch of the "white race" – i.e., the Anglo-Saxons and their "close cousins." This concept of superiority was not only racist but ethnocentric as well in positing that Northern Europeans were superior to all other Europeans/Caucasians (the Gallic, the Slavs, the Mediterranean "types"), "below" which were the other races of humankind.[14] Although most Americans are deeply troubled by this comparison, it is rather obvious that the difference between American racial mythology and the views of Adolph Hitler were/are so slight as to be meaningless.

Still, if Native Americans were contained outside the physical boundaries of the American community, African Americans were contained within those boundaries in close and often intimate contact with white Americans. Yet, paradoxically, African Americans were viewed and treated, in many respects, as being more alien to that community – and the "human race" – than were indigenous people. In this respect, there was one anomalous group without a clearly defined "place" in the American racial state that illustrates this paradox: African Americans who were *not* enslaved. As persons who were black and free in a nation where the expected status of African Americans was that of slavery, free African Americans occupied an ambiguous status in antebellum America. In this sense, despite the destruction of Native American societies and the inhumanity of slavery, the treatment of free people of color was a "litmus test" of American racial attitudes and perhaps the best example of America's opportunity and early failure to mature into a multi-racial community.

By 1830, a generation after the end of slavery in the "north," free people of color represented roughly 13.5 percent of all African Americans. Yet, in most regions of the country, they were severely restricted in their political rights and economic opportunities – and viewed generally as a degraded class. However, having been excluded from membership in the American community, free people of color both challenged the legitimacy of their exclusion and, in the interests of survival, built communities of their own. Ultimately, these "communities of exclusion," which usually included some urban slaves, achieved a "critical mass" of population size and density that triggered – in the face of white rejection and discrimination – the development of their own institutions, infrastructure, social system, and social relations with the surrounding white community. Although lacking in power and wealth, these evolved or evolving communities created opportunities for their residents to occupy roles and statuses closed to them in the larger community – for example, leadership and high status positions, property and business ownership.[15] This type of caste segregation was not a choice made by African Americans (or other people of color), but a social reality imposed upon them by whites who were determined to maintain racial subordination and social distance.

The "intermediate" status of free people of color was a prototype for the treatment of newly arrived people of color, such as Mexican Americans and Asians. Sadly, this status was extended to all African Americans after the Civil War as a blatant betrayal of the promise of emancipation. In this way, the United States, having invented itself as a "racial state," chose to remain a "racial state" even after the virtual extinction of the Native Americans and the end of slavery.

The Unresolved American Dilemma: Community, Segregation, and Desegregation

By the early 1900s, racial segregation was "a way of life" supported by American law, and "community" was defined, legally, in racially exclusionary terms. Whatever job people of color "did" in their own communities was usually invisible to white Americans and significant only when it impinged on the life of the "real" community. That community comprised those who were or could somehow become American as legitimized by custom and law – and whiteness was the minimum qualification for community membership. Ethnic European immigrants learned this lesson early and well. For example, despite centuries of oppression and discrimination, groups at the "bottom" of the European ethnic hierarchy – such as the Irish and the Jews – could be "white" in the United States. While this racial categorization did not insulate them from all discrimination, it did guarantee eventual assimilation and that there would always be "others" beneath them in the American racial hierarchy.[16] As Derrick Bell notes:

> Black people are the magical faces at the bottom of society's well. Even the poorest whites, those who must live their lives only a few levels above, gain their self-esteem by gazing down on us. Surely, they must know that their deliverance depends on letting down their ropes. Only by working together is escape possible. Over time, many reach out, but most simply watch, mesmerized into maintaining their unspoken commitment to keeping us where we are, at whatever cost to them or to us.[17]

Furthermore, because the American racial hierarchy was based on color, groups typically fairer in complexion, or fair-skinned individuals from otherwise "darker" groups, were encouraged to identify with those "above" them in the hierarchy (i.e., ultimately with white Americans), not with those who "looked like them" or who were darker. In other words, much as in Spanish America or Brazil, people of color gained status by distancing themselves from, rather than by embracing, others of their group, and certainly by distancing themselves from an identification with groups "lower" in status – i.e., darker than they.[18]

From the perspective of most whites, this type of inequality was natural, unobjectionable, and beneficial, and race relations were "good," since segregation rendered African Americans safely invisible. However, African Americans and other people of color saw segregation for what it was – not some benign system of racial accommodation, but a blatant and degrading attempt to maintain white privilege – and they responded by initiating a continuing struggle for equality and empowerment. The record of this struggle is mixed, and implicit in its outcome is the central paradox of American life for the past two generations: that a legally non-segregated society has remained a "racial state."

Unraveling this paradox requires a slightly different interpretive framework or paradigm that situates African Americans and other people of color in a global context. In this framework, the capitalist/democratic "West" (the United States and Western Europe) is the "first world." The former communist "East" (the Soviet Union and its former satellites) is the "second world." The developing nations of Africa, Latin America, and Asia are the "third world." And non-European populations, such as African Americans, living as minority groups within the geographic confines of former white settler colonies are the "fourth world," i.e., subject to internal colonialism or internal neo-colonialism.[19] Stated somewhat differently, the vital distinction between third and fourth world groups is that, while both are oppressed by whites, the oppression of the former has an external point of origin (and reaches across international boundaries), while the oppression of the latter occurs "within" the same nation, or community, or even neighborhood. Thus, the power and presence of whites are largely invisible to the majority of people in third world nations, but are visible and ubiquitous to persons living under fourth world conditions.

Fourth world groups confront unique problems, all of which would seem quite familiar to people of color in the United States. For example, as numerical minorities, emancipation and/or decolonialization does not empower them politically or economically, or enable them to promote their culture as a majority or "national" culture. If fourth world groups seek autonomy within their "host nations," they are likely to find themselves not in "separate but equal" enclaves, but on reservations or in Bantustans. Furthermore, despite the emotional appeal of nationalist rhetoric, there is no logical or historical basis for assuming that fourth world groups can control public institutions or create their own autonomous political or economic structure as though other domains of the larger state and national political economy did not exist.

Fourth world groups also exist on two planes of social reality. In the USA, one is imposed from without by white Americans through the creation of racial categories, barriers, and oppressive practices that affect all group members for no reason other than their race. The other is defined from within by the individual, gender, class, and cultural/ethnic diversity of the larger racial group.[20] As obvious examples, people classified as Latinos, Native Americans, or Asians can boast of literally hundreds of different points of national or ethnic origin. Less obvious are the regional variations between African Americans or the extent to which the African American population continues to absorb African and West Indian immigrants.[21] Thus, considerable diversity exists within and between fourth world communities and, while such rich internal diversity can be a source of strength, it can also render groups vulnerable to "divide-and-rule" tactics.

Still, while "fourth world" groups have limited power, they are far from powerless. The nature and source(s) of their power, however, are often hidden. For example, because they often exist in the wealthiest and most powerful nations, fourth world groups generally enjoy living standards superior to those of their third world cousins and even to many whites. By virtue of numbers, labor power, consumer purchasing power, and electoral power, fourth world groups, although seldom viewed as bona fide members of the host or American community, make that community possible and cannot be ignored.

Clearly, the end of legal segregation also introduced several new and unprecedented factors into the American social equation – with, in some cases, consequences becoming recognizable only now. The construct of race was updated to "fit" a society in which racial classification could no longer determine where one could live, work, attend school or college, or with whom one could form intimate relationships. Yet, changes in the law did not end segregation or, more fundamentally, did not eliminate racism and racial inequality, since, put simply, those who made the law, enforced the law, and broke the law were often the "same people." In other words, segregation, much as slavery before, was a means, not an end – and, as Berlin noted, historical constructs and their instrumentalities are constantly reformulated to fit new circumstances.[22] Nor did the removal of legal barriers create one American community, but created instead several new social "spaces" and structures on the margins of American society – i.e., on the borders between "first" and "fourth" world groups. For example, the new structures are small, multi-racial "mixing zones" within communities where whites and people of color interact – in formal settings such as school and work, and often in personal relationships – with a degree of frequency and equality unprecedented in American history. Most Americans still lead largely segregated lives, but the end of legal segregation made such "mixing zones" or proto-communities possible.[23]

Nevertheless, measurable racial inequality remains the most fundamental and intractable problem confronting fourth world groups such as African Americans and other people of color in the United States. In the final analysis, there can be no American community, plural or otherwise, as long as racial inequality and injustice persist. As Hugh Price has observed,

> The ultimate test . . . is whether we finally extend the American dream to all Americans. The foundation of this dream consists of . . . economic opportunity and ultimately economic power for those who play by society's rules, quality education that equips all young people to play . . . and compassion for those who cannot.[24]

These inequalities are profoundly real. For example, in recent years the United Nations has published a "Human Development Index" that quantifies economic and social indicators such as income, educational attainment, mortality, crime, etc., to create a "quality of life" rating for each nation. In 1993 and 1994, the "quality of life" in the United States ranked between fifth and seventh in the world – surpassed only by a few Scandinavian countries and Japan. However, when the Index data were disaggregated by race, white Americans, if treated as a separate "nation," enjoyed by far the highest standard of living in the world. At the same time and in the same nation, African Americans and Latinos, if treated as separate "nations," ranked thirty-first and thirty-fifth, respectively.[25] As a standard of comparison, the small Caribbean nation of Barbados, a former British sugar colony, ranked twentieth. Thus, viewed from a global perspective, the United States is actually three or more racially defined and dramatically unequal "nations" under one government – all but one of which exist under conditions most often found in the developing world.

As an example of the limited impact of desegregation, before 1950 the median family income of African Americans was between 40 and 50 percent of the median family income of white Americans. As a result of Civil Rights reforms, the ratio of African American to white family income rose to more than 60 percent by 1970. Correspondingly, the African American "middle class" grew in relative size from roughly 10 percent of the black population in 1950 to over 30 percent in 1970. However, progress was short-lived as African American incomes dropped precipitously in the 1980s due to the regressive and reactionary racial policies of the Reagan/Bush era. Although the economic status of African Americans rebounded under the Clinton economy of the 1990s, it only returned to 1970 levels. And because black economic gains of the 1990s occurred as a secondary consequence of a strong national economy in an otherwise conservative political era, such gains would be extremely vulnerable to any significant economic downturn.

Furthermore, even considering the gains registered since 1950, the African American "middle class" (and above) comprised only about 30 percent of the African American population compared to a white "middle and upper class" made up of about 60 percent of the white population. And while African Americans were only half as likely to earn middle-class incomes, they were three to four times as likely to live below the federal poverty line. The figures for Latinos and Native Americans are strikingly similar to those for African Americans.

When these patterns and statistics assume a "human face," the presence and the human cost of economic inequality – structured largely along racial lines – in the United States becomes truly staggering. In 1990, nearly one in seven white Americans (roughly 30 million persons) and more than four in ten Americans of color (roughly 25 million persons) had annual family incomes below the poverty line. A majority of the poor of all races were women and children, and, contrary to the popular stereotypes, the vast majority of the poor were employed.[26]

Thus, at the dawn of this new millennium, the available historical evidence indicates that the record of the American experiment in diversity is, at best, decidedly mixed. For example, at one extreme, groups relatively close to the English in racial, religious, and ethnic terms have been and are being assimilated rather easily over time. For these groups, the notion of America as a "melting pot" or an asylum has been and remains valid. At the other extreme, persons of African ancestry, because of the legacy of slavery and the visible marker of color, have been least assimilable – although, ironically, given their long and intimate association with white Americans, they are most likely to be thoroughly acculturated in their own unique fashion. In the "middle," Latinos, Asians, and "Caucasians" from outside Europe are often able to assimilate through intermarriage and simple acculturation.

Of course, the United States is more than just a "racial state," and not all white Americans enjoy full equality. Along with people of color, neither white women nor the white poor share the full benefits of American citizenship. However, inequality "works" in the post-Civil Rights era because the selective and measured extension of "opportunity" and "rewards" to small segments of the otherwise exploited groups has kept alive the myths of opportunity, diversity, and upward social mobility and has, effectively, broken the solidarity of oppressed groups by splitting off and co-opting many of the more capable potential leaders.[27] If there were a "grand strategy," it would probably include the following tactical requirements:

- the white middle class must remain a sufficiently large and sufficiently comfortable segment of the population (50 percent or more) and its members must continue to support the social and economic status quo that privileges the upper 5 to 10 percent – or, at worst, advocate limited reforms;

• the proportion of persons of color admitted to the middle class must be sufficiently large to create distinct and significant intra-racial class divisions, but sufficiently small (no more than half the relative percentage of the white middle class) to pose no real competitive threat to the white middle class;

• economic inequality by gender must be maintained as a support to male dominance, but the privilege of being white, for white women, must balance or outweigh the disadvantage of being female; and

• the illusion of upward social and economic mobility in a meritocratic society must be "sold" to each new generation of Americans, particularly to the poor and working class, who must be taught to measure success in and compete for material symbols (e.g., shoes, cars, and jewelry), which can be marketed profitably.[28]

Of course, the fact that this balance reflects the reforms and "renegotiations" of past generations can also be viewed as progress. None of these groups is as "unequal" in quantifiable terms as it was in 1950. However, none of these groups is ir has been close to parity – even under the strong Clinton economy – with elite white males. Whether by coincidence, social inertia, or conscious design, these divisions maintain the "racial state" and serve to "manage" inequality by "disuniting" American society.

The "Failure of Integration"?

Given this background, it is now possible to explore the current debate among African Americans over the alleged "failure" of "integration", and/or relative merits of "integration" versus "voluntary segregation" – a debate fraught with heated emotions and no small measure of false issues, confusion, and historical misinterpretation. Among some African Americans, this debate seems to focus on whether they should even want to join the American "community," and, at bottom, it reflects intense bitterness and anger over generations of steadfast white resistance to the full inclusion of African Americans in that community.[29]

Throughout American history, the vast majority of African Americans has been committed to the transformation of the United States from a "racial state" into a multi-racial democracy. Such a transformation meant wholesale assimilation to some, but, to most, only the removal of legal barriers to opportunity and equal protection. As DuBois, Cruse, and a host of other formidable African American intellectuals have asserted repeatedly, ending legal segregation – or "desegregation" – was the goal of the African American struggle from the Great Depression through the Civil Rights era.[30] In a "de-segregated" society, African Americans could work, learn, and associate with whomever they wished – i.e., be as "integrated" as they wished or as whites would tolerate. To most African Americans in the 1930s and 1940s, the prospect of desegregation did not include closing separate black busi-nesses, organizations, or institutions, and few African Americans believed that private race-specific groups (e.g., churches, social clubs, fraternal or-ganizations) were incompatible with life in a legally non-segregated society. Stated simply, African Americans wanted something distinctly American: freedom of choice and full access to the benefits of American citizenship with-out the loss of the traditions and institutions forged in their separate com-munities during the era of segregation.

The notion that desegregation could be achieved without an explicit strat-egy to eliminate wealth and income inequality (what Cruse terms "non-eco-nomic liberalism") derived, to a large extent, from Myrdal's *An American Dilemma*.[31] While Myrdal underestimated the tenacity of cultural racism, his optimistic assessment of the "Negro Problem" and its possible solutions was endorsed by "establishment white liberals" and most African Americans. *An American Dilemma* was also rendered more palatable to white Americans by its assertion that intimate relations with whites was a very low priority for African Americans, who were interested primarily in educational and eco-nomic opportunities.[37]

In essence, this vision of a non-segregated America assumed, beyond to-ken desegregation in the public sphere, the persistence of racial separation in the private sphere of life as the result of uncoerced personal choice(s). Of course, this vision was one of a non-segregated America in which whites could retain much of their racial privilege and exclusivity.[33] In other words, the *northern* pattern of race relations (i.e., de facto segregation, somewhat greater opportunity) would be superimposed on the rest of the nation – much as the intermediate status of ante-bellum free people of color was extended to all African Americans and other people of color after the Civil War. The direct action phase of the Civil Rights movement transformed token desegre-gation into significant reforms that impacted on enough African Americans, as noted previously, so as nearly to triple the relative size of the "black mid-dle class." This transformation was a major achievement, but one that still left most African Americans far from parity. And, in retrospect, American society was changed as much by these reforms as by their limits.

Because the United States remained a "racial state" through and beyond the Civil Rights era, legal segregation ended on terms that were usually more advantageous to whites than to African Americans. As a consequence, Afri-can Americans followed two distinct economic and social trajectories after the Civil Rights reforms of the mid-1960s. The middle class minority, regard-less of the extent to which it identified with mainstream American values, took full advantage of the new educational and employment opportunities, and partook of less restricted access to the full range of American public spaces and public/private institutions. Ironically, much as was the case with the small ante-bellum free black "elite" and the small African American "middle class" under legal segregation, slightly greater income and/or wealth allowed many members of this segment of black America to distance themselves from other African Americans. However, because American society did not become "color-blind," "middle class" African Americans soon learned that simply sharing the same level of educational attainment or income or occupational status did not render them more acceptable to most whites.

Rather, many "middle class" African Americans – again, much as the older class and "color" elites – came inevitably to consider themselves a separate group within the African American population. However, under segregation, this group was contained within the same physical space and constrained by the same racial barriers that impinged upon other African Americans and people of color. With the end of legal segregation, geographic containment was no longer possible and racial barriers were razed in some cases and strengthened in others. And the black "middle class" dispersed, whether into mixed neighborhoods or upscale segregated enclaves on the fringes of African American communities, leaving the other two-thirds of the African American population "behind." That the economic status of this two-thirds of black America – and similar proportions of the Latino and Native American populations – was never addressed left a legacy of still unresolved problems. In this context, crime, social dysfunction, drugs, and hopelessness are merely the second- and third-generation manifestations of these problems in the present.

In other words, leaving American society only "half-reformed" had unanticipated consequences. Along with the African American "middle class" discovering that it was not immune to discrimination and racial profiling, the relative isolation of poor and working-class African Americans (typically, in urban areas) had cultural and social consequences beyond purely objective measures of opportunity and quality of life. Racial isolation in the present is not synonymous with racial segregation in the past and, in communities that are now both racially and economically homogeneous, cultural values and behaviors have become disconnected in many respects from the mainstream of African American history and culture. Ironically, young African Americans, in particular, experience most of the same limiting conditions that shaped the lives of their parents and grandparents – but they lack the sense of identity and the institutional structure created and sustained in the "old" segregated black community. Thus, their responses to this unnatural social environment betray the same anger, bitterness, and frustration, but without the framework provided by a deep sense of rootedness in their culture, a framework necessary to "making sense" of their experiences and devising strategies to change the conditions under which they live. Of course, by ignoring how this unnatural environment was created, many Americans, including many Americans of color, can focus only on what the environment itself created – a "culture of poverty" with its many frightening and inchoate expressions of bitterness.[34]

Neither African Americans nor white Americans in the 1940s or 1950s could easily have foreseen the central paradox of American race relations at the beginning of the new millennium. Yet, having the dubious benefit of hindsight, a cynical observer, if well-versed in American history and racial mythology, might well have recognized that blacks and whites held fundamentally different views regarding desegregation and its anticipated benefits. These differences would result in an uneasy compromise that would sunder existing communities without reconfiguring the fragments into new and more vital structures.

As noted above, through the eras of slavery and segregation, virtually all African Americans shared, or identified with, the same broad (African and African American) heritage and the same circumstances. That these bonds may have seemed the same, but were, in fact, quite different was revealed when legal segregation ended. When African Americans were no longer forced together in "communities of exclusion" – i.e., when shared racial classification no longer ensured shared circumstances – the "old" African American community fissured along intra-racial class lines. However, while poor and working-class African Americans became increasingly segregated and isolated from the American mainstream, the African American middle (and negligible upper) class found that upward educational and economic mobility only redefined, and did not erase, the visible marker of color in the minds of most white Americans. In other words, the black poor were simply overwhelmed by the devastating power of race and poverty, and, because the white American middle class refused, for the most part, to embrace the black middle class as equals, the black middle class found that "race still mattered." Furthermore, because of the terms under which legal segregation ended and the ensuing neo-conservative reaction in American politics, no concerted group action to address either of these related problems has been initiated in the past generation.

With due deference to past leaders and thinkers, the possibility of this paradox was not seriously considered in the Civil Rights era. For example, African Americans acted on (what have proven to be) two equally problematic assumptions regarding community and culture. One assumption was that a distinctively "African American" culture and community were the legacy of slavery and segregation, and would be sloughed-off as African Americans "graduated" from second-class to full citizenship. Implicit in this assumption was the belief that white Americans, in the aggregate, would act in "good faith" and honor both the letter and the spirit of American law. Under such a color-blind system, merit and character would determine who progressed and how far.

The other assumption was that African American culture and community would persist even after the coercive force of segregation law was removed. This assumption is understandable, since few African Americans or white Americans in the 1940s and 1950s had ever known anything other than a segregated society in which black culture was reproduced, more or less, from generation to generation. Yet, implicit in this assumption was the belief that African American culture was literally "hard-wired" into African Americans, rather than a body of values and life-ways that must be taught (and modified) by one generation and learned by another. Virtually no one believed that African Americans would need to "do anything" in this arena, for example, invent new constructs and institutional structures designed to maintain group identity and solidarity, and channel group political and economic power in a pluralistic society.

The past generation has proven these assumptions wrong and, because such structures were not created, some African Americans have "succeeded" as individuals, while African Americans have "failed" to progress as a group. Desegregation changed the meaning and status of formerly all-black public institutions. Such institutions could no longer exist under American law, e.g., the "black high school" became "just another" public school or the "black hospital" became "just another" public hospital. Moreover, with the exception of African American churches and some social/civic groups, desegregation wrought equally far-reaching changes with respect to African American businesses and private organizations. Specifically, to the extent that such organizations depended on a "captive" African American market or clientele, most were either forced to adapt to new circumstances or forced to close in the 1960s and 1970s. Thus, to many African Americans – even those enjoying the benefits of a non-segregated society – the disintegration of most black institutions and the loss of a clear sense of identity and community with other African Americans was a price they had not expected to pay. And, given the fact that African Americans find themselves, a generation and more after the end of legal segregation, still far short of economic and political equality, the price of limited progress often seems too high.

Given this background, one could argue that the alleged "failure" of "integration" is, in fact, the combined "failure" to achieve or maintain community and the "failure" to achieve racial justice and equality. And, perhaps, the "failure" to achieve community in a legally desegregated society, which affects African Americans in general, often seems more fundamental than the "failure" to achieve racial equality, which affects individual African Americans to varying degrees. One could also argue that the longing for a restored sense of community rooted in a common racial heritage has become more powerful with the passing years. The many manifestations of this longing range from the proliferation of black family, neighborhood, and school reunions, to the cultural nationalism (i.e., moderate Afrocentrism) of a black middle class choosing to embrace both its "African-ness" (or "African American-ness") and the opportunities and rewards of the American mainstream, to even more extreme conservative separatist ideologies.

Consider, for example, one city where contemporary conditions illustrate the cumulative impact of these trends and the dilemma fostered thereby. By 1990, the 79,783 African American residents of Louisville, Kentucky were concentrated primarily in the western section of the city; another 44,978 African Americans were scattered throughout the metropolitan area. Local African American unemployment stood at 21.7 percent in 1987 and, by 1989, median African American family income had dropped to only 52 percent of the white median in the city and only 43 percent in the surrounding county. Violent crime had become endemic in the most segregated and impoverished African American neighborhoods, despite efforts launched by local government and financial institutions to build low-cost housing and stimulate economic development. Furthermore, mandatory busing (1975) gave way in the 1990s to a district-wide student assignment plan featuring magnet and optional school programs operating within specific racial enrollment parameters. Despite this change and the reforms engendered by the Kentucky Education Reform Act (1990), African American students remained largely segregated within local schools by tracking and program assignment, and continued to achieve decidedly unequal educational outcomes.[35]

Responding to such urgent problems, a broadly representative group of local African Americans developed an "African American Strategic Plan" between September 1996 and January 1998. This Plan identified dramatic inequalities between whites and African Americans in education, economic development and wealth-building, and health and social wellness as key problem areas requiring immediate and sustained attention. However, continued inattention to expressed African American needs prompted one group of African American parents (in 1997) to sue the school district in an effort to dissolve a 1975 desegregation order and return to neighborhood schools. Other African American parents and community activists then entered the case to advocate that the court order be retained, but modified, to address the dramatically unequal educational outcomes achieved by African American children. And, in 1999, the unresponsiveness of local officials to repeated incidents of police brutality prompted the call for "West Louisville" to secede from the larger city altogether, become a separate incorporated area.[36]

Under such conditions, the resurgence of respectable racism in the Reagan/ Bush era, the anti-affirmative action fervor of the 1990s and the persistence of seemingly intractable problems in isolated and impoverished African American communities prompted even many "successful" and assimilated

African Americans to question the value of "integration." Implicit in their frustration is the sense that white America has sent Americans of color a clear message – that white Americans have no interest in eliminating racism or racial inequality or creating an inclusive national community. However, frustration, impatience, and/or anger – while justified – cloud more often than clarify the issues facing African Americans and other people of color.

Perhaps the most difficult subjective task for people acculturated in a "racial state" is that of identifying and overcoming the effects of cultural racism – not only on others, but on themselves. For people of color, the daily stress of living in a "racial state," combined with deeply ingrained and societally reinforced negative attitudes toward themselves and others like themselves, can produce powerful emotional reactions. These reactions – among fourth world groups – while "logical," emotionally, are seldom a useful guide to the most effective strategy for group uplift or liberation. For example, some African Americans, crippled psychologically by racism, may wish to imitate or gain approval from the dominant group, while others may reject the dominant group entirely as a model and seek to find or create a real or imaginary world "without whites."

Tocqueville understood and most African Americans experience the inherent contradictions of living on the wrong side of the color line in a "racial state." His insights bear repeating:

> The fate of the Negroes is in a sense linked with that of the Europeans. The two races are bound one to the other without mingling; it is equally difficult for them to separate completely or to unite . . . prejudice leads a man to scorn anybody who has been his inferior long after he has become his equal.[37]

It is also difficult to conceive of a better recipe for frustration and anger. However, also implicit in Tocqueville's musings and his own "racial" point of view is the troublesome notion that neither full assimilation nor complete separation is a realizable goal. Racial difference blocks assimilation for most African Americans; living in the same society limits the extent to which groups can be "separate." In other words, what "feels right" as a reaction to unnatural conditions or unjust treatment can be wholly legitimate as a "feeling," but wholly misleading otherwise. For example, rejecting those by whom one is rejected is a natural reaction, but one which leads people of color to abandon the only "arena" in which racism and racial inequality are contested. Thus, much as white Americans are often blind to their racial privilege, people of color are often unaware of how their perceptions and emotional responses are affected by racism.

Not unexpectedly, the growing racial diversity of the United States, coupled with slight but meaningful reductions in the degree of racial inequality under the "good economy" of the Clinton years, has also hardened negative racial attitudes among certain segments of the white American population. In a society in which some blacks or Latinos or Asians are doing "well" – and some whites are not – the benefits of white racial privilege seem far less obvious than in the past. This anomalous group of African Americans and other people of color has long existed, but, for most of American history, has been very small in numbers and hidden behind the veil of segregation. They are not, however, hidden today. To many poor and working-class whites, the fact that some people of color are "doing better" (visibly) than they is convincing evidence not only that white privilege no longer exists, but that, because it no longer exists, America has somehow betrayed them and sold their birthright.

This is a clear example of how changes in social conditions may outpace changes in culture. Many whites born at one time in history, with one set of expectations, are now unprepared to understand or accommodate themselves to the realities – or, at least what they perceive as the realities – of the present. Furthermore, this is particularly the case with (poor and working-class) white males whose privileged racial and gender status has been challenged decisively in recent generations. This phenomenon explains why "angry white males" have been so angry and why their anger is so futile and, thus, so dangerous. This is also why, even among more privileged whites, there is so little interest in addressing racial inequality, poverty, or discrimination – they simply do not feel that their privileged position is secure.

Thus, much as the promise of emancipation was betrayed more than a century ago, the promise of desegregation has been betrayed in the past generation – for all Americans.

Conclusion: Pluralism and the Challenge of the New Millennium

The most formidable barrier to community in this diverse nation is the existence of an implicit racial covenant – a silent conspiracy of the silent and not so silent majority, a broad consensus among white Americans to defend white privilege and maintain racial inequality and discrimination in favor of whites. This is not a conscious conspiracy of millions of malicious whites conscious of "doing wrong." Rather, the operations of this racial covenant are far more dangerous because they are justified as being "right" by the "received wisdom" of cultural racism and the simple fact that long-held privileges can become confused with rights. Furthermore, this covenant exists both within and beyond the law – an arrangement made possible by the determination of segments of the white population to use the legal principle of ("winner take all") majority rule to make and interpret the law to their advantage, or simply to protect one another in outright defiance of the law. Thus, racial segregation and racial discrimination became illegal during the Civil Rights era, but, paradoxically, did not disappear. A diverse national community will not and cannot exist until the racial covenant that sustains the "racial state" is broken.

There is, as yet, no precedent for the transformation of a "racial state" into either an "integrated" or a "plural" society. Because cultural racism is one basis for "white identity" and institutional racism is the means by which white privilege is preserved, there are powerful forces working against the realization of a plural society in the United States. And the fact that such a society may be ethically and morally "right" does not render the prospect of its creation any less threatening to most white Americans.

Still, racism, as a human evil, is also a human invention and need not be as permanent a fixture in human societies as some observers have concluded.[38] However, a society in which racism and racial inequality are deeply embedded is unlikely to overcome these social evils in one or two generations – if and when that society commits itself to such a goal. Adding an indeterminate number of future generations of growing diversity and persistent inequality to the centuries now past has inescapable and unacceptable human consequences. As Martin Luther King, Jr., often stated, "Justice too long delayed is justice denied." As American and global history have demonstrated repeatedly, people forced to live "outside" the bounds of community will create, both to survive and to infuse their lives with meaning, identities and cultures and communities of their own using their gifts and the materials at hand. One consequence of the creation of these separate communities is that the longer they exist, the less attractive and more threatening the prospect – to those nurtured in such communities – of abandoning them entirely in hopes of "integration" or assimilation.

These rather dismal observations mean that true progress toward community will be difficult, but not impossible. While an "integrated" society remains a distant ideal, a plural society, which recognizes rather than seeks to suppress or obliterate difference, is achievable in the foreseeable future and may lead eventually to the realization of a truly color-blind or race-neutral social order. However, pluralism is not separatism or Balkanization and, for pluralism to exist, there must still be:

- broad consensus on core American ideals, on "what it means to be an American";
- both cultural distinctiveness and cultural fusion – i.e., along with preserving a degree of cultural particularity, there must also be a degree of openness, on a societal scale, to continuing cultural blending and cross-fertilization; and
- a degree of willingness on the part of the vast majority of citizens to share a social, cultural, political, and economic "common ground" – and to assimilate to the extent necessary to do so.[39]

None of these preconditions has been met. However, this covenant cannot be broken unless a significant minority of white Americans supports the creation or evolution of a plural society and unless African Americans (and other people of color) press assertively to achieve pluralism and equality – not as individuals, but as a group. But sharing a racial classification category and being a viable group are not the same. Consequently, for this struggle to move forward, African Americans must do what seemed unnecessary in the Civil Rights era and undertake, through conscious effort, group uplift guided by broad consensus regarding:

- the nature and meaning of group membership (i.e., who is African American and what does being African American "mean" – particularly to African Americans);
- the basic facts of group history, and the nature of social values, cultural and intellectual traditions;
- a vision of the ideal multiracial American democracy;
- the conditions, and interests created thereby, shared by all members of the group by virtue of their "race";
- the relationship between the individual and the group – i.e., what does each individual "owe" the larger group, and vice versa;
- respect for diversity within the group – i.e., a clear repudiation of ideological and/or religious orthodoxy, intra-racial classism, sexism, and homophobia;
- the relation of the group to other racially defined groups – e.g., what constitutes an ally, an adversary, etc.;
- the nature of group leadership, how leaders are selected by the group and expectations of leaders on the local, national, and international levels;
- collective strategies to combat racism and preserve group identity and culture; and
- collective strategies to achieve group political and economic empowerment, social justice, and equality.

This is not a blueprint for resegregation, but for the creation, strengthening, or redirection of the institutional structure of a viable fourth world community – a guide regarding how African Americans can preserve (and use) their ethnic uniqueness while pursuing full equality in a plural society. Because there can be no compromise with segregation and racial caste in American law and public life, these institutional structures must be private, voluntary associations, which could, under certain circumstances, be publicly subsidized to some extent. While existing cultural, religious, civic, political, and even social groups could be restructured and reoriented to serve as the nucleus of such associations, the creation of new structures should be encouraged, particularly those that "speak to" the needs and world-view of young African Americans. In essence, what African Americans were forced to do under legal segregation, they must choose to do in the post-Civil Rights era.

Obviously, reaching and acting on broad consensus across these domains will be a formidable task, a task complicated as much by intra-racial divisions as by the complacency bred by improved economic conditions. However, these difficulties can and must be overcome, since breaking the racial covenant that sustains the American "racial state" is necessary, not only to redress injustices long endured by people of color, but to ensure the future viability of this society. Beyond that, the United States does not exist in a vacuum and, in a global order in which the "have" and "have-not" nations are distinguishable primarily by race as well, achieving pluralism and equality are not exclusively "American" problems. Rather, as the world's population passes six billion, questions of how to provide a decent quality of life and maintain a reasonable degree of social cohesion in all true mass societies are no longer the province of Utopian philosophers and science fiction writers, but questions of human survival itself.

Two simple facts cannot be ignored. Both the United States and the world are still dominated, politically and economically, by persons of European ancestry. However, as this nation and the world become more populous, both are becoming increasingly non-white. Between the 1400s and 1700s, when European expansion established the colonial empires that produced, eventually, the "modern" world, global population was less than one-tenth of its current level, and technology, even in the most "advanced" nation-states and kingdoms, was not significantly beyond that used in ancient Egypt or Greece. Life was still short, still based on agriculture and trade, still moved at "a walk or a gallop," and was still dominated by superstition. The domination of the many by the few, whether brutally oppressive or benign, was an accepted fact of life and, as suggested previously, the more global construct of race (as opposed to the more local construct of ethnicity) was invented to structure and rationalize hegemony on this larger scale.

But there are limits to hegemony and, once again, the evidence of history is instructive. On the one hand, the hegemonic powers often "fall out" among themselves – a proclivity that precipitated, most recently, the First and Second World Wars. On the other, it is difficult for the few to dominate the many indefinitely. For example, in their determination to derive maximum profits from sugar cane, several European nations transported millions of enslaved Africans to the Caribbean and Brazil between the mid-1500s and mid-1800s. The Haitian Revolution (1791–1804), however, proved the ultimate folly and danger to which European greed (and assumptions of racial superiority) could lead. By creating an excessively oppressive colony in which blacks outnumbered whites by more than ten to one, the French unwittingly created a society they could not control and which, through extreme violence, became the first independent black nation of the New World. The success of this revolution signaled the beginning of the end of the African slave trade and slavery, and forced Napoleon to abandon his dream of an American empire and sell the Louisiana territory to Thomas Jefferson.[40]

A society and world, both increasingly populous and increasingly diverse, can be organized and governed in one of two ways. The first and most familiar still prevails today – a monopoly of wealth and power by the few. Beyond this fundamental social fact, labels of "capitalism," "socialism," "democracy," "autocracy," "theocracy," and the rest are more cosmetic than substantive. Today, the stability of such social formations – including the United States– depends largely on how "few" hold this monopoly and how unequal the distribution of wealth and power is across the remainder of the population. Heavily "middle-class" societies such as the United States can maintain both stability and a privileged elite by "managing" inequality as described previously. However, as in the case of Haiti two centuries ago, and most of the contemporary world, stability can only be achieved through totalitarianism and brute force.

Because of this, social stability cannot be the sole criterion for social viability. Rather, the most important criterion, and the one least valued, is the "general welfare," the well-being (i.e., the general "happiness") of the citizens of each nation, particularly non-Europeans and the poor. Implicit in this criterion is the ideal that *any human being, in a given society, should be able to "trade places" with any other human being in that same society and still be assured of living a secure, healthy, and meaningful life.* Measured against this standard of true "community," no human society would be considered fully viable – including the United States. Thus, ultimately, the choice is between a society and world that "work well" for some, or a society and world that "work well" for all (or, at least, most).

In this regard, the second approach to organizing and governing human societies is one somewhat alien to the dominant European paradigm. Examples of this alternative principle were once found in the more egalitarian and communal structures of some traditional precolonial societies in Africa and the Americas. Clearly, these societies cannot serve as entirely useful models for creating a sort of egalitarian pluralism in the postmodern world. They can, however, suggest the type of social balance toward which human societies must strive: a largely non-hierarchical balance within and between human groups. The alternative is the conflict and chaos that have shaped so much of human history.

Although not a perfect solution to an abstract problem, such a transformation would be a human solution to a human problem and would improve the quality of life for billions of people. Much as the problem of the color line dominated the twentieth century, this daunting task is the greatest challenge – the new human frontier – of the twenty-first century and beyond.

Notes

1 Alexis de Tocqueville, *Democracy in America*, ed. J. P. Mayer (New York: Harper and Row, 1969), pp. 317–413.

2 Michael Omi and Howard Winant, *Racial Formation in the United States: From the 1960s to the 1980s* (New York: Routledge and Kegan Paul, 1986), pp. 70–86.

3 Frederick Douglass, *Oration Delivered in Corinthian Hall, Rochester, July 5th, 1852* (Rochester: Lee and Mann, 1852); William S. McFeely, *Frederick Douglass* (New York: W. W. Norton, 1991), pp. 377–81.

4 Ira Berlin, *Many Thousands Gone: The First Two Centuries of Slavery in North America* (Cambridge, Mass: Harvard University Press, 1998), p. 1.

5 Raymond S. Franklin, *Shadows of Race and Class* (Minneapolis: University of Minnesota Press, 1991), p. 17; Ronald Takaki, *A Different Mirror: A History of Multicultural America* (Boston: Little, Brown, 1993), pp. 106–38.

6 Richard Wright, *White Man, Listen!* (New York: Doubleday, 1957), pp. 21–73.

7 Takaki, *A Different Mirror*, pp. 21–50, 84–105.

8 Quoted in Kirkpatrick Sale, *The Conquest of Paradise: Christopher Columbus and the Columbian Legacy* (New York: Plume, 1990), pp. 96–7.

9 Winthrop D. Jordan, *White over Black: American Attitudes toward the Negro, 1550–1812* (Chapel Hill: University of North Carolina Press, 1968), pp. 3–100; Herbert S. Klein, *African Slavery in Latin America and the Caribbean* (New York: Oxford University Press, 1986); Peter Kolchin, *American Slavery, 1619–1877* (New York: Hill and Wang, 1993); Victor B. Thompson, *The Making of the African Diaspora in the Americas, 1441–1900* (New York: Longman, 1987).

10 Benjamin Schwartz, "The Diversity Myth: America's Leading Export," *Atlantic Monthly* (May 1995): 62.

11 Reginald Horsman, *Race and Manifest Destiny: The Origins of American Racial Anglo-Saxonism* (Cambridge, Mass.: Harvard University Press, 1981), pp. 7–78.

12 John Hope Franklin, *The Color Line: Legacy for the Twenty-first Century* (Columbia: University of Missouri Press, 1993), pp. 27–52; Lani Guinier, *The Tyranny of the Majority: Fundamental Fairness in Representative Democracy* (New York: The Free Press, 1994), pp. 1–21; J. Blaine Hudson, "Simple Justice: Affirmative Action and American Racism in Historical Perspective," *The Black Scholar* 25 (1995): 16–23; Jordan, *White over Black*, pp. 315–41; Howard Zinn, *A People's History of the United States*, 2nd edn. (New York: Harper and Row, 1995), pp. 50–166.

13 Sidney Kansas, *US Immigration, Exclusion and Deportation in the United States of America* (Albany, NY: M. Bender, 1948), pp. 1–15.

14 Horsman, *Race and Manifest Destiny*, pp. 79–186.

15 Leonard P. Curry, *The Free Black in Urban America, 1800–1850* (Chicago: University of Chicago Press, 1981); John Hope Franklin and Alfred A. Moss, Jr., *From Slavery to Freedom: A History of African Americans* (New York: McGraw-Hill, 1994), pp. 148–70.

16 Jordan, *White over Black*; Gunnar Myrdal, *An American Dilemma: The Negro Problem and Modern Democracy* (New York: Harper and Bros., 1944).

17 Derrick Bell, *Faces at the Bottom of the Well: The Permanence of Racism* (New York:

Basic Books, 1992), p. v.

18   F. James Davis, *Who Is Black: One Nation's Definition* (University Park, Pa.: Pennsylvania State University Press, 1991), pp. 1–50; Klein, *African Slavery in Latin America and the Caribbean*; Wright, *Wjite Man, Listen!*, pp. 21–73.

19   George Manuel, *The Fourth World* (New York: MacMillan, 1974); Robert Staples, *The Urban Plantation: Racism and Colonialism in the Post Civil Rights Era* (Oakland, CA: The Black Scholar Press, 1987), pp. 51–73.

20   Marable, Manning, *Black Leadership* (New York: Columbia University Press, 1998), pp. 151–9.

21   *Ibid.*; Takaki, *A Different Mirror.*

22   Berlin, *Many Thousands Gone.*

23   J. Blaine Hudson and Bonetta M. Hines-Hudson, "A Study of the Contemporary Racial Attitudes of White and African Americans," *The Western Journal of Black Studies* 23 (1999): 22–34.

24   Hugh B. Price, "Gaining Access to Economic Power," in Frances Hesselbein et al., *The Community of the Future* (San Francisco: Jossey-Bass, 1998), pp. 213–15.

25   *Louisville Courier-Journal*, May 18, 1994.

26   Andrew Hacker, *Two Nations: Black and White, Separate, Hostile and Unequal* (New York: Charles Scribners' Sons, 1992); National Urban League, *The State of Black America, 1998* (National Urban League, 1998).

27   Staples, *The Urban Plantation*, p. 73.

28   J. Blaine Hudson, "Economic Justice and Social Responsibility," *Louisville Catholic Record* (April 1996).

29   Harold Cruse, *Plural But Equal: A Critical Study of Blacks and Minorities in America's Plural Society* (New York: William Morrow, 1987).

30   *Ibid.*, pp. 239–59; W. E. B. DuBois, "Segregation," *Crisis* 12 (January–June 1934); E. Franklin Frazier, *The Negro in the United States* (New York: MacMillan, 1949), pp. 687–706.

31   See Oliver C. Cox, *Caste, Class and Race: A Study of Social Dynamics* (New York: Doubleday, 1948), pp. 509–38; Cruse, *Plural But Equal*, p. 77.

32   See David Southern, *Gunnar Myrdal and Black-White Relations: The Use and Abuse of An American Dilemma* (Baton Rouge: Louisiana State University Press, 1987), pp. 293–306.

33   Cruse, *Plural But Equal*; Frazier, *The Negro in the United States*, pp. 687–706.

34   Bart Landry, *The New Black Middle Class* (Berkeley: University of California Press, 1987), pp. 67–93; Staples, *The Urban Plantation*, p. 219.

35   J. Blaine Hudson, "Civil Rights in Kentucky," *Kentucky Bar Association Bench and Bar* (May 1999): 6–11.

36   *Louisville Courier-Journal*, July 9 and 11, 1999.

37   Tocqueville, *Democracy in America*, pp. 340–1.

38   See Bell, *Faces at the Bottom of the Well*, for example.

39   R. Roosevelt Thomas, Sr., "Diversity in Community," in Frances Hesselbein et al., *The Community of the Future*, pp. 75–6.

40   Thompson, *The Making of the African Diaspora in the Americas*, pp. 301–53.

9

Renewing American Indian Nations: Cosmic Communities and Spiritual Autonomy

Duane Champagne

In Western philosophy and social science, indigenous communities are often characterized as primitive, pre-industrial, small-scale, acephalous, or precapitalist. Such characterizations provide little detail of the structure and organization of indigenous communities and present an inherently evolutionary model, where indigenous communities are allocated to the lowest rungs. Except amongst some anthropologists and environmentalists, indigenous communities are often considered doomed to destruction or at best submerged within the power of nation-states. Current theories of globalization and world-systems suggest that indigenous communities will be drawn into dependent and exploited relations with core economies and remain backwaters of economic and social organization. Melting-pot theories and multicultural views leave little room for indigenous rights, claims to territory, and political and cultural autonomy.[1] The image of the vanishing Indian continues to find subtle sway in intellectual as well as popular circles.[2]

During the 1980s and 1990s, many indigenous groups around the world increasingly found a voice in national and international fora. In particular, land rights and political recognition in New Zealand, Australia, and Canada have taken major positive turns in favor of indigenous groups when compared to conditions only several decades ago. Native communities, certainly weathered by the colonial experience, seek renewal, demand rights to self-government and cultural autonomy, and increasingly negotiate relations with nation-states. Native communities and identities have not all disappeared or assimilated, as predicted by evolutionary, integrative, and multicultural theories.[3] Native communities promise to be enduring participants in international and national affairs in the forthcoming centuries.

Indigenous communities are generally characterized from the views and interests of nation-states, and not on their own terms. Understanding Native communities from their own perspectives provides considerable insights into the construction and continuity of Native community life. Much of their continuity derives from a commitment to fundamental world-views and associated understandings of community and community relations.[4] While there are hundreds, perhaps even thousands, of indigenous communities in North America alone, Native people offer some unique ways to understand social and community relations. Despite 500 years of colonialism, many of them are loath to give up some of the primary aspects of Native life and community. Native communities offer a spiritual holism and philosophy of life that emphasizes balance in social and natural relations as well as social and individual autonomy. Even among relatively assimilated individuals and communities, the norms of balance and social and individual autonomy often persist, though the religious and ceremonial roots of these relations may no longer be explicitly acknowledged or practiced.

Native communities start with very powerful views of community and human relations. These views often persist to the present, even though considerable influences from colonial relations have moved Native communities into directions and changes that they may not naturally have taken up if left to their own devices. I propose to characterize some fundamental aspects of Native communities in terms of the conception of community and emphasis on social and individual autonomy. I will then characterize the interaction of colonial relations and comment on its influence on Native communities. Finally, I will characterize the complexity of contemporary American Indian community relations in terms of identity by descent, pan-Indian and urban communities, and the continuity of Native views of social and individual autonomy and holistic community.

American Indian communities embody social and sacred understandings that create rules and norms of social action and relations with the nonhuman world. Consequently, understanding the viewpoints of social and worldly relations is necessary for comprehending the dynamics of Native communities. Here we will restrict ourselves to communities in the United States, but to varying degrees many of the views presented here will also apply to indigenous groups in other parts of the world.

The Cosmic Community

At the start, it should be noted that there is not one "Native Community." There are hundreds of them in North America alone. Each one is organized along quite unique lines, according to its history and creation teachings. To investigate ethnohistorically even one Native community is a daunting task; community members themselves often take years to understand many of the complex aspects of their own traditions. Significant social relations in many Native communities are ordained or given in the creation and cultural teachings. Often, a trickster figure, prophet, or central intermediary, such as

Sky Woman among many woodlands cultures, provides the people with gifts of teachings and the origins of major social groupings such as families, clans, moieties, or villages.[5] Among the Tlingit, Raven is a central trickster figure. He gives the people their moiety and clan relations, the potlatch ceremony, and is generally considered to have brought civilization to the Tlingit.[6] Similarly among the Creek Indians of the southeast, the most sacred and important villages were ordained in the creation teachings. The Creek had a polity comprising village coalitions that met at the sacred central towns for purposes of managing national affairs in both war and peace.[7] Similar interpretations can be given to the Delaware, who in the 1760s were organized by three groups or phratries, each consisting of 12 clans. Each group of clans, 36 clans altogether, participated in the "Big House" religion which annually re-enacted the Delaware creation in a 12-day ceremony, each day raising the community to a higher level of heaven until unity with heaven is achieved on the twelfth and final day.[8] Again, among the Iroquois, the demigod Deganawidah offers the gift of the Iroquois confederacy to the Seneca, Cayuga, Onondaga, Oneida, and Mohawk. Deganawidah's message of peace and formation of the Iroquois Confederacy according to clans and the five nations is considered a message from the Great Spirit. Among the Iroquois, and many other American Indian communities, the social relations of community are often given to the people from the sacred realm through spiritual intermediaries.[9]

The result of having social relations constructed through the sacred realm is that the organization and relations of the community itself are considered as sacred and as gifts from the Great Spirit – the principle organizing force of the universe. In most Native cultures, the Great Spirit or ultimate force of the universe is a benevolent gift-giver. Ceremonies and social relations, such as clans, moieties, sacred villages, or other institutions, are viewed as sacred gifts. The central force of the universe is not known to humans; it is neither male nor female, its purpose or ultimate goal cannot be ascertained by humans. The Great Spirit is too busy to interfere in human affairs, and therefore relations to the sacred are conducted through intermediary figures such as trickster figures, seers, and powerful spirit beings found in nature.

The relation between social institutions and the sacred dimensions is probably not unique when compared with other communities around the world. Institutional arrangements are often considered sacred in many different cultures. In American Indian communities this sacredness is embedded in a broader sacred and moral community. The Great Spirit is the organizer of the universe and, in the American Indian view, human relations are not central to the direction and forces of the universe. Humans are one among many spirit beings in the universe, and many forces, such as the sun, moon, wind, lakes, and lightning, are considered more powerful beings than humans. The Great Spirit created or formed the universe with its many spirit beings, including the plants, animals, earth and heavens, birds – all the animate and inanimate elements that make up the universe. Humans, as spirit beings in the universe, must have relations not only among themselves but also with other spirit beings. The Native view of community extends not only to fellow humans and institutional relations but to all the spirit beings in the universe.

Humans cannot live without relations with the plants, animals, lakes, and other powerful forces of the universe. They must eat food, and in order to do so they must appease the spirits of the animals and the plants that they take for their own use and consumption. If a plant is taken for medicine, then tobacco or some other appropriate gift such as food is offered to the plant. If animals or fish are taken for food, then ceremonies must be performed in order to appease the spirits of the animals so that the people are not retaliated against for disturbing other, often more powerful, spirit beings. Humans must observe the sacred order and must maintain friendly and respectful relations with other spirit beings. If other spirit beings are disturbed, then they will retaliate by causing harm in the form of disease and will withdraw their willingness to give themselves to humans for food. In many creation teachings, the animals form an agreement with humans such that they will volunteer to give themselves up for food as long as the people treat them with respect and perform specific rituals to honor their spirits. If this agreement is honored, the animals will freely give themselves to the humans for their needs, and, through the appropriate ceremonies, the spirits of the animals will be preserved and will be reborn, so that the game and fish will be replenished and plentiful for the people. The humans, in return, perform respectful ceremonies and take only what is necessary for their survival.[10]

These covenants with the spirit beings of the universe form a cosmic community in which relations of respect and balance ideally are to prevail in order to promote harmony and order in the universe. When harmony and order prevail, then the spirit beings, including those in human communities, will enjoy peace, prosperity, health, and harmonious social and worldly relations. Of course, in any community people do not live up to the ideal and transgressions and strife occur. In those cases, individuals invite harm upon themselves from angry spirit beings, which can result in disease, death, hunger, bad luck, and disruptive social relations. Dispute resolution mechanisms within human communities and ceremonies are used to correct the consequences of breaking sacred relations with the spirit world.

The universe seen as a gift from the Great Spirit, and the rules and ceremonies for maintaining harmony and order, help point the way to understanding Native views of a cosmic community. Human community and relations cannot be understood or carried out without understanding the sacred relations and obligations that humans have toward other spirit beings. While social relations and institutions are sacred and require mutual obligations and responsibilities, Native communities are not set apart from the "natural" environment; social relations and institutions are part of a set of rules, relations, and community with all beings of the universe. Harmony and order in social relations cannot be obtained without respectful and harmonious relations with the nonhuman spirit beings. While creation traditions vary and the specific institutional relations among clans, villages, individuals, and political relations differ considerably among Native groups, the embeddedness of human community within a cosmic community of spirit beings is found quite widely among Native peoples. Here there is no radical separation between human and natural realms as there is in Western philosophy and Christian religious views, but, rather, in Native communities human relations are embedded within the entire community and relationships of universe of spirit powers. The Native view of cosmic community creates one major way to understand Native community and its internal relations.[11]

Social and Individual Autonomy

Every animate or power being in the universe must be respected, otherwise it will retaliate against the transgressor. Harmony and order are preserved through respectful relations with the animate beings of the universe. Human relations are also included in this principle that every action is countered by reaction. A harmful action against a spirit being will result in a harmful retaliation, unless the spirit being is appeased through ceremonies and offerings. Human relations operate under the same rule. Humans cannot be treated disrespectfully or they will retaliate. Each human is a spirit being and is part of the cosmic and social community. Each individual has a role to play in the cosmic order and often that role is not apparent to people, since the direction and purpose of the universe in not knowable to humans.

An individual's life role in the cosmic and social community is sought through a variety of ceremonial means. Visions, puberty ceremonies, and dreams are all ways in which men and women seek to know their role and purpose within the social and cosmic order. Visions and life tasks are often only revealed gradually to an individual and people may seek their calling through much of their lives. Often the sacred task for an individual, as it is revealed by ceremonies, visions, or the advice of spiritual leaders or elders, is kept secret. Just as every individual is a power or spirit being with a calling in the cosmic order, it is considered unruly to challenge the motivations or actions of individuals who are seeking to fulfill their sacred life tasks. One cannot know what task an individual might have and therefore considerable leeway is given to individuals who appear to be legitimately seeking to fulfill their revealed life tasks. Since others cannot vouch for the wisdom of such tasks, individuals are given considerable individual autonomy within the rules of the cosmic and social community. Actions that do not challenge the sacred rules of the cosmic order and social order are believed to be part of a person's life mission and are generally not questioned by others. An individual has a sacred right as an autonomous power being to fulfill his or her sacred life tasks as long as his or her actions conform to the rules of social and cosmic order, which, if violated, would bring retribution from angry power beings upon the social community and the transgressor.[12]

The principle of autonomy of spirit beings entails specific types of community relations and processes of decision-making. Each individual in the social community must be respected as an autonomous power being and therefore each individual has the right to provide input into any decision-making process. In every community, there might be some individual who has more influence than others because he or she may be believed to have particularly strong spirit helpers which may make the person a relatively stronger power being. Power, however, is an elusive entity: sometimes the spirit helpers are strong and at other times they may not be useful. So spiritual power and influence are fluid in most Indian communities.

A social community of autonomous power beings makes its decisions through discussion and consensus. The word "caucus" – an Algonkian expression now adopted into English – describes the process of decision-making found in many Native communities. Individuals are invited to participate through discussion of families, bands, clans, village councils, or whatever is the group's usual practice. It is often the case that there is considerable disagreement in these meetings and when no consensus is obtained there is no binding decision on the community.[13] Women often have their own councils, and, if not, they often have considerable influence within their lineages or clans. The exemplar of female political power for the feminist movement has long been the Iroquois clan matrons who have the power to appoint and impeach lineage and clan leaders.[14]

Just as individuals have the right to participate in decision-making, social groups, clans, lineages, and villages often have autonomous rights. Depending on the particular organization of the Indian community, local groups (villages, clans, lineages) might discuss issues and form positions through consensus. A majority or powerful group is not allowed to force a decision upon others if there is disagreement. Local groups retain their autonomy and national or regional decisions must also be made through the social construction of agreement and consensus. Local groups and individuals retain considerable power; they do not delegate their rights to appointed representatives or "chiefs." Among the Iroquois, the clan and lineage "chief" is a spokesperson for the consensus of the group, and no more. If he takes on more than his assigned task, which is to report the consensus of the lineage or clan to others, then he will be withdrawn from office. Political relations in Indian communities are often a process of gathering agreements from local groups and lineages who do not grant their autonomy to any central authority or to any other community.[15]

The emphasis on the individual political process and political community through consensus formation very much intrigued early colonial observers, who reported these processes back to Europe. The decentralized, egalitarian, and processual decision-making procedures contrasted sharply with the hierarchical and centralized authoritarian states of Europe. Many critiques of the old regimes in Europe used North American community examples to argue that man in nature was free and that Natives possessed natural forms of freedom and political rights that were lost in their own centralized state systems. The French *philosophes* developed critiques of the French state and offered views of freedom and democracy that were based in part on the information gathered about Native political freedoms and process. The philosophy of natural human rights helped frame United States political theory and became a unique feature of American democracy.[16]

Native social and political forms of decentralized process, however, did not derive from the theory that man had natural or god-given rights but rather from the imperative to preserve harmony and order within the cosmic community. In this view, social groups and individuals exercised considerable autonomy as part of the plan of the Great Spirit. Cosmic harmony and order were preserved through maintaining respecting relations with all spirit beings, including human groups and individuals. Native communities reflected this philosophy in a decentralized social and political organization, often with no centralized leader or delegation of power beyond local groupings. When Native communities did not arrive at a decision, colonial authorities were often frustrated and described the process as fractionated. In many cases, even in present times, Native communities exercise their local autonomy and rights to individual participation in ways that are not well understood by outside observers, who are looking for more centralized decision-making powers.

The two significant characteristics of Native communities – cosmic community order and individual autonomy – help us understand the dynamics and uniqueness of Native community relations. These relations remain important through to the present day.

The World Out of Balance

The colonial era introduced a series of rapid changes. Native communities were always changing before there was any significant colonial contact, but colonial relations initiated a sequence of greater economic incorporation, cultural interchange, and political competition. Economic relations had a lasting impact on many Indian communities, especially those incorporated into trade relations for furs and skins. The fur trade started as early as the mid-1500s, was strongly active during the 1600s, and lasted until about the 1840s, when beaver was depleted in the eastern Rocky Mountain regions. Buffalo was hunted until the early 1880s on the Plains. To a certain extent, many of the American Indian communities in the middle and eastern United States were brought into the fur trade. They became dependent on the trade relatively quickly and started trading furs and skins for a variety of European manufactured goods, such as iron tools, guns, cloth, and beads.

The fur trade threatened the covenant relations with animals as the Indians began to supply furs to traders who went to work on market supply-and-demand relations rather than through Native beliefs and obligations to maintain respectful relations with the animal nations. Most American Indians, however, treated as necessity their dependency on trade for European goods and they continued to hunt only enough animals to supply their trade and social needs they did not become capitalists in the fur trade. Although producing more furs, they were responding to their needs rather than seeking to accumulate individual wealth. Nevertheless, the fur trade by the mid-1600s was depleting game and this process continued further into the interior and was followed generally by land sales and colonists. The fur trade meant that the American Indians became specialized, spending more time hunting and curing, and harvesting more furs than they would otherwise have done.[17] Few, if any, Natives became entrepreneurs in the fur trade and Native world-views remained intact, although Natives themselves were now incorporated into European markets. When the fur and buffalo trades collapsed in the middle and eastern United States, the American Indian communities were generally impoverished and were forced to sell land and take up life on reservations.

Social contact with colonists had a considerable impact on Native communities. Colonial officials did not recognize women in political council, preferring to conduct economic trade relations with young, economically productive men. Although they struggled to regain their usual respect, women and elders were generally pushed aside, and economic and political power was largely in the hands of the young men.[18] With the fur trade and diplomatic relations in their hands, the young men had more economic and political power than previously. Reservation life nevertheless greatly attenuated the economic and political influence of productive men.

Relations with colonists ultimately led to the introduction of Christian religions and new world-views into many American Indian communities. Multiculturalism increased and members of some communities became more economically entrepreneurial, especially amongst the Choctaw, Chickasaw, Creek and Cherokee during the 1800s. Among the Iroquois in particular, the introduction of Protestant Christianity led to the formation of deep cultural cleavages between Christians and "pagans" – cleavages that continue to the present day on many of the Iroquois reservations.[19] Other groups, such as the Cherokee and Choctaw, adopted Christianity and allowed community members to make independent choices.[20] Some groups, such as the Northern Cheyenne, accepted Christianity, in the form of the Native American Church, as well as maintaining many key aspects of the Northern Cheyenne tradition.[21]

Colonial relations, then, have had a deep and significant impact on Native communities. New religions and ideas challenged traditional world-views. Many individuals, who adopted Christianity or were educated in boarding schools away from their family and communities, took on American attitudes and did not participate in the cosmic community. The old world-views were severely challenged by economic collapse, political subjugation, and religious-cultural alternatives introduced by American assimilation programs. Nevertheless, many aspects of ceremonies and the understanding of cosmic spiritual relations remained, even if forced underground and sometimes practiced only by small dedicated groups. A whole series of religious movements preserved important aspects of Native world-views, while adopting elements from Christianity. Such movements include the Ghost Dances, the Native American Church, The Indian Shaker Movement, the Handsome Lake Movement and others. Many Christian Indians created their own churches, such as among the Choctaw and Creek, where they sang songs and heard sermons in their own languages.[22] Theological understandings often reflect Native understandings of sacred relations. Some Christian Indian groups joined mainstream churches, but often mixed Native religious understandings and norms with Christian doctrine. In this way, the concept of cosmic spiritual relations and community remain among many people and are often directly and indirectly represented in Christian Indian communities, especially those led by Native ministers.

The decentralization and autonomy of individuals and social groups remains a general characteristic of most Native communities through the colonial period to the present day. Families, clans, and villages generally retain considerable autonomy in their own right or within newly constructed constitutional governments created on reservations, to a large extent by United States officials.[23] Native political processes tend to focus on consensus building, and conflict often arises when such protocols are not fitfully adopted by some leaders. Much of the present-day literature about factionalism and political conflict within Native communities underestimates the deeply embedded cultural orientations toward individual and local spiritual autonomy. What outsiders interpret as conflict or factionalism is more likely to be individuals and groups asserting their autonomy under Native rules and cultural orientations. United States officials and scholars, and even many Native leaders, try to assert more centralization of political authority in Native communities than they will culturally support given their world-view of balance among the power beings of a cosmic community. On many reservations, community members may not have a direct understanding of spiritual relations, but they have grown up in social environments where individual and local autonomy is still an implicit cultural norm.

Multiple Communities, Multiple Identities

Contemporary Native life abounds with multiple communities and situational identities. Many traces of the cosmic community are found in reservations and among urban Indian communities, where Native social and political relations remain decentralized and individual autonomy is still recognized implicitly. Some of the political difficulties on reservations, such as among the Hopi and Lakota, are caused in part by overly centralized tribal governments that run contrary to decentralized Native forms of social organization and political process. Many Native communities continue to find constitutional political forms introduced by Bureau of Indian Affairs officials to be too rigid and contrary to Native political traditions. Opposition to tribal government actions arises in Native communities and is often the result of fundamental conflicts between American and Native political processes and views of social and individual rights and obligations. Many Natives believe that while the American Indian Civil Rights Act introduced some protections, it infringed on Native political sovereignty and imposed a form of individual rights often alien to tribal communities. Although Native tribal governments are generally based on United States constitutional models, Native consensual-based rules and individual and group autonomies are ignored within such political models because decisions are made by majority rule, leaders elected by majority vote, and leaders are delegated concentrated and centralized political power. Furthermore, most constitutionally based tribal governments are secular and are separated from religious organization. Many members of Native communities feel that the separation of cosmic community from political relations is dangerous and may well lead to inappropriate guidance among secular Native leaders. In recent years, the Navajo tribal government has been an example of Native retrenchment from centralized authority. Since 1985 the Navajo court system has increasingly incorporated traditional culture and methods in their Peacemaker courts and common law. Navajo local political groups have passed legislation to decentralize the government and distribute more decision-making authority to local chapters, which generally represent local and traditional family and kinship groups.[24]

A considerable amount of conflict within tribal governments is generated by the mismatch among US-imposed political procedures and Native views of community and individual and local political processes. Such situations generate strong conflicts and often leave Native individuals and groups alienated if their normative means of handling the situation are overruled by Western forms of political order and procedure. Scholars and other observers often call such conflicts factionalism and blame the Natives for an incapacity to find workable solutions. Many Native reservation communities need to rethink their political constitutions and make them more compatible with Native orientations of political process and senses of cosmic community. Political procedures and legal orders that to a large extent represent US cultural and institutional values on reservations do not provide Natives with culturally compatible institutions. Native groups will increasingly renegotiate their political and legal institutions, as the Navajo are now doing, in order to make them more culturally compatible. Most Native communities will not strive to re-establish "traditional" cultural and political orders. Many tribal members have multiple cultural orientations, and contemporary political and economic challenges require institutional arrangements that can manage market relations and political competition from states and federal agencies. Nevertheless, as reservation communities realize self-determination, they will increasingly find ways to adopt modifications to tribal government and legal arrangements that will reflect their own philosophies of social and cultural order.

While Native communities struggle over forms of political organization and process, new forms of community and identity have emerged on the national scene and within urban areas. Pan-Indian identities emerged during the 1970s and the activism of that period.[25] Such identities have not replaced tribal identities but have added an additional layer of identity for most Native people. A single pan-Indian identity as a supra-tribal identity probably has not emerged. Many people will say they are American Indian, but often this identification is driven by the context of the situation. Most Americans recognize the name "American Indian" but they are not familiar with tribal or clan names. Terms such as American Indian are generated and used by American society as a homogeneous ethnic group label that abstracts past specific tribal identities.[26] Natives generally use the names of specific tribal or clan names when they are addressing people who have knowledge of them – usually other tribal members.

Most reservation Natives in fact would say that there is an American Indian ethnic group. Most Natives who are associated with a community primarily identify with their community group. Nevertheless, there were about 6 million individuals in the 1990 census who identified themselves as having an American Indian ancestor, about half of them claiming a Cherokee ancestor. The Native descent group probably does not form an ethnic group or community, but is, rather, a population of individuals who acknowledge some tie to Indian ancestry and often have an interest in American Indian issues. The American Indian ancestry group far outnumbers the Native population identified by race, which was about 1.96 million in the 1990 census. The number of people who live on or near a reservation totals around a half million. The ancestry group is by far the largest, but it seems not to have any social or political organization, and many have primary identities that are not American Indian.[27]

Major national American Indian organizations reflect tribal identities more so than pan-Indian identities. For example, the National Congress of American Indians (NCAI) is organized by tribal representation. Each tribe, regardless of its population size, is granted one vote in the NCAI conventions. Consequently, large tribes such as the Navajo with a reservation population of over 200,000 have the same number of votes as a small California tribe of fewer than 40 members. For this reason, some tribes like the Navajo do not participate in the NCAI. The principle of representation within NCAI preserves the autonomy rules of Native cultures. Each tribe is given the right to represent its position and vote, even if it has few members. Local cultural and political autonomy is preserved in this manner. The NCAI forms a loose coalition of tribal groups. Any effort to impose an ethnic or supra-tribal identity would most likely generate considerable opposition and dissolution of the organization, as each tribal group would insist on preserving its autonomy and would likely leave the organization.

Renewing the Cosmic Community

The colonial period did much to dislocate Native institutions and relations. While Native norms of political process appear deeply embedded in Native communities and national organizations, the holistic views of cosmic community have been disassociated from many tribal governments and institutions. Since the 1970s many tribal spiritual leaders have shown greater confidence in reclaiming the philosophies and covenants of the cosmic community through ceremonies. The revival of many ceremonies that went underground during the cultural and religious repression of the late nineteenth and early twentieth centuries[28] and the current self-conscious emphasis on preserving Native language and renewing knowledge about religion and religious practice will help to maintain the philosophy and understandings of cosmic community in many Native groups. Ceremonies that renew covenant relations with the power beings of the cosmic community are quite common among Native nations and will help restore confidence in Native institutions and revitalize Native reservation communities. Native communities and institutions that are based on specific ceremonies and cultural philosophies will do much to recreate and invigorate life on reservations. The philosophies of cosmic community were not designed to manage bureaucracies and make market decisions; nevertheless, the principles of the cosmic community can inform values and give orientation to decision-making within reservation communities. A major challenge for Native communities over the next century is to reclaim and renew cultural and institutional relations while at the same time more effectively meeting the challenges of multicultural reservation communities and competitive economic market globalization, and preserving tribal political autonomy. True self-determination in Native communities will come through forming institutional relations that are broadly informed by Native values, such as the principles of cosmic community, and, at the same time, providing the capability to engage in the global market while preserving tribal political integrity. In many Native communities, however, the combined goals of maintaining cultural philosophies with institutions capable of political and economic competition may be considered contradictory. Each Native community faces this challenge, but each has the right to meet the challenge in its own way based on its own history, contemporary community relations, and specific Native philosophies and institutional arrangements. Each Native community will move to assert its own solution in its own way. By doing so, each will be exercising the autonomy inherent in its world-view.

Notes

1   For a critique of multicultural and postcolonial views, see Arif Dirlik, "The Past as Legacy and Project: Postcolonial Criticism in the Perspective of Indigenous Historicism," in Troy Johnson, ed., *Contemporary Native American Political Issues* (Walnut Creek, CA: Altamira, 1999), pp. 73–92; Duane Champagne," Multiculturalism: New Understanding or Oversimplification?" in Diana de Anda, ed., *Controversial Issues in Multiculturalism* (Boston: Allyn and Bacon, 1997).

2   Brian Dippie, *The Vanishing American: White Attitudes and US Indian Policy* (Middletown: Wesleyan University Press, 1982); Kenya Katarine Ramirez, "Healing Through Grief: Urban Indians Reimagining Culture and Community in San Jose, California," *American Indian Culture and Research Journal* 22 (1998): 311–15.

3   Fae L. Korsmo, "Claiming Memory in British Columbia: Aboriginal Rights and the State," in Johnson, ed., *Contemporary Native American Issues*, pp. 129–30; Stephen Quesenberry, "Recent United Nations Initiatives Concerning the Rights of Indigenous Peoples," in ibid. p. 104.

4   Duane Champagne, "The Cultural and Institutional Foundations of Native American Conservatism," special issue on "North American Indians: Cultures in Motion," ed. Elvira Stefania Tiberini, *L'Uomo, Societa, Tradizione, Sviluppo* VIII (1995): 17–43.

5   Barbara Mann and Jerry Fields, "A Sign in the Sky: Dating the League of the Haudenosaunee," *American Indian Culture and Research Journal* 21 (1997): 130–4.

6   Catherine McClellan, "The Interrelations of Social Structure with Northern Tlingit Ceremonialism," *Southwest Journal of Anthropology* 10 (1954): 75–96; Duane Champagne, "Culture, Differentiation, and Environment: Social Change in Tlingit Society," in Jeffrey C. Alexander and Paul Colomy, eds., *Differentiation Theory and Social Change* (New York: Columbia University Press, 1990), pp. 58–65.

7   Duane Champagne, *Social Order and Political Change: Constitutional Governments Among the Cherokee, The Choctaw, the Chickasaw and The Creek* (Stanford: Stanford University Press, 1992), pp. 33–8.

8   Frank Speck, *A Study of the Delaware Indian Big House Ceremony* (Harrisburg, PA: Pennsylvania Historical Commission,1931), p. 75; William Newcomb, *The Culture and Acculturation of the Delaware Indians* (Ann Arbor: University of Michigan Museum of Anthropology, 1956), pp. 125–7; David Zeisberger, A. Hulbert and William Schwarze, eds., *History of the North American Indians* (Ohio State Archeological and Historical Society, 1910), pp. 92–7; Duane Champagne, "The Delaware Revitalization Movement of the Early 1760s: A Suggested Reinterpretation," *The American Indian Quarterly* 12 (1988): 107–26.

9   Arthur C. Parker, *Parker on the Iroquois* (Syracuse University Press, 1968), pp. 65–126.

10 Luana Ross, *Inventing the Savage: The Social Construction of Native American Criminality* (University of Texas Press, 1999), pp. 30–1; Ron Trosper, "Traditional American Indian Economic Policy," in Johnson, ed., *Contemporary Native American Issues*, pp. 140–2; Huston Smith and Reuben Snake, eds., *One Nation Under God: The Triumph of the Native American Church* (Santa Fe, NM: Clear Light, 1996), pp. 16–20; Reuben Snake, *Reuben Snake Your Humble Serpent: Indian Visionary and Activist* (Santa Fe, NM: Clear Light, 1996), pp. 36–9, 225–32.

11 Kenneth Morrison, "Native American Religions: Creating Through the Cosmic Give-and-Take," in Duane Champagne, ed., *The Native North American Almanac* (Detroit: Gale Research, Inc., 1994), pp. 633–41; Carol Miller, "Telling the Indian Urban: Representations in American Indian Fiction," *American Indian Culture and Research Journal* 22 (1998): 49–51, 54–6; Robert A. Williams, *Linking Arms Together: American Indian Treaty Visions of Law and Peace, 1600–1800* (New York: Oxford University Press, 1997), pp. 98–123.

12 Morrison, "Native American Religions," pp. 633–41; Smith and Snake, eds., *One Nation Under God*, pp. 16–20.

13 Bernard Stern, ed., "The Letters of Asher Wright to Lewis Morgan," *American Anthropologist* 35 (1933): 144; John Noon, *Law and Government of the Grand River Iroquois* (New York: Viking Fund Publications in Anthropology, 1949), p. 28.

14 Judith Brown, "Economic Organization and the Position of Women Among the Iroquois," *Ethnohistory* 17 (1970): 151.

15 Anthony C. Wallace, *The Death and Rebirth of the Seneca* (New York: Vintage Books, 1972), pp. 44–50; Edmund Wilson, *Apologies to the Iroquois* (New York: Farrar, Straus and Cudahy, 1959), p. 174; William Fenton, "Cultural Stability and Change in American Indian Societies," *Journal of the Royal Anthropological Institute of Great Britain and Ireland* 83 (1953): 172; Fred Gearing, "Priests and Warriors: Social Structures for Cherokee Politics in the 18th Century," *American*

Anthropologist. Memoir 93 (64)(5): 31–9; James Adair, *Adair's History of the American Indians* (Johnson City, TN: The Watauga Press, 1930), p. 406; John Swanton, "Source Material for the Social and Ceremonial Life of the Choctaw Indians," *Bureau of American Ethnology Bulletin* 103 (1932): 91.

16   Donald A. Grinde and Bruce E. Johansen, *Exemplar of Liberty: Native America and the Evolution of Democracy* (Los Angeles: UCLA American Indian Studies Center, 1991), pp. 61–72; Jeffrey Alexander, "The Paradoxes of Civil Society," *International Sociology* 12 (June 1997): 118–20.

17   E. E. Rich, "Trade Habits and Economic Motivation Among the Indians of North America," *Canadian Journal of Economics and Political Sciences* 26 (1960): 53; Arthur J. Ray, *Indians in the Fur Trade* (Toronto: University of Toronto Press, 1974), p. 68.

18   Edmond Atkins, *Indians of the Southern Colonial Frontier*, ed. Wilbur Jacobs (University of South Carolina Press, 1954), p. 10; William Steele, *The Cherokee Crown of Tannasy* (Winston-Salem, SC: Jon Blair, 1977), p. 43; Nancy Bonvillain, "Gender Relations in Native North America," *American Indian Culture and Research Journal* 13 (1989): 18–20.

19   Robert B. Porter, "Building a New Longhouse: The Case for Government Reform within the Six Nations of the Haudenosaunee," *Buffalo Law Review* 46 (Fall 1998): 805–945; Bruce Johansen, *Life and Death in Mohawk Country* (Golden: North American Press, 1993).

20   Champagne, *Social Order and Political Change*, pp. 140, 179–240; Albert Wahrhaftig, "Institution Building Among Oklahoma's Traditional Cherokees," in Charles Hudson, ed., *Four Centuries of Southern Indians* (Athens: University of Georgia Press, 1975), pp. 132–47.

21   Personal communication, and see also comments of Reuben Snake about the compatibility of Ho Chunk and Christian teachings, in *Your Humble Serpent*, pp. 109–213.

22   Personal communication, James May; Joan Weibel-Orlando, *Indian Country, L.A.: Maintaining Ethnic Community in Complex Society* (Chicago: University of Illinois Press, 1991), pp. 153–77.

23   Thomas Biolsi, *Organizing the Lakota* (Tucson: University of Arizona Press, 1992), pp. 126–50.

24   Office of Navajo Government Development, *Navajo Nation Government Book* (Window Rock, AZ: The Navajo Nation, 1998), pp. 33–40.

25   Stephen Cornell, *The Return of the Native: American Indian Political Resurgence* (New York: Oxford University Press, 1988); Joan Nagel, *American Indian Ethnic Renewal: Red Power and the Resurgence of Identity and Culture* (New York: Oxford University Press, 1996), pp. 187–205.

26   James Fenelon, "Discrimination and Indigenous Identity in Chicago's Native Community," *American Indian Culture and Research Journal* 22 (1998): 285–8.

27   Angela Gonzalez, "The (Re)Articulation of American Indian Identity: Maintaining Boundaries and Regulating Access to Ethnically Tied Resources," *American Indian Culture and Research Journal* 22 (1998): 200–3.

28   Ross, *Inventing the Savage*, 38–41.

10

Nations and Nationalism: The Case of Canada/Quebec

Frank Cunningham

If the recently proclaimed "end of history" dampened theoretical interventions in the contest between socialism and capitalism, it certainly has not impeded debate about the other prominent feature of twentieth-century historicity: nationalism.[1] Instead, the journals and academic bookstores, as well as the educated popular press, are replete to an unprecedented extent with lively exchanges on this subject.[2] As in all such politically relevant discussions, normative controversies are embedded in putatively non-normative questions of definition. Thus, current extensions of earlier debates over how to define nationhood have focused on the question of whether nations are, in Benedict Anderson's phrase, "imagined communities," and these have merged with attempts to define "nationalism." The normative debates encapsulated in these controversies have to do with the justice (or rightness, or goodness, or appropriateness, or importance) of nation-favoring policies, attitudes, and practices by states, groups, or individual citizens.

Within the tangled web these discussions constitute are to be found some useful ideas and distinctions. The more engaged of the debates have forced nuanced deployment of communitarian and individualist theory which has opened space for liberal communitarianism in the one case and group-supportive individualism in the other. Historical interrogations have illuminated differences between ethnic and civic nationalisms (or between ethnic and civic dimensions of nationalism). While older debates distinguished between state and nation and problematized the relation between them, more recent exchanges have introduced multicultural realities and policies into the mix. Discussions that have focused on national loyalties or identifications have shown these to be more complex matters than atavistic commitment to nationalist values or the like.

At least these are among the notions I have found useful in attempting to think through the constitutional conundrum faced by me and my compatriots in Canada. Less useful have been deductions and dichotomies either affirmed or supposed in much, if not all, of the theoretical literature – for example, that if nations are constructed, national loyalties are misplaced, or that civic and ethnic nationalism are mutually exclusive alternatives. In what follows I shall describe a perspective on the current Canadian case that is "nation-friendly" in one respect, drawing on material from the theoretical debates where appropriate. As will shortly be seen, I do not think that the perspective described is simply derived from philosophical principles. Nor is it offered as a test case for some particular abstract theory about nationalism (or group rights and individual rights or justice).

The analysis that makes up the rest of this chapter is, rather, an attempt at philosophically informed political prescription or of the application of philosophy as opposed to "applied philosophy" as the latter is often undertaken. Acceptance of the prescriptions in the Canadian case would no doubt lend presumptive weight to their transferability to other situations (or to Canada in a future situation), but it would not provide a sure guide to prescriptions regarding other circumstances. They, like that of Canada, require closer analysis than is typically found in work of political philosophy. It is of the nature of such an analysis that it makes reference to local events and actors, which, at the risk of boring readers acquainted with the Canadian case, I shall summarize as required.

The Conundrum of Canada/Quebec

As reported in the foreign press, the ongoing tug of war between Canadian federalists and Quebec nationalists is often reported as an exceptional paradigm of peace and reason. If the contrast is the Balkans, there is something to this picture; however, Canadians themselves are not wont to boast of our constitutional crises. In part this is due to fatigue: the crises and succession of legally ingenious but politically messy schemes to meet them never end. And in part it is due to apprehension about the future. In a referendum held in Quebec in October 1995 the governing, sovereigntist Parti Québecois (the PQ) very nearly gained a mandate to begin negotiations with the federal government for sovereignty. The vote was 51 percent to 49 percent against the sovereigntists, with 93 percent of those eligible casting a ballot.

Watching the results come in we in English-speaking Canada – alternatively called RoC, "the Rest of Canada," or CoQ, "Canada outside of Quebec" by political scientists groping for accurate and neutral descriptions – knew that 60 percent of Franco Quebeckers had voted for the sovereigntist position. When the PQ acknowledgment of defeat was broadcasted from Montreal, we saw a hall full of young and evidently uncrushed people. The assurances of our Prime Minister that defeat in this referendum would put an end to future pressure for sovereignty were believed by virtually nobody.

What if the sovereigntists had won the referendum? There is no constitutional provision for secession. A very large portion of Quebec territory is claimed by Aboriginal bands, who shortly before the referendum had unanimously declared that in the event of a sovereigntist win they would not leave the Canadian confederation. Would the PQ have used police force? (The Quebec Provincial Police had shortly before engaged in armed combat with the Mohawks at Oka.) Would the federal government have responded to a Native request for military assistance? (Quebec had been put under federal military control in 1970 when then Prime Minister Pierre Elliot Trudeau claimed to have discovered an "apprehended insurrection" and invoked an emergency powers act.) Luckily, we did not have to confront such scenarios, but their potentialities remain. Within Quebec, Anglophones and "Allophones" – that is, those whose maternal language is neither English nor French (about 10 percent each of the total Quebec population and concentrated in the large cities, mainly Montreal) – voted heavily against sovereignty. This would have left a sizable and highly disaffected minority within a sovereign Quebec.

The response of Parliament was to introduce legislation designating Quebec a "distinct society" and giving veto power over future constitutional changes to it along with Ontario, British Columbia, the Atlantic Provinces, and the Prairie Provinces (each grouped as a single vetoing unit). Franco Quebeckers, however, have not been placated by the distinct society appellation, which they consider to be without substance. Regional and provincial veto powers are welcomed by some devolutionists, but seen by others as a dangerous step toward balkanization of the country and as consistent with an economic policy that puts countrywide planning and centrally financed social services in jeopardy.

Moreover, the Parliament that enacted this legislation and was supposed to heal the country's wounds was anything but coherent, dominated by the Liberal Party, the parliamentary majority of which masked persisting divisions regionally and along lines of social and economic philosophy. Bizarrely, the official opposition was the Bloc Québecois, earlier formed and elected to Parliament exclusively by voters from Quebec. This party led the sovereignty referendum in partnership with the Parti Québecois and Action Démocratique (a party formed when members of the youth wing of the Quebec Liberal Party broke away from it). Next in number of parliamentary seats was another newcomer, the rightwing populist Reform Party, based in Alberta but with not insignificant support elsewhere and since the last federal election the official opposition.

The social democratic, New Democratic Party and the Tory, Progressive Conservative Party, which with the Liberals had previously been our only significant parties, held and continue to hold relatively few seats. In Quebec, the PQ, led by Lucien Bouchard (formerly head of the Bloc Québecois) has been tending to economic problems – waffling between neoliberal and social democratic positions, with an emphasis on the former – and regrouping for another run at sovereignty.

Against this background (accurate at the time of drafting this contribution), I wish now to introduce some prescriptions by situating the Canadian constitutional conflict within the framework of what I take as its political landscape. The first prescription is, therefore, that the conundrum should be thus situated.

The Landscape

This landscape may be conceived of as comprising actors, on the one hand, and candidates for being objects of action on the other. Identification of each of the possible actors and "actees" is problematic, and debates about their characterization and significance is implicated in the political process itself. This has been especially evident regarding a claim of nearly all Quebec sovereigntists that the most important objects of action are nations. From the 1960s Trudeau and all subsequent federal leaders have not only contested this claim, but have denied that Quebec constitutes a nation. This seems to have derived from a fear that nationhood confers at least a presumption of statehood. They point out, in addition, that Quebec is not homogeneously French. Moreover, there are concerns about whether there are any other national objects of action such that a nation-focused politics could make sense. For reasons shortly to be given, I am sympathetic to the idea that the land called Canada comprehends three national groupings: a Franco nation, an Anglo nation, and the ensemble of Aboriginal nations. However, each designation is problematic.

Quebec is ethnically and linguistically heterogeneous, and French-speaking people live in every region of Canada (a fact recognized in our official policy of bilingualism), not all of whom identify with Quebec as a national homeland. Many English-speaking Canadians think of Quebec as integral to a Canadian identity and accordingly resist its separation on this score. This, plus the fact that many in the economic or political elite of Franco Quebec, such as Trudeau, are strong federalists make our situation more complex than some other countries, such as Czechoslovakia, that have also been struggling with national divisions.

English-speaking Canada itself comprises many linguistic communities, some of them, such as the Dutch and German, dating to pre-confederation times and many more to the turn of the century; hence the awkward CoQ and RoQ designations. Also, nothing like the strong nationalist sentiment to be found in the United States or in Quebec exists in English-speaking Canada. Aboriginal peoples constitute a "community of fate" (to use an expression of

Robert Michels) due to their terrible common treatment by European settlers and their descendants, but are by no means a single nation.

Provinces and regions constitute two more actees on the Canadian political landscape, and much of the history of Canadian politics may be seen as a
tension between federalist centralism and regional/provincial decentralization. However, there is also a tension between regions and provinces, as provincial boundaries do not exactly coincide with regional ones, and the
Northern Territories are not provinces at all. Both provinces and regions are
divided along southern/northern lines, which, furthermore, typically coincide with urban/rural divisions.

In addition to nations, provinces, and regions, there are ethnic groups, of
which there are very many and which, at least from the 1970s, have not
been encouraged to follow the US melting-pot practice (currently challenged
in that country) of assimilation into the majority culture. Finally, there are
individuals. The importance accorded to ethnic groups is reflected in Canada's policy of multiculturalism, which in 1982 was entrenched as official
policy in the Constitution (patriated from Britain in that year). Never as militantly individualistic as US political culture, Canadian attitudes have nonetheless evolved in a direction favoring individual rights to the extent that in
1985 a "Charter of Rights and Freedoms," earlier attached to the Constitution and similar to the US Bill of Rights, came into force. It should be noted,
however, that provisions of this Charter may under certain circumstances
be overridden by a province or by Parliament.

The principal political actors on this landscape have been federal and provincial politicians: the Prime Minister and the provincial premiers. Following recommendations of a succession of commissions struck by them, these
elected leaders have either acted unilaterally, or they have negotiated with
one another to arrive at propositions to put before federal and provincial representative assemblies or to put directly to a popular vote. These efforts resulted in the Meech Lake Accord of 1987 and the Charlottetown Accord of
1992 (named after the places where politicians met to negotiate them). The
first of these failed to receive the required endorsement of each of the provincial legislatures, when Manitoba and Newfoundland did not ratify it. I shall
later return to the significance of the fact that Manitoba's Legislative Assembly was   single-handedly blocked from endorsing the Accord by its sole Aboriginal member, Elijah Harper. The Charlottetown Accord was defeated in a
countrywide referendum.

Other actors are: business and labor organizations, political parties, social
movements, leaders of the Aboriginals communities, and ordinary citizens.
Typical of most other modern-day democracies, the last-mentioned group
has had the indirect influence of electing provincial and federal governments
and the further limited input of voting on referenda, though without a say
on their timing or wording, indeed, the campaign for a "oui" vote on the

Quebec sovereignty referendum was begun several weeks before its question had been formulated. A 10,000-person-strong demonstration in Montreal on the eve of the 1995 referendum on sovereignty by Canadians from all over the country no doubt reflected strong popular sentiment outside of Quebec against sovereignty, but its appearance of being a spontaneous exercise in participatory democracy was compromised by the fact that it was organized and financed by the Federal Liberal Party.

An example of the fragile hold that elected representatives and their establishment backers have on the constitutional process is seen in the fate of the 1992 Charlottetown Accord. The provincial first ministers (including of Quebec, then with a Liberal government) and Brian Mulroney, Prime Minister at the time, put to a referendum a proposal, which, like the current federal policies, tried simultaneously to placate Quebec and the other provinces by devolving federal powers to all the provinces. With the ministers stood the three traditional political parties, the head of the Assembly of First Nations (an umbrella group for Native bands), the principle business associations, organized labor, and the press. But, in what must be an anarchist's dream, this elite consortium was massively defeated at the polls.

Because I take defeat of the Charlottetown Accord as a pivotal moment in the recent conduct of democratic politics in Canada,[3] I shall introduce the recommendations below by a brief report about how this Accord was discredited in the public mind. The Accord was already in disrepute among Franco-Quebeckers, who resented the fact that it did not acknowledge their nationhood, instead reiterating the "distinct society" description mentioned above and tried out in the earlier defeated Meech Lake Accord. It was also in popular disrepute among those Anglo-Canadians, especially in Newfoundland and the West, who resented even this measure of singling Quebec out from the other provinces. Further opposition was sparked by the conservative Reform Party, which correctly declared the process whereby cloistered ministers played such a crucial role democratically deficient. Reform's success in draping itself in the democratic mantel was, however, short-lived when several social movements (environmental, anti-poverty, and especially the strong and widely supported coalition of women's movements, the National Action Committee on the Status of Women) took up the "no" side of the referendum. Their concern, quite at variance with that of the Reform Party, was that devolution would weaken social services.

The final nail in the Accord's coffin was driven by Native tribal councils, which rejected its endorsement by the leader of their own Assembly. The Accord went further than any previous initiative in recognizing an "inherent right to self-government" for Native peoples. Still, band leaders recommended to their members that they vote negatively. The reason for this could not be that the Native leaders disagreed with the substance of the Accord's stand on Aboriginal rights; rather, they did not like the process whereby it and several provisions for making concrete and testing the extent of these rights was being entrenched. Individual voting on such monumental matters after limited public debate was out of keeping with an Aboriginal conception of democracy, which involves protracted discussion aiming at consensus. In addition, Aboriginal women wished to insure that women's rights would be protected in the new arrangements. This was not the first time that people of European ancestry had made take-it-or-leave-it offers to Aboriginal peoples. There are insufficient numbers of Native peoples for their vote to have sunk the Accord, but their negative stance alienated many who might have voted for it out of support for them.

Some Questions of Methodology

I, myself, did vote for the Accord, chiefly because I considered entrenchment of the right to Native self-government a substantial gain in an otherwise flawed document and process, but I took a lot of flak from fellow academics, left and right, as a result. Reflecting on both my motives and the motives of my colleagues who voted against the Accord, it now seems clear that, despite rhetoric we used in classrooms and academic conferences, we did not proceed in the deductive mode typical of political theorists in general and of political philosophers in particular. That is, we did not apply a favored general ethical theory (utilitarianism, deontology, contractarianism, etc.) to the case at hand, eager to see the result so we would know what political position to support, nor did we devise a stand on the general question of the right of nations to self-determination and then ask whether Quebec had such a right and whether it was adequately recognized in the Accord or justifiably overridden.

Rather, I have the impression that the theorists thought through the merits or otherwise of voting for the Accord from positions initially anchored in some political or social concern: to protect social services, to advance Quebec national interests, to resist elite decision-making, to support Native peoples, and so on. These "anchors" meld normative intuitions, assessments of fact, and predictions about alternative futures. No doubt the normative dimensions of the resulting attitudes are themselves partly shaped by the earlier attention of political philosophers to foundational theories, but so are the theoretical commitments affected by intuitions and empirical views in the manner of "wide reflective equilibrium" (to employ the phrase of some neo-Rawlsians).[4]

Since most people had several concerns differentially affected by the Accord, and since the critical dimension of political philosophy mandates that at least those trained in it be prepared to question even their most cherished values and prioritizations, the anchors themselves stand in need of interrogation and defense. More traditional political philosophy can play a role in helping one in an such endeavor. However, I doubt that appeal to such abstract theory alone suffices, and in any case what contribution it can make depends on the contexts within which appeals are made to it. The landscape sketched above is such a context. But appropriate prescriptions for policies or actions do not directly spring forth from the description of a context. Required is an *orientation* within which solutions might be most fruitfully sought and appropriate modes of intervention identified.

In Defense of a National Orientation

Two Canadian philosophers who have been active intervenors in the recent debates are Charles Taylor and Will Kymlicka.[5] Each has endorsed some version of group, and especially national, rights: Kymlicka from an individualist perspective and Taylor from that of a liberal democratic communitarian (though Taylor, himself, tries to avoid this appellation, due to its association with moral relativism). Also, they agree politically, as each is a federalist who acknowledges Quebec's claims to nationhood. Both also give general arguments in favor of individualism or communitarianism, but the aspect of their contributions I wish to focus on is the way they make explicit the orientations from which they argue. Kymlicka illustrates some often overlooked strengths of approaching the political problems of Canadian confederation from an orientation that put individuals at its center, while Taylor's focus on nations. This is one of the useful contributions that I believe political philosophers can make to debates over nationalism. Kymlicka and Taylor are especially good examples, because each challenges an assumed view that community- and individual-based orientations must be diametrically opposed. If their theories are regarded as articulations of perspectives, rather than as necessarily opposed sets of prescriptions, then one can evaluate the relative advantages of the perspectives without being hostile to or dismissive of the uses to which each is put. Viewed this way and with reference to the current situation of Canada/Quebec, I believe the national orientation has more to recommend it than an orientation centered on individual citizens or one that takes as its point of departure the other objects of action (ethnic groups, provinces, or regions) described above.

Kymlicka's argument shows how somebody who is not him or herself a nationalist, but who favors the liberal pluralist view that individuals should be able as far as possible to pursue their own goods in their own ways, can at least presumptively respect the aspirations of those whose good is participation in shared national projects. Its weakness is that it does not sanction a sufficiently robust notion of national identification to extend this respect in the areas most important to a nationalist. Such a person is not concerned just to be able individually to enjoy the benefits of national group membership, but to see his or her nation survive through future generations. This is why Franco-Quebeckers have taken such extraordinary measures to preserve the French language in Quebec, even for a time making public advertising in other languages illegal. Aboriginal peoples have certainly pressed for measures to ameliorate the lives of currently living Native persons, and Aboriginal women have leveled just charges of sexism against some aspects of Aboriginal practices themselves. However, both Aboriginal men and women have also made it clear that they want to avoid cultural assimilation or loss of the means to transmit their ways of life to subsequent generations.

Taylor's nation-centered approach does not lack the requisite robustness, but has as its burden – recognized and wrestled with by Taylor – to show how nationalism can also be pluralistic. In the face of all-too-many examples of intolerant and fanatical nationalism, nobody could argue that any form of nationalistic sentiment is also respectful of individual rights and differences. However, it does not follow from this that any form of national identification and resulting national politics is bound to be chauvinistic any more than it follows that an individualistic culture must always promote alienation or the legalization of human relations just because it sometimes does.[6] Also, Taylor's argument does not require a general defense of nationalism. He only sets out to show that Franco-Quebec nationalism includes liberal and democratic principles, some of which are identical to those found in the rest of Canada. Others are subject to alternate interpretations, but they can have the same desired effects. Nor does Taylor need to claim – what would, alas, be false – that Quebec nationalism is void of intolerance. He need only show that there are resources within Quebec political culture for a tolerant form of nationalism.[7]

Most debates about the relative merits of individualism or communitarianism concern themselves with two questions: the normative problem of whether or when community-promoting policies or activities should take precedence over the protection of individual rights, and the social-scientific question about whether or how individuals can rise above socially conditioned values in choosing or revising life plans.[8] The task of designating appropriate "actors" within the current Canadian political landscape, or at least that portion of it germane to the current constitutional conundrum, intersects with these questions but is of a different, less philosophically or theoretically abstract order.

I assume that principled liberal democratic politics involves a continuing effort to strike balances and seek ways to minimize mutually destructive conflicts between protection of individuals against group pressures, on the one hand, and preservation of the ability of people to act in accord with group-related goals (when this is required for them to pursue their own goods in their own ways, without confronting a state-sanctioned concept of the good), on the other. I also assume that on any but the most fatalistic social theory and in any but the most educationally impoverished and monolithic cultures, people are able to evaluate norms implicated in whatever of the many group identifications give sense to their lives. On these assumptions the task at hand is to decide whether, with respect to countrywide, constitutional issues, an individual or a national focus is most conducive to confront the liberal democratic tensions in part by empowering people to evaluate their group-based identifications without always delegitimizing them. To these ends, an individualist perspective will emphasize politics centered on the formulation and promotion of legal or morally sanctioned individual rights, while the national perspective will pre-eminently encourage cultural politics within national groupings (neither of them exclusively). In my view, a ground for preferring a nation-centered to an individual-centered orientation in the Canadian context is that there is more room within the former for active politics, including cultural politics, to nurture liberal and democratic national sentiments – not only in Quebec but among English-speaking Canadians and Aboriginal Peoples as well – than there is an analogous potential in the case of individualism. One reason for this is that "nationhood" is flexible, subject not just to different interpretations as a concept but to alternative constructions in actual life. The fact that nations are "imagined" in this context thus supports a nation-friendly orientation.

I suppose that among the conditions for something to be a nation are (a) that the people making it up have the will and the ability collectively to carry on large-scale transgenerational projects to preserve and promote that about their nation with which they identify (in the case of Quebec centrally, but not exclusively, its French language); (b) the realistic ability to be an independent state; and (c) the preparedness at least to entertain the possibility of seeking statehood if this is required to pursue national projects. Note that this is weaker than requiring the will to become a state, but stronger than mere capacity for statehood.[9] The Catholic Church and the United Church (the union of Presbyterians and Methodists in Canada) possess some measure of the first of these conditions, but not the second. The Province of Ontario or the region of Atlantic Canada possess the state potential, but while each of them, like the other Provinces and regions, possesses some historically inherited cultural traits distinguishing them from the others, with the possible exception of Newfoundland, in no province or region is there some one unique trait or cluster of traits with which a significant number of people identifies or identifies strongly enough to make its preservation a matter of seriously contemplating state sovereignty.[10]

Those Quebeckers who do seek sovereignty often appeal to a general right of nations to self-determination. Some federalists respond in the way referred to above by denying that Quebec constitutes a nation (thus unwittingly endorsing the general right) while others either deny this right or allow only a weak form of it, for instance, as articulated by Allen Buchanan.[11] It is unlikely that philosophical victory (somehow ascertained) regarding one of these positions could have much effect on the actual politics of sovereignty. Lucien Bouchard has already announced, with support from the Franco population of Quebec, that his government does not consider decisions of the Supreme Court about the legality of secession to be binding.[12] More germane to the question of secession is whether would-be seceding peoples have the ability and the will to form a state: hence the significance of this definitional aspect of nationhood.

Assuming both the ability of Quebec to function as an independent state and the preparedness to do this if it were deemed to be required to preserve national traditions, the question to ask is not whether they have a right to do so but whether this is a good idea. From a pragmatic, geopolitical point of view, I, for one, think there are reasons why this is not a good idea: Canada and Quebec sleep together (if fitfully) next to an economically and culturally powerful giant, and division into separate states could weaken each in their respective efforts to protect their economies and cultures in this circumstance. Setting such considerations aside, I wish to focus on some questions where normative and practical-political matters intersect. Being a multicultural society, Quebec statehood would be both morally repugnant and politically shaky to the extent that it was premised on intolerance toward Anglo- and Allophones.

Multiculturalism

The prospects for a tolerant Quebec nationalism would be doomed if Franco-Quebeckers regarded people of non-French origins or cultures as unworthy of Quebec nationality. That there are some Franco-Quebeckers who think this way there can be no doubt. The former head of the PQ, Jacques Parizeau, was thus charged by many for a comment blaming the failed referendum in part on Quebec's Allophone communities. However, the issue here is deeper than a question of intolerant attitudes on the part of some leaders. Tensions between Francophones and Allophones verging on mutual hostility are exacerbated by a siege mentality that seems to constitute part of the national identity of Franco-Quebeckers.

Beginning with the British military conquest of French forces in Quebec in 1759, and continuing through the 1960s when Quebec industry and many of its commercial enterprises were owned by Anglophones and English was the unofficial language of work, Franco-Quebeckers have seen themselves as dominated by English-speaking Canadians, thus putting their language, and through it their culture, at risk. The "quiet revolution" beginning in the 1970s to resist this and becoming increasingly loud (leading to the first election of the Parti Québecois in 1976) represented resistance to this erosion. However, during this period Quebec included people from Southern Europe, whose languages were neither French nor English and who wished their children to function in English to maximize their options in an English-speaking continent. Many Quebeckers accordingly came to see these Allophones as allies of the "enemy" Anglophones.

Quebec is no longer monolithically dominated by Anglo capital, however, and vigorous efforts by the PQ and also by the Provincial Liberal Party have arrested the erosion of French. This does not mean that the siege mentality and its concomitant suspicion of Allophones has been expunged from Quebec nationalism: national identities, like the subconscious phenomena Freud addressed, seem to function within their own time frame. But not everyone who shares Quebec national aspirations sees them as threatened by the allophone presence. Parizeau has resigned as head of the PQ not just because the referendum was lost, but because his comments were resented, among others by some sovereigntists themselves.

This latter group, including many church, labor, and social activists, participate with all other Quebec nationalists in wishing to preserve the French language and to support key Quebec political and legal institutions, such as parliamentary democracy and Napoleonic law. They do not require, in addition, that somebody's Native culture be foregone or that elements of a variety of cultures cannot be incorporated, through time, into Franco-Quebec traditions.[13] This has initiated a contest among Quebec nationalists between what might be called pluralist and antipluralist forces, into which Quebec intellectuals, drawing on the work of David Miller and Yael Tamir, among others, have introduced the notion of "civic" or "liberal" nationalism. According to this version of nationalism, loyalties of Quebeckers would be primarily as citizens bound together by shared commitment to liberal democratic political and legal institutions.[14] The weakness of civic nationalism in a pure form – not advanced by Miller or Tamir and found in Quebec by those whose commitment to sovereignty is weak at best – is that it risks losing touch with national sentiments altogether. Imagine a world where everyone spoke Esperanto while adhering to the values of civic nationalism. Neither nationalism nor nations would have a place in such a world. It is dubious that they would have a place in a world which only differed from this imaginary one in being divided into linguistic communities. To say that the two worlds would be different because languages are not just instrumental but carry cultural meanings would reintroduce ethnic nationalism. It is in recognition of this that some sovereigntist intellectuals now seek to combine liberal and ethnic nationalism or to supersede a dichotomy between them.[15]

Such a combination would clearly be impossible for the blood-based nationalist, as it would for a strong advocate of the melting pot. That it is possible (having rejected these conceptions) is evidenced by its being actual, among other places in English-speaking Canada and, increasingly, in the larger cities of Quebec itself. In addition to a requirement that immigrants should conduct their public affairs in either English or French, it is expected that they should encourage their children to learn the history of their adopted nations, and that where there are deeply divergent cultural attitudes pertinent to the public life of the adopted nation (for example, theocratic attitudes) the divergent attitudes must give way. But these requirements and expectations do not extend to other aspects of immigrant culture.

In one respect civic nationalism can be said to presuppose a measure of ethnic nationalism. According to the latter conception, people of the dominant national "ethnicity" should be tolerant of values and aspirations of minority ethnic groups and, even more strongly, prepared to allow themselves and their children to adopt some features of the minority cultures. These dispositions are in fact manifest, if unevenly, in Canada outside of Quebec and also in French-speaking Quebec, in each of which the dominant culture is quite different from that of previous generations in virtue of the influence of recent immigration. But what is different are aspects of the *ethnicity* of the dominant culture beyond a disposition to tolerance. What makes this tolerance substantial is not just that it is culturally internalized but that it opens up the pre-existing ethos to transformation by sympathetic contact with other cultures.

The conclusion of these observations is that Franco-Quebec nationalism and multiculturalism need not be in conflict. In practice, however, they have been set against one another partly because of the reluctance of immigrants in Quebec to assimilate to a culture which is itself a minority one in Canada, let alone North America, and partly because of Federalist political manipulation of multiculturalism. It is largely for this reason that I do not favor an orientation focused on ethnic diversity, which in the Canadian context means multiculturalism. Trudeau set himself vigorously against any form of Quebec nationalism. He also initiated the eventually successful effort to include a charter of individual rights and freedoms to the Constitution, and was the key force in making bilingualism and multiculturalism official Canadian policies.

These initiatives were seen by Quebec nationalists, not without some reason, as efforts to diffuse their project: French was to be one of the countrywide languages, thus muting its special place in Quebec culture; individuals were to be protected from group-based intrusions; Franco-Quebec culture was to be one of many (indeed hundreds) in the Canadian multicultural mosaic. There are, of course, other motives for promoting multiculturalism, and in agreement with the Quebec "pluralist" nationalists referred to above, I consider it most unfortunate that these things have been pitted against one another.

Still, to single out from the Canadian landscape its ethnic diversity and accordingly to prescribe that multiculturalism be the orienting perspective from which to address the current problems would be to adopt the viewpoint that Franco-Quebec, like English-speaking Canada and the Aboriginal group-ings, is no more than a large ethnic group. In addition to creating hostility in Quebec as a result of the history just mentioned, this is inaccurate. Accord-ing to the characterization of nationhood given above, a strong case can be made that Quebec, unlike, for instance, the East Asian communities in Van-couver, the Italian or West Indian communities in Toronto, or the Ukrain-ian communities in Winnipeg or Edmonton, qualifies as a nation.

It is true that Aboriginal peoples are geographically dispersed, some on reservation lands, some off reservation, and that they comprise a large number of different self-described nations: Dene, Micmac, Ojibwa, Cree, Mohawk, Seneca, Nisga'a, and so on. Also, the nature of "statehood" would likely be different for Aboriginal peoples granted full self-governance than it would be for people with European political traditions, and it could itself in-volve confederations, for instance, into something approaching originating linguistic groupings such as the Iroquois or Algonquin. Political plans for Aboriginal self-government have also been proposed, most recently in an impressively comprehensive report by a Royal Commission on Aboriginal Peoples co-chaired by a leading Native spokesperson (George Eramus) and in close dialogue with Aboriginal groups.[16] Some recent initiatives to pro-vide zones of Aboriginal self-government – the partition of the Northwest Territories to create Nunavut as an Inuit homeland and an (impending) treaty in British Columbia with the Nisga'a – offer models and make other initia-tives live options. The aspirations and efforts for preservation of their na-tional traditions and identities is truly remarkable among such beleaguered peoples.

The (Anglophone) Canadian Nation

Summarizing how, in my view, Canada outside of Quebec constitutes a na-tion will help to sharpen the notion of nationhood being employed and di-rect this chapter toward its major conclusion. One can safely say that at least into the 1960s the aspect of Canada, outside of Quebec, that commanded national loyalties was primarily if not exclusively its English linguistic herit-age and its political culture of "peace, order, and good government," also inherited from Britain, combined, in generations prior to mine, with a ritual attachment to the British crown. These associations were adumbrated with a frontier spirit, not of the rugged individualist variety but rather a special fondness for the natural beauty and expanse of the land and with a com-parative dimension differentiating Canada from the USA for being non-chauvinistic, less prone to violence, and more egalitarian.

With the exception of monarchist attachments, I believe that at least strong traces of these loyalties persist. Under pressure of neoliberal politics and US mass entertainment and news media, some of these things, and in particular egalitarianism considered as a motivating value, are threatened. Were egalitarian and related values to atrophy altogether, would this mean that Canadian identity had changed? On the viewpoint of one theorist of nationalism, Wayne Norman, probably not. He observes that national loyalties and identifications do not entail and often diverge from shared values.[17] This is one of those places where theoretical dichotomization fails to do justice to national realities. To some extent Norman is clearly right, otherwise it would be impossible for people with divergent values to share national loyalties: when Canadian politicians or notable figures perform laudably in international forums, I and my compatriots with different religious, political, or personal values alike feel a certain pride that we would not feel in the case of foreign representatives, just as we feel shame for ignoble performances. This does not, however, preclude some convergence of national loyalties and values. For example, when I and my conservative compatriots disagree about active support by our government for policies of global marketization, we may appeal to common national loyalties and berate each other for not understanding what is in Canadian national interests, but should this difference become too deep and merge with other differences, for instance, should the conservatives come to adopt militaristic stances as well, berating charges could turn to those of being "un-Canadian" (the scare quotes indicate that this is a nationally foreign phrase), pawns of international capital in the one case or of international socialism, or perhaps today, of social democracy in the other.

I speculate that most values are not identity-determining, but exceptions are those values that justify public economic, political, or cultural policies, where "justifying" in this context means that they are appealed to for popular justification of such policies.[18] To the extent, then, that values and identifications may affect one another, we see a contest wherein either Canadian national identifications prompt rebellion against threats to things like egalitarian policies, or give way to them, thus leading to a   situation (often, but erroneously, claimed by foreign visitors to Canada already to obtain) where Canadian and US national identities are largely indistinguishable.

A different and also complex problem concerns non-Anglo-originated communities, about which two questions are pertinent. What stance toward them is implicated in Canadian national identity? And what, if any, Canadian identifications do they, themselves, harbor? Full answers to these questions would take an enormous space, and in any case extends beyond my sociological expertise. One need only read the histories or listen to the stories of almost any Canadian of non-Anglo origin to conclude that there has been and still is a stream of Anglo, indeed, Anglo-Protestant, chauvinism, not excluding racism and antisemitism by virtue of which large and long-standing parts of the population are not considered true Canadians.

Against this stance are the attitudes referred to above ranging from toleration to inclusive adaptation of people from a diversity of linguistic, religious, and cultural backgrounds, where toleration or inclusion are themselves defining characteristics of Canadian identity. Such attitudes are reflected both among those who favor multiculturalism for advocating the protection of a variety of cultures and among critics who fear what they see as a ghettoizing tendency of multiculturalism. As one approaches the inclusive pole of this range of attitudes, Anglo culture is not given pride of place per se, though certain political institutions and values that historically accompanied it are retained, and the English language is seen instrumentally, as a lingua franca. Unlike the chauvinistic sentiment, this one is compatible with people of non-Anglo origins sharing a Canadian national identity.

The relation of Quebec to Anglo-Canadian national identity is problematic in yet another way. A common bumper sticker that began appearing after the 1994 election of the PQ reads, "My Canada Includes Quebec." In some cases this slogan is no more than a mean-spirited threat, which, whether intended or not, could only fuel the siege mentality in Quebec. Indeed, hostility to Quebec nationalism has itself taken on the character of an analogous siege mentality on the part of many in English-speaking Canada to the extent that anti-Quebec sentiment is part of their own national identity. Such sentiment, however, is not hegemonic. The bumper slogan no doubt also expresses a widespread sentiment, according to which many Canadians think division of the country would be an end not only to a state but also to a nation: the English-speaking Canadian nation for which cohabitation with Quebec is an important symbol.

Some federalist Franco-Quebeckers seem to harbor a reciprocal sentiment; however, it is my impression (gained largely from interaction with Franco-Quebec colleagues and students when I taught there for a term a few years ago and reinforced by the strength of the "oui" side in the 1995 referendum) that the reciprocal attitude is not shared by the majority of Franco-Quebeckers. Separation from the rest of Canada would be accomplished without the slightest diminution of their sense of Quebec nationhood. This makes for the unfortunate situation where Canadian national identity partly demands a forced marriage. Moreover, the dominant alternative attitude, especially prominent among supporters of the Reform Party, that favors "letting Quebec go to get rid of it" is even worse, articulating as it does the open hostility that many Quebeckers fear.

"Tri"-Nationalism

One function of an orientation is to suggest criteria that legal and political institutional solutions must meet. The national orientation endorsed here invites one to seek solutions within which national projects in each of

Quebec and Canada, outside of it, can simultaneously be pursued. This means that Quebec requires a high degree of autonomy over cultural matters and over those economic and foreign policy matters that have a significant bearing on the preservation of its language and culture, but that this not be purchased at the expense of such provincial or regional balkanization of the rest of Canada that it loses the ability to maintain its own national identity. Sovereigntists claim that this condition can only be met by separation. Canadians and students of the Canadian scene will recognize as an alternative one of the several plans for "asymmetrical federalism" advanced during the constitutional debates, whereby a single state is composed of national units, as coherent within themselves as they wish, but with differential political powers and legal entitlements.[19]

Of these options, asymmetrical federalism has two advantages: it would preserve that aspect of each nation's identity which includes state partnership with the other nation stronger, as mentioned, in Anglo-Canada than in Quebec; and it would facilitate cooperation in the face of continental and global economic threats. Asymmetrical federalism, however, is not entirely at odds with the sovereigntist option. In order for it to function well, such federalism would not only have to be entered into but also maintained voluntarily; hence it would have to include provisions for secession. Also, the sovereigntist option of the 1995 referendum was probably realistic in not exactly calling for complete separation. Rather, it would empower the provincial government of a sovereign Quebec to negotiate a new form of association with the rest of Canada in some ways modeled on plans for the European Union. (That asymmetrical federalism and nuanced sovereignty, though surely different options, are not entirely antithetical is evidenced by the similarity of each to an earlier proposal, initially made by the Parti Québecois, for "sovereignty association," which, like a reversible figure, could be seen from either of these two directions.)

As the first ministers who drafted the Charlottetown Accord found out, it is easier to draw up institutional plans than to secure public support for them. The same is true of any plan for asymmetrical federalism or for qualified separation. General public acceptance is needed as a prerequisite for any such proposal. From the national orientation endorsed in this chapter, this means that two aspects of Anglo-Canadian and Franco-Quebec national identities must be overcome: the dimensions in which the national identity of each is constructed in part by seeing the other as an enemy and those aspects which inhibit full participation of Allophone communities in the national life of Quebec or of Anglo-Canada. How might these attitudes be at least marginalized in the relevant national communities? Of course, as in the case of any effort to transform values, there is no easy answer to this question. In general, those with some access to means of cultural production – writers, teachers, journalists, religious leaders, and so on – need to nurture whatever charitable sentiments already exist in their communities. I would, however, like to urge that one part of the solution, and it is an essential part, is to insist upon a "tri"-national and not just a binational approach (where the scare quotes are to register recognition of the multinational nature of Aboriginal peoples). Some academics were urging this prior to the Charlottetown Accord,[20] and though the Accord resisted reference to nations, it did, as indicated earlier, highlight Aboriginal concerns in a new and positive way. The report of the Royal Commission on Aboriginal Peoples (issued in November, 1996, but as yet largely not acted on) made detailed recommendations in favor of Aboriginal self-government and documented a case for its justice and feasibility. These initiatives should be pressed.

That anti-aboriginal values and concomitant activities exist in each of the other nations, there can be no doubt. However, these negative values do not, or at least do not yet, form part of their respective national identities in the way, for example, that they have in societies which pursued genocidal policies toward Aboriginal populations more proudly and overtly than in Canada/ Quebec. Moreover, historically, provincial governments have been more dismissive of Aboriginal needs than the federal government, which has, at least sometimes and in some ways been protective of them. This is another reason to resist a Provincial orientation in addressing the national question in Canada, and it suggests that Canadians qua Canadian citizens are more sympathetic toward Aboriginal peoples than they are qua provincial citizens.[21]

Native claims for redress of past wrongs, for land rights, and for humane treatment remain alive on the political agenda everywhere in Canada, despite the fact that Aboriginal peoples account for only about 3 percent of the total population. The reason for this is mainly that Native people enjoy such popular moral support that citizens will not let the issue go away. This support is reinforced by a growing international awareness of Aboriginal issues and the sometimes successful appeal of Aboriginal peoples to international bodies such as the World Court.

With the exception of the Charlottetown Accord's recognition of an "inherent right to Native self-government," stances toward Aboriginal peoples in the constitutional debates so far have been less than constructive. In Quebec, despite the relatively generous legislation regarding Native entitlements of that province, the announced refusal of the Cree to leave the Confederation has been met with hostility on the part of separatists; while federalist political leaders have cynically and ominously played "the Indian card" to intimidate Quebec. A tri-national perspective, as envisaged here, would tap popular sympathy for Native peoples, attempt to reinforce it by highlighting the way that Aboriginal peoples have legitimate, if largely thwarted, national aspirations, and try to effect a union of Quebeckers and Canadians from the rest of the country to address with First Nation and Inuit peoples the moral and territorial problems they face in common.

The claim that such common efforts would help to break down attitudes of mutual animosity among Canada's nations is based on the assumption that people who work together toward a common goal and with some shared values grow together as a result.[22] In keeping with recent viewpoints on the origins of racism, I suggest that the abysmal treatment of indigenous peoples of the Americas by our European ancestors fueled a pernicious disposition that persists as a source of racism and intolerance generally – comparable in terms of its tenacity and depth of grasp to sexism.[23] The suggested project would directly confront this source of intolerance and, in striving finally to put an end to it, have desired cultural effects beyond the attitudes of Ango- and Franco-Canadians/Quebeckers toward Aboriginal peoples and toward each other to include more tolerant attitudes toward people from other ethnic origins as well.

Addressing the Aboriginal question is not just a matter for Anglo- and Francophones, but concerns people from all of the country's ethnic groups, who should be no less engaged in this project than those of English and French origin.[24] In this connection, it is worth noting that while nations, races, and ethnic groups are importantly different from one another, national chauvinism, racism, and ethnic chauvinism are, if not identical in origin or character, kindred phenomena. It is, thus, no surprise to find the rightwing in Canada opposed alike to Aboriginal rights, multiculturalism, and Quebec self-determination.

Not to count entirely on altruism, two further motivations for a joint approach to the situation of First Nation and Inuit peoples suggest themselves. One of these is that given the high level of organization and the militancy of these peoples, this problem *must* be addressed. Moreover, it must be addressed in a way acceptable to the Aboriginal peoples themselves. Unacceptable alternatives would not only create more painful and (as in recent times) armed conflict, but justified international censure of a relatively small country, which in today's world can hardly afford it. Regarding specifically confederation-related problems, it should not be forgotten that Aboriginal interventions have twice had major impacts and upset the plans of white politicians: first when Elijah Harper blocked the Meech Lake Accord and then when Native band leaders declared themselves unprepared to support the Charlottetown Accord.

Yet another motivation concerns the land claims. At first sight, final resolution of these claims looks to be an impossibility, thanks to their location and extent. However, solving this problem may well be easier from an Aboriginal perspective than from a European one. The reason for this is that sovereignty is regarded differently in Aboriginal traditions, where there are ways that it can simultaneously be retained and shared, than in European traditions, which associate it with exclusive use.[25] Perhaps solutions to problems affecting the land claim issue drawing upon these alternative conceptions of sovereignty can be transposed for use in confronting problems of sovereignty between the remaining two nations.

Actors

I wish now to return to the actor side of the Canadian landscape. Who from Anglo-Canada and Quebec are to work together and with Aboriginal peoples to seek rapprochement among the land's national groupings? As rejection of the Charlottetown Accord shows, there exists among the citizenry a strong democratic impulse. According to polls taken at the time, a major source of resistance to the Accord was anger not just at the top-down way it was prepared and presented, but at the unresponsiveness of federal and provincial political leaders generally. In Canada, as in too many other places in the world proclaiming themselves democratic, people are frustrated at their lack of power to decide their own fates even within institutions designed to facilitate this. So popular democratic expression typically takes the form of negative voting just to punish politicians and governments.

The alternatives to this sort of democratic activity – which is obviously inadequate to the task here being addressed – divide into two categories: to seek undemocratic solutions or to deepen democratic ones. When politicians in Canada have been the primary actors, they have sometimes acted as representatives of provincial interests (and regarding federal politicians, power-brokers among them), or they have attempted, as in the Charlottetown meetings, to stand above such politics and to act as a tribunal making judgments about what is in the best interests of the country. In neither role have solutions been democratically sought.

When provinces act as if they were interest groups, with narrowly defined and usually exclusively economic interests, entering into power-political negotiation, we have a sort of political market. As in the case of an economic market, the result is often unpredictable and seldom optimal even regarding the players' narrowly defined interests individually considered, let along regarding the larger body politic. The Charlottetown attempt was unable to subdue the provincial political market, to which excessive power was devolved. More significantly, popular rejection of the Accord showed that this approach can only work if it is combined with effective democratic input (thus vitiating its necessity) or dictatorially.

This leaves democratic alternatives – the citizens themselves. But simply calling on the citizenry to address these problems of national reconciliation is a strategy unlikely to succeed. In fact, some such strategy has been tried in Canada when, shortly after the Meech Lake episode, the federal government set up the commission charged with initiating local discussions in living-rooms and workplaces throughout the country. While some interesting sociological information concerning Canadian values was acquired by this means, no convergence of views about solutions to the problems of confederation was discovered. Moreover, neither provincial nor federal government leaders seems to have heeded one of the concerns on which there was strong consensus, namely that countrywide social services not be diminished.

Just as referenda, majority voting, direct participation, or other ways that democracy might be exercised are sometimes efficient for this purpose and sometimes not, depending on the context, so are such attempts at local consensus building. The problems of national reconciliation are at once too multifaceted and too grand in scope for such a direct appeal to citizen input to be effective. One possible alternative would be for citizens to participate in selecting and mandating delegates to a constitutional convention. Such an admittedly large undertaking could take one of several forms and its legal force could be more or less dramatic. But in any case, for it to be a truly democratic exercise, such a convention would have to be preceded by widespread and informed debate and discussion about such matters as the designation of constituencies and options that might be put before such a convention. Similar considerations pertain to any analogous new effort at constitutional reform.

One locus for democratic input to such a venture is citizen activity in and through non-governmental organizations. This sort of activity was especially evident around the time of the Charlottetown Accord in the mobilization of the large number of popularly based groups referred to earlier in the chapter. Not only were the groups individually active to this end, but they also conjoined their efforts through a coordinating organization, the Ottawa-based Action Canada Network.

To my way of thinking, it is through such groups that citizen participation in the task addressed here is initially best pursued. Each of the labor, women's, environmental, municipal, anti-poverty, and other such groups in Canada outside Quebec have analogues within Quebec, with whom they already share some common interests. To these might be added such things as educational or religious institutions, which, while not specifically issue-oriented, are important organized sites of citizen participation. In each of Anglo-Canada and Quebec such organizations, individually or in coalitions, should make contact with their counterparts in the other nation for the purpose of projecting models and working out strategies starting from matters on which they can agree. Since the groups all have organizational structures and are independent of government, they could act unilaterally to initiate such interchanges.

One hopes that among such groups' shared concerns is that Anglo- and Franco-Canada finally discharge their obligation to right the historic wrongs committed against our Native populations. The recommendations of the Royal Commission on Aboriginal peoples provide an excellent occasion and a starting place. Jointly pursued efforts of people from all three of the country's national communities to address the Canada/Quebec question specifically from the point of view of restoring dignity and equal partnership to our Aboriginal peoples would have several advantages. At the very least these would provide forums for self-education: an undertaking for which the six volumes of the Commission Report provides invaluable resources. They would also strengthen the ability of non-governmental groups to articulate political preferences and to apply pressure to politicians and political parties. They might even provide the impetus and some crucial advance thinking for another run at constitutional reform, this time from the bottom up.

Political Theory

Political theorists, philosophers in particular, do not (perhaps mercifully) constitute a social movement, but some of their students, people influenced by the fruit of their research, and some theorists themselves are to be found within the organizations of people whose initiative in constitutional matters is entreated in this chapter. This means that theorists might contribute to the prescribed democratic project from "within the cave" in the engaged sense described by Michael Walzer.[26] In this chapter I have alluded to five relevant topics addressed by political theorists pertinent to a national perspective: civic and ethnic nationalism, the notion of nationhood, the right of nations to secession, the nature of nationalism, and the construction of nations.

Theorizing from within the democratic cave of the current situation of Canada/Quebec can make useful contributions with respect to each of these topics: combining or, more ambitiously, superseding civic and ethnic nationalism; conceptualizing nationhood in a way that does not pit nations against individuals and ethnic groups; identifying acceptable conditions for national self-determination; and participating in the normative dimension of national identity construction and hence of the nation itself. These last-mentioned tasks pertain to the chapter's major prescription in favor of nationally joint campaigns finally to right the wrongs committed against Canada's Aboriginal peoples and to address their contemporary concerns.

I suggested that there exists a general sympathy for these concerns on the part of Canadians, but also that neither of the dominant traditions in Quebec and in Canada outside of Quebec is free of intolerance even extending to racism. The benign attitudes give normative philosophical intervention a foothold, but to be effective the philosophers must come to grips with what Charles Mills (himself a Jamaican Canadian) calls the "racial contract." Mills shows how our political philosophical ancestors – Locke, Hume, Kant, Mill, et al. – were complicit in an agreement whereby rights and norms of justice applicable to white Europeans and their colonial progeny were carefully denied to others, and in particular to Native inhabitants of colonialized lands.[27] What better contribution to nation-constructing in Canada/Quebec could there be than for its political theorists to expose and tear up or (if they are contractarians) rewrite this contract?

Notes

1   This contribution incorporates parts of an earlier essay, "The Canada/Quebec Conundrum: A Trinational Perspective," *Constitutional Forum* 8 (1997): 119–29. In preparing both the earlier essay and the current one, I have profited from help by Mel Watkins and Shin Imai.
2   The supplementary volume no. 22 of *The Canadian Journal of Philosophy, Rethinking Nationalism*, ed. Jocelyne Couture, Kai Nielsen, and Michel Seymour (University of Calgary Press, 1996), includes an impressively thorough bibliography of recent writings on nationalism, as well as a good cross-section of differing political philosophical approaches to it.

An interesting exchange regarding nationalism between Francis Fukuyama (who announced the end of history) and Ghia Nodia and Shlomo Avineri (who see the announcement as premature) is in Larry Diamond and Marc F. Plattner, eds., *Nationalism, Ethnic Conflict, and Democracy* (Baltimore: Johns Hopkins University Press, 1994), pp. 3–31. Fukuyama sees Quebec as a test case for his thesis. Being a liberal democratic society within another liberal democratic society, Quebec national aspirations should, on his view, whither.
3   I see defeat of the Accord as significant because it marked a shift in the conduct of democratic politics and public attitudes toward such conduct. In all modern democracies, political leaders, governmental and otherwise, are expected both to represent the wishes of those to whom they are ultimately responsible (legislators with respect to voters, party leaders to party members, union officials to the rank and file, and so on) and also to act independently of such wishes in their members' objective interests and in that of the body politic as a whole, the balance between these two expectations varying polity by polity.

In Canada the emphasis has traditionally been on the paternalistic side, and has functioned best when political leaders have formulated policy in consociational-like negotiations among themselves. Meanwhile, Canadian publics in the mainstream have typically passively accepted such leadership, if not always enthusiastically. It is hard to imagine a more complete consociational agreement than the Charlottetown Accord, and yet this was not only rejected but rejected partly as a result of active popular-level organization, as people from all constituencies broke ranks with their representatives. The result has been a confused mix of efforts to replace older political habits with more directly responsive government, though so far this has mainly been exercised in a demagogic or populist way by conservative political parties playing to short-term, localized preferences, and by increasingly strained attempts by the Federal and some provincial governments to negotiate in the former way (as in a current effort to forge a "social union" governing distribution of social services), but this time without support from extragovernment political leaders and in the face of strong public cynicism.

4   This interactive approach is called "wide reflective equilibrium" by some neo-Rawlsian political philosophers. See Norman Daniels, "Reflective Equilibrium and Archimedean Points," *The Canadian Journal of Philosophy* 10 (1980): 81–103.

5   The theoretical views informing Taylor's several public interventions are collected in his *Reconciling the Solitudes* (Toronto: Queen's-McGill Universities Press, 1993), see chs 7, 8, and 9. One of these, "Shared and Divergent Values," is also reproduced in the Watts/Brown collection cited in note 19 below. Kymlicka has published several commentaries on specific issues of the constitutional debate in *Network Analysis*, an Ottawa-based publication dedicated to this topic. His liberal individualistic defense of nationalism is in *Liberalism, Community, and Culture* (Oxford: Clarendon Press, 1989), ch. 8. A paper going a bit further than Kymlicka in giving a liberal justification for secession is by Guy Laforest, "Le Québec et l'éthique liberale de la sécession," *Philosophiques, Numéro Spécial: Une nation peut-elle se donne la constitution de son choix?* 19 (Autumn 1992): 199–214.

6   Russell Hardin expresses an extreme version of the view that national and other such group identifications are unavoidably exclusionary and, indeed, violence-prone in *One for All: The Logic of Group Conflict* (Princeton: Princeton University Press, 1995); I criticize this view in a critical review of Hardin's book in *The Canadian Journal of Philosophy* 27 (December 1997): 571–94, and more generally in "Group Hatreds and Democracy," in Daniel Avnon and Avner de Shallit, eds., *Liberalism and its Practice* (New York: Routledge, 1991), pp.127–45.

7   See Taylor's alternative to what he takes as Parizeau's stance toward minority communities in Quebec: "Les ethnies dans une société 'normale'," *La Presse* 21/22 (November 1995).

8   Each dimension of this debate is nicely summarized by Will Kymlicka in his text *Contemporary Political Philosophy: An Introduction* (Oxford: Clarendon Press, 1990), ch. 6, to be sure, from his nuanced, individualist perspective.

9   David Copp usefully cites as indices of national identifications that one feels pride or shame in actions or events considered central to one's nation (as opposed to simply approving or disapproving of them as one might toward actions of another nation): "Do Nations Have the Right of Self-determination?" in Stanley French, ed., *Philosophers Look at Canadian Confederation* (Montreal: The Canadian Philosophical Association, 1979), pp. 71–96. His complex definition is largely backward-looking, appealing in part to nationals' identification with a history and tradition. The characterization I employ agrees, but adds the proactive dimension of a will to carry national projects into the future.

David Miller, *On Nationality* (Oxford: Clarendon Press, 1995), writes in terms of shared values in a way that Norman rightly resists, but adds the useful notion that one way nations are thought of by their members as active is through national representatives. While Copp requires that those making up a nation must aspire to statehood, Miller refers just to an aspiration to be self-determining (p. 19). In my view this correctly distinguishes between national self-determination and separate statehood. I take it that an aspiration to a high degree of self-determination must exist for something to be a nation, as must the (objective) ability to be a state and the (subjective) will to become one if this is required to satisfy the aspiration to protect and preserve that about the nation which is taken as important.

In general, I think that enough theorists have thought about the notion of nationhood long enough that we are very close to having an adequate and full-blown definition.

10   The criteria of will and ability interact, since geographic, economic, and demographic conditions place limits on what could be a state, even if a population wanted to become one, but at the same time determined popular will can compensate to a large extent for deficiencies in such conditions. It is thus that Newfoundland, though "objectively" less well suited to statehood than Alberta or British Columbia, is a more likely candidate than either of these provinces, notwithstanding occasional declarations of separatist sentiments in the latter (usually, I believe, made more as expressions of antagonism, sometimes justified, toward central Canadian obliviousness to Western needs than of actual intentions to seek independent statehood).

11   Allen Buchanan, *Secession: The Morality of Political Divorce from Fort Sumter to Lithuania and Quebec* (Boulder, CO: Westview Press, 1991). Buchanan's view is weaker than that preferred by pro-sovereigntists because, while he admits a right to national self-determination, he does not think that this extends to a claim right (or even a presumptive claim right) to secession; rather, secessionists must demonstrate that they suffer wrongs that can only be escaped within separate statehood.

12   Early in 1998 the Supreme Court of Canada delivered a "Reference" on the question of whether unilateral secession of Quebec would be constitutional (determining that it would not, but that if a clear majority of Quebeckers opted for secession, the rest of Canada would be well advised to negotiate with Quebec over the issue). Prior to release of this decision, Bouchard announced that Quebec would not consider itself bound by it. The content of this reference, Quebec's *ex ante* reaction, and the escalation of political intervention by the Court have been matters of debate among analysts of and participants in the constitutional controversies. See the essays in Barbara Cameron, ed., *The Supreme Court, Democracy, and Quebec Secession* (Toronto: James Lorimer, 2000), including a contribution of mine, "The Court on Democracy and Secession."

13   In 1994 a coalition of social movements, community, and labor groups published a Charter after several years of hearings across the province and endorsed by more than 300 secular and religious organizations, many of them large and mainstream. Section 19 calls for recognition and preservation of Quebec's "multiethnic and multicultural" nature, which is seen as compatible with the affirmation of a common national identity characterized by "the French language, democratic values, and distinct social and political institutions," *La Charte d'un Québec Populaire*, published by Solidarité populaire Québec, 1600 ave De Lorimier, Montreal, Québec (H2K 3W5), 1994. A similar sentiment is expressed in a declaration issued just before the October 1995 referendum by a group calling itself "Intellectuels pour la souveraineté," *La Presse*, December 15, 1995.

14   Yael Tamir, *Liberal Nationalism* (Princeton: Princeton University Press, 1993);

Miller, *On Nationality*. A collection of essays largely organized around the viability of civic nationalism (or, "liberal nationalism" as Yael labels the viewpoint) is François Blais, Guy Laforest, and Diane Lamoureux, dirs., *Libéralismes et nationalismes* (Les Presses de l'Université Laval, 1995).

15 See Couture, Nielsen, and Seymour, "Liberal Nationalism Both Cosmopolitan and Rooted," in Couture et al., *Rethinking Nationalism*, pp. 579–662. And see Dominique Schnapper, "Beyond the Opposition: Civic Nation versus Ethnic Nation," in the same collection, pp. 219–34.

16 The Commission developed and justified its recommendations in an impressively documented, six-volume document, *Report of the Royal Commission on Aboriginal Peoples* (Ottawa: Canadian Communication Group Publishing, 1996).

17 Wayne Norman, "The Ideology of Shared Values: A Myopic Vision of Unity in the Multination State," in *I* Joseph H. Carens, ed., *Is Quebec Nationalism Just?: Perspectives from Anglophone Canada* (Toronto: McGill-Queen's University Press, 1995), pp. 137–59.

18 Each of the Federal Liberal Party, the Reform Party, and the Provincial Tory parties in Alberta and Ontario currently pursues neoliberal policies (downsizing government, tax cuts for the rich, diminution of social services, free-market economics, and the like) with the difference that the Liberals accompany their policies with egalitarian rhetoric, while the others are explicitly anti-egalitarian. Polls show the federal appeal still better received, but slipping.

19 An example is Alan C. Cairns, "Constitutional Change and the Three Equalities," in Ronald L. Watts and Douglas M. Brown, eds., *Options for a New Canada* (Toronto: University of Toronto Press, 1991), pp. 77–102.

20 One such intervention was a statement composed by a group of Toronto-based political theorists, "Three Nations in a Delicate State," and published among other places in *The Toronto Star*, February 4, 1992. See, too, a postmortem of the Charlottetown vote by members of this group, including a contribution by myself, in *Canadian Forum* 71 (December 1992).

21 On this topic, see, Tony Hall, "Aboriginal Issues and the New Political Map of Canada," in J.L. Granatstein and Kenneth McNaught, eds., *"English Canada" Speaks Out* (Toronto: Doubleday Canada, 1991), pp. 122–40.

22 I take it as a hopeful sign that intellectuals who actively intervene in the Constitutional debates and from a variety of political and national orientations concur on the importance of addressing the aboriginal question. Some examples are: Tony Hall, "Aboriginal Issues"; Michel Seymour, "Le nationalism Québécois et la question autochtone," in Michel Sarra-Bouret, ed., *Manifeste des intellectuels pour la souveraineté* (Montréal: Fides, 1995), pp. 75–99; Henri Dorion, "Au delà de la dialectique majorité/minorité: la voie non gouvernmentale à la convivialité," in Jean Lafontant, ed., *L'état et les minorities* (Sanit-Boniface, Man.: Les Éditions du Blé, 1992), pp. 187–99; and Peter Russell, "Aboriginal Nationalism and Quebec Nationalism: Reconciliation Through Fourth World Decolonization," *Constitutional Forum* 8 (Summer 1997): 110–18.

23 The connection between racism and colonial subjugation of aboriginal peoples is made by nearly all the recent authors concerning themselves with the origin and nature of racism. Examples may be found in Charles W. Mills, *The Racial Contract* (Ithaca: Cornell University Press, 1997), Theodore Allen, *The Invention*

of the White Race (New York: Verso, 1994), and Kenan Malik, *The Meaning of Race: Race, History, and Culture in Western Society* (New York: Routledge, 1998).

24   Ross Poole makes this point regarding immigrants of non-British origin in Australia with respect to Aborigines there in "National Identity, Multiculturalism, and Aboriginal Rights: An Australian Perspective," in Couture et al., *Rethinking Nationalism*, pp. 407–38. I consider it non-accidental that Poole's perspective is similar to the one I am urging (without opposing either individual rights or multiculturalism, he prescribes a nation- based orientation), since a core motivation of the two endeavors is the same, namely, to promote justice for our respective Aboriginal peoples.

25   James Tully discusses alternative conceptions of sovereignty in Canada in his *Strange Multiplicity: Constitutionalism in an Age of Diversity* (Cambridge: Cambridge University Press, 1995). Examples from Aboriginal literature of the special place afforded the land in this culture may be found in Geary Hobson, ed., *The Remembered Earth: An Anthology of Contemporary American Indian Literature* (University of New Mexico Press, 1980); see in particular Paula Gunn Allen's "Iyani: It Goes This Way," pp. 191–4.

26   Michael Walzer, "Philosophy and Democracy," in John S. Nelson, ed., *What Should Philosophy Be Now?* (State University of New York Press, 1983), pp. 75–99.

27   Mills, *The Racial Contract*, see chap. 1 for a summary of the argument.

11

Love Care, and Women's Dignity: The Family as a Privileged Community

Martha Nussbaum

Giribala, at the age of fourteen, then started off to make her home with her husband. Her mother put into a bundle the pots and pans that she would be needing. Watching her doing that, Aulchand remarked, "Put in some rice and lentils too. I've got a job at the house of the *babu*. Must report to work the moment I get back. . ."

Giribala picked up the bundle of rice, lentils, and cooking oil and left her village, walking a few steps behind him. He walked ahead, and from time to time asked her to walk faster, as the afternoon was starting to fade.

Mahasweta Devi, "Giribala", 1982[1]

Accused Md. Jahangir Alam was found after marriage to be a ruthless, cruel and greedy person. Accused petitioner Selema Khatun is mother and accused petitioner Md. Solaiman is younger brother of accused Jahangir Alam. Accused petitioner Thanda Mia is father and accused petitioner Abdul Mannan is maternal uncle of accused Jahangir Alam. Accused petitioner Md. Hashim is a close friend of accused Jahangir Alam. All the accused persons in collusion with each other started torturing complainant Ferdousi Begum both mentally and physically after the marriage with a view to squeeze money (as dowry) from the guardians of complainant Ferdousi Begum. . . . Finally on 30.9.85, accused Jahangir Alam asked his wife Ferdousi Begum to bring 20" Coloured T.V. Set, Radio, Wrist Watch and cash money amounting to Taka 25,000 from her brothers. . . . Complainant Ferdousi Begum expressed her inability to go to her brothers with such demand. At this stage all the accused persons . . .became furious and started beating Ferdousi Begum with rod, lathi, etc. At one stage accused Md. Jahangir Alam caught hold of her throat and attempted to murder her by throttling. Accused Jahangir Alam also kicked her several times and caught her hair and pulled her down on the floor, pressed her and dragged her out of the house. Then all the accused persons snatched away her gold ornaments from the body and left her with one cloth in the courtyard where she lost her senses due to inhuman beating and torturing by the accused persons for the whole day. As a result of this beating by all the accused persons she lost hearing capacity of her right ear. Both her legs were so severely injured that she felt difficulty in walking. . . .The spinal chord showed traumatic collapse in X ray and dislocation of bone was also found in the X ray.

Salema Khatoon vs. State (F. H. M. Habibur Rahman J.)[2]

A Home for Love and Violence

Women are givers of love and care.[3] In virtually all cultures women's traditional role involves the rearing of children and care for home, husband, and family. These roles have been associated with some important moral virtues, such as altruistic concern, responsiveness to the needs of others, and a willingness to sacrifice one's own interests for those of others. They have also been associated with some distinctive moral abilities, such as the ability to perceive the particular situation and needs of others and the ability to reason resourcefully about how to meet those needs. These virtues and abilities need to find a place in any viable universalist feminism. Feminists have long criticized male universalist theories for their alleged neglect of these important values, and have frequently argued that universal approaches based on liberal ideas of dignity and equality cannot make sufficient room for them. They have worried that liberal theories of justice would turn havens of love and care into collections of isolated mutually disinterested atomic individuals, each bargaining against the others with a view to personal advancement.

On the other hand, it would be difficult to deny that the family has been a, if not the, major site of the oppression of women. Love and care do exist in families. So too do domestic violence, marital rape, child sexual abuse, undernutrition of girls, unequal health care, unequal educational opportunities, and countless more intangible violations of dignity and equal personhood. In many instances, the damage women suffer in the family takes a particular form: the woman is treated not as an end in herself, but as an adjunct or instrument of the needs of others, as a mere reproducer, cook, cleaner, sexual outlet, caretaker, rather than as a source of agency and worth in her own right. The cases in my epigraphs show this tendency clearly. For Giribala's husband, she was as a domestic servant, rather than a person.[4] Her role was to walk a few paces behind, carrying the lentils. For the family of Jahangir Alam, Ferdousi Begum was little more than a device to extract money from her brothers; her bodily well-being was worth less to them than a 20" color TV set, a radio, a wristwatch, and a small amount of cash.

Family, then, can mean love; it can also mean neglect, abuse, and degradation. Moreover, the family reproduces what it contains. Just as it is often a school of virtue, so too (and frequently at the same time) it is a school of sex inequality, nourishing attitudes that not only make new families in the image of the old, but also influence the larger social and political world. (This influence goes in both directions, clearly, since the family and the emotions it contains are shaped by laws and institutions regarding such matters as marital rape, child custody, children's rights, and women's economic opportunities.) It is implausible that people will treat women as ends in themselves and as equals in social and political life if they are brought up, in the family, to see women as things for their use.[5]

The family is frequently romanticized as a home of virtues that rise above mere justice, a "haven in a heartless world." But, like all forms of community, the family is typically hierarchical: it contains asymmetries of power and opportunity. When contemporary theorists praise "community" and criticize "individualism," they sometimes seem oblivious to the fact that communities are composed of individuals, and that they do not treat all individuals equally. If we are inclined to give a group such as the family special privileges, we ought to consider the damage done to people when things go badly there. Even without settling the question whether the conventional family is inherently patriarchal, we can see that it frequently is, and that it has done great harm to women and girls. If we keep Giribala and Ferdousi Begum firmly in mind, we will be prevented from swathing injustice in a rosy glow of romance.

In this chapter I shall confront the questions posed by the presence of the family, and the roles it constructs for women, at the heart of a society that is attempting to promote human capabilities – prominently including the capability for various forms of love and care. I shall argue that a liberal approach to the family that treats each individual as an end is in no sense incompatible with the appropriate valuation of love and care; indeed, it actually provides the best framework within which both to value care and to provide it with the necessary critical scrutiny. By thinking of people's affiliative needs, as well as their needs for the whole range of the human capabilities, we can best ask questions about how the family should be shaped by public policy, and what other affiliative institutions public policy has reason to support. I shall argue that an approach aimed at promoting "human capabilities" provides an even better framework for analysis, here, than standard liberal proceduralist approaches, since it is explicitly committed to a prominent place for love and care as important goals of social planning and as major moral abilities – within a life governed by the critical use of practical reason. At the same time, the capabilities approach avoids a common defect of at least some liberal theories, in that it does not rule any institution "private" and so off-limits for purposes of public scrutiny. Individuals have privacy rights, in the form of associative and decisional liberties. But there is no institution that, as such, has privacy rights that prevent us from asking how law and public policy have already shaped that institution, and how they might do so better. Personal liberty is a central social goal, whether or not it is exercised inside the home; personal dignity and integrity are also central social goals, no matter where the threat to them is located.

Capabilities: Each Family Member as End

In order to reflect about the contribution of the family, we need to set before us some of the central capabilities that it is plausible to think a just society will promote for all its citizens. Let me therefore introduce my own account of these, to give the argument a set of parameters to which we can refer in the subsequent discussion:

The central human capabilities

1   Life: being able to live to the end of a human life of normal length; not dying prematurely, or before one's life is so reduced as to be not worth living.
2   Bodily health: being able to have good health, including reproductive health; to be adequately nourished; to have adequate shelter.
3   Bodily integrity: being able to move freely from place to place; to be secure against violent assault, including sexual assault and domestic violence; having opportunities for sexual satisfaction and for choice in matters of reproduction.
4   Senses, imagination, and thought: being able to use the senses, to imagine, think, and reason – and to do these things in a "truly human" way, a way informed and cultivated by an adequate education, including, but by no means limited to, literacy and basic mathematical and scientific training; being able to use imagination and thought in connection with experiencing and producing works and events of one's own choice, religious, literary, musical, and so forth; being able to use one's mind in ways protected by guarantees of freedom of expression with respect to both political and artistic speech, and freedom of religious exercise; being able to have pleasurable experiences and to avoid non-beneficial pain.
5   Emotions: being able to have attachments to things and people outside ourselves; to love those who love and care for us, to grieve at their absence; in general, to love, to grieve, to experience longing, gratitude, and justified anger; not having one's emotional development blighted

by fear and anxiety. (Supporting this capability means supporting forms of human association that can be shown to be crucial in their development.)

6 Practical reason: being able to form a conception of the good and to engage in critical reflection about the planning of one's life. (This entails protection for the liberty of conscience and religious observance.)

7 Affiliation:

(a) being able to live with and toward others, to recognize and show concern for other human beings, to engage in various forms of social interaction; to be able to imagine the situation of another. (Protecting this capability means protecting institutions that constitute and nourish such forms of affiliation, and also protecting the freedom of assembly and political speech.)

(b) having the social bases of self-respect and non-humiliation; being able to be treated as a dignified being whose worth is equal to that of others. (This entails provisions of non-discrimination on the basis of race, sex, sexual orientation, ethnicity, caste, religion, and national origin.)

8 Other species: being able to live with concern for and in relation to animals, plants, and the world of nature.

9 Play: being able to laugh, to play, to enjoy recreational activities.

10 Control over one's environment:

(a) Political: being able to participate effectively in political choices that govern one's life; having the right of political participation, protections of free speech and association.

(b) Material: being able to hold property (both land and movable goods), and having property rights on an equal basis with others; having the right to seek employment on an equal basis with others; having the freedom from unwarranted search and seizure; in work, being able to work as a human being, exercising practical reason and entering into meaningful relationships of mutual recognition with other workers.

What human capabilities are at issue, when we think of the family structure? As the case of Ferdousi Begum shows us, they are: life, health, bodily integrity, dignity and non-humiliation, associational liberties, emotional health, the opportunity to form meaningful relationships with other people, the ability to participate in politics, the ability to hold property and work outside the home, the ability to think for oneself and form a plan of life – all these things are at stake in the family, and the shape of the family institution influences all these capabilities, for both women and men. The family is indeed a home of love and care, and we should not ignore these capabilities when we assess what different family structures contribute. But we should also remember that the family has a tremendous influence on the other capabilities. Indeed, it influences them pervasively and from the start, since children are born into such groupings, for better or for worse. On this basis, the family has an especially great claim to be regarded as what John Rawls has called the "basic structure of society," an institution, that is, to which principals of justice most especially ought to apply if our goal is to promote justice for all citizens. In a similar way, my capabilities approach suggests that public policy should devote particular attention to any institution whose influence on the formation of capabilities is profound, since a bare minimum of social justice will involve bringing citizens up to a threshold level of capability.

When we look at the family, whose capabilities do we look at? Here we must repeat: we look at the individual. Here as in the case of religion, a *principle of each person's capability* should guide us. It is not enough to ask whether the family promotes a diffuse and general kind of affection and solidarity. We must ask in detail what it does for the capabilities of each of its members – in the area of love and care, and also with regard to the other capabilities. Such a focus on the individual has sometimes been held to slight the worth of love and care. But really, it does no such thing. If liberal individualism urged people to be egoists, putting their own concerns first and those of others second, or to pursue a solitary conception of the good, in which deep attachments to others play no role, then we might well accuse such a theory of indifference to the intrinsic value of love and care. But liberal individualism really involves none of these things;[6] indeed, all the major liberal thinkers have in their different ways emphasized the intrinsic worth of love and care. To give just one example: for John Rawls, the model of moral impartiality that is provided through the Original Position, including its Veil of Ignorance, is intended as a model of the virtue of fraternity;[7] and the Rawlsian account of moral development gives attachments in the family a central role. My own view, similarly, gives capabilities for love and affiliation a central role in the political conception itself, as central social goals.

The liberal *principle of each person as end* does entail, however, that the person, not the group, should be the basic unit for political distribution. Basic political principles mandate that society secure a threshold level of the central goods of life to *each*, seeing *each* as deserving of basic life support and of the basic liberties and opportunities; that we do not rest content with a glorious total or average, when some individuals are doing badly, whether in liberty or in material well-being. Such a principle is especially urgent when we think about the life of women and girls in the family. For, all too often, women have lost out on the basic goods of life because they have been seen as parts of an organic entity, such as the family is supposed to be, rather than as political subjects in their own right. In concrete practical terms, this has meant that too few questions have been asked about how resources and opportunities get distributed within the family. For women such as Giribala, her daughters, and Ferdousi Begum, an emphasis on individual rights and entitlements, far from removing opportunities to love and care, would seem essential in order to promote more fruitful and less exploitative styles of caring.

Instrumental and male-focused ways of valuing women are amazingly persistent, even in lives that are elsewhere characterized by profound moral reflection. Any reader of the *Autobiography* of Mahatma Gandhi, for example, is likely to be very struck by the strange combination of a rare moral depth and radicalism, which questions not only colonialism, but also the entire foundation of the Hindu social order, with attitudes to his wife that are extremely traditional and male-centered. Although Gandhi repents of his personal jealousy and his sexual demands on his wife, he never shows the slightest sign of a thought that she might also be a sexual agent, or that one of the things wrong with his sexual demands on her was their extremely egocentric character. And even when, by his own account, he attains a purer and more harmonious relationship with her, he continues to praise her, above all, for conventional wifely traits of obedience and reverence, rather than for any traits that would suggest that he respected her as a source of agency in her own right. Seeing this moral intransigence even in one so morally outstanding, should we not believe all the more in an approach that insists on treating each and every person as an end?

We can see this point from another angle if we now consider the different approaches economists have taken to the family. The most prominent economic model of the family, that of Gary Becker,[8] assumes for purposes of descriptive modeling that the family is a harmonious organic unit held together by altruism; the head of the household takes adequate thought for the interests and privileges of its members. It has frequently been objected that this approach is not individual-focused enough even for purposes of description and prediction (as Becker now acknowledges[9]); still less does it serve as the basis of an adequate normative approach. Conflicts for resources and opportunities are ubiquitous in families. For this reason economists have increasingly turned to a different, and more individual-focused strategy, modeling the family as a *bargaining unit*.[10] In this approach, it is not denied that the members may be linked by bonds of love and cooperation; they may pursue shared ends, and view one another's well being as among their very most important ends. But they are seen to be distinct individuals, to some extent also in competition with one another. Used descriptively, such an approach can tell us what conditions strengthen the bargaining power of different family agents, and help us to predict what changes, public or private, will alter those relations, and in what ways. A normative approach based on such a descriptive/predictive model would be a model of a *fair* bargain, in which the interests and rights of each member are respected. Obviously enough, there is a natural fit between a normative approach based on the *principle of each person's capabilities* and an economic approach of this type.

The *principle of each person's capabilities*, although endorsed in some form by most of the major liberal theories of justice, has a striking consequence that liberal theorists have not always acknowledged. It is that the family *as such* has no moral standing within the core of the political conception. It is persons who have moral standing. We are interested in the family as a locus of individual development, expression, education, and so forth. But it has no standing qua organic unit. If politics decides to recognize certain groupings as enjoying a special status, my approach does not forbid this.[11] But the moral question behind the political choices should always be, "What do these groups do for people, thinking of each person as an end?" This focus should guide us when we ask which groupings of individuals, if any, deserve special protection in a political structure.

The Family: Not "by Nature"

Sometimes these questions are not asked about the family, because it is taken to be a "natural" unit. If this means a unit whose form is invariant across cultures, the claim is evidently false. Even the briefest study tells us that there are enormous cultural variations in family structure, even within a single nation. To focus, again, on the case of India, we find regions with patterns of dowry and exogamous marriage; we also find, especially in the south, regions where residence is matrilocal and property transmission is matrilineal. Virtually all regions of India, however, differ in some ways from the norm of family typically considered in US discussions: for a single dwelling will typically house several generations, and the upbringing of children will be the function of this extended unit, and also of a larger network of friends, relations, and neighbors, rather than of the nuclear father–mother unit. Our nation, too, exhibits great diversity of family structures: our political focus on the nuclear unit is more than a little influenced by immigration policies, which have sought to limit the definition of who counts as a family member.[12]

This brings us to the next issue we should bear firmly in mind: family, as such, is a creation of state action. It is evident enough that laws and institutions influence the shape of the family in many ways, by defining what marriage and divorce are, what counts as rape and child abuse, by making education compulsory and child labor illegal, and so forth. So much is also true of voluntary associations within civil society, such as churches and universities, which are shaped by law in many ways. But the family is a creation of state action to a far greater extent than these groupings.[13] For there is really no thing, "the family," into which the state either does or does not intervene. People associate in many different ways, live together, love each other, have children. Which of these will get the name "family" is a legal and political matter, never one to be decided simply by the parties themselves. The state constitutes the family structure through its laws, defining which groups of people can count as families, defining the privileges and rights of family members, defining what marriage and divorce are, what legitimacy and parental responsibility are, and so forth. This difference makes a difference: the state is present in the family from the start, in a way that is less clearly the case with the religious body or the university; it is the state that says what this thing *is* and controls how one becomes a member of it.

To see this more clearly, let us consider the rituals that define a person as a member of an association: in the university, matriculation (and, later, the granting of a degree); in a religious body, baptism, conversion, or some analogous entrance rite; in the family, marriage. Now it is evident that the state has some connection with university matriculation/graduation and with religious baptism/conversion: it polices these rites on the outside, by defining the institution as enjoying a particular tax-free status, by preventing the use of cruelty or other illegalities in the ritual,[1] and so forth. As Rawls says, it polices these associational rites on the outside. But marriage is from the start a public, state-administered rite. There are state laws defining it, and these laws restrict entry into that privileged domain. The state does not simply police marriage on the outside; it marries people. Other very similar people who don't meet the state's test cannot count as married, even if they satisfy all private and even religious criteria for marriage. (Thus, same-sex couples whose unions have been solemnized by some religious body still are not married, because the state has not granted them a license.) Marriage has not always been a state function, and there is no necessity that it be so. But in the modern world it pervasively is. Even in India, where marriage and divorce are the business of each separate religious system of law, these systems of law are part of the public sphere, in the sense that they are constituted by the basic structure of laws and institutions in society, people are assigned to them by a system of public rules, and individuals do not have the option to contract a marriage in whatever way they wish, apart from these rules.

Given this large state role, it is unacceptable to treat the family as if it were an institution with its own form, into which the state might or might not intervene. Since the state is present in the family from the start, it had better take that role seriously, and consider how it may execute this function well.

Political Liberalism and the Family: Rawls's Dilemma

We see that the family both fosters and undermines human capabilities. Our question is, how may law and public policy insure that it does more fostering and less impeding? On the one hand, we must take seriously the possibility that important values of personal affiliation and love will be sacrificed if the family is made too directly the subject of a theory of political justice. On the other hand, we must not lose sight of the obvious fact that the family has a profound influence on human development, an influence that is present from the start of a human life. It thus has a very strong claim to be regarded as part of the basic structure of society and among those institutions that basic principles of justice are most directly designed to regulate.

A vivid sense of how this dilemma tugs at liberal political thought can be found in John Rawls's article "The Idea of Public Reason Revisited."[15] Responding to questions from feminist critics, Rawls makes two claims, which are difficult to render coherent.[16] First, he repeats the old claim, first made in *A Theory of Justice*, that the family is a part of the basic structure of society, that is, one of the institutions to which, by definition, the two principles of justice primarily apply. Second, he makes a new claim that his two principles of justice do not "apply directly to the internal life of families." In this respect, Rawls says, the family is like many other voluntary associations, such as "churches and universities, professional or scientific associations, business firms or labor unions." Just as principles of justice do not require that principles of ecclesiastical governance be democratic, although they do supply some essential constraints that bear on ecclesiastical governance, so too with the family: principles do not regulate its internal governance, but they do supply some important constraints on it. Thus, the family need not internally obey the Rawlsian difference principle, with regard to the distribution of resources and opportunities; nor need it obey the priority of liberty, with regard to basic political and religious liberties. On the other hand, the fact that its members are in a society in which the lives of all citizens are governed by institutions based on these two principles will regulate, in many ways, what can and cannot go on there.

Where the two principles of justice are concerned, what Rawls appears to have in mind is the following idea. Even if society as a whole is governed by the difference principle, this does not require the internal distribution of income and wealth in the family to obey this pattern, inequalities being tolerated only where they raise the level of the worst off. Where liberty is concerned, it is a little hard to know what restrictions Rawls's cautious formulation would permit, since any absolute ban on certain types of religious exercise, speech, and political action on the part of a patriarch – at least when we are considering adult female citizens – would seem to run afoul of public liberty principles straightaway. But perhaps Rawls is thinking of cases in which one partner might say, "I'll divorce you if you convert to Judaism," or, "I cannot stay with you if you vote for Bill Clinton." If public officials restricted liberties of citizens in this way, it would clearly be illicit; in the family (Rawls may wish to argue) such coercive tactics, while unpleasant, are not violations of basic justice, so long as the threatened party can leave and is not physically threatened.

It is of course important to assert that the principles of justice apply to the basic structure taken as a whole, and that this does not directly entail that they apply to each of the institutions that forms part of the basic structure, taken one by one. Thus it is a little difficult to imagine what it would mean for the principles of justice to apply directly to the family *taken as part of the basic structure*, and whether this would be the same as for the principles to apply directly to the family as one institution that is in the basic structure. Other institutions that form part of the basic structure do not raise this problem, because the basic constitutional structure has no "inside" life to which principles can apply, until it is given shape in the form of more specific institutions that are created only at the constitutional and legislative stages. So we are not troubled by the question, what is it for the principles to apply to these other institutions as parts of the basic structure, and is it or is it not the same as for the principles to apply to each and every one of the institutions? So the family raises a unique question. Rawls's strategy in answering the question is to turn to other institutions: churches and universities.

The difficulty with the parallel between families and universities, as Rawls is aware, is that the family is part of the basic structure and churches, universities, etc., are not.[17] That means, in terms of Rawls's conception, that the family has been judged to be one of the institutions that dictates people's life chances pervasively and from the start, and a university obviously does not have this character.[18] Rawls is clearly torn between the idea that the family is so fundamental to the reproduction of society and to citizens' life chances that it must be rendered just, and the equally powerful idea that we cannot tolerate so much interference with the internal workings of this particular institution.

Rawls's solution is to try to make the external constraints tough enough to deliver genuine equality to women as citizens. He denies that there is any such thing as a private sphere "exempt from justice," insisting that law must intervene to protect the equality of women as citizens and of children as future citizens.[19] "The equal rights of women and the basic rights of their children as future citizens are inalienable and protect them wherever they are. Gender distinctions limiting those rights and liberties are excluded."[20] One concrete proposal Rawls appears to endorse, at least for our historical circumstances,[21] is that the law should count a wife's work in raising children as entitling her to an equal share in the income that a husband earns during marriage, and in the increased assets during the time of the marriage, in the case of a divorce. "It seems intolerably unjust," Rawls concludes, "that a husband may depart the family taking his earning power with him and leaving his wife and children far less advantaged than before." On the other hand, Rawls maintains that we should allow traditional gendered division of labor within families, "provided it is fully voluntary and does not result from or lead to injustice"[22] – words that are honorable but difficult to apply to reality.

Rawls's approach seems to me to stop somewhat short of what justice requires. The family is indeed part of the basic structure.[23] Children are its captives in all matters of basic survival and well-being for many years. Women are frequently its captives out of economic asymmetry. It is difficult to know whether anything children do in the family could be described as "fully voluntary,"[24] and of course this is true for very many women also, especially those without independent sources of material support. Nor is a child's choice to be a member of such a unit at all voluntary, as membership in a university is, and as membership in a church is apart from the issue of family pressure. So more needs to be said about how the dilemma is to be addressed, compatibly with preserving an appropriate degree of space for personal choices in matters of love and care.

The dilemma has a form similar to that of a dilemma that arises in dealing with tensions between sex equality and religion (indeed, it is frequently bound up with that dilemma). I shall now therefore make use of a framework that I have introduced to treat that dilemma,[25] although we shall find a crucial difference. As in the case of religion, we have, on the one side, respect for an intrinsic value: in this case, the value of the capabilities for love and care; on the other side (at least sometimes) we have the claim of the other capabilities, which pushes us toward critical scrutiny of the family and its agents. We now have two orienting principles. With the family, as with religion, we must observe the principle of each person's capability. We must, that is, ask at every point not just whether love is preserved but whether the capability of each person to select appropriate relations of love and care (and the other central functions) is preserved. Love that exists at the expense of the emotional freedom of others does not deserve public protection, any more than religious freedom that exists by tyrannizing over the religious freedom of others. Nor should public action protect an organic unit as such; what it should protect are the affiliational capabilities of its members.

A principle of moral constraint can also be invoked: anything that is cruel and unjust, though it takes place in the family, does not deserve to be included in what we value when we value and protect family. A person who thwarts and denies the capabilities of family members puts himself outside the moral community for which "family" rightly stands, insofar as it belongs in our normative political conception; he does not deserve to be permitted to invoke its name in his defense.

With all this in place, our analogous principle would seem to be: the state should not intervene in the conduct of family members without a compelling interest, but such a compelling interest is always supplied by the protection of the central capabilities – including, of course, the individual capabilities to choose relationships of love and care.

Here, however, the symmetry with the religious case begins to break down. For, as we have noted, religions have a life outside the state, as do universities; families do not. So the dilemma might more plausibly be construed as one between the associational liberties of citizens, on the one hand, and the claim of the other capabilities, on the other. In addressing this dilemma, I am claiming, the state should give family actors considerable liberty of association and self-definition, but within constraints imposed by the central capabilities – which should, insofar as possible, be built into the legal structure that constitutes and regulates the family.

My approach, unlike Rawls's, recognizes this difference and makes it salient. There is no point in urging that the state may regulate the family from without, the way it regulates a private university. Because of the nature of the state's relation to marriage, as well as because of the pervasive influence of the family on the opportunities and liberties of citizens, the family simply is part of the basic structure of society, and capability-based principles of justice should apply to it directly as a part of that structure, within limits set by the other capabilities, especially the personal liberties (associational, dignitary, and choice-related) of citizens.

This approach differs from Rawls's, although the differences are subtle. Rawls, for all his eloquent criticism of the idea of a private space free from justice, nonetheless begins from the assumption that "the family," understood in a highly conventional way, is to remain a part of the basic structure and to play a basic role in the reproduction of society. To judge both from his remarks in the 1997 article and from the extensive account of moral development in *A Theory of Justice*, he appears to envisage that unit as a Western-style heterosexual nuclear family, although he does not explicitly rule out other groupings (same-sex couples, for example).[26] He gives this unit, vaguely specified, a high degree of centrality and support, and he never asks what other affiliative groupings of individuals might for related reasons deserve state protection and support. Thus, despite his attack on the private–public distinction, he retains the picture of a society of people divided into nuclear home units that has frequently been used to underwrite that distinction. He strongly suggests that the family has a pre-political form and that politics can regulate it on the outside, rather than constituting it from the ground up – although at the same time he insists that a sphere of life is not a "place or space" exempt from justice. Rawls may also retain, in a related way, a distinction between state action and inaction that suggests that the state is not acting when it does not interfere with the traditional shape of the family, whereas it would be acting were it to attempt to change modes of family governance.

My approach, by contrast, begins by focusing on the capabilities and liberties of each person, and does not assume that any one affiliative grouping is prior or central in promoting those capabilities. People have needs for love and care, for reproduction, for sexual expression; children have needs for love, support, and education; and people also enjoy a wide range of associational liberties. But at this point my approach urges us to look and see how different groupings of persons do in promoting these capabilities. Women's collectives of a type common in developing countries play a valuable role in giving women love and friendship, in caring for children, and in fostering the other capabilities. Conventional families often do less well. Sometimes a women's collective appears to be more truly a child's family than its nuclear home, as when, as often happens, women's collectives protect children from sexual abuse, or arrange for children at risk of abuse, or child marriage, to be protected through state-run schools. Giribala's children would have done well to have had the support of a women's *sangham*, rather than the nuclear family that isolated them from protection and left them vulnerable to their greedy and corrupt father's schemes. Rawls seems to give state protection to the privacy of families, but not, similarly, to other affiliative groupings. My approach would urge that this choice be a contextual one, asking how, in the given history and circumstances, public policy can best promote the claims of the human capabilities. The only thing that stops state intervention are the person and the various liberties and rights of the person, including associative liberties, the right to be free from unwarranted search and seizure, and so forth. The family has no power to stop this intervention on its own, as though it were a mystical unity over and above the lives of its members.[27]

Similarly, my approach urges us to question whether the distinctions between outside and inside, and between action and inaction, are really coherent. Laws governing marriage, divorce, compulsory education, inheritance – all are as inside as anything can be in the family. Nor should the criminal justice system know a distinction between inside and outside, in the definition and ranking of criminal offenses: it should treat rape as rape, battery as battery, coercion as coercion, wherever they occur. To let things take their status quo ante course is to choose a course of action, not to be completely neutral. In short, the state's interest in protecting the dignity, integrity, and well-being of each citizen never simply leads to external constraints on the family structure, whatever appearances may be; it always leads to positive constructing of the family institution. This constructing should be done in ways that are compatible with political justice.

Thus Rawls's position recommends, in effect, accepting certain groupings as given and not interfering with their internal workings, simply policing them by a system of tough external constraints. This approach does not answer the question how the state ought to define which groupings count as families, and what it should consider as it attempts to answer this question. I have argued that there is no reason for the state to take traditional groupings as given: in light of the human capabilities, the state should consider what groupings it wishes to protect, and on what basis. And I have argued further that there is no way in which the state can really avoid constructing the family unit in accordance with some norms or other; so it had better do so self-consciously, with full awareness of the goals in view.

In practical terms, my approach in terms of the promotion of capabilities and Rawls's approach, which views the two principles of justice as supplying external constraints on the family, will give many of the same answers. Laws against marital rape, laws protecting marital consent, laws mandating compulsory education, laws banning child marriage and child labor, laws ensuring an appropriate material recognition of the wife's economic contribution to the family, laws providing child care to support working mothers, laws promoting the nutrition and health of girl children – all these laws, I think, we would both support as appropriate expressions of state concern for citizens and future citizens. But the grounds on which we would support them will be subtly different. Rawls sees the laws as supplying external constraints on something that has its own form, the way laws constrain a university or a church; I see them as contributing to the constitution of an institution that is in the most direct sense a part of the basic structure of society.

Furthermore, my approach, like Rawls's, would permit the state to give conventional family groupings certain special privileges and protections, just as it gives religious bodies certain privileges and protections. It will probably do so in many cases, since the family does promote the rearing of children, as well as serving other needs of citizens. Thus parents may be given certain limited kinds of deference in making choices regarding their children. And tax breaks for certain types of unit are not ruled out, insofar as these units promote human capabilities. But for me, the reason the state will choose such policies, as in the religious case, is to protect the central capabilities of individuals; the definition of family, and the policies chosen, should be chosen with this aim in view. Rawls does not ask how "family" should be defined, nor does he make it clear on what basis it should have special privileges, although the state's interests in its future citizens would appear to be one such basis.

Most important of all, because Rawls takes the family as given, he does not ask what my approach urges us to ask at all times: what other affective ties deserve public protection and support? It is not at all clear, then, what role women's collectives could play in his account of society's basic structure. In my approach, though all such inquiries should be contextual, a role for such collectives is built in from the start, since the aim is not to protect any institution that is customary, but rather to protect and foster those forms of association that promote human capabilities, within limits set by the associational and other liberties of citizens.

Notice that here, as in the case of religion, I do not give the traditional form of a practice exclusive privileges: I ask what capabilities it serves, and extend privileges, insofar as is practicable, to other similar institutions that promote those same capabilities. In practice, such an approach, as with religion, would usually involve both defining family broadly[28] and also supporting other organizations, prominently including women's collectives, which are important in a given cultural context in promoting the well-being of women and children.

Again, my approach would forbid certain types of interference with the family structure that Rawls's approach would also forbid. For me as for Rawls, it is wrong for the state to mandate the equal division of domestic labor or equal decision-making in the household. But again, the reasons for this shared conclusion will differ. Rawls judges that it is wrong to interfere with the internal workings of a particular institution, deemed to exist apart from the state – whereas I judge simply that there are associational liberties of individuals, and liberties of speech, that should always be protected for citizens, no matter where they occur. (Rawls might have reached a result similar to the one he does reach by relying on the priority of liberty; but, significantly, he does not use that argument.) It just seems an intolerable infringement of liberty for the state to get involved in dictating how people do their dishes. Indeed, for me, dubious forms of conduct get less prima facie protection if they are in the family than if they are in a purely voluntary association, since the family (for children at any rate) is a non-voluntary institution that influences citizens' life chances pervasively and from the start. Furthermore, the state has a legitimate interest in children, as future citizens under its protection, which it does not have in adults who elect membership in a church or a university.

In a wide range of areas, our approaches will support different choices of public policy. In my approach, the central capabilities always supply a compelling interest for purposes of government action. Thus it will be alright to render dowry illegal in India, given the compelling evidence that the dowry system is a major source of women's capability failure. I believe that Rawls would have a difficult time justifying this law – because he is thinking of the family as pre-political, and dowry as one of the choices it makes in its pre-political state. For me, by contrast, the family is constituted by laws and institutions, and one of the questions to be asked is whether dowry-giving is one of the things it should be in the business of doing. Permitting dowry is not neutral state inaction toward an autonomous private entity; it is another (alternative) way of constituting a part of the public sphere. (As in the case of religion, my approach admits the possibility of loss and even tragedy. If we should judge that the liberty to give dowry is a significant protected liberty, the choice to curtail the practice will have a tragic dimension. I am inclined, however, to think that this is no more a core area of protected liberty than would be the liberty to pass on one's estate to one's children without taxation.)

Again, interference with traditional decision-making patterns in the family will be much easier to justify on my approach than on Rawls's. Consider the Mahila Samakhya Project in Andhra Pradesh, in southern India. This project, funded and run by the national government, is explicitly aimed at increasing women's confidence and initiative, and empowering them in their dealings with employers, government officials, and husbands, by setting up and fostering women's collectives. There is no doubt at all that the government is attempting to reconstruct the family by altering social norms and perceptions. No community and no individual is forced to join, and this is a reservation I would support. Nonetheless, it seems likely that there is more in the way of endorsing a particular conception of family governance than Rawls would consider acceptable. Apart from the content of the teaching, the very existence of the women's collectives as a focus for women's affective lives transforms the family profoundly, making it no longer the sole source of personal affiliation. It seems likely that Rawls would oppose government support for such collectives on that account, thinking of it as the endorsement of one conception of the good over another – for much the same reason that he has opposed government support for music and the arts. For me, the fact that women's capabilities are in such a perilous state, together with the fact that empowerment programs have shown great success in giving them greater control over their material and political environment, gives government a compelling interest in the introduction of such programs. Meeting with other women in groups is, once again, of the first importance in gaining a sense of strength and effective agency. As a woman in Andhra Pradesh put it, "A single voice is not heard. Together we demanded and negotiated an increase in wages." A woman in a rural literacy program said to Chen: "If anybody's mind is depressed, after participating in the meeting, her mind will be refreshed."[29] The importance of this factor cannot be underestimated: for women who have typically been isolated, each in a separate household, finding strength in group solidarity is a major source of change in self-perception.

Indeed, it would appear that in India at the present time, the single most effective way for government to promote women's sense of their worth and their entitlements is to promote women's collectives. The Mahila Samakhya Project is not a very expensive project; it involves a small staff, and relies heavily on local trainees. Its efficiency in getting women thinking about their lives has been tremendous. Once such thinking begins, it is difficult to go backward, and so such collectives, once started, have a transformative power all their own. These women's collectives are communities of equality and agency, rather than hierarchical communities that define women as passive before their destiny. Moreover, these new relationships of care also make positive changes in the family relationship, giving women new strength to bargain against domestic violence, winning them new respect from husbands and sons. Often there is a valuable synergy between networks of care outside the family and a positive restructuring of that institution. My approach supports such restructuring to an extent that Rawls's does not.

Or take similar programs that involve giving women access to credit. For Rawls, such a focus on economic self-sufficiency, together with the usual accompaniment in such programs, education in confidence and leadership, would be, I surmise, an impermissible interference by government into the family structure. The very idea that government would support an all-women's bank would be highly suspect. For me, while I think it is very important for a program like this to be non-coercive, it seems quite all right for government to act in ways that aim at changing social norms that shape the family, and at promoting capabilities in those who lack them. For after all, and this is the crux of the matter, government is already in the business of constructing an institution, the family, that is part of the basic structure of society. It had better get to work and do this job well.

Even in the area of property, Rawls's approach seems to me to offer uncertain guidance, whereas mine offers clear guidance. Property rights in India have traditionally belonged to families as organic wholes, and women have little or no control over the family unit or "coparcenary," which is run by its male members. Demands by women for land rights of their own have frequently been greeted with the claim that this would "break up the family."[30] And certainly the demand, if accepted, would transform the internal governance of that structure. Rawls might or might not hold that the transformation was necessary to make women equal citizens; but the fact that the change in family governance would equalize women's bargaining position in the family would, by itself, supply an insufficient argument for the change. In my approach, by contrast, we get to the conclusion very directly, since control over property is one of the central capabilities that cannot be abridged unequally on the basis of sex. What Rawls would say, at best, is, "This so-called breakup of the family is an appropriate constraint supplied by external justice." What I would say is, "You didn't just find the family lying around, you constituted it in one way, through the tradition of property law; now we shall constitute it in another way, one that protects women's capabilities."

The largest difference in the two approaches will be in the treatment of female children. It is here, especially, that my approach recognizes the pervasive and non-voluntary nature of family membership, and gives the state broad latitude in shaping perception and behavior to promote the development of female children to full adult capability in the major areas. This means not only the abolition of child marriage and (where practically possible) child labor, and (where practically possible) compulsory primary and secondary education for all children. Rawls would presumably also favor these changes. It also means encouraging the public perception that women are suited for many different roles in life, and are active members of the political and economic communities, something that Rawls is likely to see as too much promoting of a definite conception of the good. Thus the content of public education should include information about options for women, and about resistance to women's inequality. (One terrible problem India is now having is that government has no money for new textbooks, with the result that outdated images of women must be used in primary schools despite the fact that nobody likes them.) In addition to regular schooling, the Indian government also supports special hostel programs for young girls who are at risk of child marriage, to remove them from their homes and give them education and job training. Rawls would be likely to see this as too much state intervention with the family, even if the mothers consent to the girls going away: after all, government is saying, "I will support you if you leave this dangerous structure." My approach judges that the protection of girls' capabilities warrants this interventionist strategy.

Rawls's approach to the family and mine are very close: both of us define the person as the basis of distribution; both of us see an important role for liberties of association and self-definition; both of us recognize the intrinsic value of love and care. But Rawls remains half-hearted, I think, in his realization of the important idea that the family is a part of the "basic structure of society," and in his recognition of important asymmetries between the family and other voluntary organizations. I have tried to show how an approach through the central capabilities would capture that idea, while still valuing family love and the insights it affords.

Love, Dignity, and Community

I have argued that the family, like other communities, does not exist "by nature"; even more than others, it is the creation of laws and institutions. Moreover, such communities are not organic entities: they are made up out of people, each of whom has needs for food, and love, and opportunity, and freedom, each of whom has a separate path in the world from birth to death. In all such groupings of people, but most obviously in the family, some typically do well at the expense of others. A society concerned about justice and opportunity cannot afford to neglect this problem. I have argued that a liberal approach that focuses on each person as an end is the best way to approach the tensions that arise when people's needs for love seem intertwined with differences of power that deny some people an equal chance in life.

But I have also argued that love is among the most important of human capabilities, and that the most appropriate type of liberal approach will be one that insists on promoting affiliation to a place of importance among the central goods that all citizens have a right to enjoy. I have suggested that an approach based on the idea of human capabilities can balance these concerns more adequately than a Rawlsian approach.

When we apply the capabilities approach, we may find some instances of loss: as when a way of life that seems rich in value goes out of existence over time because the public political conception changes attitudes in ways that lead people to turn from tradition. Many traditions are not worth weeping over; we should not be upset if female malnutrition, domestic violence, and many other ills endemic to the family should perish from the scene. But we should also not assert a priori that nothing of value will be lost as women realize to a greater degree the capabilities on my list. We should also remember, however, that the new ways of life that a capabilities approach will promote are also complex forms of human affiliation, rich in value. Women's collectives, in particular, seem to exemplify virtues of love, reciprocity, and mutual care that are valuable, and not so often found in traditional families, except in a skewed and hierarchical form.

In short, we are not forced to choose between a deracinated type of individualism, where each person goes off as a loner, indifferent to others, and traditional types of community, which are frequently hierarchical and unfair to women. The fact is that justice and friendship are good allies: women who have dignity and self-respect can help to fashion types of community that are no less loving, and often quite a lot more loving, than those they have known before. Human capabilities provide essential support for love, even as love is among the most important human capabilities.

Notes

1   Translated from the Bengali by Kalpana Bardhan, in *Women, Outcastes, Peasants, and Rebels: A Selection of Bengali Short Stories* (Berkeley: University of California Press, 1990), p. 274.

2   38 DLR (*Dhaka Law Reports*) (1986). Although this case is from Bangladesh, it is typical of the phenomenon of dowry extortion as it commonly occurs in India as well; legal efforts to stem the tide of dowry abuse have been very similar in the two nations.

3   This chapter is based on chapter 4 of my *Women and Human Development: The Capabilities Approach* (Cambridge: Cambridge University Press, 2000). The book defends an approach to the formulation of basic political principles that can underlie fundamental constitutional guarantees, based on an idea of human capability and functioning. I argue that all societies ought, as a matter of justice, to provide their citizens with a threshold level of all the capabilities. I focus on India throughout the manuscript, because that is where my own work with women's development groups has focused; I feel that it is better to analyze one cultural situation in detail than to draw in examples from all sorts of places. But the approach, suitably specified in accordance with local conditions, is intended to be fully cross-cultural, a close ally of the human rights approach. All the abuses mentioned here are prominently exemplified in our own society – and indeed I shall argue that we can learn a lot from India about how to address them. For comments on this portion of my project, I am especially grateful to Jasodhara Bagchi, Martha Alter Chen, Joshua Cohen, Leela Gulati, Susan Moller Okin, and Cass Sunstein.

4   The story primarily concerns the later history of the marriage, in which the husband, viewing his daughters, too, as commodities for his use, sells two of them into prostitution. Giribala (who all along has been the family's primary economic agent) leaves him before he can sell the third.

5   This point was forcefully made by J. S. Mill in *The Subjection of Women* (1869), ed. S. M. Okin (Indianapolis: Hackett, 1988), p. 87; Okin herself develops the idea further in her important *Justice, Gender, and the Family* (New York: Basic Books, 1989).

6   See my "The Feminist Critique of Liberalism," in *Sex and Social Justice* (New York: Oxford University Press, 1999).

7   For references and discussion, see my "Rawls and Feminism," forthcoming in Samuel Freeman, ed.,*The Cambridge Companion to Rawls* (New York: Cambridge University Press, 2000). An important discussion of these issues is in Susan M. Okin, "Reason and Feeling in Thinking About Justice," in Cass R. Sunstein, ed., (Chicago: University of Chicago Press, 1990), pp. 15–35.

8   Gary S. Becker, *A Treatise on the Family* (Harvard University Press, 1981).

9   In his Nobel Lecture, "The Economic Way of Looking at Behavior," in R. Febrero and P. Schwartz, eds., *The Essence of Becker* (Stanford: Hoover, 1995), pp. 633–58.

10   See Amartya Sen, "Gender and Cooperative Conflicts," in I. Tinker, ed., *Persistent Inequalities* (New York: Oxford University Press, 1991), pp. 123–49; Bina Agarwal, "'Bargaining' and Gender Relations: Within and Beyond the Household," *Feminist Economics* 3 (1997): 1–51; Shelly Lundberg and Robert A. Pollak, "Bargaining and Distribution in Marriage," *The Journal of Economic Perspectives* 10 (1996): 139–58.

11   In chapter 3 of *Women and Human Development* I discuss the related case of religious groups.

12   See Martha Minow, "All in the Family and In All Famlies: Membership, Loving, and Owing," in D. Estlund and M. Nussbaum, eds., *Sex, Preference, and Family: Essays on Law and Nature* (New York: Oxford University Press, 1997), pp. 249–76.

13   See Frances Olsen, "The Family and the Market: A Study of Ideology and Legal Reform," *Harvard Law Review* 96 (1983): 1497–577, and "The Myth of State Intervention in the Family," *University of Michigan Journal of Law Reform* 18 (1985): 835–64.

14   See chapter 3 of *Women and Human Development* on dilemmas involving the use of drugs in religious ceremonies.

15   *University of Chicago Law Review* 64 (1997): 765–807. Rawls here revises ideas developed in *Political Liberalism* (Columbia University Press, expanded paper edition 1996), but that work did not include discussion of the family. For an analysis of all Rawls's statements on this issue, see my "Rawls and Feminism."

16   See section 5 of the article, "On the Family as Part of the Basic Structure," pp. 787–94.

17   Rawls has nowhere suggested that churches and universities are parts of the basic structure, and he probably would be strongly opposed to such an idea. Institutions that form part of the basic structure can be subsidized by the state, and he would appear to be opposed to state subsidies for churches and universities. An excellent discussion of this whole problem is in G. A. Cohen, "Where the Action Is: On the Site of Distributive Justice," *Philosophy and Public Affairs* 26 (1997):

3–30. Cohen discusses the family and the market as two examples of pervasive institutions in which people cannot help participating and that influence their life chances pervasively and from the start – but which are treated by Rawls as outside the institutional framework that principles of justice directly govern.

18   Churches may, if a child is born into one, and in that sense the case is an intermediate one; but the case remains different from the family, since every child that is born is for years at the mercy of its family in all basic matters of survival and well-being.

19   "The Idea of Public Reason Revisited," p. 791: "A domain so-called, or a sphere of life, is not, then, something already given apart from political conceptions of justice. A domain is not a kind of space, or place, but rather is simply the result, or upshot, of how the principles of political justice are applied, directly to the basic structure and indirectly to the associations within it. The principles defining the equal basic liberties and opportunities of citizens always hold in and through all so-called domains. The equal rights of women and the basic rights of their children as future citizens are inalienable and protect them wherever they are. Gender distinctions limiting those rights and liberties are excluded. . . . If the so-called private sphere is alleged to be space exempt from justice, then there is no such thing."

20   Ibid.

21   Ibid., p. 793. The proposal was made by Susan M. Okin in *Justice, Gender, and the Family*.

22   Ibid., p. 792.

23   Rawls seems to waver on this question when, on p. 791, he writes, "Even if the basic structure alone is the primary subject of justice, the principles of justice still put essential restrictions on the family and all other associations."

24   On p. 792 n. 68, Rawls notes the slipperiness of the idea of voluntariness, as applied to religion, and he states that he describes religious choice as voluntary only from the point of view of "objective conditions," not subjective ones. But even objectively, children's membership in the family is not voluntary.

25   See *Women and Human Development*, chap. 3.

26   In "The Idea of Public Reason Revisited," he explicitly states that he does not presuppose a heterosexual form of family.

27   In this respect (though not in all respects!) my approach is close to that of Richard Epstein, in articles regarding homosexual marriage and surrogate motherhood: see "Caste and the Civil Rights Laws: From Jim Crow to Same-Sex Marriages," *Michigan Law Review* 92 (1994): 2456–78; and Richard Epstein, "Surrogacy: The Case for Full Contractual Enforcement," *Virginia Law Review* 81 (1995): 2305–41.

28   See the proposal in Minow, "All in the Family," who observes that narrower definitions, rather than reflecting social reality, frequently are simply devices to limit immigration.

29   Martha A. Chen, *A Quiet Revolution: Women in Transition in Rural Bangladesh* (Cambridge, Mass.: Schenkman, 1983), p. 155.

30   See a statement by the Minister of Agriculture quoted in Bina Agarwal, "'Bargaining' and Gender Relations: Within and Beyond the Household," p. 3.

12

Community and Society, Melancholy and Sociopathy

Osborne Wiggins and Michael A. Schwartz

Communities and Persons

The loss of community is frequently seen as a personal loss, i.e., as a loss for persons as social beings. The loss of community entails the loss of certain kinds of social relationships, and the loss of these relationships is a difficult personal experience. At least, so say the advocates of community.[1] But perhaps these advocates do not realize how much persons differ, even at the most basic levels of their relationships to the world and to other people. Fundamental human differences can make life in communities ideal for some people and almost unbearable for others. Conversely, the loss of the possibility of life in a community may be hardly felt by certain persons and the cause of a deep despondency and eventual suicide by others. If this is so, then praise of the benefits of communities and laments over their vanishing need to be sensitive to and tempered by recognition of these basic human differences.

It will be our contention that there are certain types of person who are so constituted that living in a community is extremely difficult and uncomfortable for them. These people do much better and can even thrive in modern societies. Moreover, there are other individuals who thrive precisely as members of communities. These people find life in society stressful, if not unendurable; they may even fall into depression and attempt suicide. A corollary of these contentions is that modern society – with its inherent powerful tendency to erode communities – presents grave difficulties for persons of the latter type, while it affords unprecedented opportunities for individuals of the former type. The advocates of community are not entirely mistaken, however, when they imagine a kind of person who can benefit from both life in communities and a simultaneous life in society. Many such people do exist. We simply wish to prevent this kind of person from being seen as Human Nature writ large: the person who lives a "well rounded" and happier life by participating in both communities and society is only one type of person.

There are other types of people, and we need to appreciate what fates they can expect in a mass society like ours in which communities are disappearing.

A Phenomenological Distinction between Community and Society

The concepts of community and society, as we shall define them, denote two ends of a continuum. Many social groups fall between the concepts; i.e., these groups to varying degrees share features of community and society. Thus some social groups will be more communal than societal, but these groups will nonetheless exhibit to some degree certain features of societies. Other groups will have predominantly societal features but will also manifest to some extent certain features of communities. Our concepts of community and society are thus unalloyed "ideal types" or "pure types" in Max Weber's sense.

We call our characterization of community and society "phenomenological" because we shall focus on these realities as they are experienced by the people who participate in them. Thus, our account proceeds from the social participant's subjective point of view. For this reason too our approach could also be deemed Weberian in its methodological orientation. Both communities and societies will thus be seen as intersubjectively constituted realties. As I live in either a society or a community, I encounter other people, and I therefore experience them as experiencing me in certain ways. Their ways of experiencing me shape my self-experience. It is this sort of intersubjective constitution of self and other that we shall examine.

Community

Communities are composed of relatively small numbers of people who regularly encounter one another in face-to-face relationships. These interactions among them are informed by basic values and beliefs that all parties share. Some values and beliefs may vary from individual to individual, but underneath these more individual values and beliefs lie common ones. Following Peter Berger and Thomas Luckmann, we shall call these sets of values and beliefs a *nomos*.[2]

Communities are non-voluntary forms of human association. Individuals do not choose to become members of communities: one is born into a community. One is thus born into a family or a church. Today, of course, many people "choose" their churches, but this simply demonstrates that this contemporary sort of church membership cannot be called communal; it is, rather, societal.

Because one is born into a community, membership in the community is expected to be life-long. Therefore, leaving a community with finality but while still alive is an event of very significant proportions, both for the individual and for the community. (In communities children, of course, grow up and "leave" the family, but they are expected to maintain contact and to return periodically. "Leaving the family" thus means living elsewhere; it does not mean losing one's family membership. When living children for some reason depart from a family "once and for all," i.e., forfeit their family membership, this is a highly significant event.)

Because one is born into and grows up in a community, the nomos of that community is experienced by the individual as "given" and unalterable. The nomos of the community is imposed on the individual and is experienced by the individual as the only conceivable one. The communal nomos is not considered a matter of choice.

Because one is born into a community, other (older) members of the community have known one all of one's life. Communities are those social groups into which one is born, in which one grows up, and in which one is expected to live. It is expected that leaving a community with finality will occur only at death. And usually even at death the individual is viewed as "living on" somehow, e.g., in group memory or in ancestry worship, in the community. The community therefore includes the entire life of the individual: one is *always* a member of the community.[3]

Because communities are composed of relatively small numbers of people, one is repeatedly encountering the same persons. In the different encounters these persons perceive the individual as *the same individual,* whether she is performing the role of church leader, mother, or president of the town council. The different roles that one plays, of course, require different actions and are governed by different norms. But one is still expected to be (and is seen as) the same person in performing these different roles. The woman who hosts the church reception is the same woman who is William Davis's wife, the mother of two lovely children, and the town council president. Thus, individuals experience a considerable amount of "role overlap": in any given situation they play several different roles at once. If the woman who is hosting the church gathering is perceived to be noticeably intoxicated, this reflects on her being as William Davis's wife and the mother of Linda and William Davis, Jr., as well as her being as president of the town council. The "same person" is thus perceived in all the roles that he or she performs, and a person is always perceived as the unitary bearer of *all* of his or her roles. In short, one *is* all of one's roles at once.

Such "role overlap" occurs because of "group overlap." The church member who encounters Mrs. Davis hosting the church reception is also a parent whose children play with Linda and William Davis, Jr., and who is County Sheriff. Different groups compose communities, but the members of these groups are to a considerable degree the same individuals. In the different groups these individuals, of course, play different roles; but precisely because they are the same individuals in the different settings, they are perceived by one another as "the same while different."

Since a person is perceived as the same person in all of his or her role performances and since members of the community live in accordance with a common set of beliefs and values, there is a "transparency" to one's actions and one's self as perceived by others. Members of communities feel that they know why people do what they do. Opacity of a person's motives arises only when that person behaves contrary to the shared nomos. As long as people behave in accordance with the common nomos, people "immediately understand" one another. (This "immediate understanding" of one person by another, like all cases of one person understanding another, may be mistaken, of course.)

This pervasive, unspoken agreement on fundamental matters with one's fellows produces a sense of "one-ness" with them. One "feels at home" among them. The individual feels that his or her life is rooted in the community: one belongs in and to the community.

Society

Societies are composed of large numbers of persons. These persons meet one another in varying situations and in various groups. Societies are thus composed of a large number of groups which have significant, insignificant, or no relationships with one another. These groups also have varying life-spans, from minutes to decades.

In society people become members of groups because they have individual interests which they believe the group will serve. Group membership is thus a means to the end of one's own personal interests. Group membership is accordingly voluntary or chosen. And, hence, one's membership in the group is conditional upon the group serving one's personal ends. When the group fails to serve the person's individual ends, the person is free to leave the group. Such self-interested choices to abandon the group are deemed perfectly legitimate.

In society, an individual is a member of groups that have little or no relationship to one another. Since the person plays different roles in these different groups, the person participates in a group with only a separate part of him- or herself. The "whole person" is never perceived as involved in the group. The members of the group may not even know about the other parts of the individual's life. This encourages "the compartmentalization" of one's life and a fragmentation of the components of one's personality. For example, the individual may be going through a divorce and a court battle over the custody of her children without other members of the business knowing anything about it. Integration of oneself is thus a matter to be achieved by oneself, if it is to be achieved at all. The perceptions of other people play little role in the integration of this self.[4]

Because society is composed of a plethora of different groups, there is only a minimal overarching nomos shared by all members of society. Different groups may have their own internal norms and expectations, but the general societal nomos consists simply in non-interference: groups and individuals are required to leave one another alone unless some sort of relationship is freely invited and freely accepted. Relationships are thus founded on the conscious, voluntary consent of the related parties. Human relationships are perceived as based on contracts. One party would freely contract to interact with another party only because such interaction is seen by each party as serving its own interest.[5]

In a society, then, values and beliefs are not perceived as imposed but rather as chosen. Beliefs and values are viewed as subjectively relative and as otherwise groundless. The laws of a society thus tend toward a tolerance for a plurality of beliefs and values. This nomic pluralism results in disagreements among people regarding even the most fundamental beliefs and values. Such intractable disagreements eventually lead to uncertainty in the minds of many people. If well-meaning people disagree so fundamentally over issues of primary importance, the dubiousness of one's own personal values and belief seems obvious. The individual thus begins to experience *anomie*, i.e., a pervasive sense of normlessness and value-disorientation. This constant lack of agreement with one's fellows produces a vague mood of alienation from them. One feels a rootlessness or a lack of belonging in the society in which one lives.[6]

Not all members of society can bear the arbitrariness of relativism, pluralism, and subjectivism, however. As a result, some members of society will tend toward a nomic absolutism. Adherents of this nomic absolutism will thus find themselves opposing the ethics of tolerance that permits a wide variety of lifestyles and value viewpoints. Adherents of this absolutism will see this ethics precisely as unethical.

As we turn now to address the topic of how certain personality types deal with life in either a community or a society, we shall address it in terms of the self and the social roles it performs. To focus on the self and its social roles is to select only one aspect of the large problem of the self in community or the self in society. But the large problem cannot be adequately explicated here. We shall thus limit ourselves to the self and its social roles, and in this way hope to adumbrate in one of its core aspects the larger picture of the person participating in either community or society.

The Self and its Social Roles

The problem of the relationship between the self and social roles is a complex and elusive one. Numerous experiences, however, show that the self and the roles that it performs are not identical even though the distinction is difficult to pinpoint. The same person can enact different social roles, and this in itself seems to show that the self transcends the roles it plays. On the other hand, it does appear that while the person is enacting that role, the person *is* the role and nothing else. But another experience leads us to doubt this identification of the person with role even during role performance, namely, the experience of "role distance." Roles can be played with different degrees of identification with them. I can enact my role of university professor while fully identifying my personal being with the role, or I can play it while at the same time maintaining a distance from it. Such inner distance from the role that one is performing demonstrates that the self is not identical with its roles.

We would like to explicate some of the essential characteristics of social roles, and on the basis of this explication delve further into the question of the relationship of the self to the social roles its plays. *Social roles consist of both modes of behavior and modes of experience.* In other words, *social roles are constituted of both objective (behavioral) and subjective (psychological) components.* The person playing the role must engage in the behavior prescribed by the role. Moreover, the person enacting the role *may* have the experiences appropriate to the role. But with this "may" we meet the crux of role distance, for the person performing the role may not have the subjective experiences prescribed by the role. Such role performance, namely, a role performance in which the person actualizes the role-required behavior but not the role-prescribed experiences, manifests role distance. On the other hand, a role performance in which the person actualizes both the role-dictated behavior and the role-prescribed experiences would evince role identification. I *fully identify* myself with the role when my states of perceiving, valuing, and willing are those prescribed by the role and nothing but these. And in certain limit cases such full identification does occur. But in most cases of role performance the mental states of the actor are more complex than those prescribed by the role. In addition to having the experiences prescribed by the role the actor may have other (extra-role) experiences as well. In this case the person would achieve partial role identification but also some degree of role distance. Role identification and role distance are therefore matters of degree. We shall thus define them as matters of degree: *role distance* occurs to the extent that the actor's subjective states differ from the subjective components of the role, even when the actor's overt behavior accords perfectly with the role; and *role identification* occurs to the degree that the actor's subjective experiences are identical with the subjective components of the role and moreover the actor enacts the behavior.

The possibility for role identification and role distance clearly depends on the human being's capacity to determine his or her overt behavior and subjective experiences. Overt behavior can be determined by oneself sufficiently to enact the objective components of the role. One's subjective experiences, however, can be controlled by oneself only to a limited degree. And moreover, even if one can control one's experiences, one may nevertheless allow oneself to have experiences different from those required by the role. In sum, role distance and role identification can be only partially determined by us because of our limited capacity to determine our own subjective states.

Dispositional Vectors and the Shaping of Personality

Certain types of persons do well in communities, and other types of persons do well in societies. We can, of course, imagine an individual who can live well in both communal relationships and societal structures. That person would appreciate the stability, familiarity, and sense of belongingness available in a community, while also wanting the freedom and variety available in society. This person, however, would also have to tolerate the limitations imposed by communities and the rootlessness and anonymity of society. This would require a person who can sincerely play social roles and find satisfaction in adhering to communal norms but who can also distance himself from his role even when he is playing it and can occasionally find ways around communal norms. This individual would therefore need an inner flexibility in his or her personality so that he or she could be "different selves" in different situations while still maintaining a sufficiently coherent sense of personal identity.

We shall turn now to consider two kinds of person who lack such flexibility: they cannot shift back and forth between role identification and role distance. One kind, the kind we shall call *typus melancholicus*, overidentifies with social roles and remains incapable of role distance. The other kind, the sociopathic personality, underidentifies with social roles and therefore always experiences extreme role distance. This characteristic of being "fixed" or unfree in one's basic relationship to one's social roles will result in these two different types of person having difficulty living either in community or in society.

The reader should be warned, however, that while we shall refer to these persons as being of two different "types," we are again using the word "type" to signify "ideal type" in Max Weber's sense. We shall define the "pure" or "clear-cut" case. In fact, our descriptions are idealized fictions in the sense that real persons fit these types only to different degrees and in very different ways. What we seek to capture in human beings by depicting these types is what we prefer to call "dispositional vectors" in people. *Hypernomia*, for instance, is a tendency in people; it is a particular direction in which individuals are pulled. It signifies the tendency of certain people to overidentify with social roles and norms. Most people may have this tendency to some degree. But some people have it very, very little. Other people have this tendency to a great degree. *Hyponomia* signifies the tendency to underidentify with social roles and norms. Again, many people may have this to some extent, however slight. But other people may tend in this direction to an extreme degree. And human nature is even more complex than this. In some individuals there will exist tendencies toward both hypernomia and hyponomia; some people will be highly hypernomic and only mildly hyponomic, some people may be neither, etc. Hence our "ideal types" portray only directions in which people are drawn – some persons strongly, other people weakly. It is of paramount importance, however, that the reader, as he or she reads our definitions of these ideal types, keep in mind that we are not describing real people. We have only selected certain features of real people and characterized them in an idealized form in order to convey some basic human differences.

The *Typus Melancholicus* Personality

We shall construct a pure type of a personality that has been shaped by a particular "dispositional vector." Following Alfred Kraus we shall call this dispositional vector "hypernomia."[7] The personality that is shaped by this vector has been labeled *typus melancholicus* (usually referred to henceforth as TM) although it is sometimes difficult to perceive the "melancholy" in this person.[8] Some psychiatric researchers have obtained evidence that this kind of person is the "pre-morbid personality type" for depression. In other words, this type of personality is prone in certain difficult circumstances to develop severe clinical depression and to require psychiatric treatment. In still other words, this person is especially vulnerable to depression.[9] We shall describe only the structure of the "pre-morbid" personality.

The *typus melancholicus* personality exhibits an excessive dedication to particular social roles and norms. Indeed, there is an overidentification with certain social norms. To state our point negatively, we might say that the TM remain incapable of role distance. The TM's striving is thus marked by its conscientiousness, by its determination to live up to these social norms. One performs one's duties, whether agreeable or disagreeable. The TM will not settle for less than complete fulfillment of them. The TM tends to feel guilty or valueless when she fails to fulfill her duties completely.[10]

In the above descriptions we have employed the phrases "*particular* social roles" and "*certain* social norms." We need to specify what we mean by "particular" and "certain." The social norms to which the TM ceaselessly strives to conform are primarily the nomos of her childhood. Hence it remains incomplete to characterize this person as overidentifying with social roles and norms. What she rather does is overidentify with the *cultural tradition* of which the roles and norms form a part. She views herself and her life as a part of a tradition, namely, the tradition she internalized in her childhood. This tradition has had a worthy history which preceded her and into which she was born and initiated. This cultural tradition will have a future, however, only if she and other members of it work to preserve it. Therefore she views herself as co-responsible for the continuing existence of the worthy tradition of her childhood.

This is so because one of the main characteristics of the TM personality is its relative lack of development in time. The TM's core self exhibits very little historical development. The TM personality is from childhood on relatively unadaptable to changing circumstances in the sense of assimilating and adapting to the new values that one encounters as one continues to live. Some components of the TM's personality do change and develop, but the normative roots of childhood remain basically unaltered and powerfully determinative. For the far greater part, then, the nomos in accordance with which the TM lives is the nomos internalized in childhood.[11]

To say that the TM's personality, at least in its fundamental nomic structure, lacks temporal development is to say that the TM is firmly rooted in the past. For the TM, the present and future are viewed primarily in terms of the imposition onto them of the nomos of her past. In overly simplified terms, we may say that, for the TM, the normative past endlessly repeats itself: the future is merely a projection of the nomos of the past. For the future to be like the past, the TM will have to work hard to realize the ideals; the future will not of its own accord preserve the tradition of the past. *Only firmly committed acts of will can make the future what it ought to be, namely, like the past.* The willpower of the TM, then, is called upon to perform resolutely and even heroically.

Another central characteristic of TM experience is, as Kraus has pointed out, its *intolerance of ambiguity*.[12] The meanings and values that the TM bestows on persons and actions are unambiguous, univocal, and definite. A particular action, for example, is either good or bad; it cannot be both good and bad. Colloquial English allows us to say that the TM inhabits a "black-and-white world": everything is either black or white; there are few shades of gray.

These tendencies of the TM to view the future as needing to replicate the nomos of the past and to view this in an unambiguous, unconditional manner leads to what we would like to call "the utopian demand of the TM." Nothing less than full realization of the past nomos will suffice. For this reason the TM requires that her environment be kept orderly and well structured. Disorderliness in the TM's environment is deemed a personal failing and hence unacceptable.

There is an obvious gap between the TM's utopian demands and the imperfections of reality. Because of this often wide and persistent gap, the TM's determination to realize her ideals may require serious sacrifices in the present. The present, then, because it necessitates hard work for the sake of the future, may be experienced as a time of considerable difficulty and striving. But this difficulty and striving are experienced as the prices that *must* paid to create the utopian future. We may thus describe the phases of the TM's lived experiences of time as follows: (1) the past was the time of the ideal, (2) the present, aimed firmly as it is at the future, requires strenuous effort that may now lead to disappointment; and (3) the future will embody the idealized past if one only strives diligently enough.[13]

Finally we would like to add that as a matter of empirical fact there is another trait that is usually associated with hypernomia. This person's threshold for emotional stimulation is unusually low. In other words, external stimuli need not be very forceful or sudden in order to arouse strong emotions in this person. Such an individual will become unusually anxious in situations that objectively involve relatively low levels of risk. This person therefore desires to live in environments in which the occurrences are familiar, predictable, manageable, and risk-free.

Having now sketched the basic personality structure of the *typus melancholicus*, we would like to characterize aspects of this person's daily life with somewhat more specificity.

The relationship of the TM to her social roles is complicated. On the one hand, we can truly say that she overidentifies with her social roles: she definitely sees herself as, for example, a dedicated vice-president, an effective political activist, a loving and helpful wife, and a devoted mother. Seeing herself as completely fulfilling these roles, she sees herself as sincerely experiencing the feelings that are appropriate to the role. But she has many other feelings too. Because she strives so hard to fulfill her roles, she sees other people and her life circumstances as obstacles. Her complete dedication to her work is hampered by what she views as incompetent and unintelligent people with whom she must work and on whom she must rely. She therefore feels frustrated and angry in her job. These negative feelings prevent her from experiencing the pleasant gratification of successfully engaging in her work. Because her husband, she thinks, does not help enough with the children, she feels stress and acts short-tempered when she picks them up after orchestra rehearsal, and then the love and devotion she feels for them becomes submerged.

This woman could probably endure this stress and anxiety if she lived in a community which consistently affirmed her in her roles. If she were regularly seen by those around her as a hard-working, astute, and successful businesswoman, she could endure the annoying incompetence of her fellow-workers. If she were always recognized by members of her community as a loving and devoted mother, she could put up with the many time- and energy-consuming tasks of rearing her children. But in a society she is not likely to be seen this way by many people. In a pluralistic society, other people see us through value-lenses that are not our own. Her fellow workers, because they have different values regarding work, see her as a workaholic who is determined to do the job her way. Her friends are not entirely sympathetic with her plight as a devoted mother because they see her as a woman who, if she wanted a successful career in business, was foolish to try to have children too. Her problem is that in a pluralistic society her values are not the values of the people around her. And when she therefore strives dutifully to actualize her values, she is not consistently confirmed in this by others.

It is quite different for the TM in communities. Let us look first at the function that the TM can perform in communities that are only beginning to take shape. With her concern for the ideal, she will take the emerging structures of the community and organize and systematize them. She will not be an innovator except through her determination to complete and regulate the emerging order. She sees that the rules of the new community are set firmly in place and that all people act in accordance with them. In this crucial way she *builds* the community: she takes structures that are only beginning to take shape and makes sure that people treat them as solid and compelling. Other members of the community will usually then appreciate her dedicated efforts to make the new community succeed.

But let us look again at the TM's experiences in a society. We stated above that the TM experiences herself as the bearer of a tradition which depends on her for its maintenance. Because of the cultural pluralism of societies, however, the particular tradition with which she identifies (indeed overidentifies) is only one among many others. Living in a society, the woman confronts manifold forces in it that are inimical to her tradition. She perceives her tradition as threatened on all sides, both internally and externally. Participating in a society, therefore, involves a constant struggle to defend and fortify the tradition against strong, antithetical cultural forces.

If this person lived in a community, she would share the overarching nomos taken for granted by others. Her values would be the sole tradition. She would therefore receive help from others in faithfully upholding and maintaining this tradition. She would be appreciated and respected for her work on the church board of deacons, and other people who knew and admired her as vice president, wife, and mother would cooperate with her as she carries out her duties as church deacon. All of her hard work, all her ceaseless striving, would be recognized and confirmed as right and remarkable. Because of her personality structure she would ask nothing less of herself than the highest achievement, but such high achievement would be acknowledged and applauded in a community. Her overidentification with social roles would make her stand out as a leader.

If the TM is really the pre-morbid personality type for depression, when the precipitating circumstances are sufficiently severe, this person is likely to fall into depression. The precipitating circumstances could become sufficiently severe in a society. Because of the multirelationality that people experience in societies, this woman could assume too many social roles. And she might industriously perform these roles in a social world that not only refused to appreciate her but that also negated the values she holds dear. She could finally reach the point at which she "couldn't do it all" and undergo a psychological breakdown. If she did, she would experience herself as a personal failure. In other words, she would blame herself for her inability, seeing herself as a incompetent businesswoman, an inadequate wife, and a useless mother. Now she views herself as failing entirely in her role performances. Such a self-image is common in depression. This kind of depression, if it persists and especially if it grows more severe, could precipitate suicide.

The Sociopathic Personality Type

The personality type that we shall discuss now has been known by several names: psychopath, sociopath, and antisocial personality. We shall use "sociopath" because it expresses what we view as the central characteristic of this type of person.

In many respects the sociopathic personality type proves to be opposite of the typus melancholicus. The sociopathic personality can be characterized as "hyponomic." The sociopathic person is someone who can enact the behavior prescribed by a social role very effectively while maintaining an extreme subjective distance from the role. In his role-performance the sociopathic person can be very convincing to others: other people believe in the sincerity of the role performance. But the sociopathic person himself feels none of the subjective states appropriate to the role. In fact he performs the role only out of some ulterior self-referential interest, and the manipulation of the other person serves his self-interest.

The sociopathic person can be extremely perceptive of other people's experiences. But this awareness of others is almost entirely cognitive and not at all sympathetic or emotional. The sociopathic person's attachment to self overwhelms any emotional attachement to others. Hence the standard psychiatric reference to the sociopathic person's "incapacity for love."[14] This perceptive cognitive understanding of other people's mental lives, however, permits the sociopathic person to know how to manipulate them quite effectively. One of the predominant ways in which other people experience the sociopathic person is as charming.[15]

The subjective distance of the sociopathic person from the social nomos is shown in his inability to feel guilt, remorse, or shame – or any moral emotions – for his violations of the nomos.[16] The person appears to be "without conscience."[17] Nevertheless, as we have indicated, other people can be thoroughly taken in by the sociopathic person's outward conformity to the social nomos.

The sociopathic person lives largely in the present. He or she feels no ties to or roots in the past and no duties to the future. Hence the standard characterization of this person as unable to follow any life plan. This lack of any connection with his own past is also manifest in the person's apparent inability to learn from experience.[18]

The sociopathic person's threshold for emotional stimulation is unusually high. In other words, external stimuli must be extraordinarily forceful or intense in order to arouse emotions in this individual. As a result, he frequently places himself in situations in which there will occur unusually high levels of stimulation. Compared to other people, then, this person will appear to be sensation-seeking and risk-taking to an extraordinary and even dangerous degree.

The permanent role distance combined with the extremely high threshold for emotional stimulation of the sociopathic person eventually leads to problems with other people. Because of his extremely high threshold for stimulation, the sociopathic person can outwardly conform to the requirements of the social nomos for only so long. After carrying out proper role behavior for a certain period of time, the sociopathic person grows unbearably bored. In order then "to feel something," the sociopathic person will almost intentionally violate the social nomos, thereby offending and disconcerting other people. In the midst of the interpersonal conflict and stress caused by the norm-violation, the sociopathic person can for a while "feel something." Moreover, this urge to violate the social nomos goes inwardly unchecked because of the person's emotional detachment from the nomos.

In a society the sociopathic person can "move on" if such conflicts become severe. And because he feels no attachment to the roles he plays, he can shed past roles and assume novel ones without difficulty. He can change who he is. That is to say, he can change "who he is" in terms of the self he presents to others. He can even take on a new profession, marry a new wife, have children, and associate with different companions. He can "recreate himself anew" to fit the new circumstances in which he finds himself. And when, because of his antisocial behavior, this new situation becomes difficult for him, he can immediately leave it and move on without feeling qualms, regret, or guilt. Because of his hyponomia., all of these changes are, to him, merely superficial.

In a society the sociopathic individual enjoys a significant advantage over the *typus melancholicus*. The sociopathic person does not feel bound by social norms, but in a society deviation from these norms is less easily detected. Moreover, the sociopathic person can pretend, at least for a while, to conform to social norms; and with the many shifting relationships within a society the difference between reality and pretense can go unnoticed. Finally, as social values change, the sociopathic person, having no personal attachment to any social values, can readily change along with them. He can thus recreate himself in order to be in tune with or even leading the wave of the future. This ability to change with the times or to even be on the forefront of that change can, in an unstable society, impress other people. The TM person, by contrast, feels powerfully bound by values of the past; and, consequently, this person will be left behind as social values change. Striving to preserve these values of the past, the TM individual works tirelessly to fulfill ideals that other people no longer appreciate. And convinced as she is that these are still the "true values," she will work even harder to prevent their complete dismissal. The sociopathic person has no commitment to the past, not even to his own personal past. If it serves his self-interest, he can recreate himself to become "the man of the hour."

The sociopathic person will have great difficulty living in a community. In a community he is likely to be seen as unbearably deviant. Hence, if he remains in the community, he will probably become the town brawler and/or drunk. Communities do have some functions for the sociopathic person to perform. He could, of instance, play the role of protector – e.g., soldier or policeman – because of the daring and stimulating nature of the job. As a policeman, however, he will probably be the "outsider" cop – e.g., the policeman who violates even the rules of the police force. But in a truly stable community this person is likely to violate the social nomos far too often for others to tolerate him. Hence, when the time comes for this person to "move on," he could probably not simply move to another neighborhood, change professions, marry a new wife, and lead a different life. In a community there would be no "new" place for him to go and become someone else. He would have to leave the community. In the United States in the second half of the nineteenth century he could have "headed west" and become a gunslinger, either the town marshal or outlaw. In the USA today he has to head for the city.

Of course, the kind of man our "ideal type" depicts is an extreme case. We can imagine several kinds of person who basically resemble this man but in whom the pull of hyponomia is not as strong. These people too would not identify themselves with the roles they perform. For this reason they would find it much easier to live in a society. Society, after all, tends to place only a minimum requirement on role performance: one must overtly enact the role behavior but one need not necessarily have the subjective experiences proper to the role. In a society the insurmountable distance between the sociopathic self and its roles need not matter or be discovered.

We would like to mention one additional reason why the sociopathic person would have great difficulty living in a community. Existence in a community, would be experienced as unbearably boring by this person. Because of the simplicity and routinized sameness of the community when compared with the complexity and variety of a society, the sociopathic person will find life more interesting and stimulating in a society.

Conclusion

There are, of course, people who have the internal flexibility or "freedom" to identify with roles as well as to remain inwardly distant from them. They experience great satisfaction in identifying themselves with their roles as father, husband, and football coach. Such people need to live in communities. They also need to maintain a distance from their roles when the role performance is constantly frustrating or merely unfulfilling. Moreover, they value the freedom that comes with the variety of opportunities in society. They even sometimes enjoy the anonymity offered by society.

Quite often, however, personalities fall somewhere along the spectrums of types that we have described. And when they do, community is no unalloyed good, just as life in society can prove to be destructive.

Notes

1   See Amitai Etzioni, ed., *New Communitarian Thinking: Persons, Virtues, Institutions, and Communities* (Charlottesville: University Press of Virginia, 1995); Amitai Etzioni, ed., *The Essential Communitarian Reader* (Lanham, MD: Rowman and Littlefield, 1998).
2   Peter L. Berger and Thomas Luckmann, *The Social Construction of Reality: A Treatise in the Sociology of Knowledge* (Garden City, NY: Doubleday, 1966).
3   See Aron Gurwitsch, *Human Encounters in the Social World*, trans. Fred Kersten (Duquesne University Press, 1979).
4   See Peter L. Berger, *Facing Up to Modernity: Excursions in Society, Politics, and Religion* (New York: Basic Books, 1977).
5   See Berger and Luckmann, *The Social Construction of Reality*.
6   See Berger, *Facing Up to Modernity*; Peter L. Berger and Thomas Luckmann, *Modernity, Pluralism and the Crisis of Meaning* (Gutersloh: Bertelsmann Foundation, 1995).
7   Kraus, *Sozialverhalten und Psychose Marisch-Depressiver*.
8   See Hubertus Tellenbach, *Melancholy: History of the Problem, Endogeneity, Typology, Pathogenesis, Clinical Considerations*, trans. Erling Eng (Pittsburgh: Duquesne University Press, 1980); Alfred Kraus, *Sozialverhalten und Psychose Manisch-Depressiver* (Stuttgart: Ferdinand Enke Verlag, 1977).
9   Derlev Von Zerssen, "Zur Pramorbiden Personlichkeit des Melancholikers," in

C. Mundt, P. Fiedler, H. Lang, and A. Kraus, eds., *Depressionkonzepte heute* (Berlin: Springer-Verlag, 1991), pp. 76–94.

10   Michael Schwartz and Osborne Wiggins, "Pathological Selves," in Dan Zahavi, ed., *Exploring the Self* (Philadelphia: John Benjamins, 2000), pp. 257–77.

11   Ibid.

12   See Kraus, *Sozialverhalten und Psychose Manisch-Depressiver*.

13   See Schwartz and Wiggins, "Pathological Selves."

14   See Hervey Cleckley, *The Mask of Sanity: An Attempt to Clarify Some Issues about the So-Called Psychopathic Personality* (Augusta, GA: Emily S. Cleckley, 1988); Donald W. Black, *Bad Boys, Bad Men: Confronting Antisocial Personality Disorder* (New York: Oxford University Press, 1999).

15   Ibid.

16   See Black, *Bad Boys, Bad Men*.

17   See Robert D. Hare, *Without Conscience: The Disturbing World of the Psychopaths among Us* (New York: Guilford, 1993).

18   See Cleckley, *The Mask of Sanity*; Black, *Bad Boys, Bad Men*.

PART III

Community, Culture, and Education

13

The Role of Art in Sustaining Communities

Marcia Muelder Eaton

Many claims have been made about the power of the arts. As the title of my chapter annouces, one of the things I believe art can do is contribute to conditions required for the sustainability of communities. But I also want to alert the reader to some limits of making this and other claims about the power of art. In an age of hyperbole, more measured avowals are called for. For this reason, I have chosen to begin by considering a speech made by Evan Mauer, the Director of the Minneapolis Institute for the Arts, early in 1998. It was a clearly written, heart-felt articulation of many of the claims that are generally made for the power of the arts. The occasion – a Minneapolis mayoral inauguration – made it natural for the speaker to stress the role of the arts in community building, making it particularly useful for the purpose of this chapter.

Mauer began by citing and agreeing with the claims made by persons who supported the establishment of cultural and artistic institutions (civic libraries, museums, symphonies, etc.) in nineteenth-century America. The arts were alleged to elevate, humanize, educate, refine, uplift, ennoble – generally to make those who come into contact with them better people and citizens. Mauer's claims, he acknowledged, fit solidly into this tradition. Here's what he asserted the arts do:

1 Through an expression of peoples' most important values, art ties people to nature, history, and to each other.
2 The arts embody and express religious beliefs, foundation myths, and civic ethics.
3 By embodying essential elements of humanity, the arts allow persons to understand themselves and others better. ("Better," one assumes, than we could do without the arts and the more we engage with the arts.)
4 Arts can unite culturally diverse American cities.
5 The arts are the best way to achieve bonds of communication, understanding, and respect.
6 The arts can improve academic achievement.

At the end of his talk, Mauer claimed to have "shown that [the arts] can ... be the most effective means of bringing together our diverse population and of helping our children become better students, better citizens, and better future achievers."[1] I contend that he did not *show* anything, in the sense of providing the sort of proof philosophers seek. Rather, he simply made a series of claims. This is, unfortunately, true of most arts advocacy. Eliot Eisner, one of America's foremost art educators, discusses this tendency in his paper, "Does Experience in the Arts Boost Academic Achievement?" His answer is that very little in the way of solid research supports a positive answer. It has not been definitively proved, for instance, that art courses increase test scores in math or reading, or even serve to keep some students from dropping out of high schools. "I cannot help but wonder if we sometimes claim too much," he worries.[2] His review of the research done between 1986 and 1996 justifies his concern. "At this moment I can find no good evidence that [the transfer of achievement in arts classes to other disciplines] occurs if what we count as evidence is more than anecdotal reports that are often designed for purposes of advocacy."[3]

Eisner's concerns, which I share, are directly relevant to the view expressed in Mauer's sixth claim; I fear that these concerns apply to the other five as well. To begin with, many are overstated. Are the arts the best or most effective way of expressing values or uniting diverse societies? I have heard people (a former governor of Minnesota, for instance) give this role to sports. Indeed, it is extremely interesting to substitute "baseball" for "the arts" in Mauer's claims. (One will, of course, have to revise the claims for countries where other sports reign.) Baseball certainly expresses basic American values. It ties people to history, each other, and, at least in places where it is still played outside, to nature. Obviously spiritual values and civic ethics are expressed. The playing of the game is more important (or at least is supposed to be more important) than the success of any individual. "All people are created equal" applies (except, one might argue, for the designated hitter rule), but with all of the issues of justice that come with that principle. Tensions between equality of distribution and differential distribution of rewards based on differential merit are manifest. No one gets more than three strikes, but people with better hand–eye coordination score more runs and get more recognition. Perhaps baseball does not express our foundation myths (I leave it to the reader-fan to show how it might), but it certainly unites diverse communities. Few artists have done more that Jackie Robinson on this score. Baseball can also be credited, I think, with enhancing communication, understanding, and respect. It is certainly arguable that it has kept as many students from dropping out of high school as have art courses.

In fact, claims made for the arts can be made for a wide range of human pursuits, from cockfighting in Bali[4] to World War II to dealing with El Niño. Eisner correctly observes that what is need is a *theory* that relates the arts with the effects that they are purported to have. What we need is an *explanation* of what it is about art that makes it possible for it to contribute to the sustainability of communities. Eisner calls for empirical research. This is, of course, needed. But a theoretical foundation is also required, and I hope to begin to construct that here.

This demands, of course, that I say what I mean by the terms "art" and "community." Elsewhere I have offered a detailed account of my theory of art, so I shall only state key definitions here.

X is a work of art if and only if
- X is an artifact;
- X is treated in aesthetically relevant ways; that is, X is treated in such a way that someone who is fluent in a culture is led to direct attention to intrinsic properties of X considered worthy of that attention (perception and reflection) within that culture; and
- when someone has an aesthetic experience as a result of attending to X, he or she realizes that the cause of the experience is an intrinsic property or set of intrinsic properties of X considered worthy of attention within the culture.

By "intrinsic" I refer to properties such that it is necessary to inspect directly an object or event in order to verify a claim that the object or event has that property. One must look at a painting to know if the colors are balanced, must listen to a sonata in order to know if it is unified, and so on.[5]

"Community" has been defined in a plethora of ways, and writers have also offered theories that subdivide the notion – distinguishing political from religious communities, market from domestic communities, healthy from sick communities, voluntary from involuntary communities, free from unfree communities. I do not want to add another theory of community per se. Rather, I want to focus on one aspect of some communities which contributes, I will argue, to their sustainability. This aspect, I will try to show, can be integrated with my theory of art in such a way that the explanation urged by Eisner is forthcoming. That is, I will offer an answer to the question, What is it about art that accounts for the role it plays in sustaining communities? (And bear in mind that this is a much more modest claim than is often made. I simply claim that art *sometimes* and by no means exclusively plays this role. Sports, wars, natural disasters can as well.) Art's contribution is special; that is, the nature of art is such that when it plays a positive sustaining role in communities, it does so in its own unique ways.

I do claim that art makes a special kind of contribution to one necessary feature of sustainable communities: In a sustainable community, individual members are aware of other members and take some responsibility for their "well being."[6]

A great deal of philosophical blood has been shed on what constitutes human well-being, so settling the multifarious issues that have been raised along the way goes well beyond the scope of this chapter (not to mention my capabilities). I rely on readers' intuitions here, in some confidence that what I say will not contradict them. If it does, no discourse on well-being that I can provide here will be much help. The notions of taking some responsibility for others of whom one is aware also deserve more attention than I can provide here. Brief reflection on what happens when communities, big or small, more or less durable, come into being will have to suffice.

Erving Goffman's concept of a focused group has helped me consider what it is that can turn a mere collection of individuals into a community, and how artistic activity turns a collection of people into a focused group. Goffman suggests that games provide a helpful case study in this regard. He gives a detailed analysis of the conditions operative in board games, for example, which turn the players into a group with a shared focus. Several things operative in board games also function in baseball, and, more importantly, in art.[7] But more important than the specification of the particular rules in operation is Goffman's characterization of what happens when people do what is required to play a game and thus become a focused group. Involvement in joint activity results in each individual becoming "an integral part of the situation, lodged in it and exposed to it, infusing himself into the encounter."[8] A consequence of this is that the activity is made stable, or, as I would say, is sustained or at least sustainable. Goffman says that in focused groups a "euphoria function" keeps things going.[9] In games, this may require new recruits and subsequent reallocation of resources. It also requires that a certain level of participant interest be maintained, and it is essential that the participants remain "at ease." "To be at ease in a situation is to be . . . entranced by the meanings [the activities] generate and stabilize; to be ill at ease means that one is ungrasped by immediate reality and that one loses the grasp that others have of it."[10]

Does art have the effect of creating focused groups in this sense? I think the answer is clearly "yes." Fans of Bach or The Spice Girls may, as individuals, derive pleasure from what they listen to in the privacy of their own rooms. But for most people there is also a sense of connection to others who derive similar pleasure, and this in itself yields another special kind of pleasure. History has shown that Bach's fan clubs are more likely to be shaped by euphoria functions than those of pop groups, more likely, that is, to feel pleasure over a considerable length of time. Art certainly provides occasions for becoming entranced by meanings. And when individuals are left cold by artworks, it is impossible to be "at ease," to be grasped by realities that seem to enthrall others.

But how does artistic activity function to create focused groups of the sort that are or might become communities? Imagine a collection of individuals who are not jointly focused on anything. How might art turn them into a focused group and ultimately into a community? My characterization of community demands awareness of others and a sense of responsibility for their well-being. There are two sorts of activity that are readily recognized as artistic – creation and contemplation – which can contribute to creating focused groups.

Creation, to put it very simply, is what art-makers do. By "contemplation" I mean to include the wide range of things audiences do: perceive, reflect, describe, evaluate, display, make purchase decisions, etc. (All of these things, of course, once more cry out for further discussion, and again I will have to rely on readers' intuitions.) There may be some occasions of artistic creation in which the maker is not aware of and does not care about the audience. These are rare, I believe. However, since I am concerned about the role art *can* play in producing sustainable communities, it is sufficient to claim that sometimes artists are aware of and are concerned with and for potential contemplators. (I will say more later about the ways in which failure to be aware of a sufficiently broad audience and to care about it has been a divisive factor in contemporary society – a destroyer rather than a builder.)

If a member of a collection of individuals creates something with an awareness of other members of the collection, a first step is taken in the direction of making it possible for the collection to focus as a group. If the creator also takes responsibility for the good of the group – concentrates on exposing what is made in a way that will infuse the experience of others and produce feelings of pleasure or generate solidarity (as Goffman puts it, generates "relatedness, psychic closeness, and mutual respect"[11]) – another necessary condition of community is met. Not all artists do this; but many do. And many do so successfully. I am certain that Bach did it; I expect The Spice Girls do as well. Much everyday activity of human beings exhibits the same structure. On a beach with strangers, someone picks ups a shell and alerts general attention by saying, "Boy, look at this! Isn't it beautiful?" In this simple act we find a basic element that makes creation of a focused group possible, even likely.

Contemplation is also essential. Obviously individuals can all by themselves savor objects and events aesthetically – enjoy a shade of blue or consider the intrinsic properties of a lily of the field or the sound of a slit-gong. But this has not typically been the extent of what I mean by "contemplation." Human beings by nature engage in descriptive and evaluative commentary. When they do, it is rarely just to hear themselves talk. They do so in awareness of others and often in the belief that others will benefit. Fans of Bach, The Spice Girls, or of songs written for Efe ceremonies in Yoruban cultures describe and evaluate as well as enjoy their individual encounters. Back on the beach one imagines strangers responding to the speaker's call for attention to the beauty of the shell. Some come closer, ask to hold it for themselves, inquire whether there are many others like it in the area. For however fleeting a time, a focused group exists. The focus will be maintained if, for instance, some contemplators decide to go shelling together or to establish a shell museum. Focus will have to be maintained even longer if what is undertaken is the building of an earthen mound, a pyramid, or a cathedral. But maintained and sustained, a focused group turns into a community.

Activities such as shelling in groups or setting up formal or informal institutions for presenting or displaying suggest how focused groups differ from communities – a difference, I think, of degree not of kind. Rituals or traditions direct and intensify awareness of other members of the group. When individuals consciously and conspicuously participate in these they begin to take responsibility for the group's continued existence and well-being. They are concerned with what has often been called "the good of the commons."

Eliot Eisner says that effective justification for including the arts in education requires looking at the arts themselves and asking what "demands they make on those who would create, perceive, or understand them."[12] His own answer is complex.

- The arts produce a feeling for what it takes to transform one's ideas, images, and feelings into a specific medium and form.
- The arts refine awareness of aesthetic qualities both in art and in the world and life more generally.
- The arts teach connections that have been made between form and content across cultures and times.
- The arts promote imagination of possibilities, desire and tolerance for ambiguity, recognition and acceptance of multiple perspectives and resolutions.

I agree that the arts can do all of these, and that all enhance awareness of others and provide a fertile soil in which a shared sense of responsibility can flourish.

But my answer to Eisner's question about how the demands the arts put on us produces certain effects is grounded in my definitions of "art" and "aesthetic." When one *creates* art of the sort that transforms focused groups into communities, one does it in the awareness of others and with the intention that they will respond when, and because, they attend to intrinsic properties of what has been created and to the fact that someone created it with that intention. Both creators and responders are also aware of and respond to the fact that the other members of the group are responding in (some) similar ways – or at least that their response results from attention to some of the same intrinsic properties. Members also engage in those forms of contemplation – pointing, discussing, displaying, etc. – in the belief that they will bring others to respond to certain intrinsic properties. Art can teach and refine skills required for awareness and contemplation. It provokes further acts of creation that in turn encourage more occasions for awareness and contemplation. By embodying rituals and traditions, art can instill a sense of responsibility. People engage in creation and communal contemplation at least in part for the good of others, and hence tend to act out of a sense of responsibility for the well-being of the group.

Some art forms and artworks contribute more than others to sustaining communities. Judgments about which these are require broad and deep cross-cultural awareness and knowledge. Considerable progress has been made in recent years with respect to the diversity of cultures whose art is presented in schools, museums, concert halls, the media, and other public arenas. But many people fear that this has contributed to an entrenchment of sub-cultures that works against the creation of unified communities that can be sustained over the long haul. Even if sub-cultures respect one another (which, of course, we cannot assume), confronting and respecting do not automatically result in acceptance, let alone enjoyment. *Looking* at artifacts does not necessarily produce an ability to participate in the aesthetic pleasures of cultures others than one's own, for this requires *seeing* as the members of those other cultures see. Can theories of art and beauty that recommend specific artistic practices contribute to the deepened understanding required for responding with sustained pleasure as well as respect? If so, how? And what theory or theories are most likely to contribute to the creation of sustainable communities? I am not so presumptuous as to pretend to know the complete answers. But thinking about the role of good art as well as the general role of art is certainly one condition for beginning to articulate an answer.

I believe that good art is more likely to contribute to sustaining communities than bad art. Good art, I have argued elsewhere, is art that repays sustained attention.[13] Individuals return again and again to aesthetic objects and events that reward perceiving and reflecting upon intrinsic properties therein. As I recognized above, sometimes individuals feel pleasure and the activity stops there. This value should not be denied or sniffed at. But art that sustains evokes more. When personal pleasure leads individuals to invite others to attend to those properties, communal practices and institutions that generate and regenerate attention develop. The more often and the longer that attention is paid, the more likely a focused group is to develop and continue to exist. A non-oppressive community is sustained only as long as the well-being of the commons is believed by members to be a mutual concern. As an individual I will only invite others to attend to intrinsic properties that reward me and that I believe will reward them; that is, I try to contribute to the well-being of others of whom I am aware. (Notice there is a difference between *inviting* and *forcing* others to attend; forcing is not typically done out of a sense of obligation for the good of those forced.) As I have argued elsewhere, intrinsic properties that one values are valued-in-a-community.[14]

The more and the longer that a particular artwork inspires me to invite others to engage in similar perception and reflection, the more and the longer I and those others will tend to maintain our interrelationship. Goffman's "euphoria function" is satisfied. But this is precisely what constitutes sustainability. Group contemplation and discussion require that members enter into relationship with the objects and with each other. When this is combined with the ways in which artworks present the shared ideas, values, myths, metaphors, and feelings that characterize flourishing communities, sustainability is enhanced.

The claim made for art – that it provides windows across cultures that invite deeper understanding of world-views that differ from one's own – is, of course, true. But within single communities it is not always the case that art objects and events present diverse views. The provision of multiple perspectives in a single work is culture-specific; even in the West it is a relatively recent phenomenon. One simply cannot show that cultures are most sustainable when their arts challenge viewers to consider various viewpoints. This was not true, for example, of Christian art of medieval Europe; and although the communities therein did not last forever, they were sustained over several centuries. The art of the Sepiks of New Guinea expresses only the ideas and emotions (fears and hopes) of the males who have dominated in what seems to many outsiders an almost appallingly sustained manner. Again, one must be very careful about making claims for the arts that are too strong. My own liberal insistence on the value of a marketplace of free artistic ideas is challenged by cultures such as the Sepik's, where art undeniably permeates daily life and helps to hold the communities together.

The difficulty that many Westerners, especially women, have with making sense of, let alone admiring, art of such different cultures as the Sepik's, indicates how careful one must be in making claims for art's power to illuminate, let alone unite, diverse communities. I have written elsewhere about the "deep fluency" I believe is required before one can arrive at the level of entry into a culture that is a condition of understanding and respect.[15] Nonetheless, art does provide access and helps us to see the world through others' eyes. This comes about both by looking at others' art and by learning how others see our own art. In *No Mercy: A Journey to the Heart of the Congo*, Redmond O'Hanlon relates an experience in which his guide and companion, Dr. Marcellin, becomes insulted at O'Hanlon's amusement at African "superstitions." Marcellin angrily responds with a catalog of what he perceives as white men's superstitions: the fetishes (crosses) worn around many of their necks, the cannibalistic rites they euphemistically call "eucharist," etc. "You white men – we don't even know how you breed. You had a god born without any sex! And then he never had a woman! And what about the god's mother – in those fetish statues you have everywhere – a woman who'd never had a man, with that idiot smile on her face and a baby in her arms? If that's not just plain silly, if that's not stupid, I don't know what is."[16] Seeing others' art and our art as others see it is an excellent way to remain open to the revisions demanded by sustainability in a changing world .[17]

I believe that in my *own* culture good art is more likely than bad art to develop the kinds of community-enhancing skill that Eisner and I claim good art requires. Something that challenges and rewards repeated attention is more likely to challenge one to exercise careful, nuanced attention. Inferior or sentimental art allows for laziness – for *anaestheticized* rather than heightened, *aestheticized* attention. Daniel Jacobson writes:

> The ethical function of narrative art lies in its ability to get us to see things anew. . . . How much to hope for from art, and how to fear it, will hang on one's diagnosis of our condition. Are we, as some believe, suffering from a surfeit of contrary ethical views? Or are we still often talking past each other, unable to imagine other ways of seeing than our own, and hence incapable of confronting them?[18]

Isaiah Berlin has insightfully worried along similar lines. There is no guarantee that diverse communities will be able to achieve means for harmonizing different values and projects, he says.[19] Art *can* present diverse ideas in ways that engage discussion rather than threaten dissolution. Communities are more likely to sustain themselves if they achieve a delicate balance between the tolerance for new ideas that allows for revision necessary for continued existence and a chaos that may result from a Babel of competing voices. Great art often repays attention precisely because it embodies not simply multiple perspectives, but even contradictions. But one must recognize the possibility of great art that expresses and entrenches a single shared worldview.

Art can express a sense of shame as well as a sense of pride, often at the same time and with the same goal of regeneration. A public project in southwestern Pennsylvania exemplifies a community struggling to sustain and regenerate itself. Success demanded coming to grips with "a company-town mindset that waits for The Company to take the lead, [and where] residents can be history-proud, history-shamed, anxious about their future, yet incredibly passive."[20] Acid mine damage had created deadly streams and a starkly degenerated landscape. The single-minded industrial focus of the mid-twentieth-century community that produced these could not sustain itself into the final decades of that century. Historians, scientists, designers, and artists are working together to turn this graveyard into a park – into an aesthetic environment in which art plays a key role. It will "re-energize" the area and its inhabitants if it succeeds. What is clear, as one reads about this and similar projects, is that the aesthetic activity permeates a sense of awareness and shared responsibility for others.

What communities cannot stand, as Jean Behke Elshtain says, is cynicism, for this undercuts any possibility of regeneration.[21] Art that feeds cynicism (and there are many examples of this in contemporary technological societies) is not likely, therefore, to contribute to sustainability – unless it also encourages revisions of harmful institutions and practices. Nor, I think, can communities stand for long when art contributes to factionalization or to putting power in the hands of a few who may, like Machiavelli, be aware of others but concerned only for their own personal well-being or for the well-being of a chosen minority. Art can oppress as well as liberate. What counts as well-being for a group allows for, indeed demands, diverse answers. But coupled with the notion of the *commons*, I believe (hope) it is less likely to be restricted to vested interests of a single class, race, gender, or religion.

Perhaps powerful forces in general can be beneficial only if they are capable of malevolence as well. Art can destroy as well as build. This empirical claim calls for more evidence, of course. The story will have to be complex. William McNeill warns against simplistic reductionism in a review article on Jared Diamond's *Guns, Germs and Steel: The Fate of Human Societies*. Diamond argues that since one cannot explain Europe's outpacing of other societies in technology in terms of intelligence, the main factors must have been environment and bio-geography. McNeill considers this an oversimplification:

> I do not accept Diamonds's dismissive appraisal of "cultural idiosyncrasies unrelated to environment." A more persuasive view might be to suppose that in the early phases of our history, when technical skills and organizational coordination were still undeveloped, human societies were indeed closely constrained by the local availability of food, as Diamond convincingly argues. But with the passage of time, as inventions multiplied and more effective modes of coordinating collective effort across space and time were adopted, the course of human history became increasingly autonomous simply because our capacities to reshape actual environments to suit our purposes became greater and greater. Cultural idiosyncrasies – systems of meaning constructed out of nothing more tangible than words and numerical symbols, and largely independent of any external reference whatever – came into their own. This is the ordinary domain of history. . . . Introspection surely tells us that conscious purposes and shared meanings govern much of human behavior; and a science of history that leaves this dimension out, as Diamond's does, is unlikely to explain satisfactorily the modern world or any other part of the human record.[22]

The question of the "superiority" of technology aside, McNeill is surely correct that purposes and meanings are factors that matter as much as environment and geography. A full understanding of the role of art in sustaining (as well as undermining) communities demands careful case studies of the ways in which artistic symbols and activities serve to establish and perpetuate forms of life One must, as it were, put art into the proper context. Formalist theories that locate art's value exclusively in emotions generated by a work's intrinsic properties deprive art of its sustaining role, for such a role can only be played when art is clearly connected to the multifaceted activities of a community and when it is realized that members of the community recognize that connection.

Murray Edelman provides a detailed analysis of one specific social function art has played in communities (to both good and bad ends), namely, politics. By supplying images that enable individuals to become part of a focused group (or as Edelman puts it in this context, "a politically conscious group"),

> Works of art . . . construct and periodically reconstruct perceptions and beliefs that underlie the political actions in the news, even when their role is concealed, as is usually the case. They create diverse levels of reality and multiple realities. . . .At other times they construct beliefs in one true reality, as do both positivist and scientific writings and fundamentalist religious tracts.[23]

Art helps individuals to define themselves as insiders and to distinguish themselves as outsiders. Art can also be a tool in the hands of those in power who act to create shared perceptions, and often, as Marx warned, those perceptions constitute a false consciousness. We are all familiar with sentimental pictures of loving, well-fed healthy families that purpose to express universal American family values:

> Current as well as past conditions, events, and anxieties make people susceptible to particular ways of seeing and understanding realities, including the outcomes of political processes. . . . It is artists who provide the ways of seeing, the categories, and the premises that yield modes of understanding everyday life. Twentieth-century art has been especially explicit in revealing the premises that have dominated contemporary thought. The wars, genocides, homelessness, and other conspicuous public events of the century have inspired a great deal of shock, fear, and outrage, which works of art have objectified and so made more readily available for expression in everyday activities and political statements.[24]

Myths and narratives "justify and rationalize the power, incomes, and perquisites of people who hold high positions."[25] Works of art can broaden perspective but can also narrow them. In getting members of a group to classify in terms of what is heroic, calamitous, even funny, governments and political candidates serve their goal of getting constituencies to see things from a particular point of view. I am more interested here in considering how art generally contributes to sustainability. But Edelman's very interesting discussion of specific ways in which specific arts are used by political parties and authorities for specific purposes supports my more abstract assertions, I believe.

Individual communities have special needs: things, and hence art, that will work to sustain one community will not necessary work in others. Up to this point I have tried to avoid the imperialism that comes with making universal judgments about what in general is sustaining about art. However, I want to conclude by saying more about what I think "we" need. I confess that issues of diversity and attempts to deal justly with them have often left me not quite knowing who "I" am, let alone who "we" are. I am white, but female, economically well-off, but fat, an American, but a Minnesotan, a Minnesotan, but one whose first 21 years were spent in Illinois, heterosexual, but post-menopausal, and so on. Thus I will speak for a group Cass Sunstein has called "enlightened citizens of a free democracy."[26] Putting aside questions of degrees of enlightenment and of freedom (questions that other contributors to in this volume rightly refuse to put aside), one can ask: what does this "we" need from art in order to sustain ourselves?

In trying to answer this question, I rely heavily on ideas presented about a century ago by Leo Tolstoy. He defined art as the communication in a medium of feelings so sincerely felt and skillfully presented by the artist that members of the audience who experience the work come to feel the same way.[27] The upshot is that artists and audience members are united in a spiritual community, or, as I would put it, are aware of and have a sense of responsibility for the well-being of the commons. The unabashedly moral character of this view is present, though perhaps less explicitly in all of the concepts in the phrase "enlightened citizens of a free democracy." A different moral aspect of art has recently been articulated (in a different context) by Yuriko Saito. In discussing the questions of whether or not there are correct and incorrect interpretations of art, she argues that we have a moral obligation to try to experience works of art correctly, to attempt to do more than simply get as much aesthetic pleasure from an object or event without regard to what the artist meant or what it meant when it was produced, and without regard to the category to which the work belongs. Doing otherwise, she insists, shows a selfish, self-centered, close-minded attitude, "an unwillingness to put aside our own agenda, whether it be an ethnocentric or present-minded perspective or the pursuit for easy pleasure and entertainment."[28] One ought (morally ought) to respect each work, give it a chance to open our eyes and minds. I agree with Saito, but hers is, admittedly, a very strong position. Whether one is ready to go as far as she does, one must admit that art can open eyes and minds; and to this extent it is highly recommended, perhaps required, to sustain a democratic society of enlightened citizens. This returns us, of course, to Eliot Eisner's point that the arts should be required in democratic societies' educational systems because of their propensity to create a tolerance and even enthusiasm for multiple perspectives. The arts can also play a related and significant role in a market-place of free ideas.

Art, particularly good art, also develops the skills required for the enlightenment that we consider a necessary condition for sustainable free democracies. There is no guarantee, of course, that the existence of great art alone will make for a more sustainable community. Works must be reflected upon – e.g., read, but read carefully, seen and heard, but seen and heard with attention and repetition. Two of the most frequently assigned fictional works in America's high schools are *To Kill a Mockingbird* and *The Color Purple*. This must be because teachers believe that they encourage and challenge students and because they are worthy of their attention. There is a difference between reading *a book* and *reading* a book. *Reading* is engaging in aesthetic activity of the sort that contributes to the development of skills necessary for becoming an enlightened citizen – critical analysis and moral imaginativeness, to name just two. But not just anything can be *read* in such a way. One can read but not *read* a Harlequin romance. These are books, but not books that demand much of the reader. Enlightened citizens of a free democracy need precisely the things that good art demands: powers of observation, organization, puzzle-solving, imagination. In order to be a member of a focused group, one must be able to focus. In order to be a member of an *enlightened* focused group, one must be able to focus in enlightened and enlightening ways. In short, one must know what is justifiable and how to express the ideas and attitudes that sustain awareness of and responsibility for the well-being of other free democrats.

Both internal and external forces can work against sustainability. A community is sustainable when insiders' practices perpetuate those positive features that enhance awareness and responsibility for the good of the commons. But this requires knowledge of what is really good. A community that requires and inspires total celibacy, for instance, will not last long. Even apparently admirable practices may have a dark side. A flourishing society on Easter Island was brought to a level of squalid subsistence by their own obsession with bringing huge rocks from the inner island to the coast, for the practice required logs to roll the stones laboriously from one spot to another. This in turn resulted in such deforestation that the delicate biosystems that once supported abundant food sources disappeared. We admire the religious, aesthetic zeal these stones still exhibit today – but one asks oneself with a self-conscious glance over one's shoulder at our own environmentally unfriendly practices, "How did they fail to see what they were doing?" In our own culture, many artists have, unfortunately deliberately separated themselves off from the majority of the population. They seem increasingly unaware of others and cannot or will not seriously heed obligations for the general good. Mass art is too often contemptuously taken as incompatible with good art.[29] Art that is used to drive wedges between groups within a community will not contribute to but will act against sustainability.

At the same time, communities cannot sustain themselves in the face of overwhelming external human forces. Powerful external forces must either ignore a community or treat it with sufficient respect if it is to survive. Richard Anderson, in a discussion of Aztec art and aesthetics, describes this culture's preoccupation with apocalypse and the elaborate ways in which their rituals and ceremonies aimed to forestall its inevitability in the hands of powerful gods:

> There is some irony in the fact that the Aztec's world *was* soon destroyed – not by an earthquake sent by the gods, but by the conquering Spanish; the irony is heightened when one realizes that the essence of Aztec culture *did* survive this experience largely through art works such as architecture, the illustrated codices, stone sculpture, and so on.[30]

Even if art cannot by itself sustain the ideas that keep cultures alive long enough to attain and maintain what we might call "the flourishing point," it does make a contribution. The very outsiders who act to destroy a community often borrow those artistic forms and practices that made them worth attacking. The Spanish borrowed from the Aztecs who had borrowed from the Toltecs. The Romans copied Greek architecture, Europeans incorporated in their paintings the art forms of the Africans they subjugated, White Americans imitate Black American music, and so on.

Art advocates have high hopes for art's ability to encourage intercultural respect. There is much about art that justifies such hope. If communities cannot stand in the face of too much cynicism, neither can they stand in the face of too little hope. In his novel, *The Discovery of Heaven*, Harry Mulisch expresses one kind of hope that art seems to generate.

> In a world full of war, famine, oppression, deceit, monotony, what – apart from the eternal innocence of animals – offers an image of hope? A mother with a newborn child in her arms? The child may end up as a murderer, or a murder victim, so that the hopeful image is a prefiguration of a pietà: a mother with a newly dead child on her lap. No, the image of hope is someone passing with a musical instrument in a case. It is not contributing to oppression, or to liberation either, but to something that continues below the surface: the boy on his bike, with a guitar in a mock-leather cover on his back; a girl with a dented violin case waiting for the tram.[31]

A child with a musical instrument is not the only cause of hope, of course; a child with a baseball glove or ballet slippers may be as well. But surely Mulisch is correct in identifying implements for making art as paradigmatic sources for the creation of the focused groups that ideally engender awareness of and responsibility for the well-being of others.

Notes

1   Evan Mauer, "Keynote speech at Inauguration of Major Sharon Sayles-Belton," January 2, 1998. Typescript available from Minneapolis Institute of Arts, Minneapolis, MN, p. 6.

2   Eliot Eisner, "Does Experience in the Arts Boost Academic Achievement?" paper delivered at conference on Arts in the Workplace, sponsored by Getty Education Institute, Los Angeles, 1997, typescript, p. 1.

3   Ibid., p. 8.

4   For an analysis of the aesthetic and other social aspects of this, see Clifford Geertz, "Deep Play: Notes of the Balinese Cockfight," in *The Interpretation of Cultures* (New York: Basic Books, 1973), pp. 412-53. I am grateful to Ronald Moore for this example.

5   I have developed these definitions in several books and articles. For the most recent discussion, see "A Sustainable Definition of 'Art'," in Noël Carroll, ed., *Theories of Art* (Madison: University of Wisconsin Press, 1999).

6   I have been tremendously influenced here by the work of Robert Terry. See his *Authentic Leadership* (San Francisco: Jossey-Bass, 1993).

7   Erving Goffman, *Encounters, Two Studies in the Sociology of Interaction* (Indianapolis: Bobbs Merrill, 1962). In board games, rules of relevance dictate which features of the situation matter. In chess, for example, the material out of which the pieces are made is irrelevant; initial placement of tokens on the board is relevant. Rules of realized resources tell us what is real; for example, the queen in chess is not a real queen outside the boundaries of the game; within the game only "she" can move in certain ways. Transformation rules allocate resources. In chess, usually each player gets the same number of pieces, but if the group decides that handicapping will create a better game, then one player may receive or take fewer pieces. Obviously, in terms of these particular rules, the board game model does not apply directly to art. Something like rules of relevance are at work (the colors of a painting matter, its temperature does not), as are rules of realized resources (in one sense a painting may *really* be Queen Elizabeth I, in another sense obviously not). Transformation rules, at least interpreted as resource allocation, are not applicable. (There may be activities within the general rubric of artistic activity, say museum going, in which this is relevant.)

8   Ibid., p. 38.

9   Ibid., p. 44.

10 Ibid.

11 Ibid., p. 40.

12 Eisner, "Does Experience in the Arts Boost Academic Achievement?", p. 15.

13 Marcia Muelder Eaton, *Art and Nonart: Reflections on an Orange Crate and a Moose Call* (Cranbury, NJ: Associated University Presses, 1983).

14 "A Sustainable Definition of Art," in Carroll, ed., *Theories of Art*.

15 Marcia Muelder Eaton, "Philosophical Aesthetics: A Way of Knowing and Its Limits," *Journal of Aesthetic Education* (1994): 19–32.

16 Redmond O'Hanlon, *No Mercy: A Journey to the Heart of the Congo* (New York: Alfred A. Knopf, 1997), p. 336. I am grateful to Laurie Hall Muelder for this example.

17   For discussions of ways in which the artists John T. Scott and Kosen Ohtsubo have interpreted the necessity for using traditions from the past to meet present and future needs of a community, see Marcia Muelder Eaton, *What About Beauty?* (Minneapolis: University of Minnesota Press, 1998).

18   Daniel Jacobson, "Sir Philip Sidney's Dilemma," *Journal of Aesthetics and Art Criticism* 54 (Fall 1996): 335.

19   Isaiah Berlin, "The Romantic Revolution," in Henry Hardy, ed., *The Sense of Reality, Studies in Ideas and Their History* (New York: Farrar, Straus and Giroux, 1996), pp. 168–93.

20   T. Allan Comp et al., "A Place of Regeneration," *Forecast* (Spring/Summer 1997): 15–18.

21   See Jean Bethke Elshtain and Christopher Beem, "Communities and Community: Critique and Retrieval, " chap. 1 in this volume.

22   William McNeill, Review of Jared Diamond's *Guns, Germs and Steel: The Fate of Human Societies, New York Review of Books*, May 15, 1997, pp. 49–50.

23   Murray Edelman, *From Art to Politics: How Artistic Creations Shape Political Conceptions* (Chicago: University of Chicago Press, 1994), p. 9.

24   Ibid., p. 40.

25   Ibid., p. 102.

26   Cass Sunstein, "A New Deal For Free Speech," Talk delivered at the Understanding Communities conference at the University of Louisville, May 27, 1998.

27   Leo Tolstoy, *What Is Art?* (1896).

28   Yuriko Saito, "The Aesthetics of Unscenic Nature," *Journal of Aesthetics and Art Criticism* 56 (1998): 103.

29   For an excellent discussion of mass art and the generally bad rap it has gotten from philosophers, see Noël Carroll, *A Philosophy of Mass Art* (Oxford: Oxford University Press, 1998). With Carroll, I believe that there is nothing incompatible about having mass art that is also good art.

30   Richard Anderson, *Calliope's Sisters: A Comparative Study of Philosophies of Art* (Englewood Cliffs, NJ: Prentice Hall, 1990), p. 152.

31   Harry Mulisch, *The Discovery of Heaven*, trans. Paul Vincent (New York: Penguin, 1996; originally published in Dutch, 1992), p. 56.

14

Images of Community in American
Popular Culture

Eileen John and Nancy Potter

Although the content of American popular culture is strikingly individualistic, one also finds images that signify, or are meant to signify, something like
a community. This chapter analyzes images as they are found in television,
radio, and film. The chapter has three aims: (1) to analyze the meaning of
community and disaffiliation, taking those meanings to be constructed and
under revision; (2) to hypothesize about the desires to have images of community, with particular attention to the different social positions and contexts from which the desires arise; and (3) to investigate the interconnections
between images of community and the moral and political domain. Can these
images direct us toward a better sense of our social positions and relations?
Can they motivate us to address conflicts between different communities?
How do we and how should we respond to these images? The chapter argues
that images of community are powerful in part because they function as
mnemonic devices for complex ideological structures – as abstract reminders of our attempts to organize and evaluate our fundamentally messy social
existence. Although apparently superficial and simple, many images also
function to destabilize our customary ways of conceptualizing communities
and so can help us to constitute a radical pluralist society.

Let us begin by explaining further our focus on images of community in
popular culture. First, by popular culture, we mean something rather complex: popular culture is a large domain of human creations and activities
that are widely available and are to varying degrees widely recognized; that
at least partly function as entertainment, social commentary, or self-expres-
sion; and that primarily emerge from "everyday people." The creations and
activities that become part of popular culture contribute in some informal
way to the contemporary population's sense of what ideas, concerns, styles,
people, historical events, and so on are vital to ordinary folks (for example,
as a kind of currency in everyday conversation and thought) and to their
sense of what is currently accessible for public reference. So, all of the images
we consider come from broadcast media, which make them widely avail-

able, and they all have some role as entertainment (though this role is perhaps supposed to be subordinate in the cases of the news broadcasts of Princess Diana's death and the self-help show *Loveline*). Furthermore, the popular culture sources we have chosen are ones that we think count toward establishing the ideas about communities that are currently accessible.

Second, by an *image* of community, we mean something that displays the life of a particular community, not necessarily in visual form. An image of community may do this through forming an actual community. For example, one might say of the hosts and audiences for MTV's *Loveline* or for public radio's *Prairie Home Companion* that they actually constitute communities. We treat such cases in which communities are instantiated as *images* because they offer prominent public models of how a community can function. These communities are open to display in a way that most communities are not. This means we are treating them as *exemplars*, to use Nelson Goodman's term. As exemplars, they *are* communities, but in their public role they also refer to or symbolize the features of communities, just as, in Goodman's illustration, a fabric sample *has* the qualities of the fabric and also *refers to* or *symbolizes* those qualities.[1]

The special importance of images of community, as opposed to theories of community, lies in the different kinds of simplicity and complexity that images offer and in the various forms our responses to them can take. Images are in some ways simple to encounter because there is something in an image to be immediately acquainted with – we can hear voices, see human interaction, register details of setting or context, and sense moods, tension, pace, and patterns. So we can feel fairly directly exposed to the life of a community through an image, whereas a theory of community normally does not aim to and cannot provide that experience. The features we experience in an image thus often have a powerful presence for us – we remember them vividly, we readily put different components of the image together, and we may respond to the experience emotionally or with subtler kinds of affect and assessment. Viewers of *Seinfeld* have a very strong, apparently effortlessly acquired, sense of what it is like to hang out in Jerry's apartment.

As that example illustrates, however, images also display extremely complex ideas, feelings, and social patterns. To know what it is like to hang out in Jerry's apartment is in part to have a basic sensory awareness of the space and of movement within it and of its boring governing aesthetic. But viewers who know what it is like to hang out there also have an awareness of operative social and moral expectations, central ambitions and worries, what counts as funny and disastrous, and so on. In general, in an image of community, a huge amount of information about the nuances, the guiding assumptions, and the values of a community can be conveyed without being discursively articulated. The lack of articulation means that our understanding of the communities on display can be both very rich and very superficial.

We may be in some sense intimately acquainted with the social dynamics of *Seinfeld*, but we may never have isolated and scrutinized their guiding assumptions and values. Part of our task here is to articulate some of the complex information we receive from images of community. The work of articulating, scrutinizing, and evaluating what is conveyed in these images is crucial, if the images are to do more than simply remind us of familiar ideas about community.

One reason that images of community have the potential to do more than this is that they can engage our desires and emotions. They can display ideals of community that make us want something new in our own communities. They can prompt us to enter into the affective life of a particular community, and that emotional engagement can be extremely important to understanding the dynamics of a community. In watching the coming out episode of *Ellen*, discussed below, the viewer must feel some of the emotional pressures involved in order to appreciate what it means and what it costs for Ellen to come out in a community of heterosexual friends. These images can also be disturbing and unsettling, and that kind of gut response is usually significant – it indicates that the image is posing questions we do not yet know how to answer. Our discussion of particular examples will spell out further how our affective and motivational responses shape how images of community function.

We take as our starting point two accounts of community, offered by Trudy Govier and Robert Fowler. Govier's definition of community is as follows.

> A community is a group that attempts to be an inclusive whole and can celebrate different callings and the interdependence of private and public life. People in a community mutually respect each other despite their differences, and are able to understand that the community has long term interests and must provide for the needs of future generations. People in communities have commitments to each other and to common projects and causes. They have a kind of rootedness, a connection to the place where they live with others.[2]

Govier gives a quite rich, normative account of communities, seeing them as social groups whose members share mutual moral responsibility and respect, are committed to each other's and the community's well-being, celebrate differences within the community, and feel a sense of rootedness. But Govier says:

> [M]any Americans experience tremendous difficulty identifying their activities meaningfully with the efforts of others. In the contemporary mass culture of America there is no generally accepted conception of community involvement, responsibility, and identity that would lead them to do so. . . . It is extraordinarily difficult to get a picture of the whole society and how one fits into it. This phenomenon has been referred to as the problem of invisible

complexity. We tend to see, and are encouraged by many media accounts to see, only contending groups with contending claims based on rights, entitlements, and special interests. What should be – and in many ways is – a society of interdependent people is seen instead as a marketplace wherein people contribute only by competing with one another.[3]

Govier diagnoses contemporary culture as failing to provide us with good, sustaining and illuminating images of community. Instead, communities are usually presented as superficial "lifestyle enclaves," where groups with similar lifestyle choices band together for survival to the exclusion of others. Govier thinks the images we encounter through the popular media primarily present social interaction as a marketplace of mutual competition, and she suggests that our encounters with community both in experience and in representations ultimately feed distrust and pessimism about social change.

Fowler emphasizes that there are different kinds of communities which function differently (a point we will return to below), but he makes several general points about what sustains communities: they are vulnerable to the tyranny of powerful paradigms, they need to embrace the inevitable messiness of community life rather than have idealized expectations of perfection, participation in community is partly affective in nature, and communities are sustained partly through providing examples of how communities function – how a community is modeled, say in images of community, is important to the life of that community.[4] In Fowler's view, sustaining communities on these terms is a difficult, ongoing project, requiring what he calls "existential watchfulness" to guard against tyranny.

Fowler categorizes community into three kinds:

1 *Communities of ideas*, where people decide together, face to face, conversing with, and respecting each other in a setting which is as equal as possible.
2 *Communities of crisis*, where people band together in resistance to some public or global problem.
3 *Communities of memory*, which are communities shaped around long-established belief systems that link present to past. Fowler identifies this kind with tradition and religion, demarcating it from (2), where group members are centering their commonalities around ethnic, racial, or national identities.

We suggest the addition of (at least) three more kinds of communities:

4 *Communities of home*, where "home" is not necessarily a location but instead is a mutually nourishing group where each member can, in significant ways, be himself or herself among others.

5   *Communities of transience,* where people who were formerly strangers
    come together quickly and temporarily but, while together, form bonds
    that are fairly comprehensive, are concerned for one another's well-be-
    ing, and come to hold (for a time) some common goals or interests.
6   *Outlaw communities,* where members are brought together, in part,
    through identification with law-breaking. Our hunch is that outlaw com-
    munities will typically also be communities of crisis and perhaps of home,
    so that members will bond around similar things as in those other kinds.
    But members of outlaw communities also bond around their relation to
    the law as law-breakers. We are calling them "outlaw" not because the
    members are outlaws but because that is how society typically views
    the formation of "law-breaking" people into cohesive groups.

Although Govier and Fowler each point us to some useful thoughts about
community, both assume a grounding that we are hesitant to endorse.
Govier's description of a community strikes us as more homogeneous and
unified than we think is politically desirable; Fowler emphasizes the centrality of virtue and character in communities.[5] We take Govier and Fowler to
be exhibiting features of the political ideology of communitarianism and,
while we share some of the concepts of such theories, we don't identify our
interest in communities as communitarian.

Communitarianism as an ideology celebrates participation in communities, in contrast to various liberal assumptions about the self and the goals of
social and political institutions. Although there are many versions of liberalism, some of which are quite subtle and complex, in general the liberal takes
the individual to have basic rights, interests, and conceptions of the good life
that establish the identity of the self as an autonomous agent who acts in
social contexts. Social relations, then, involve the interaction of these individually constituted selves, and social and political institutions should promote individuals' free, self-determined activity. Liberal theorists often take
seriously the value of participation in communities and may even acknowledge the embeddedness of individuals in social networks. Nevertheless, the
individual is the primary unit of society, and structures and institutions ought
to be shaped so as to protect and foster the individual. Communitarians, in
contrast, see individuals as existing through their participation in social,
communal life and through commitment to the values defined by their communities. On a communitarian view, social and political institutions need to
encourage this richer form of socially constituted individual and to discourage the development of the rights-bearing autonomous individual whose own
interests come to dominate his or her choices to the extent that civic relations, familial ties, and societal obligations are eroded.

We agree with Habermas that contemporary communitarianism, as it has
developed from its basic critique of liberal assumptions, constricts political

discourse in that it labors under a kind of "ethical overload."[6] It has emerged as an ideology that gives priority to the objective of communal consensus or unity and to the entrenchment of core moral values. For example, communitarian advocate Amitai Etzioni defines community as a shared set of social bonds that include shared moral and social values, and he adds that such communal values must be arrived at by free and open dialogue. But, he says, "these values must be assessed at some level for their legitimacy . . . communal values are only legitimate insofar as they are not in tension with overarching core values."[7] But what are the external and overriding criteria by which we judge values, and where do they come from? In "The Responsive Communitarian Platform: Rights and Responsibilities," more than 50 thinkers set out core values of communitarianism, which include statements about the value of family and education and the role of government. Moral anchoring, the Platform states, begins at home, in the family, where "family" seems to be understood implicitly as rooted in two-parent, heterosexual marriage.[8]

By celebrating the value of consensus and the governing role of moral commitments, communitarianism has the potential to function in politically constrictive and oppressive ways. Penny Weiss, articulating specifically feminist criticisms of communitarian ideals, points out that "communitarians are concerned with the *loss* of 'traditional boundaries,' while feminists are concerned with the *costs* of those boundaries, especially for women. Nostalgia for communities of the past almost forces nonfeminist communitarians to gloss over or ignore those social forces and structures that have allowed and justified exclusion, oppression, and hierarchy."[9] Our critical focus on communities and their images thus attempts to balance the communitarian insight that our identities emerge within social, communal relations, with recognition of the harms that can be sustained and marginalized within these relations.

We can further express the distinctly non-communitarian spirit of our project by saying that we take pluralism, rather than consensus, to be both a reality and an ideal with respect to social relations. Pluralism entails, in Chantal Mouffe's terms, "the end of a substantive idea of the good life, what Claude Lefort calls, 'the dissolution of the markers of certainty'."[10] This is not to reject the idea that it makes sense for individuals and communities to conceive of and pursue the good life on their terms, but rather to reject the notion that there is *one* conception of the good life that applies to all human beings.

Pluralism in this basic sense embraces human life as appropriately guided by different conceptions of the good, reflecting the realities of our different subject-positions. This value, however, has the potential to support a conception that Mouffe labels "extreme pluralism," where there is "only a multiplicity of identities without any common denominator." The stance of extreme pluralism, in "its refusal of any attempt to construct a 'we,' a collective identity that would articulate the demands found in the different struggles against subordination, partakes of the liberal evasion of the political."[11] Mouffe's preferred pluralist vision, which we share, is one of "radical democracy," in which the basic commitment to pluralism is allied with an insistence on the essential but problematic role of power relations in shaping individuals and communal entities. We identify ourselves and our communities in part by the exclusion of others, and these exclusions both reflect and help establish divisions of power. A central part of the process of exclusion involves the construction of others as "different" from ourselves – as others – and the valuing of that difference unequally – as others, but not other *subjects*. Another way of explaining this point is to say that when we conceptualize another person as different from ourselves, we are taking ourselves to be the paradigm case and using our characteristics as the standard by which to measure the degree of commonality with the other person. But the demarcation lines for deciding similarity and difference arguably are not natural kinds but, rather, artifacts of history and culture. Yet we inscribe meanings in these differences that entrench relations of domination and subjugation. Difference, then, is an asymmetrical relation (magazines and journals are more like books than are books like magazines and journals; gay people are more like straight people than are straight people like gay people) and the asymmetry expresses and embeds a power relation.

While it is crucial to acknowledge the role of power in constructing differences as inequalities and to unravel the meanings given to difference, pluralists also worry about the dangers of eliding differences and proclaiming similarity and unity. And everyday, ordinary people – for example, people who participate in popular culture or who are interested and intrigued by it – may experience themselves as caught in a forced choice between noticing difference or attending to sameness. *Radical* pluralists are rightfully wary about the play of power expressed in either alternative, and point, instead, to the ways in which binaries such as these do not exhaust the possibilities for the construction of subjectivities.[12] In Derridean terms, there is always an excess, a remainder – what Derrida calls *différance*. It is this idea that Mouffe takes to be central to the possibility of radical democracy.

The notion of *différance* is employed in the context of radical democracy, then, to allow for the development of conceptions of identity that do not entrench simple (and illusionary) binary oppositions of sameness and difference. In Derridean terms, the identity of an individual or community is always constituted in part by *différance*, meaning that there is an excess or remainder in the qualities of that subject that are not captured by accounting for how it is the same or different from other such subjects. While we have not made *différance* a central analytic tool in our analysis, putting it directly to work in only one case, we want to note it as a valuable route into thinking about identity, community, and pluralism that goes beyond the approaches usually taken in discussions of liberalism and communitarianism.

The problems of difference and sameness are not merely conceptual, either. Unequal distributions of power make a genuine, healthy pluralism extremely vulnerable; the ideology of radical democracy aims at imagining and constituting forms of power that are compatible with democratic values and supportive of pluralism. In more concrete terms, the radical democrat aims to establish communities and institutions in which power is not abused through domination and violence. This means radical democracy too carries with it an ethical demand. This does not amount to an "ethical overload," however, since its ethical demand does not take for granted the social and political worth of any particular forms of social and political relations – as an ideology it does not tell us how to structure our social and political lives. The demand is rather that the structures we develop be assessed in terms of the value of communication, conflict, deliberation, and cooperation across differences, where power relations are both acknowledged and contestable.

Our approach to specific images of community will reflect the concerns of pluralism and radical democracy through our examination of the boundaries, exclusions, hierarchies, and visions of normality held within these images. Do these images help us find some interesting middle ground between the extremes of celebrating the benefits of communities and exposing their oppressive potential? Do these images open up spaces for us to play with and, perhaps, flaunt the power of the dichotomous subjectivities and oppositional world-views that we encounter? We will not in general offer the sort of condemnation of contemporary images of community that Govier gives. She emphasizes their disappointingly crude, clumsy, and shallow form and content. While that sort of condemnation is indeed frequently understandable, we have found that even images that are crude and shallow in some respects are usually complex in others, and we find that one image may easily be both constructive and flawed. In articulating this kind of complex response to an image, we will take Fowler's approach in recognizing different kinds of community and assessing corresponding images in terms of the needs and goals of the kinds of community they model.

For these reasons, our assessments of the images discussed below are not terribly neat. We try to approach each case by being open to the diversity of things we can want from an image of community. Here are a few of the questions we have been asking ourselves, as we consider these images.

1   Do the images tell us something about how we should conduct ourselves in relation to others in order to flourish?
2   Do they give us some idea of the "glue" necessary for making a community survive? ("Glue" includes things like conventions, norms, a moral

framework, or pragmatic considerations.)

3   On the other hand, we don't want the glue to be superglue. So, do the images help us negotiate what Fowler calls the tyrannical potential of communities to enforce paradigms? Can we learn something about how to foster pluralism within communities, in Mouffe's sense, while still maintaining cohesiveness? Fowler says community members need to have a kind of "existential watchfulness" to guard against tyranny; are there images of this watchfulness? To what extent do we find positive images that go against the grain of homogeneity and unity?

4   Along similar lines, do the images help us understand the advantages of separation and the disadvantages of exclusion? When is it good for a community to have permeable or fluid boundaries, and what does it take to have permeable enough boundaries? Do any images hint at Derridean excess?

5   Do the images tell us something about how to evaluate communities to which we are outsiders?

6   Do they make any headway toward combating the pessimism Govier describes, without being overly idealistic?

These questions guided us in approaching our examples, and, while we have not answered any of them in a fully satisfying way, we offer them here to suggest some issues we take to be interesting and important in approaching any image of community. In the following sections, we consider a variety of images. We can only gesture at a few of the features of our examples that support our analyses of these images. Ideally, readers will have some familiarity with these cases, enabling them to extend and perhaps contest our claims.

Table 14.1   *Images of community in popular culture*

Example	Kind
Seinfeld (network television)	community of home
Waiting to Exhale (film)	community of crisis; home
Ellen (network television)	community of crisis; home
Princess Diana's funeral (special news broadcast)	community of memory
Prairie Home Companion (public radio)	community of memory
Boyz N the Hood (film)	outlaw community; crisis
Loveline (MTV)	community of ideas; transience

Seinfeld

This show, which ran from 1990 to 1998, was an extremely popular television show. It concerns a community of adult friends, each portrayed as nearly entirely self-interested. They are relentlessly petty, shallow, insecure, and tactless; they frequently harm, deceive, and disgust people outside the circle of friends; and they show little if any regret, shame, or compunction for their behavior. What binds them together as a community? Perhaps in some cases a television viewer's experience of a weekly show creates an illusion of community – the sheer regular association of characters, the familiar format and plot lines, the place in our weekly routine, may allow us to feel as though we are encountering an image of a community, without having sufficient basis in the actual functioning of the social group.

But in the case of *Seinfeld*, there are grounds for seeing this group of people as forming a specific kind of community, which we are calling a community of home. The central bond that unites them is that they are able to be at home with each other. They can be honest about their pettiness, shallowness, and lack of moral scruples. They thoroughly know each other, and while the knowledge is generally unflattering, it does not lead them to be harshly critical of each other. Criticism is registered very mildly, perhaps in annoyance, or in very grudging cooperation, or in bemusement at the lengths to which someone goes in a self-centered scheme. The bond of mutual honesty is also supported by what might be called a bond of taste, in that they tend to share a sense of what is funny, irritating, outrageous, and so on.

Given this community of home, the four characters have a mutual interest in preserving the community, to keep out others who would not find the community standards acceptable or who would take away their freedom to expose their fully shallow selves. This interest shows up, for instance, in an episode in which Jerry unthinkingly suggests that Elaine ask Susan, George's fiancée, to go to a show with her. Susan, despite being a fiancée, is not a member of the community, and George is desperate to avoid having her join it through friendship with Elaine. George berates Jerry, "If [Susan] is allowed to infiltrate this world, then George Costanza as you know him ceases to exist!" George is not comfortable in his relationship with Susan, who is an apparently decent, sweet person who is unable to see him for what he is. So he cannot bear to have these two "worlds collide" because that would leave him no place to be himself.

The community is threatened in another episode when Elaine encounters a parallel "bizarro world" of three men who resemble Jerry, George, and Kramer in names, appearance, and in their habits of hanging out together, but who are in contrast caricatured as genuinely "nice guys." They read books, do charitable works, are polite and considerate, and show respect for each other. Elaine admires this principled, mature form of community, and she tries to join it. But she discovers that she cannot behave with the freedom she enjoys in her old community: in the "bizarro world" she is criticized and not understood for following her basic impulses.

What is the appeal and significance of the *Seinfeld* image of community? In part it reflects a legitimate need for a community of home, for associations with people in which we do not have to disguise ourselves and in which we are both known and accepted. In its exaggerated and sometimes excruciating way, it thus gives us an image of something genuinely desirable and difficult to achieve in human community. On the other hand, it is significant as an image because it also shows a community in which moral commitments and standards play a very minor and over-rideable role. While the members of the community do abide by some standards of loyalty to each other, they do not seem to need a sense of shared moral goals as "glue" for their community. They are not shown wrestling with full-fledged moral problems; their problems concern practical obstacles, how to avoid doing things they don't want to do, saving social face, issues of etiquette. This is just not a community that depends for its survival and flourishing on its members having and meeting moral expectations. Is this then part of its appeal as an image? Is this a fantasy we have about communities of home: that there could be a community in which consistent failure to have moral aspirations would not lead to criticism and rejection by the community? Or is it not even a fantasy, but an exaggeration of something realizable in actual human communities? To the extent that *Seinfeld* provides an image of a flourishing but amoral community, it raises the question of how necessary moral standards are for sustaining a community and perhaps allows us, while we laugh, to imagine what we would stand to gain and lose by pursuing such a community of home.

It is also worth noting that the *Seinfeld* community is distinctive in the extent to which it is self-referential, constantly reflecting on itself as a community. One thing we might want from an image of community is insight into the expectations and boundaries of that community, and the humor of *Seinfeld* frequently depends on exploring exactly that.

Waiting to Exhale

While this movie also portrays a community of home, by showing the friendship of four African American women who know and accept each other, we can also describe it as portraying a community of crisis. Each of these women wants to find a decent man to share her life with, but each has a long and still unfolding experience that makes that desire seem unattainable. They are extremely wary of men, seeing them simultaneously as attractive and as terribly likely to be exploitative, unprincipled, unreliable, and insensitive. The story provides numerous examples of "problem men" who lie, cheat, steal, and generally waste the women's time and affection. It seems at certain low points in the movie that, if you want to have a relationship with a man at all, you may have to settle for being a woman on the side for a man already involved with another woman. They want to be able to exhale with a man – to relax and feel trust and shared affection, to feel at home with a man – but instead they experience that desire as the defining problem of their social world.

The movie image of this community illustrates various kinds of concrete response to this crisis, all of which are portrayed as good responses (be yourself with the widowed nextdoor neighbor, have a child on your own, get a tough divorce lawyer, decide that being alone is better than being with a married man). Although the movie does not do a great deal to show how having this community of friends leads the women to these responses, it certainly seems to be the assumption of the movie that sharing the crisis and their accumulated experiences was crucial to their finding a way to deal with their desires and options constructively. The image is intended to combat pessimism about the possibilities for heterosexual, African American women, without being naive about those possibilities, and to that extent it seems we should count this as a potentially helpful image of community. It may even be true that features of the movie that seem heavy-handed (the bad men are sooo bad; the women's drive to find men is sooo unceasing) are in fact important for setting up a clear, paradigmatic image of a social crisis, where the image is indeed crude but is therefore also memorable and provocative.

Viewers may want to complicate their thinking about the provocatively clear image in various ways. For one thing, it portrays a strongly heterosexual community of women. The desire to have sex with a gorgeous man is made prominent and pervasive. Perhaps it is unfair to ask of a movie which focuses on African American women, as so few popular movies do, that it also offer a more complex view of sexuality, as so few popular movies do. Still, it seems useful to have in mind that awareness of the heterosexual tyranny that this movie image seems to take for granted.

A different kind of complication can arise, when the audience for the image is not a member of the kind of community portrayed. Do we have special problems and responsibilities when we encounter images of communities to which we do not belong? *Waiting to Exhale*, for instance, raises a number of difficult questions for white female viewers. The movie image seems to reinforce ideas that have near-stereotype status in American culture – most prominently, the idea just outlined that there is a crisis of trust between African American women and men. But a second, less prominent theme concerns how white women are perceived by African American women. In a number of scenes in the movie, white women are portrayed as contributing to these women's crisis. The stereotype in play is that white women take eligible men away from African American women, and that they are resented for this and are perhaps generally viewed with suspicion within this community. White women seem at best remote and uninteresting, from the perspective of the central characters, and at worst they seem like malicious, threatening rivals; either way they are part of the "constitutive outside" of the community portrayed in the movie.

What can white female viewers make of this image? We are not raising this question because we think the white female response is especially important in this case; it is just an example of a problem everyone faces in different contexts, of how to assess an image of a community to which one is an outsider. Is it appropriate to object, say, to the whole notion of white women "taking men away from" black women? Is it appropriate to argue with the suggestion that white women are distant from and are unlikely to worry about the interests and problems of black women? It seems that a white female viewer has a responsibility to react very cautiously to such an image. Keeping in mind that this is a Hollywood production, with many goals other than that of portraying real conditions and attitudes in communities of African American women, it nonetheless seems that an outsider should assume that the clear themes in the movie reflect real conditions and attitudes in some way. This assumption can then be a starting point for questioning one's responses and one's standing as a critic of this image. A white female viewer should ask herself, "Is my response to the portrayal of white women defensive rather than well considered? Do I insist that I am not remote and indifferent, even though I have no ties to communities of non-white women? Have I tried to imagine what it would be like to be an African American woman who is left by a man for a white woman? What social meaning would it have for me to pursue a relationship with an African American man? Am I uncomfortable with a movie image that, glowing with Angela Bassett and Whitney Houston, uses the power of movie glamour to upend relations of social power with which I am comfortable? In general, do I have life experiences that are relevant to the interpretation and evaluation of this image? If not, should I wait until I have changed my life and become more qualified, before I judge this image?"

Whether or not these questions are apt of course depends on the nuances of one's own responses to the movie. But for some viewers a movie like this can be eye-opening, in revealing one's social isolation from the kind of community the movie portrays. If that is one's position as a viewer, then the movie image is a useful starting point for reflection about what is not known and what is hard to imagine from one's current social position. And that sort of reflection can be a useful starting point for seeking relevant changes in one's social relations.

Ellen

Ellen was a prime-time television show that ran from 1994 to 1998. It featured a lesbian in a community of straight people. But during the first seasons, Ellen was closeted on the show while, at the same time, viewers "in the know" were interpreting the subtext and double entendres correctly as lesbian. This episode is the famous "coming out" show that received months of advance notice. Earlier in this episode, we learn that Ellen's friends are privy to her plans to date an old male friend and, although Ellen rebuffs his sexual advances, she tells everyone else that she had a voracious appetite for him. She does this for two reasons: (1) because – we learn from a later conversation with her therapist – it is easier to tell our friends what they want to hear; (2) because she is sexually attracted to a woman and is confronted with her own fears about what it means to be gay. At this point, Ellen is having a dream in which she is grocery shopping and everything is now marketed differently for her. For example, a grocer tells her that the store is running a special on melons this week for lesbians. A product promoter says of her snack that it is perfect "whether you're on the go or in the closet." The bagger asks, "Do you need some help loading that in your gay car?"

We selected *Ellen* to illustrate two points about communities. One point is that being at home as a member of the community she has, for so long, taken herself to be part of – the straight community – and being comfortable with herself requires that she tell others about her "private desires." But telling others results in her straight friends now seeing her "as a lesbian" and assuming a narrow and stereotyped version of "lesbian life." This episode thus works with the tyranny of paradigms that we mentioned earlier and how they can frighten us into deception, on the one hand, and reduce us to classes of things, on the other. It also highlights how much it matters in our culture which community we belong to. Particularly interesting is seeing Ellen epistemologically and psychologically negotiate her individual crisis in terms of the consequences to being out: she doesn't want to be discriminated against. As Ellen talks about her concerns with her therapist – Oprah Winfrey – she says, "You don't understand! Do you think I want to be discriminated against? Do you think I want people calling me names to my face?" Oprah says, nodding, "Have people commit hate crimes against you just because you're not like them?" "Thank you!" Ellen says, relieved that Oprah understands Ellen. But Oprah continues, "Have to use separate bathrooms and separate drinking fountains and sit on the back of the bus?" "Oh, man," Ellen groans, "we have to use separate water fountains?"

Ellen sees that Oprah empathizes with her concerns about being viewed as an outsider, an other, at the same time that Ellen has a fresh appreciation about what it is like to be racially discriminated against – something that marks them as different from each other. So in this episode, viewers see the possibility for interconnections between different communities who variously experience discrimination without denying difference.

The second reason we focus on *Ellen* concerns the phenomenon of the unifying potential of the media. Millions of Americans watched this episode of *Ellen*; public viewings and discussions took place across the USA on campuses and in various organizations. There were gay, lesbian, and bisexual viewers; gay-, lesbian-, and bisexual-supportive viewers; and the curious. We suggest that this phenomenon (not necessarily the content of the episode itself) is, on the whole, positive, for two reasons: (a) it functioned to bring together and affirm together lesbian existence; and (b) it functioned as an educational tool for "outsider audiences" (viewing audiences external to gay and lesbian communities.)

On the other hand, we also recognize that, like television in general, this episode is only one story of one person that is being told and it leaves many issues in lesbian lives untouched – such as intersections of race and class. So it is a gloss that may, in fact, alienate many lesbian viewers rather than unite them.

Consider the examples shown in figure 14.1, which are examples of simple "universal" symbols created to be recognizable by everyone. The overly simplistic image of lesbian life seems to function like these symbols: they can give sympathetic "outsider" audiences the impression that they now understand "what it is like to be a lesbian" rather than just a glimmer of what it is like to be this lesbian.

Special News Broadcasts

While we are discussing the power of the media to unify a society and create a feeling of something like community, we want to mention special news broadcasts. The example we have in mind is Princess Diana's funeral. In Brit-

Figure 14.1

ain alone, 31 million people watched the funeral on television. According to Durrants, the coverage of the funeral in the world's magazines and newspapers by far exceeded that generated by any other event, anywhere in the world, at any time in history.

What was going on with this phenomenon? Was it a public grieving that is both resonant of communities of memory and of home – a kind of belongingness to what is good in human beings? Or was it what Ian Jack calls it "an oppression of grief"? As he puts it: "People had not only to grieve, they had to be seen to grieve."[13]

This example suggests another way in which a community – even a false one – can function tyrannically: by setting out norms for appropriate emotional responses. The creation of "transcommunity feeling" demands the display of certain signs of membership. But genuine community feeling comprises meaningful affective signifiers, does it not? As Ian Jack writes about the public grieving for Princess Diana's death:

> Outside the personal sorrow of those who knew the princess, what kind of grief were people feeling? And how many people were feeling it? To judge the quality of other people's grief may be a risky enterprise, but my guess about the first is this: that it was recreational grieving ("look me grief" was how the writer Julian Barnes described it), that it was enjoyable, that it promoted the griever from the audience to an onstage part in the final act of the opera, which lasted six days. The dead heroine had provided the most marvelous story, and the grief of her spectators may have been genuine in the sense of unfaked. But it was grief with the pain removed, grief-lite. When people telephoned each other that Sunday morning, they spoke eagerly – 'Have you heard that . . . ?' – and not with the dread – 'How can I tell him that . . . ?' – familiar to bearers of seriously wounding news, which the hearer may recover from only in months or years or sometimes never at all. It was possible, after all, for the readers of Dickens to weep at the death of Little Nell, whom they too felt they knew.[14]

We suggest that, although Fowler is right to include the criterion that affect is part of community, he couldn't mean just any affect: the affect that is part of community has to be meaningful.

Radio Programs

Other sources of community-building include radio programs. We have in mind things like the stations that foster a listening relationship, such as *Prairie Home Companion*, a Public Radio Broadcast that we think fits the category of popular culture. *Prairie Home Companion* weekly describes a fictional small rural midwestern town of (mostly) white Scandinavian Lutherans. In one story, for example, Tina has grown up and moved to The Cities where she has lived for 20 years, when her Uncle Ed comes to visit. Listeners hear Garrison Keillor gently poke fun both at city attitudes and at midwestern provincialism, which allows them to view their pettiness and their differences with affection and forgiveness. A central part of *Prairie Home Companion's* appeal is that it gives hope to combat the sort of pessimism Govier talks about: we need not be entirely alienated urban dwellers, it is good to remain connected to the old ways, not all is lost as society becomes more technologically advanced. While often sentimentalizing about tradition, Keillor also interjects the oddness and the modernity of an occasional person, thus destabilizing the very homogeneity he romanticizes.

But the audience for *Prairie Home Companion* is very select. Not only is it primarily for those who like nostalgia (and folk music) but for those who like to dwell imaginatively in community with white Scandinavian Lutherans. *Prairie Home Companion* may expose some of the subtle complexities of small community living, but the categories of difference seem surprisingly reductive: Lutheran versus Catholic; Norwegian bachelor farmer versus the assimilated town dwellers; The Cities versus Lake Woebegone.

Outlaw Communities

We want to mention a kind of community for which there are very few images in popular culture: outlaw communities. We have in mind, as examples, gangs and women in prison.

These communities are feared by society not only because they are considered morally unacceptable (like a gay community, which is feared to bring all sorts of catastrophes to the morals of society) but because outlaw communities are known to be on the fringes of obedience to the law and therefore potentially or actually dangerous. A popular film with images of outlaw communities is *Boyz N the Hood*, which shows the development of a neighborhood gang and tells what it takes for Tre, the main character, to choose how he is going to affiliate with other black males. But this film is an anti-gang film, and therefore an anti-outlaw community film. It tells viewers which affiliation is better.

Talk Shows

Loveline is a national radio and MTV talk show of sorts which is on each weeknight. The theme is love and sex, and the purpose of it is for audience members to ask questions and receive advice. It is hosted by two men, Dr. Drew and Adam Corolla (and a newer addition of a woman), and then a featured guest, usually a television celebrity. It also has a studio audience and various technological devices for linking up with a national audience. The callers and other audience participants are typically not anonymous, in that viewers can see them and learn their first names, but they are strangers. We think this could count as a kind of community because hundreds of thousands of teenagers and young people tune into it regularly and because it is interactive in the way a soap opera, say, is not.

For example, in one episode, a caller who identifies himself as a lawyer poses a question about the appropriate frequency of masturbation. He reports to Dr. Drew and Adam, as well as thousands of listeners, that he has to leave his law office several times a day to masturbate – even sometimes when he is conferring with a client. He seems just the slightest bit concerned that his autoerotic activities are beginning to interfere with his work life. Should he be worried about this behavior, he asks *Loveline?*

Communities have different conventions, and *Loveline* is no exception. Conventions we want to call your attention to are (a) that the topics are typically considered either taboo or in too bad taste to discuss openly; (b) there is an expectation that sensitive questions will be treated lightly but seriously (there is a considerable amount of joking going on, some of it on the offensive side, some just downright dumb, but nearly every question eventually gets answered thoughtfully and often helpfully); (c) there is an expectation that callers are not trying to deceive the viewers with a trumped-up problem; and (d) a central project is to identify norms of psychological health. Twenty years ago, this kind of show would have been framed around moral norms but now, although moral expectations sometimes are explicitly stated, for the most part they play only a minor role.

Secondly, *Loveline* is a place where people can come together when they are trying to understand their behavior and choices (or that of other people). Thus it is a kind of normalizing community. It functions as a community-forming device for setting up the boundaries for acceptable behavior.

This is a community of ideas, but it is also, by and large, a transient community – a community of strangers who are talking about things that are usually kept private. So an important question is, how does trust arise? One way is through another convention, that the hosts and special guests give the illusion of mutual vulnerability by revealing superficial "facts" about their lives. The humor we mentioned earlier also seems to build trust, as it functions as an icebreaker to put people at ease.

Our position is not so much that talk shows are a good source of images of community but that by paying attention to *Loveline* we can learn about a particular need for community that is, for many people, not satisfied in other communities, or in families or friendships – namely, being able to ask and listen to embarrassing questions about love, sex, and violence and figure out, together with other confused or uncertain people, what is weird, abusive, self-degrading, or nothing to worry about.

On the other hand, its normalizing features may function repressively. Boundaries keep people in, but they also keep people out. Consider Gayle Rubin's "Charmed Circle," where she identifies the "appropriate" boundaries of sexual behavior as, for example, heterosexual, monogamous, with bodies only, at home, and vanilla, and activities outside the "charmed circle," which she terms the "outer limits," as, for example, homosexual, involving exchanges of money, sexual activities done alone or in groups, with manufactured objects, and sadomasochism. Sexuality in the context of the outer limits, Rubin argues, is deemed bad, abnormal, unnatural, or damned.[15] Still, whether or not the normalizing image functions repressively depends on the dominant sexual context and, right now, it seems that the community displayed on *Loveline* is still breaking down barriers even while it reminds us of limits.

For a different take on talk shows, we want to briefly discuss Joshua Gamson's marvelous and highly readable analysis of talk shows that amounts to a kind of ironic defense. In *Freaks Talk Back: Tabloid Talk Shows and Sexual Nonconformity*, Gamson argues that TV shows such as Phil Donahue, Oprah Winfrey, Jerry Springer, and Jenny Jones give visibility and credibility to people whose lives are usually invisible – that is, to the "misfits, monsters, trash, and perverts" – in a way that challenges class distinctions and blurs the lines of normality and difference.[16] Through an excess of emotion, sexual difference, and advice, "the deviant isn't readily distinguished from the regular person, class stereotypes melt into the hard realities on which they rest, what belongs in private suddenly seems to belong in front of everybody, airing dirty laundry looks much like coming clean."[17]

In fact, TV talk shows exhibit many of the postmodern markers that attract us to Mouffe's position on radical democracy. The explicit emphasis on performance and the ensuing confusion over the "true" self; the flaunting of categories to the degree that the categories themselves appear to be absurd; the insistence in exposing individuals' subjective experiences and voices and reveling in indeterminacy; the refusal to allow audiences the illusion of generalizations; all these features suggest the presence of Derridean excess and the possibility of pluralism centered on *différance*. As Gamson states, "with its postmodern 'constellation of voices,' its tendency to 'juxtapose rather than integrate multiple, heterogeneous, discontinuous elements,' and to 'explode the notion of any one authentic self,' the genre multiplies and destabilizes truths."[18] But, Gamson adds, talk shows "do not so much refuse patterns of meaning as propose overarching patterns while making 'proof' impossible."[19] That is, Gamson cautions us that it is a mistake to read too much postmodernism into the TV talk shows: whatever else they are, talk shows are also "an awkward patchwork of old-fashioned class cultural fragments."[20]

Nevertheless, TV talk shows can shake us up rather than reaffirm institutionally regulated boundaries and (participate in) normalizing discourse. As Gamson writes:

> Those people who straddle categories, even though for the most part they do not themselves identify as freaks and monsters, do indeed knock open mind doors here and there, as we have seen. The farthest-out of sex and gender non-conformists, the most stigmatized, can cause meaning crises. They awaken in audiences the sneaking, sleeping suspicion that perhaps they do not get it, that the differences they are used to are not making sense, that maybe all brides are drag queens and some females are men. You too are monstrous, they announce, since you and I are the same. Their us-ness makes them potentially potent messengers of new ways of thinking about sex and gender, much more potent than any run-of-the-mill lesbian or regular-guy gay man.[21]

TV talk shows, as Gamson argues, are often conceptually challenging to viewers in ways we aren't always cognizant of. But talk shows are also exploitative: producers, advertisers, and networks profit from people's deviance and difference and often *demand* exaggeration. Thus in an odd twist on Derridean discursive practices, talk show guests must *perform excess*. Whatever benefits may be derived from being a talk show viewer, then, must be understood in the context of this profit and performativity. Jerry Springer and other shows may be unsettling partly because they upset our concepts of truth and reality, but it is also the case that the viewing audience – at least at some level – knows the guests are pretending to bigger emotions than fit the situation. If a characteristic of community is that it have meaningful affect, then it looks like TV talk shows mostly miss the mark. And in their larger-than-life depictions of deviance, viewers may come away with more of a mnemonic than an appreciation of the complexities of individual difference – let alone *différance*.

Conclusion

It is difficult to draw unified conclusions from such an array of images. We find each of these examples to be interesting in its own right and, in part, we hope this discussion prompts further concrete thinking about these and other specific images. While we do not see these cases as all fitting into the same mold or as raising the same questions, we do see a few useful general ideas emerging from the discussion.

First, we think the dismay Govier expresses over the shallow, cynical nature of contemporary images of community is largely misplaced. While it would, of course, be good to see more rich and thoughtful images displayed in popular culture, the images we already have available show people forming communities for many reasons, seeking much more than "lifestyle enclaves." Even the most cynical image we considered, *Seinfeld's* community of friends, displays what we take to be the positive value of communities of home. And even when these images are superficial, unsatisfying, or actively misguided, we find their inadequacy to be a fruitful source of provocation. It can indeed be good to encounter images that fail, that set up a simple model we know is wrong, as long as we try to understand and move beyond their inadequacies. If there is reason for dismay, it will be due to a lack of critical, imaginative response to these images. The empirical question of whether people tend to absorb these images uncritically is beyond our scope; our tendency is to assume people are at least fairly sophisticated about the artificiality and glibness of much popular culture. People know many things are missing or off-target in these images, and all of us need to be encouraged to use that knowledge constructively.

In our attempts to work constructively with these images, we found that many of them have an interesting double effect of opening up some possibilities while simultaneously closing off others. The *Ellen* episode, both in its fictional story and in the public event it became, clearly took steps to liberate us from images of community in which homosexuality is invisible – except as something to be caricatured. Yet the episode also displayed such a "safe" image of lesbianism – the white, educated, middle-class lesbian surrounded by a circle of liberal heterosexual friends – and displayed it with so much media attention, that it has the power to normalize that version of lesbianism. Other more socially challenging possibilities may seem still quite inaccessible as a result. *Loveline* opens up a forum for examination of issues of sex and relationships that are very difficult to discuss in other contexts, but it also rather explicitly has the function of prescribing what is normal in that domain. *Waiting to Exhale* explores a positive model of women-centered community, while also entrenching divisions between heterosexual and homosexual, and black and white women. *Prairie Home Companion* integrates the disturbances of the modern world into an apparently tradition-bound community, but still depends for its humor on rather rigid social categories. In these images, boundaries are usually signaled, and possibilities closed off implicitly, through what is omitted or taken for granted. This means that we usually do not get a satisfying exploration of what possibilities are ruled out and why. We are left without a positive account of how the new boundaries around the communal spaces are constituted. (*Seinfeld's* preoccupation with its own conventions as a community makes it something of an exception on this score.) We found that these double effects have a destabilizing power: the experience of having possibilities open up and limits unexpectedly signaled inevitably creates an unstable cognitive space. We leave behind a familiar sense of how a given kind of community can function, but we do not understand exactly what the new possibilities are or how they should be limited.

A form of destabilization occurs with respect to our affective responses as well. We often respond emotionally to these images while having a sense that the emotion is staged or not clearly "authentic." While feeling moved by the coverage of Diana's death, we are also able to wonder about why we are moved and about what sort of community is being formed around this prominent public grief. People may feel nostalgic in listening to stories about Lake Woebegone, even though they are urban dwellers through and through, with no ties to Scandinavian Lutheran traditions. The hyperbolic, obviously performed emotions on TV talk shows likewise have the capacity to call into question the authenticity or reality of emotion. In various ways, these images and our responses to them have a useful ability to expose us to emotion as something we *do* rather than as something we merely experience. That is, the peculiar nature of some emotions in response to these images illustrates our role in constructing and entering into emotionally compelling contexts. Being aware of this role may, in turn, give us a better awareness of how we construct the emotional bonds important to community life.

Finally, how do these images fit into the pluralist rejection of a substantive idea of THE good life? How do they support or complicate Mouffe's view of the constitutive role of power relations in a pluralist radical democracy? By their sheer diversity, these images show the many different goods we seek as social beings, and they show our need for different structures of social inter-action: we need transient affiliations, forums for sharing ideas rather than building bonds of affection, affiliations responding to crises and exclusions, and imagination-invoking constructions of history and tradition. In theorizing about communities, at any rate, we need a multiplicity of models for how communities function, and we assume the categories used here lay out just some of the models called for in a fully developed theory.

These images also clearly illustrate the ways in which power relations are central to our forms of community and to the problems faced within particular communities. Why do we need communities of home, if not to experience a release from forms of social control and vulnerability? How do the crises around which we form communities reflect facts about social domination and discrimination? How does the need for special communities to discuss certain ideas reveal standards asserted by those in power? In these and many other ways which we have not pursued, these images document the implication of power relations in the features of our communal lives.

However, we would also emphasize that, while issues of power are pervasive, they do not exhaust what is interesting about the functioning of communities. We also need to appreciate features of our communities that need not have any direct bearing on understanding communities as sites of power and vulnerability. It is important, for instance, to understand the role of bonds of taste in community formation, such as the bonds established by a shared sense of humor. Or, in understanding the roles of communities of memory and of transience, we should think not just about how such communities reflect possession of and desire for power, but also about our struggles to have meaningful pasts and presents. In general, the non-reductive approach that is elicited by these images counteracts the goal of neatness that we tend to aim for in theory-building. This is not to say that the images stymie theorctical work. We think consideration of these images can stimulate better theoretical work – as long as, again, we respond critically and imaginatively to their powerful, liberating, constricting, crude, and complex messages.

Notes

1   Nelson Goodman, *Languages of Art* (Indianapolis: Hackett Publishing, 1976), pp. 52–3.
2   Trudy Govier, *Social Trust and Human Communities* (Toronto: McGill-Queen's University Press, 1997), p. 174.
3   Ibid., pp. 172–3.
4   See Robert Booth Fowler, "Community: Reflections on Definition," in Amitai Etzioni, ed., *New Communitarian Thinking: Persons, Virtues, Institutions, and Communities* (Charlottesville: University Press of Virginia, 1995).
5   Ibid., p. 94.
6   See Jurgen Habermas, "Three Normative Models of Democracy," in Seyla Benhabib, ed., *Democracy and Difference: Contesting the Boundaries of the Political* (Princeton: Princeton University Press, 1996).
7   Amitai Etzioni, "Old Chestnuts and New Spurs," in Etzioni, ed., *New Communitarian Thinking*, p. 17.
8   Amitai Etzioni et al., "The Responsive Communitarian Platform: Rights and Responsibilities," in Etzioni, ed., *The Essential Communitarian Reader* (New York: Rowman and Littlefield, 1998), pp. xxviii–xxix.
9   Penny Weiss, "Feminism and Communitarianism: Comparing Critiques of Liberalism," in Penny Weiss and Marilyn Friedman, eds., *Feminism and Community* (Philadelphia: Temple University Press, 1995), p. 167.
10   Chantal Mouffe, "Democracy, Power, and the Political," in Benhabib, ed., *Democracy and Difference*, p. 246.
11   Ibid., p. 247.
12   For example, see Bonnie Honig, "Difference, Dilemmas, and the Politics of Home," in Benhabib, ed., *Democracy and Difference*, p. 273.
13   Ian Jack, "Those Who Felt Differently," *Granta* (New York: Granta /Penguin, 1997), p. 16.
14   Ibid., pp. 16–17.
15   See Gayle Rubin, "Thinking Sex: Notes for a Radical Theory of the Politics of Sexuality," in Linda S. Kauffman, ed., *American Feminist Thought at Century's End: A Reader*, (Cambridge, Mass.: Blackwell, 1993).
16   Joshua Gamson, *Freaks Talk Back: Tabloid Talk Shows and Sexual Nonconformity* (Chicago: University of Chicago Press, 1998), p. 4.
17   Ibid., p. 18.

18   Ibid., p. 99.
19   Ibid.
20   Ibid., p. 42.
21   Ibid., p. 167.

15

Virtual Communities: Chinatowns Made in America

Gary Okihiro

The author Will Irwin, in the foreword to a book of photographs by Arnold Genthe published in 1908, addressed the German-scholar-turned-photographer: "You, the only man who ever had the patience to photograph the Chinese, you, who found art in the snap-shot – you were making yourself unconsciously, all that time, the sole recorder of old Chinatown." That old Chinatown, Irwin lamented, had been obliterated by the 1906 San Francisco earthquake, and what had arisen from the ashes and rubble was a "new, clean Chinatown."[1] Irwin's claim that Genthe's carefully crafted photographs constituted the sole record of San Francisco's pre-earthquake Chinatown, the memories and accounts of Chinatown's residents notwithstanding, likely failed to register as suspect or unusual among his mainly non-Chinese readers, because to the vast majority of them Chinatown was more a representation than a lived and experienced reality.

Another writer in another time and place, Gwen Kinkead, made a similar claim for her account of New York City's Chinatown. She was curious, Kinkead began, at the "anomaly" of a community "splitting at its seams" in the city in which she lived and yet had "never heard or read anything about Chinatown." How was that possible, she asked, and "why was it mute?" Asian Americans, she noted in 1992, were the fastest growing US minority, and yet were "the least enfranchised" and "the least understood." Indeed, she wrote, there was widespread ignorance on both sides of her binary of "Americans" and "Asians," a condition in which "neither side makes the effort." But Chinatown's residents, Kinkead stated, bore a special blame in this matter, because of their silence and isolation. Research for her book, she claimed, was "like opening oysters without a knife," and, she lectured, "Chinese can learn that they can't have it both ways – they cannot charge mistreatment and racism and, at the same time, refuse to talk to outsiders, or vote, or lend a cup of sugar to their neighbor."[2]

Although not the claimed sole recorder of New York City's Chinatown, Kinkead could write with confidence that she, an outsider like Genthe and

Irwin nearly a century earlier, could represent a Chinese American community to its neighbors, serving as a cultural broker across her imagined divide of "Asians" and "Americans." The texts that Kinkead, Genthe, Irwin, and others like them produced, in words and photographic images, created virtual communities – Chinatowns – that existed in the ether of the imagination, bore certain fixed natures, exerted themselves upon the social relations and material conditions, and were rejected and struggled over and accepted and deployed by Chinatown's residents for their own ends. Genthe, Irwin, and Kinkead produced travel narratives that transported their non-Chinese readers from the self to the other, from the familiar to the exotic, from the domestic to the international. Even as Chinatown was simultaneously local and global, its residents were both citizen and alien. Venturing into Chinatown might have entailed merely crossing the street, but it might as well have been the journey of a lifetime. As a self-proclaimed last white resident of New York City's Chinatown told Kinkead when she first began her adventure, "Walk through Chinatown. You're not in the United States. You're in Hong Kong."[3]

Of course, "discovery," as many have shown, is oftentimes really a projection of self and already known or conjured visions of differently constituted peoples and distant lands. As Neil Rennie has pointed out about travel literature of the South Seas, the European gaze or first-sight upon "discovered" peoples and places was a "knowing" even before the encounter and it turned upon "what was new to what they knew" and "what they 'knew' about the beginning of the world was textual, not empirical" and was "only what they had read and believed." In that way, Rennie observed, European travel was regressive insofar as the traveler discovered not "a new land so much as a new location for old, nostalgic fictions about places lost in the distant past, now found in the distant present, found and confirmed, it seemed, in the form of exotic facts."[4] Will Irwin's nostalgia for a lost, pre-modern Chinatown and Gwen Kinkead's timeworn, formulaic rendition of New York City's postmodern Chinatown exemplify the acuity of Rennie's observation.

The "knowing" of European travel literature is foremost an authorial "knowing," and emanates from power relations endemic to the colonial project. Mary Louise Pratt revealed travel literature's attachment to the science of classification, thereby accruing to itself the authority of an ostensibly value-free, universal knowledge, while displacing allegedly value-laden, parochial forms of naming and classifying. Expansionist literature, noted Pratt, generally advances the claims of the colonizer over the colonized and works to delegitimate indigenous cultures and expressions. That literature, thus, comprises hegemonic discourses.[5] Further, those discourses are constitutive of the social relations. Writing about tourism's impact upon indigenous cultures, anthropologist Davydd Greenwood argued that cultures become commodities, like the natural resources that are similarly packaged and sold to visitors. Culture is an integrated system of meanings by which reality is established and maintained, Greenwood noted, and when a culture is commodified it has fundamental consequences for that people's identities and behaviors and is essentially destructive and is indicative of and results in an unequal distribution of power and wealth.[6]

Those material relations, nonetheless, are neither simply unidirectional nor singular, as the theorization of tourism shows. Daniel Boorstin launched a critique of tourists, as opposed to travelers, as empty-headed consumers and seekers after "pseudo-events" or caricatures, preferring the fake over the real. In disagreement, Dean MacCannell offered that tourists were modern-day pilgrims seeking authenticity, even "staged authenticity," and the sacred, and Jonathan Culler added that tourists could be seen as "armies of semiotics" in search of signs, "reading cities, landscapes and cultures as sign systems." Those signs might mediate and mask tourism's economic exploitation, cautioned Culler, but they can also expose its inner workings and thereby allow for interventions in that transnational system of signification.[7] Hence, instead of culture, the significations of culture succumb to the tourist gaze and that gaze, like culture, is socially situated within time and place.

In addition, staged culture (or the "front") produced for tourists by indigenous peoples not only shielded those peoples' identities and behaviors (or the "back"), but also those performances generated revenues for those groups.[8] In that way, exploitation and gain went both ways. And the fact that the nature of tourism has changed over time in concert with the rhythms of social relations, especially the articulations of race, gender, and class, suggests that culture and its significations are not easily surrendered by their owners and instead undergo constant negotiations, reinscriptions, and transformations.[9] In the move from modernity to postmodernity, thus, theorists have identified the emergence of "post-tourists," who delight in the inauthentic and in playing the tourist game, believing that there is no authentic or fixed culture or tourist or absolute cultural differences and boundaries.[10]

What I contend in this chapter is that travelers and tourists have created textual and imaginary communities – "virtual communities" – of Chinatowns in the United States, and that those constructions arise from and have had effects upon the social relations and historical contexts. I see those conditions not simply as hegemonic on the part of external "colonizers," but also as resisted and deployed by Chinatown's "colonized" peoples for their own ends. By virtual communities, I don't mean to suggest computer-generated realities, but the characteristics of that process, involving an apprehension or a knowing of the "real" world and an interaction or negotiation between the knower and the apprehended, but in the end, an exercise of power or authority of the creator over the creation.[11] And I understand communities to be entities delineated by those both within and without them, and as social defense systems that serve to inhibit, avoid, and mitigate fears and anxieties of differentiated others. Communities, thus, are simultaneously mechanisms of inclusion and exclusion, and they are historically situated and subject to change.[12]

A lost world – San Francisco's pre-earthquake Chinatown – emerges from the pages of Arnold Genthe's *Pictures of Old Chinatown.* Genthe's photographs have been critically examined by historian John Kuo Wei Tchen.[13] I herein offer a brief reading of Will Irwin's accompanying word-text. Although complementary and mutually reinforcing, Genthe's photographs and Irwin's writings offer two representations of an early twentieth-century Chinese American community in two distinctive genres. "Where are those broken, dingy streets, in which the Chinese made art of rubbish?" asked Irwin. Where is St. Louis Alley, "that tangle of sheds, doorways, irregular arcades and flaming signs," and Ross Alley, "that romantically mysterious cleft in the city's walls," and Fish Alley, "that horror to the nose, that perfume to the eye?"[14] A warren of alleyways, Irwin's Chinatown drew its readers into the dim reaches of the other and of self.

At times, that recognition grew out of a shared intimacy. Chinese manservants, Irwin explained, like African American women in the South, "watched at the cradle above most of them [new generations of white Californians], rejoiced with the parents that there was a baby in the house, laughed to see it laugh, hurried like a mother at its cry." For the Chinese man, the nursery was the "heart of the house. He was a consoler and fairyteller of childhood. He passed on to the babies his own wonder tales of flowered princesses and golden dragons, he taught them to patter in sing-song Cantonese, he saved his frugal nickels to buy them quaint little gifts." Chinese men were, in Irwin's racialized, gendered, and sexualized portrait, "unobtrusive" and "comprehending in all its subtleties the feminine mind," "shy," "gentle familiar," "versed in the arts of friendship," "gracious," "a feudal retainer," and a willing servant "in a voluntary slavery."[15]

At other times, self-recognition for Irwin's readers dawned from an awareness of distance. On his nights off, Irwin observed, a Chinese domestic went to Chinatown to gamble, smoke opium, and witness gang violence. He became unrecognizable to his white masters. Hidden from the white gaze was the Chinese soul and what "lay under those yellow skins, under those bizarre customs and beliefs." In Chinatown, whites became invisible to the Chinese, who treated whites with "a passive contempt," saw them as objects and not persons, and would "notice you no more than a post."[16] Having witnessed a night of debauchery, testified Irwin, "I thought I watched of wars of the past; these were not refined Cantonese, with a surface gentility and grace in life greater than anything that our masses know; they were those old yellow people with whom our fathers fought before the Caucusus [*sic*] was set as a boundary between the dark race and the light; the hordes of

Genghis Khan; the looters of Attila." And yet, despite that fleeting moment of recognition, Irwin continued, the revelers of "young bloods and soiled women" committed "not one unseemly or unlovely act" and behaved as Chinese gentlemen and "ladies."[17]

Still, "we shall never quite understand the Chinese, I suppose;" confessed Irwin, "and not the least comprehensible thing about them is the paradox of their ideas and emotions." On the one hand, he explained, Chinese men behaved like women. But on the other hand, "underneath their essential courtesy, fruit of an old civilization, underneath their absolute commercial honor, underneath their artistic appreciation of the grace of life, runs a hard, wild streak of barbarism, an insensibility in cruelty which, when roused, is as cold-blooded and unlovely a thing as we know." Chinatown, admitted Irwin, "lived not only by tea and rice and overalls and cigars and tourists, but also by the ministry to dissipation." "Tough citizens" prowled its streets and "priests of vice" presided over its gambling houses.[18] That was the "vicious" side of Chinatown, its cultural interiors and not its tourist façades.

The alleged underground maze that criss-crossed Chinatown might have served as a metaphor for that hidden side of Irwin's Chinatown and Chinese culture. Subterranean tunnels, Irwin surmised, hid from topside view Chinese workers, women, the sick, diseases, and the dead, and they were the means by which criminals escaped detection and capture. "What tragedies their earthen walls must have witnessed," speculated Irwin, "what comedies, what horror stories, what melodramas! There it was, below everything . . . whose circumference was darkness and whose centre death."[19] Beneath the veneer of normality lay an entire network of deviance. But that world was breached and buried by the great earthquake, and a new Chinatown replaced the old. "Gentle figures," Irwin returned to his initial rendition of the Chinese, "seen bright through the sunset scarlets of a youth that is past, do you linger yet, now that your old environment is gone?"[20]

Like his Chinese man who was both woman (within the domestic spaces of white homes) and man (within the alien alleys of Chinatown), Irwin's Chinatown was a hybrid tangle of irregular shapes, mysterious recesses, and horrific smells that repelled but also attracted. Chinatown, he claimed, was "the real heart of San Francisco, this bit of mystic, suggestive East, so modified by the West that it was neither Oriental nor yet Occidental – but just Chinatown."[21] A manufacture of the West, Irwin's Chinatown was both culturally distant and physically immanent and constituted a racialized other, a feminine "cleft" insofar as Chinese men were rendered woman-like and sexuality and criminality seeped from the flesh-pots of passion and excess, and a confused site of deviant heterosexuality where men outnumbered women and where only women prostitutes walked the streets.[22] And it was impossible – a racialized, gendered, and sexualized penetration by white, heterosexual men of Chinatown's similarly racialized, gendered, and sexualized dark, concealed, and deadly tunnels.

Even as Chinese men were figured as womanly and manly, virtuous and criminal in Irwin's Chinese America, Chinese women appeared as "lily woman" and "soiled." That paradox was captured in Irwin's verbal snap-shot of a peek through the "latticed window" of a brothel – "a confusion of painted, flowered, Chinese women, all squalling together."[23] That gaze was imaginatively through the eyes of Donaldina Cameron, who had organized a police raid on the brothel in her attempt to "rescue" Chinese prostitutes.[24] Described by Irwin as "a pretty, fair-spoken Scotch maiden," Cameron zeal-ously pursued "the lives and souls of Chinese women" and in the process encountered adventures, "the material of a dime novel." But even this social reformer failed to dent the doorway of Chinese clannishness, reported Irwin, and she "usually lost her girl in the end." Indeed, noted Irwin, Cameron saw "girl after girl, who had welcomed rescue in the beginning, crumple up on the witness stand and swear herself back into Hell." And Chinatown's un-derground passageways, he told his readers, comprised that literal hell. To escape Cameron's raids, Irwin wrote, prostitute owners dragged their prop-erty into secret tunnels and punished those who sought escape "down there in the bowels of the earth."[25]

The contemporary writer, Gwen Kinkead, might be likened to Cameron, the social reformer of Chinatown's isolation. Both assumed "manly" roles of rescuers of "womanly" peoples by penetrating the "fronts" of Chinese Ameri-can communities and exposing their "backs" or interiors. Their authorial gazes were thus a racialized and gendered "knowing" with the force of a moral mandate of social uplift. As Kinkead explained it, misery in New York City's Chinatown was the product of its oyster-like impenetrability. Chinatown's "crooked streets" and smell of "salt and fish and orange peel" alert the "Ameri-can" to a distant and alien place and people, described Kinkead. "This boom-ing, chaotic little piece of China, overflowing with new immigrants, is a remarkably self-contained neighborhood – virtually a nation unto itself." Although within America's borders, Chinatown was foreign to America. Added Kinkead: "to a degree almost impossible for outsiders to comprehend, most of its inhabitants lead lives segregated from the rest of America."[26]

Roaming Chinatown's bustling streets, Kinkead recalled, she encountered an insuperable barrier. The Chinese, most of whom are foreign-born and many of whom are illegals, Kinkead claimed, considered her, an "Ameri-can," a "barbarian" and "an object of fear, distrust, indifference." Unchanged since the 1870s, she explained, Chinese ethnocentrism manifested itself in calling whites "barbarians" "with the sting of bitterness." Her father, a writer for the *New Yorker*, received that treatment from Chinatown's residents dur-ing the 1930s, and upon seeing her, Kinkead reported, they treated her simi-larly, giving her "white eyes" by turning up their eyeballs "which is the

Chinese way of ignoring strangers." Generally, she observed, "people shut off automatically at the sight of a white person," and the universal use of "barbarian" was "my first sign of its [Chinatown's] closed and secret life."[27]

There are several sources for that silence, Kinkead reasoned. Chinese come from repressive societies such as communist China where silence is a matter of survival and where alienation from government is widespread. But culturally, she mused, the Chinese also "prize self-effacement" where the individual "is of no account." Hence, they refuse to defy the collective group and rarely reach out beyond their community. Whether in the USA or in Southeast Asia, offered Kinkead, the Chinese isolate themselves and resist assimilation. Uppermost in their minds is work and making money, not assimilation, not "merging with America." That choice, she charged, conspired with the aims of the tongs and organized crime to keep Chinatown "cohesive and isolated" wherein the code of silence is woven into the social fabric for fear of gang violence and reprisals. In truth, Kinkead confided, the community's social order is "so ruthless that its very existence seems to be against the law, but, because the area is so isolated from the rest of society, most of the people who live here accept it as normal."[28]

As if to complement their illegal status as immigrants, charged Kinkead, Chinatown is a cash economy to avoid taxes. That underground economy was carried out in broad daylight on the streets, where peddlers and stalls with foul-smelling fruit and exotic fish flown in daily from China offer a profusion of produce. "Gagging smells" rise from the sidewalks and gutters, and water from overflowing vegetable and fish stands spill out onto the sidewalks and streets. Herbalists sell strange concoctions of ground antler, starfish, and roots, and in the numerous jewelry stores African American patrons try on "medallions and gold chains and chunky, gold-plated door-knocker earrings." Gangs of youth with the latest punk haircuts mingle with Chinese objects made "a hundred years ago." In a noodle shop, boxes of noodles lay stacked on the floor. Looking in, Kinkead remembered, "a giant rat ran across the floor to the storage racks. It paused there, sneaked ahead carefully until only its tail, slender and quivering, was visible, and there, in a flash, slid between the boxes."[29]

The Chinese, observed Kinkead, live cheaply and their mantra is "work, work, work" to save "a pile of money." They will do "everything for the US dollar."[30] In addition to that fanaticism wherein they devote "every waking hour to making money and saving it," Chinese migrants appear especially selfish and sinister in Kinkead's rendition because they constitute an alien presence. "When I make the money," she quotes a Chinese worker, "I go home. That's all." "Home," of course, is Asia and not America, although "home" is also bred here in America by the spreading tentacles of the yellow peril. "Liu smiled like a Cheshire cat," Kinkead recalled of a conversation with Albert Liu, a former president of the Asia Bank in Flushing. "'We chose

this block, and many Orientals moved to it, and it is now all Chinese. Look at
the signs – no English!' He laughed heartily." And describing an interview
with the man who controls the majority of the world's supply of opium, Khun
Sa, she wrote, "laughed and laughed" as he boasted that his opium was more
powerful than America's nuclear arsenal. "It was like laughter in a fun house,
full of crazy echoes. Each time in the interview that Khun Sa mentioned death
or defying the United States, he laughed in the same crazy fashion. He seemed
to enjoy himself." Funneled through Chinatown, drugs smuggled and pushed
by Asian organized crime, a 1990 Senate judiciary committee declared, was
a "vast and frightening threat to our cities and our communities," Kinkead
noted.[31]

Chinatown's isolation, thus, is more than an exotic stop on a tourist's itin-
erary. It conspires, in Kinkead's version, to drain America of its resources
and energies. But it also enslaves and exploits its residents – equally
unAmerican. Chinese business and criminal classes prey upon captive migrants and workers who feel trapped and form "an intimidated labor pool."
Abused by Chinese and suspicious of whites, recalled Kinkead, "I met many
prisoners of Chinatown . . . isolated, upset about the community, but resigned
to making a buck and to always being strangers in America." And yet the
gilded cage was built by its own inmates, according to Kinkead's version of
history. From the beginning, she stated, the Chinese "lived apart in
Chinatowns to avoid white barbarians, and they smoked opium, wore their
hair in queues, burned incense before idols, and didn't bother to learn English, because they were only here to find fortune." In Kinkead's Chinatown,
the oyster of community resists exposure, whether from Chinese arrogance
that ignores whites or Chinese leaders who counsel against Americanization or Chinese tongs who overwhelm the residents with violence. As a New
York City police officer exclaimed, according to Kinkead, "'It's crazy here.
These people strangle each other.'"[32]

Fittingly, Kinkead ends her guided tour where it began – in Chinatown's
isolation. On Sundays, she wrote, half a million people descend upon
Chinatown, and "a burden lifts from this desperate community, strangled by
miserable wages and organized crime." Families stroll, the temples are full,
businesses hum. Yet amidst that crush and appearance of familiarity, Kinkead
felt keenly a sense of loneliness and alienation. No one, she testified, spoke to
her, a white devil. She wandered up an alley to a courtyard. "It is a gritty,
gray, forlorn place," she recalled, "a patch of old Chinatown more or less
untouched since the 1880s." Like an explorer in an unmapped and timeless
land, Kinkead ascended a staircase to a second floor apartment. "I knock. A
frail old man, like a withered moon appears. He greets me quizzically. He has
lived in Chinatown for sixty years, he says, and has never spoken to a white
person."[33]

Those snapshots of the Chinese and Chinatown, of course, are yellowed, dog-eared, and well-worn, and they are not naively displayed by late twenti-eth-century writers like Kinkead, who are knowing projectionists having learned from the various civil rights protest movements of marginalized mi-norities during the preceding decades. "Today, liberal Chinese, influenced by the Asian-American movement," Kinkead poked, "skip over this period [the times when Chinatown was allegedly ruled by criminals who controlled gambling, opium, and prostitution] or ridicule it as an invention of white journalists for the titillation of their readers." On the contrary, she asserted with the confidence of an ethnographer, those features of Chinese American life were a veritable reality, and "there is no question that Chinatowns were tough."[34] In truth, earlier mythmakers like Will Irwin were likewise aware of skeptical readers, who might doubt the veracity of their claims as wildly outlandish or as mere fabrications. Thus, Irwin sprinkled his account with assertions of an insider's familiarity with insular, paradoxical Chinese America along with recognitions that tourists only see the surfaces of Chinatown – the "prepared show" – whereas he depicted the community as it truly was – "a real life of homes and quiet industry."[35]

Besides the commonality of their ostensibly sympathetic, but authorial gazes, Irwin's and Kinkead's representations share elements that constitute and reinscribe a formulaic tradition of Chinatowns made in America. Chinatowns and their residents are racialized, gendered, and sexualized si-multaneously in their prominence and isolation, transcendence and imma-nence, surfaces and interiors, attractions and repulsions, passion and materialism, familiarity and distance. Those apparent polar positions are collapsed and confused in this impenetrable, contradictory, anomalous place and people. Perhaps their logic, as Dean MacCannell has suggested, rests in the notion that Chinatown, like all tourist meccas, contains representations of both good and evil and offers complex, but orderly and universal codes that signify and affirm modernity.[36]

Textual Chinatown is as familiar to whites as it is to its Chinese residents, who surf daily in the breakwaters of that virtual reality. Indeed, many of those surfers not only ride those waves, but have helped to generate and sustain them. Thus, for instance, exoticism might entrap and enslave the cultural other, but also serve to lure the self. Frank Marshall White reported in 1907 that for the past 30 years "tens of thousands of sight-seers, the great majority from out of town" have descended upon New York City's Chinatown, "inhaled the odor of incense in the joss-houses, made purchases in the quaint shops, partaken of weird aliments in the georgeous tea-houses, looked in on the interminable and incomprehensible performances of the Chinese thea-tre, or witnessed by stealth bogus opium orgies in mysterious basements." Tourist dollars drop from orientalist trees; social constructions have mate-rial reality. And Chinatown's isolation and marginality allowed Tammany politicians to stuff the ballot boxes and buy the votes of disenfranchised Chinese in this "banner district," White alleged, and it enabled Chinese, who were being pursued by the law, to hide and elude capture and punishment. Lacking individuality insofar as to many whites all Chinese looked alike had its advantages, and English-language disability might cripple equal access to racial privileges, but it might also be used to obscure harmful testimony or deny service to intrusive whites.[37]

Sociologist Ivan Light has shown the careful and deliberate crafting of Chinatown by its business class to net tourist dollars. During the late nineteenth century, Light stated, prostitution, gambling, and opium-smoking flourished in the San Francisco and New York City Chinatowns. Those businesses catered mainly to men, both Chinese and white, and were run by Chinese gangs, but also in partnership with whites – the police, landowners, and government officials. In New York City, Light noted, Irish competitors sought to muscle in on the action, and whites, blacks, and Chinese lived and hustled in Chinatown. In 1885 San Francisco, reports cited 150 gambling joints and 70 houses of prostitution, and an 1880 visitor observed that the Chinese theatre attracted hoodlums and "scamps of the worst type from the entire city." In that setting, violence was commonplace. Explained Light: "The combination of police laxity, syndicated vice resorts, and inter-ethnic friction created a boisterous and volatile climate on Chinatown streets."[38]

Merchants, he continued, held class interests at variance with those criminal elements in Chinatown. They relied upon white, middle-class tourists to patronize their shops and restaurants, and Chinatown's violent streets kept them away. During the first several decades of the twentieth century, thus, Chinese businessmen struggled to eliminate the vice traffic and ultimately prevailed. Restaurants replaced gambling parlors, and curio stores, bordellos. Even the displaced gangs joined in the new prosperity, opening shops and restaurants, and toughs became tourist guides, who promised to show the hidden, lurid side of Chinatown. Some guides hired Chinese to put on shows for the tourists, according to Light, and a favorite theme was a fight among "opium crazed fiends" over a "slave girl." Chinese New Year became a major cultural event and tourist attraction, and the streets and building façades were designed to convey that oriental feeling. "They built Chinatown to suit the taste and imagination of . . . the American public," a study observed.[39]

Indeed, Chinatown's transformation from vice district to tourist attraction, in Ivan Light's study, or vice district and tourist trap, in the ahistorical orientalist tropes of writers like Will Irwin and Gwen Kinkead, exemplifies complicity on the part of both white and Chinese authors and the material rewards of those projects. And yet, they were unequal partners – whites and Chinese – in that the power to name was held by whites, who not only designated and classified the Chinese and Chinatown, but who thereby identified and positioned themselves. Vancouver's Chinese and Chinatown, explained geographer Kay J. Anderson, illustrated the constructedness of those categories of race and place, but also revealed the power of the state and institutional practice in the making of those malleable yet rigidly fixed ideas. Chinatown, Anderson argued, was "an idea with remarkable social force and material effect – one that for more than a century has shaped and justified the practices of powerful institutions toward it and toward people of Chinese origin."[40]

Chinese migrants, observed Anderson, brought with them notions of kinship and community and built their own consciousnesses and neighborhoods within this new setting of Vancouver. Still, "without the acknowledgement or acceptance of the residents," whites apprehended and located Chinatown through their cognitive categories and established a boundary between white and Chinese, Vancouver and Chinatown. Whites thereby isolated and distanced themselves from those they named Chinese, and Chinatown was properly "an arbitrary classification of space, a regionalization that has belonged to European society." Further, Anderson contended, Chinatown or the place have become racialized such that racial ideology "has been materially embedded in space . . . and it is through 'place' that it has been given a local referent, become a social fact, and aided its own reproduction." Chinatown as symbol, thus, informed and institutionalized the racialization process of both Chinese and white, and helped to structure and maintain the wider social relations.[41]

The rebuilding of San Francisco's Chinatown after the 1906 earthquake and fire that produced Will Irwin's "new, clean Chinatown" modifies Anderson's stresses around race, place, and the relations of power. Unlike Arnold Genthe's moody, orientalized vision, old Chinatown was an architecturally unremarkable place of Victorian buildings and American styles. Visitors, revealing as much about themselves as about what they saw, described Chinatown as "neither picturesque nor Oriental . . . the pagoda as a building is wholly absent . . . the majority of the buildings are of brick . . . two or three stories high and with the cellars or basements . . . the architecture is thoroughly American."[42] The city's board of supervisors appointed a subcommittee to study the relocation of Chinatown after the earthquake. The plan to remove Chinatown from its central location to the city's outskirts was vehemently opposed by Chinese merchants, who moved quickly to rebuild a fanciful, new oriental city of "veritable fairy palaces," according to one of those businessmen.[43]

The merchants hired white architects, who had shallow understandings of Chinese construction styles. "Their exposure to Chinese architecture was limited to images of pagodas and temples with turned-up eaves and massive curved roofs, forms and expressions that were already centuries old," noted a historian of that undertaking. In the process, they invented "an exotic Asian form in architecture" and "a Sino-architectural vocabulary using Western methods of construction and local building materials in accordance with local building codes." That orientalizing of Chinatown worked for its creators. White San Franciscans welcomed this "Oriental city," and writers extolled it as one of the most notable places in America.[44] Chinatown remained where it was before the earthquake, and became the tourist destination that the Chinese merchants desired. In promoting a hegemonic, orientalist discourse, a class of Chinatown's residents advanced their material self-interest.

Chinatowns have been studied in numerous ways. In the United States, scholars have seen Chinatowns as ethnic enclaves exemplary of ethnic solidarity or discrimination, of segregation or assimilation, of stagnation or social mobility. They depict them as homogeneous concentrations and heterogeneous populations, and have considered them from the outside as well as from within. The literature is deep and diverse.[45] In this brief study, I have, like social geographer Kay J. Anderson, stressed the constructedness of the ideas of Chinatown and the Chinese and referenced some of their material manifestations. Representations have palpable effects. They also reveal the sources and articulations of power. Chinatown virtual communities are apprehensions of racialized, gendered, and sexualized selves and spaces over racialized, gendered, and sexualized others and spaces. But they are also complicated by the interactions and negotiations between and among the knower(s) and the object(s) in the forms of acquiescence, modification, and resistance. Orientalism can work both ways, and virtuality itself can be a complicitous creation.

Notes

1   Arnold Genthe, *Pictures of Old Chinatown*, with text by Will Irwin (New York: Moffat, Yard and Company, 1908).
2   Gwen Kinkead, *Chinatown: A Portrait of a Closed Society* (New York: HarperCollins, 1992), pp. ix and x.
3   Ibid., p. x.
4   Neil Rennie, *Far-Fetched Facts: The Literature of Travel and the Idea of the South Seas* (Oxford: Clarendon Press, 1995), p. 1.
5   Mary Louise Pratt, *Imperial Eyes: Travel Writing and Transculturation* (London: Routledge, 1992), pp. 10 and 15–107.
6   Davydd J. Greenwood, "Culture by the Pound: An Anthropological Perspective on Tourism as Cultural Commoditization," in Valerie L. Smith, ed., *Hosts and Guests: The Anthropology of Tourism* (Philadelphia: University of Pennsylvania Press, 1977), pp. 129, 130–1, and 137.
7   Daniel J. Boorstin, *The Image: A Guide to Pseudo-Events in America* (New York: Atheneum, 1971); Dean MacCannell, *The Tourist: A New Theory of the Leisure Class* (New York: Schocken, 1976); John Urry, *The Tourist Gaze: Leisure and Travel in Contemporary Societies* (London: Sage, 1990), pp. 7–9; and Jonathan Culler, *Framing the Sign: Criticism and Its Institutions* (University of Oklahoma Press, 1988), pp. 154, 155, and 164–7.

8   MacCannell, *The Tourist: A New Theory of the Leisure Class*.

9   See Urry, *Tourist Gaze: Leisure and Travel in Contemporary Societies*, for a clear discussion of tourism's changing natures and its location within the social relations.

10   Ibid., pp. 11 and 82–8.

11   Marie-Laure Ryan, "Immersion vs. Interactivity: Virtual Reality and Literary Theory," *Postmodern Culture* 5 (1994).

12   David Morley and Kevin Robins, *Spaces of Identity: Global Media, Electronic Landscapes and Cultural Boundaries* (London: Routledge, 1995), pp. 182 and 192–3.

13   *Genthe's Photographs of San Francisco's Old Chinatown*, photographs by Arnold Genthe, selection and text by John Kuo Wei Tchen (New York: Dover, 1984).

14   Genthe, *Pictures of Old Chinatown*, pp. 2–3.

15   Ibid., pp. 6, 7, 8, and 9.

16   Ibid., pp. 6, 8, 24, and 25.

17   Ibid., pp. 28–32.

18   Ibid., pp. 32–4.

19   Ibid., p. 48.

20   Ibid., p. 57.

21   Ibid., p. 2.

22   For an explication of deviant heterosexuality, see Jennifer Ting, "Bachelor Society: Deviant Heterosexuality and Asian American Historiography," in Gary Y. Okihiro et al., ed., *Privileging Positions: The Sites of Asian American Studies*, (Pullman: Washington State University Press, 1995), pp. 271–80.

23   Genthe, *Pictures of Old Chinatown*, pp. 51 and 53.

24   For sympathetic treatments of Cameron, see Carol Green Wilson, *Chinatown Quest: The Life Adventures of Donaldina Cameron* (Stanford: Stanford University Press, 1931); and Mildred Crowl Martin, *Chinatown's Angry Angel: The Story of Donaldina Cameron* (Palo Alto: Pacific Books, 1977). For a critical view, see Laurene Wu McClain, "Donaldina Cameron: A Reappraisal," *Pacific Historian* 27 (1983): 25–35. For a comprehensive view of white women's missionary activities, see Peggy Pascoe, *Relations of Rescue: The Search for Female Authority in the American West, 1874–1939* (New York: Oxford University Press, 1990).

25   Genthe, *Pictures of Old Chinatown*, pp. 50–2.

26   Kinkead, *Chinatown: A Portrait of a Closed Society*, p. 3.

27   Ibid., pp. 5–7.

28   Ibid., pp. 5 and 7–11.

29   Ibid., pp. 11, 14–15, and 17.

30   Ibid., pp. 19 and 21.

31   Ibid., pp. 21–2, 24, 133–4, and 155.

32   Ibid., pp. 32, 35, 45, 46, 63, 70, and 82.

33   Ibid., pp. 200 and 204.

34   Ibid., pp. 47 and 48.

35   Genthe, *Pictures of Old Chinatown*, pp. 13 and 14.

36   MacCannell, *The Tourist: A New Theory of the Leisure Class*, pp. 40 and 46.

37   Frank Marshall White, "The Last Days of Chinatown," *Harper's Weekly*, August 17, 1907, p. 1208.

38   Ivan Light, "From Vice District to Tourist Attraction: The Moral Career of Ameri-

can Chinatowns, 1880–1940," *Pacific Historical Review* 43 (1974): 367–75.

39   Ibid., pp. 377–91.

40   Kay J. Anderson, "The Idea of Chinatown: The Power of Place and Institutional Practice in the Making of a Racial Category," *Journal of the Association of American Geographers* 77 (1987): 581.

41   bid., pp. 583, 584, and 594. See also, K. J. Anderson, "Cultural Hegemony and the Race-Definition Process in Chinatown, Vancouver: 1880–1980," *Environment and Planning D: Society and Space* 6 (1988): 127–49.

42   Quoted in Philip P. Choy, "The Architecture of San Francisco Chinatown," *Chinese America: History and Perspectives* (1990): 39.

43   Ibid., p. 49.

44   Ibid., pp. 49 and 54.

45   See, e.g., Peter Kwong, *Chinatown, New York: Labor and Politics, 1930–1950* (New York: Hill and Wang, 1987); Chalsa M. Loo, *Chinatown: Most Time, Hard Time* (New York: Praeger, 1991); Victor G. and Brett de Bary Nee, *Longtime Californ': A Documentary Study of an American Chinatown* (Boston: Houghton Mifflin, 1972); Paul C. Siu, *The Chinese Laundryman: A Study of Social Isolation* (New York: New York University Press, 1987); Bernard P. Wong, *Patronage, Brokerage, Entrepreneurship, and the Chinese Community of New York* (New York: AMS Press, 1988); Min Zhou, *Chinatown: The Socioeconomic Potential of an Urban Enclave* (Philadelphia: Temple University Press, 1992).

16

Villages, Local and Global: Observations on Computer-Mediated and Geographically-Situated Communities

Samuel Oluoch Imbo

In our age more than any other, our world has increasingly and unalterably become a global village in which the fate of the global community is shared. This increased interdependence calls for a re-evaluation of our ideas about what constitutes community, a re-examination of our commitments to other members of the global community, and some level of individual sacrifice for the collective good. The issue of the relationship of individuals to their communities has typically been discussed from either a standpoint of liberalism or that of communitarianism. I begin with an explanation of both these theoretical orientations.

The term "liberalism" means different things to different people. Instead of understanding the term as representing one doctrine, it is better to understand "liberalism" as denoting a family of doctrines built around two core liberal values. The first value is the primacy of the individual. In evaluating any political, social, or economic arrangements, liberals hold individuality to be the ultimate value. The test of a good arrangement is its impact on individual human beings and to what extent the arrangement fosters respects for individuals and their rights. An extreme version of this value is that only individuals count. Such extreme forms of liberalism do not discount the importance of groups or cultures, but claim only that any evaluation of the group or subculture must be from the standpoint of specific individuals. Whether moderate or extreme, liberals uniformly reject the views of group theorists who identify individuals primarily as parts of entities larger than the individuals themselves. The second liberal value is freedom of choice. Liberals of all shades stress voluntary agent-centered choice and indeed hold that only uncoerced choice has moral significance. The point here is that social and political institutions are evaluated primarily on their impact on individual autonomy.

From these two core values, liberalisms of all kinds have been constructed. John Locke and John Stuart Mill both exemplify the liberal concern with the promotion of individuality and the insistence that societies serve the interests of citizens who come together in voluntary association. Adam Smith's economic liberalism is the insistence that the state should leave individuals to their own devices if the creation of wealth is to be maximized. In this chapter I refer particularly to the contemporary versions of liberalism in the work of John Rawls, Ronald Dworkin, and Robert Nozick. Nozick stresses individual autonomy so radically that he concludes that no state, or, at worst, a minimal state, can be justified by liberal principles.[1] John Rawls offers an example of a political liberalism according to which individuals imagining themselves in an "original position" would endorse liberal principles of justice as the basis for a well-ordered society. A crucial feature of Rawls's political liberalism is that for the individuals in the original position liberal values of individuality and autonomy emerge as paramount foundations for a legitimate social arrangement if any actual inherited epistemological and metaphysical presuppositions are completely set aside.[2] The prolific writing of Jürgen Habermas has an underlying message that at the core of a well-ordered society must be a commitment to the promotion of undistorted communication. Democratic societies must have structures that enable the interests of all citizens to be voiced. The validity of the structures depend on their ability to incorporate all relevant interests in society. Dialogue must be unconstrained by factors of politics and economics and must be open to all autonomous rational individuals. Anyone must be able to participate in the discussion on equal terms of symmetry, reciprocity, and reflexivity.[3] Thus the Habermasian concern for societies characterized by diversity and conflict is undergirded by the liberal principle of freedom of speech and of assembly.

Liberal political theorists are influenced by the two core values of individuality and autonomy in the views of community and institutional arrangements they advocate. It becomes easy to see why there are so many liberal theories precisely because there is disagreement on the interpretations of the fundamental principle that only individuals count. The classic free market liberalism of Adam Smith and the libertarian ideals of Robert Nozick agree that any political authority over individuals is unfair and illegitimate if that authority extends to rights that individuals can secure for themselves. The egalitarian liberalism of John Rawls is anchored by the idea that individuals are free and equal and therefore the first order of business for any state is the promotion of equal opportunities. The rights-based liberalism of Ronald Dworkin begins with the straightforward claim that individuals have rights that may not be abridged in the name of society or common good.[4] Given these variations in the interpretation of what constitutes liberal thinking, there is a corresponding variation in the institutional arrangements liberals recommend. Most generally, these institutions include valid structures for the incorporation of all interests in the public discourse, mechanisms to allow the toleration of diverse philosophical, religious, and moral positions, a system to ensure political representation and the enforcement of valid laws, the will to enable the unhindered exchange of goods and services, and, most importantly, political mechanisms to protect the core values of individuality and autonomy.[5]

On the other side of the divide stand theorists such as Charles Taylor, Alasdair MacIntyre, and Seyla Benhabib, who may collectively be called "communitarians." As with liberalism, it is difficult to agree on a fixed meaning of the term communitarian. Communitarianism is at once a political theory, a movement, and a framework for public policy. These are the different facets that conjure up in the popular mind a picture of the communitarian as a citizen whose children attend public rather than private schools, a citizen who prefers public transportation, libraries, and recreation parks, one who does volunteer work in her community and is familiar with her neighbors.[6] From these ordinary examples of family, school, and neighborhood, one begins to glean the relationship communitarians make between individuals, social groupings, and the environment. Communitarians find agreement around three issues: challenge to the liberal claim concerning the priority of individual rights over the public good, conceptions of the self as a moral agent, and the justifications of political ideals and institutions.

Communitarians such as MacIntyre, Taylor, and Benhabib make a number of claims about the nature of individuals, their identity, and their relationships. One of these claims is that individuals are embedded in community in the sense that "personal identity" is defined by their membership in community. Communitarians mean that an individual's character is shaped, though not completely determined by, social roles and relationships. The account MacIntyre gives in *After Virtue* of inherited traditions, histories, and narratives reinforce the theme that the moral agent is constituted by membership in communities.[7] Charles Taylor makes the same argument in *Sources of the Self: The Making of the Modern Identity*.[8] His main criticism is that liberalism is blind to the fact that "personal identity" is made possible only within the context of a community and can only be exercised within community. Neither MacIntyre nor Taylor propose the extreme position that our most important attachments are unchosen or severable at will. They restrict their arguments to the difficulty of detaching oneself from inherited roles and the constitutive nature these in turn have on the question of "personal identity." Seyla Benhabib is not usually categorized as a communitarian, though I interpret the theoretical positions she takes in *Situating the Self: Gender, Community and Postmodernism in Contemporary Ethics* as attempts to reassess the notion of the moral self in a communitarian spirit.[9] She argues that "the abstract and disembedded, distorting and nostalgic ideal of the male ego" fostered by liberalism fails to capture crucial aspects of community and is particularly incapable of explaining the contemporary loss of public spiritedness and sense of community.[10] Starting from the premise that the modern person belongs simultaneously to multiple sub-communities, the participatory communitarianism advocated by Benhabib encourages "non-exclusive principles of membership among the spheres . . . and the sense that we have a say in the economic, political, and civic arrangements which define our lives together, and that what one does makes a difference."[11]

Central to the debate between liberals and communitarians are divergent conceptions of community. Both sides would agree with St. Augustine's characterization of a community as a band of people bound together by the love of a common object. Their disagreements would revolve around what the common object should be. Liberal theorists emphasize individuality and autonomy, communitarians peg their arguments on the indebtedness of individuals to their societies for their personal identity.

Liberal theories that have an excessively individualistic conception of the person cannot successfully meet the challenges of our age because these theories seem to presume that persons ought to pursue their autonomy by being wary of interdependent relationships that compromise personal independence. Communitarian theories err in the opposite direction when they paint pictures of individuals embedded in community in ways that spell danger for the concepts of autonomy and moral agency. In this chapter I want to discuss two traditional communities and make a case that computer communication gives us a way to extend the range of the notion of community. While traditional communities are usually limited by such factors as ethnic or national boundaries, computer-mediated communities help us reconceptualize the notion of community to transcend the usual limitations of place, time, and physical attributes.

The primary challenge of the new millennium will be to understand the bonds of community that unite the people of the world as one. A feature of our time is the rapidity with which those bonds are changing. If change is good, we live in exceedingly good times. The chief agent or culprit, depending on the perspective one adopts, responsible for the unprecedented change is the computer. Computers are changing the ways in which we use language. Windows, rams, megabytes, applications, programs, compressing files, logging on, hard drives, cutting and pasting – now all these mean different things. According to a joke currently making rounds in the internet, gone are the days when if you had a 3½-inch floppy you hoped nobody would find out. Bytes, bandwidth, routers, domain names, and viruses might as well be words in a new language. Understanding that language means evolving new forms of communication and the alteration of some social arrangements. All world cultures are forced to confront this new reality; nation-states watch as their boundaries become increasingly porous, and human conventions must adapt to these new realities or become outdated. Striking examples of change may be seen in two traditionally community-building activities – commerce and education. Setting up shop on cyberstreet gives a wholly new meaning to traditional forms of commerce. In the same way, new forms of electronic communication radically affect the ways learning and teaching happen in societies around the world. There are obviously benefits and pitfalls, opportunities and obstacles, attached to these reconfigurations.

The central concern of this chapter is the extent to which these reconfigurations affect notions of community. Computer-mediated communities stand in contrast to geographically situated communities such as the Luo of Kenya or the Japanese. Geographically situated communities come with a built-in sense of their own authenticity and identity. Yet it is these same aspects that may be problematic about these communities. The Luo and Japanese communities complement each other well for this discussion, because they are different kinds of communities commonly acknowledged as "real" (that is, as opposed to computer communities). While the Luo are mainly traditional and non-industrialized, the Japanese are modern and industrialized. Both of these communities are structured around specific geographical spaces. Computer communication focuses attention on precisely those questions about how we experience both ourselves and other persons in real and virtual environments. The transphysical "places" of cyberspace can have a role in extending the range of authentic social relations because such electronic interactions focus attention on the relations between virtual worlds and traditional communities.

I intend the term "community" in its widest possible extension – the global village. This is not to ignore the diversity to be found in specific communities to which the people of the world belong. But I consider it crucial that all traditional communities that are well-ordered point beyond themselves to something larger. I take that "something larger" to which all specific communities prepare their members to be the essential sense of the term community. In the modern world these specific communities will be able to sustain themselves to the extent that they prepare their members for, in the words of Maria Lugones, "world-traveling."[12] With Lugones, I think it is crucial that our communities equip us with the ability to feel at ease in other real and virtual worlds. The chief pressure of world-traveling is to find one's place in a community with no national boundaries but in which all members are rooted in specific cultures, countries, and traditional communities. I argue that computer-mediated communities point to ways in which we can usefully meet the challenges of our age by reconceptualizing the notion of community to transcend the usual limitations of place, time, and physical attributes.

The Luo Model of Community

The Luo, currently living mainly in Uganda and Kenya, are speakers of a Nilotic language (distinguishing them from the other main linguistic groups in East Africa, Bantu and Cushitic speakers). According to their oral traditions, the Luo migrated from Sudan. The precise dates of their migrations are unknown because the oral traditions of the Luo are not overly concerned with documenting precise beginnings and endings. Attempts by historians and anthropologists to reconstruct the Luo migrations have resulted in a clear distinction between the Northern Luo (in Sudan), the Central Luo (in Uganda), and the Southern Luo (in Kenya). The oral traditions and cultures of all the Luo groups still exhibit striking similarities. Each group has also understandably developed in its own unique ways since the separation from the cradle land in Sudan. In view of those differences, the term "Luo" is here used to refer to the Kenya Luo.

There are four features about membership in the Luo ethnic group that I think both liberals and communitarians would benefit from:

- personal identity is defined by an intricate web of biological and social
- group interests are considered to override personal ones;
- membership in the community is not to be understood in contractual terms;
- it is impossible to opt out of group membership.

Two caveats are in order before this discussion of the Luo, and indeed any African ethnic group. I think it is possible to make statements about African ethnic groups, African cultures, or even African peoples without at the same time implying homogeneity or conformity of these entities throughout the continent. Of course African ethnic and cultural groups differ in their particulars. Reference to the Luo is to the most common and general features members of the group themselves take as defining their membership.

Secondly, there is no implication that what is said about the Luo is fixed or unchanging through time. While acknowledging that the Luo and other ethnic groups are dynamic, the features to which I call attention here are those that pre-dated colonialism. African ethnic groups have survived that colonial experience in varying degrees. In any case, it is fair to note that the Luo, like many other African ethnic groups, currently exhibit very strong effects of their interaction with the West. I have attempted to reflect the state of the groups' ideas prior to the colonial experience. It therefore bears repeating that my comments take precolonial Luo community (and Africa) as the point of reference for only this reason.

One last preliminary comment needs to be made. No implication of cultural purity is intended by the choice of the precolonial ideas about membership in Luo community as the point of reference for the discussion. The precolonial period in Africa is not to be understood as a glorious past whose purity of traditions was adulterated by colonial contact. This is merely a starting point that allows for the discussion of the Luo community with as little outside influence as possible.

The aspect of the Luo community that I start out with is the conception of the individual in the social context. Two Luo sayings capture this point about interconnectedness: "Hulu bende oro ngege" (Even the tilapia can run errands for the anchovy) and "Kik iidh yath ma malo to iweyo ma piny" (Do not climb the taller tree while neglecting the shorter one). These are proverbs about sociality and one finds throughout the African continent the idea that individual persons are defined by an intricate web of biological and social relations. Consider the Sotho saying "Motho ke motho ka batho" or the Xhosa saying "Umuntu ngumuntu ngabantu" – both of which translate to "Man is man by his fellowmen." These sayings have certain underlying conceptions. In the social context the individual is not conceived as the singular, personal, and impenetrable entity, living in glorious isolation, and who finds hell in the words of Sartre, to be other people. The individual's existence is not fully meaningful unless in the context of being part of a larger totality. The individual's life cannot be disentangled from the web of biological and social relations. It is as if by one's life one is saying, "I am because we are. Because we exist, I exist as well."

This social feeling finds expression in many ways. One way is in the opinions about the extended family. Another way in which this expression manifests itself is the idea that the community, and especially the leader, has the duty to help or to let the less fortunate share in the riches of the wealthy. In post-independence Africa this idea has found expression in various formulations which have been loosely collectively subsumed under the rubric of "African socialism" or "African humanism." Kwame Nkrumah, Julius Nyerere, and Kenneth Kaunda are famous exponents of these versions of African communalism.

For the Luo, as for other African groups, collective interests normally are accorded precedence over individual interest. In terms of ethics, the most outstanding wrongs are sins against the group. In the African setting the group revolves primarily around kinship and so therefore the sins against the group are essentially those that undercut the rules of harmony that define the system of group values. Another exemplification of the precedence of group interests can be deduced from the importance, on the positive side, of social prestige and, on the negative side, the dread of shame.

The obvious question this leads to is exactly what kind of community the ethnic group is. Groups can be divided into two kinds, aggregates and conglomerates. Aggregates are loose-knit groups whose members share a short-lived interest. The interest does not abide long enough for the group to form a leadership structure. Conglomerates are highly structured groups whose members may share narrow but long-lasting interests. The two kinds of group share an assumption about the centrality of the principle of freedom of association. In a broad sense, both kinds of group may be called interest groups because they are voluntary associations of individuals with common interests.

This assumption about the importance of the principle of freedom of association remains largely unquestioned in contemporary discussions about community by both liberals and communitarians mentioned earlier. In these discussions, particularly Rawls in *A Theory of Justice* and Nozick in *Anarchy, State and Utopia*, it is usually implicitly taken that communities are necessarily voluntary associations of individuals who have chosen to "journey together". Hence there is a predominance in the discussions by Rawls, Nozick, and other liberals of groups such as labor unions, social and welfare clubs, interest groups, corporations, and nations. The members of a trade union come together to further their obvious common interests in higher wages, satisfying work, safe working conditions, and vigilance about justice in the workplace. Economic corporations have an interest in producing their goods or services as cheaply as possible, cornering as much of the market as possible and in maximizing profit. The state brings together people, for the most part, individuals with a common ideology, history, culture, and system of government. All these groups assume voluntary participation, with the consequence that as soon as the common goal has been achieved or the factions within the larger alliance become powerful enough, the interest group ceases to have reason to stay in existence. The theory here seems to be that if these groups continue to stay in existence it can only be because the individuals in these groups are primarily interested in their own welfare and choose to pursue those interests collectively. There is an implicit acceptance in such a theory of interest groups that what drives the group to action or the glue that holds it together are the twin considerations of choice and self-interest.

But are liberal and communitarian orientations capable of explaining ethnic groups such as the Luo, other groups with non-economic interests, or even communities in which membership is not voluntary? Contemporary liberal discussions about community can best be described, following Virginia Held, as being "in the grip of contractual thinking."[13] Held is right to lament that the prescriptions of Rawls, Nozick, and Dworkin have seeped into all spheres of social discussion so that one finds the same basic assumptions about individuals everywhere one turns. The main negative effect of such seepage is the "economic man" – the disinterested individual who is representative of all humanity and whose social relations are calculated on the basis of rational choice. As Virginia Held argues, this vision of contractual relations ignores or fails to take into account the experience of women. Similarly, I want to argue that such contractarianism is inadequate in understanding the model of community exemplified by groups such as the Luo and Japanese. It is impossible to understand the relationship of kinsmen and women in contractual terms. The main reason that kinship relationships are not in perpetual danger of erosion is because members of the same ethnic group "find themselves" in relationship and do not place themselves there contractually. The crucial element in kinship relationships, I suggest, is the lack of voluntariness.[14]

A court case in Kenya raised the twin issues of the non-voluntariness of Luo membership and the inability to opt out of that membership in clear form.[15] The case involved Silvanus Melea Otieno (S.M. Otieno), a Luo and a distinguished Nairobi criminal lawyer, who died at the age of 55 in 1986. According to (unwritten) Luo customary law, a deceased Luo adult male must be buried in his ancestral home. The issues revolved around who was entitled to bury him and what law (Luo customary law or the laws of the government of Kenya) applied in the case. His widow's lawyer sought to demonstrate that S. M. Otieno, by marrying a Kikuyu woman (a member of Kenya's largest ethnic group) and by his modern lifestyle, had put himself beyond the reach of the traditions and customary Law of the Luo community. By these actions, the lawyer argued, Otieno had clearly signaled his intention never again to be subject to Luo customs. The modernizing influences on his life were said to be his having spent his entire working life in the metropolis of Nairobi, in the practice of law, in the marrying outside his own ethnic group, and in the practice of Christianity. At the end of a long trial, the High Court of Kenya concluded that at the practical level of implementation, Luo practitioners of tradition act as if the customs which bind them are not made so contractually. This lack of voluntariness, among other things, serves to sustain such groupings in the promotion of specific ethnic interests such as transmission of culture, a sense of order, and pride in a shared history.

Rights-based liberalism with its emphasis on individuality and freedom of association, cannot adequately account for Luo conceptions of community or membership in an African tribal group – groups in which one finds oneself. Individualist concepts are inadequate tools with which to fully capture what it is to be a Luo. One "finds oneself" a Luo and that membership defines one's very identity. The choice of membership which social contract theorists make their foundation is not the primary feature of these groupings. One cannot opt out. To be a Luo is to have a deeply social nature.

Ifeanyi Menkiti puts the case succinctly.[16] One of the crucial distinctions he notes between African and Western views of the person is that in the African view it is the community that defines the person as person, and not some isolated static and abstract quality as rationality, will, or memory.

Menkiti concludes that personhood in the African context, since it is dependent on the community, cannot be assumed to be given at birth. It has to be attained. Personhood is attained in proportion as one participates in the community and fulfills the obligations of the social networks previously mentioned. He echoes Nyerere when he says, "whereas the African view asserts an ontological independence to human society, and moves from society to individuals, the Western view moves instead from individuals to society."[17] It is in this context that Julius Nyerere is to be understood when he made the theme "I am because we are" the cornerstone of his thought on African socialism.[18] The focus is on the family, the village, the collectivity. Contrast this with the seemingly disembodied Cartesian thinking self. Beginning with the family, African personhood progresses through membership in the village, the clan, and extends into a vast social network encompassing both living and dead. There are mutual claims that are generally assumed. In the traditional setting, one could always count on the help and hospitality of co-members. The bonds of mutual claims cover all aspects of life – economic, education, religious – a sum total of traditions, ideas, customs, modes of behavior, patterns of thought, ways of doing things that are passed on. The crucial features about the Luo model of community are the non-contractual nature of membership and the inability to opt out of that membership. These two features strike me as cornerstones of a view of community that would promote world-traveling. The knowledge that we are in relationships we cannot get out of must be the beginning of an understanding of those bonds and the construction of a more adequate theory of membership in a global community.

The Japanese Model of Community

The same element of non-voluntariness is seen in the Japanese communitarianism to which I next turn. The discussion of Japanese communitarianism, however, adds a new element. In Japanese society one finds a group-oriented community that is at the same time industrialized and urbanized. This element is important, because one of the challenges for communitarian theorists has been to show that communitarianism is compatible with the values of industrialization and urbanization. In the popular mind and in contemporary debate, liberalism has been closely associated with the democracies and free enterprise systems of the West, while collectivism was associated with the former communist countries of the former Soviet Union and the then communist Eastern Europe.[19]

The same caveats made in discussing the Luo are applicable here. There seems to be no way to discuss Japan and "the Japanese" briefly without oversimplification or implying a static social arrangement. Conscious of the danger of oversimplification, I defer to the work of two scholars of Japan Hajime Nakamura[20] and Chie Nakane.[21] Both include in their discussions some features that capture Japanese reality. These include the predominance of Shintoism, a commitment to the social (as opposed to individualism), a preference for nonverbal communication, a deep respect and love for nature, an unwillingness to rock the boat, always doing the pleasing thing, and keeping all the rough edges underneath.

Commitment to the social can be seen to be deeply ingrained in both traditional and modern Japan. The literary evidence as well as the popular sayings, proverbs, songs, mythologies, and folklore lack any emphasis on individualism, self, and self-consciousness in the manner or to the extent these are visible in Western culture. It would be misleading to suggest from the foregoing that Japan does not have its share of assertive and introspective individuals. Much nearer the truth would be to observe that individualism as it is known in the West, accompanied by such manifestations as the emphasis on explicitly guaranteed freedoms and rights, or extreme forms of alienation, has not developed in Japan. At a very superficial level this commitment to the social expresses itself in the homogeneity of dress and conformity to generally accepted standards of behavior. These manifestations are in turn rooted in the similarity of beliefs, values, cosmologies, and general life experiences. As such, the cultivation of idiosyncrasies in terms of personality is impeded by the more important social factors of family membership and clan membership. Tradition mediates between roles and regulates social interaction. As in the case of the Luo, personhood is defined in terms of social roles. In this communal web outsiders see a near total absorption of the individual by the group because the boundary between self and society is not as distinctly drawn as it is in the West. It would be hasty to conclude from this observation that the Japanese view of community is wholly detrimental to the individual or that it necessarily encourages a "tyranny of the majority."

Another of the ways in which the emphasis on social relationships exhibits itself among the Japanese is in the form of highly elaborate greetings. There are rules of propriety that are both detailed and comprehensive. These rules extend to all areas of the social and personal, the political and the moral. The stress on propriety is guided by what may be called a "collective conscience." "Collective consciousness" stands in need of explanation. From a radical individualist's standpoint, it implies, at the very least, an anti-individuating "tyranny of the majority." For liberals, collective consciousness is anathema because of its uniform and homogenizing overtones. The principle of freedom of association, as has been noted, is crucial to the liberal viewpoint. On the liberal view, membership in professional, social, or international associations must be the result of choice on the part of an individual. The result is a series of chosen relationships of individuals with common or shared wants.

Since the chosen relationships are entered into voluntarily, the individuals retain the right to extricate themselves from them by exercising their choice at any moment. Community on this view becomes wholly contingent on the common purpose or interest of those concerned – a view of community which communitarians find unsatisfying and unstable because, as the communitarian theories of MacIntyre and Taylor insist, the starting point for any discussion of community is the ontologically socially embedded individual. On the liberal view, however, only groups formed out of the dynamics of personal consciousness are capable of consistently resisting sublimation into the "group mind" that is collective consciousness.

The level of common interest or purpose among the Japanese, on the other hand, surpasses the limited overlap of interests found in aggregates and conglomerates. The Japanese share mythologies, folklore, proverbs, songs, beliefs, values, cosmologies, and general life experiences. From this shared world-view it becomes clear how the interests of individuals are intertwined in one big communal web. Health, job satisfaction, self-image – these are all intertwined with the interests of countless other fellow community members. On this point Nozick and Taylor come to different conclusions. The former suspects that such a widespread overlapping of interests will lead inevitably to authoritarianism and totalitarianism. Taylor would see such a thorough confluence of interests in a community as the height of collective consciousness – thus a positive development.

Since their lives intersect at so many points, special feelings arise among the members of the community toward each other. These feelings hardly have a chance of coming to life in aggregate groups because of the limited time spent together, whereas in the more organized groups the narrowness of the range of common interest prohibits such special relationship. Brought together by family, clan, tradition locality, and institutions, the Japanese have a very wide range of shared experiences. A common history and, more importantly, a shared fate, enhance the collective consciousness of a group whose members, by dint of tradition and interconnected interests, share in each other's successes and failures. Shared fate is much stronger than merely overlapping interests. To use the analogy of a sports team, a success or a defeat is attributable as much to the team as to individuals.

In this respect, one may think of the importance of the practice of vicarious shame or pride among the Japanese. So too the practice of "saving face.". Individuals are proud, and can be ashamed, of their ancestors, families, and clans. An unseemly act done by a distant clan member is capable of arousing shame or embarrassment in a co-member who hears about it. The company executive who resigns because the company is not doing well financially is expressing shame at having failed the dependent members of the community. This, then, is the essence of collective consciousness. Joel Feinberg discusses this same collective consciousness, but calls it "solidarity." It is the result when "the plural possessive 'our' more naturally comes to the lip than the singular 'mine.' "[22] I would go further than Feinberg and say that the degree of collective consciousness increases in proportion as the chance of opting out of the group decreases. Understood in this sense, then, the Japanese are thoroughly collectively conscious. The collective consciousness is the crucial element of a good community.

As an example of collective consciousness among the Japanese, an integral part of introducing oneself to any new acquaintance is some reference to a group one has membership in – some connection with others. Nakane calls this a frame, by which he means localities, institutions, or relationships that bind individuals into a group. For example, the question "Who are you?" is rarely answered with a simple "my name is Kenji Sumi." Kenji is more likely to invoke a frame by answering, in addition to the name, "I belong to Nissan." Similarly, the Samurai who calls out "I am Wada Shojiro Yoshishige, 17 years old, grandson of Miura Taisuke Yoshiaki, not far removed from a princely house, the eleventh generation from Prince Takamochi, descendant of the emperor Kammu" is invoking several layers of frames.[23]

The family, neighborhood, clan, and workplace in Japan are frames that have brought about a measure of homogeneity and cohesion that makes social isolation a most serious handicap. Collective consciousness is, at the first level, rooted in the family as the dominant unit of social organization – a family system understood extensively enough to include ancestors. Associated with this view of family are the practices of ancestor worship and family shrines. Extending outwards, but building on family as society's dominant unit, we are led into a kind of clan consciousness. In ancient Japan the consciousness came from real clans where the rural farming communities were actually co-members in clans. However, it is important to note that the collective consciousness survived the collapse of the clan system. It has further been noted by many commentators that the pervasiveness of the collectivity orientation is such that even such relations as those between landlords and tenants or owners and workers in factories are based on simulated family ties.[24] Nakane goes so far as to declare it the basic scheme: "It seems, then, that an organizational principle in terms of parent–child relationships constitutes the basic scheme of Japanese organizations. This principle is to be found in almost every kind of institution in Japan."[25] In this way a major university will align itself with smaller outlying colleges, a big factory or industrial plant links itself to several others in the same line of business.

Commitment to the social is exhibited in the moral sphere too. The tendency of social relationships is to surpass the individual on the scale of importance. From the foregoing discussion of family and clan, consciousness of the individual as an entity comes to be only in the light of the wider spectrum of clan consciousness. In other words, although the individual remains important, that importance derives from one's social class or role and is therefore lessened when a comparison of the individual is made vis-à-vis the social. In this way, what may be called a social morality arises. Good and evil, instead of being determined by the rational individual using abstract reason as proposed by Kant, are seen more in terms of effects on the group. The highest virtue becomes sacrifice of the self for others (one's prince, parents, family, clan, or one's community at large). One thinks here of the executive who voluntarily bows out as a result of poor organizational performance or in extreme circumstances, Kami Kaze soldiers, and the practice of Hara Kiri.

The Japanese sense of community prompts two observations. The first has to do with the pervasiveness of the family model. Japanese society remains one that has a relatively homogeneous configuration. The ethnic group is at the same time the nation. Few other ethnic groups in the world double up as nation-states and parallel the same high degree of cohesion, conformity, and consensus. One finds in Japan a collective conscience at its most extensive – a true ethnic society. We noted earlier that society as a whole in Japan takes on the appearance of a family.

The second observation has to do with Japan being the paradigm case of a communally organized society that evolved into a modern industrial society. The Japanese are an ethnic community that has mastered the processes of urbanization and industrialization. Japanese society has developed from small localized farming communities. Industrialization in Japan was not followed by the chaos and anomie that have plagued other communally organized societies in their bid to industrialize and urbanize. Japan has become notable for this ability to function effectively in a thoroughly modern way – without abandoning deeply held ontological attitudes toward society, relationships, and the individual.

Japan's example is instructive for a variety of reasons. It is an example of a communally organized non-liberal society that is both very large and is a first-rate capitalist economy. This is a dimension of the liberalism/communitarian debate not quite understandable if one falls back on the usual framework of the debate. There are those who would argue that Japan exemplifies an isolated case that cannot be generalized. Japan had a history of being isolated from the rest of the world so that even when the society borrowed from China and other nations it was possible to hold on to traditional social organization even while mastering the processes of urbanization and industrialization. However, Japan has been on the international stage since the end of World War II. This is, hence, a case of combining collective values with a modern industrial economy. The two did not prove to be incompatible. In a sense, the modern Japanese man or woman, while retaining a communitarian attachment to the group, nevertheless functions effectively in a modern industrial economy. On the basis of a traditional role-centered hierarchical social structure, a society has been built that is enormously economically successful.

Japanese close affiliation and conformity have proved more conducive to teamwork than liberal individualism, which is by its nature short-term goal-oriented and adversarial. In recent years, with the exception of 1998 and 1999 when the Japanese economy nearly collapsed, the Japanese have been better capitalists than Americans and Europeans. Lest the near collapse of the Japanese economy be taken as proof of the incompatibility of communitarianism and industrialization, one only needs to look at the counter-examples provided by the recent near-collapse of Mexico and Brazil which are not communitarian societies. These different examples show that there is no direct connection between economic problems and either liberalism or communitarianism. And here we can draw lessons for the global village. With the interconnectedness of the world, there has grown unregulated global competition which has usually been hailed as the best or even the only alternative in a world becoming one. A result of globalization is that speculation at the New York Stock Exchange affects stock prices in Hong Kong, Tokyo, and the rest of the world. Market speculation and competition based on self-interest and short-term goals have had predictable results – global corporations roaming the world in search of cheap labor. To attract investments, local communities around the world have had to make concessions about their environmental, social, and labor regulations, with the result that such investment has been followed by deterioration of the environment and social conditions. Economic globalization on the model of Adam Smith's self-interest is therefore to be rejected. One has only to think of Mexico's maquiladoras (border factories), New York City's garment sweatshops, and Disney's merchandise "Made in China." Economic globalization on this model has resulted in, among other things, the exploitation of people of color, especially women and children – the bulk of workers in the sweatshops being drawn from these segments of the population. Japanese collective capitalism may serve to show that our visions of the global village need not be constrained by the old frameworks of the individualism of Adam Smith and John Locke. On the global scale, if one thinks of the different countries as individuals and the whole as the team, it is not difficult to see that "individualism" leads to statism and dire economic consequences. Attempts to superimpose teamwork on a model designed to undercut it cannot be as successful as basing the teamwork on a model that takes the collective as the point of reference. From evidence at the present time, the collectivistic capitalism of Japan would seem a much better approach in the global market.

New Ideas About Community

These preceding observations about Japan sidestep the whole issue of whether capitalism is to be preferred to socialism or some other social and economic arrangement. The point here is that defenders of individualistic capitalism have often presented it as the supreme economic arrangement among all alternatives. The collapse of the Berlin wall, the failure of non-liberal models in Eastern Europe, and the disintegration of the Soviet Union have admittedly made it more difficult for communitarians to argue that a large industrial society can be built along communal lines. With the liberals, led by Rawls and Nozick, arguing that their model is superior to any realizable alternative, the implication for the new countries of Eastern Europe and the former Soviet Union searching for new models was obvious. The Japanese model makes it less obvious that the only alternatives are capitalism or socialism.

The idea that times are changing is, of course, not a new one. The signs of the impact of technology are everywhere – a stepped-up pace of life, a throwaway society, increased geographical mobility, lack of commitment in personal relationships, weakening and disintegration of family bonds, and increasing obsoleteness of centralized hierarchies. In the spheres of economics, politics, and family life, telecommunication technology empowers the individual user of technology to control and shape change. Part of the change is the breakdown of community noted by Robert N. Bellah et al. in *Habits of the Heart: Individualism and Commitment in American Life*.[26] Their observation led to the view that in American life the primary emphasis on self-reliance had the result of producing a fragmented citizenry. *Habits of the Heart* calls for a cultural transformation – a prescription which, if followed, would move America towards the pursuit of the public good and away from the pursuit of merely private goods. The crucial question is what constitutes the public good when the idea of community is itself becoming increasingly elastic. One ideal of community is a backward-looking approach, a view of community as purely retrospective. *Habits of the Heart* discusses these "communities of memory"[27] as being constituted by their past and sustained primarily by retelling their constitutive narratives. When such a community injects visions of the future into the narrative it evolves into a "community of hope." Community can also be invoked as a descriptive concept, for example when the term captures the "communities of interest" such as the diverse computer-mediated discussion groups that interact for recreational, religious, and other social purposes. Obviously, each time "public good" or "community" is invoked should also be an occasion for examining whether the proposed ideal is one to be celebrated or whether the ideal is exclusionary. If an invoked sense of community falls back on a past not widely shared, the proposed ideal obstructs the very notion of a community that promotes diversity.

Computer-mediated communities are to differing degrees simultaneously communities of memory, hope, and interest. Their crucial feature is that they force us to rethink the issue of what separates genuine community from illusory community. Computer technology raises new questions about the "reality" of a "community" of people engaged in a shared activity (or series of activities) in cyberspace (which is not a "real place"). Are cyberspace communities real or merely apparent because they not only lack physical realities such as a "place" and "people" but also operate asynchronistically? The classical liberal and communitarian ideas discussed earlier are unhelpful in answering this question and seem only to lead to a false dichotomy. Rawls and Nozick, by arguing for the priority of liberty and individual rights over any common good, leave room primarily for communities of interest. In contrast to these communities in which individuals with previously defined interests get together to further those interests, communitarianssuch as MacIntyre proceed from a substantive idea of the common good. The various liberal and communitarian positions present our choice as being between individuals without a common public sense or a community organized around a single substantive idea of the common good. Computer communities inspire us to go beyond this polarity, and offer a way to reformulate liberal and communitarian conceptions by building on their insights. The number of computer-mediated groups doubles each year and this trend discourages the conception of community as groups organized around a single substantive idea. The diversity of gender, class, race, ethnicity, and sexual orientation in cyberspace evokes a community (with ever-increasing sub-communities) held together not by a common good but by a common bond. In this community without a definite shape, "loss of community" takes on the meaning of losing sight of the common bond that ties together the global community.

There is little doubt that the traditional communities with which we are more familiar are worth saving. Increasingly, there are calls for renewal in our commitment to religious associations, sororities, fraternities, honor societies, professional and international organizations, and even nation-states. What is also becoming increasingly clear is that any renewed commitment must be based on new ideas about membership in community. In recent times, traditional communities have had to adjust to membership that accounts for multiple identities. Even though membership in these communities has continued to be understood as flowing from the principle of freedom of association, increasingly communities are thought to be more well-ordered and valuable to the extent that they can integrate ethnic, religious, sexual, and geographical diversity. Conversely, communities that exhibit aspects of fundamentalism, especially a strong central decision-making structure that decreases the possibility for diversity in membership, are less valuable.

The challenge of modern times is to provide alternative theories of community that remain sensitive to the differences within communities. Computer communication provides the basis for such alternative theories. Computer-mediated communities are particularly instructive because they call into question the assumptions of communities built on the foundation of the principle of freedom of association. There is a sense in which membership in one form of computer-mediated community or another is not a matter of choice at the start of the twenty-first century. There may indeed be persons who have arranged their lives to be free of any interaction with computers. The point is that such an arrangement comes at too high a price and is therefore not a viable option. In a world in which most day-to-day transactions are computer-mediated, no individual or country can adequately function away from the information superhighway.[28] Further, the individuals and countries in cyberspace communication must confront the question of diversity and community membership. Such cyberspace communication takes place in virtual environments, and thus also calls into question the connection between community and place. That communication also alters the status of the individual as author of actions in one's community, hence calling into question relations of power in society. Electronic communication holds possibilities for understanding what kinds of community appear in cyberspace, and also how the lessons learned from cyberspace communities may strengthen traditional communities.

The Luo and Japanese societies are examples of traditional communities that I think remain worth preserving. While there is much to recommend these forms of community, they nonetheless carry within them features that systematically discourage world-traveling. Traditional communities may contain frameworks that make possible self-critique but none of them allows the articulation of that self-critique to the extent that electronic interaction does. There are limited ways to be a "good" Luo or Japanese while at the same time being a good citizen of multiple other worlds (real and virtual). Computer-mediated communities expand the range of what "good membership" means. Further, the changed experiences of time and space in virtual environments transform the status of the individual as agent and moral actor. Cyberspace alters the public and private realms, affects the representations of truth and falsity, and thus ultimately must change our ideas of society. Computer communication, because it calls into question issues of meaning and validity, holds great potential for advancing our understanding of the idea of community. The potential is both for strengthening our traditional communities of memory and for a proliferation of communities of interest and hope.

Notes

1   Robert Nozick, *Anarchy, State and Utopia* (New York: Basic Books, 1974).
2   John Rawls offers the most influential contemporary philosophical discussion of liberalism in *A Theory of Justice* (Cambridge, MA: Belknap Press of Harvard University Press, 1971) and *Political Liberalism* (Columbia University Press, 1996).
3   I find these themes particularly articulated in his *Legitimation Crisis*, trans. Thomas McCarthy (Boston: Beacon Press, 1975), pp. 104 ff.; and *The Theory of Communicative Action, Vol. I: Reason and the Rationalization of Society*, trans. Thomas

McCarthy (Boston: Beacon Press, 1981), p. 89.

4   Ronald Dworkin, *Taking Rights Seriously* (Cambridge, Mass.: Harvard University Press, 1978).

5   For detailed discussions of various aspects of the liberal tradition, I found the following sources both eloquent and accessible: David Johnston, *The Idea of a Liberal Theory: A Critique and Reconstruction* (Princeton: Princeton University Press, 1994); Charles W. Anderson, *Pragmatic Liberalism* (Chicago: University of Chicago Press, 1990); and Richard E. Flathman, *Willful Liberalism: Voluntarism and Individuality in Political Theory and Practice* (Ithaca: Cornell University Press, 1992). A sharp criticism of liberalism is offered by Paul Wolff, *The Poverty of Liberalism* (Boston: Beacon Press, 1968).

6   *The Nation*, July 18, 1994.

7   Alasdair MacIntyre, *After Virtue*, 2nd edn. (Notre Dame: Univeristy of Notre Dame Press, 1984).

8   Charles Taylor, *Sources of the Self: The Making of the Modern Identity* (Cambridge, Mass.: Harvard University Press, 1989).

9   Seyla Benhabib, *Situating the Self: Gender, Community and Postmodernism in Contemporary Ethics* (New York: Routledge, 1992).

10   Ibid., p. 3.

11   Ibid., p. 81.

12   Maria Lugones, "Playfulness, World-Traveling, and Loving Perception," *Hypatia* 2 (Summer 1987).

13   Virginia Held, "Mothering versus Contract," in Jane J. Mansbridge, ed., *Beyond Self Interest* (Chicago: University of Chicago Press, 1990).

14   I am grateful to Larry May (Washington University, St. Louis) for pointing out to me that being a Luo would seem to be quite different from being black. Whereas one cannot stop being black, a Luo community member could "pass" as a member of another tribe or the larger national community or even act as if he/she had no connection to the tribe. Having exercised this choice, others would then treat the person as if he/she were not a member of the Luo community. It may be objected that one can "opt out" of these relationships and thus it is problematic to characterize them as really non-voluntary. The objection is that one can "pass" as a member of another tribe or even the larger national community. A further part of the objection is that being a Luo is different from being black because one cannot stop being black. One may begin acting as if one had no connection to the group and would henceforth be treated by others as if one had stopped belonging to the group. I disagree with the objection because the same lack of voluntariness characterizes both being black and being Luo. It is true a Luo may pass as a member of another tribe. However, this is in the same sense in which a black person may pass as white. In both cases the "passing" is successful only because of an element of deception or lack of information. There is something about the passing individual that is not known to the wider community. In that sense, then, these are not true instances in which an individual voluntarily renounces one identity for another. The true test would be a situation in which there was full disclosure by the individual of his/her intention. My contention here is that such a declaration would not be enough to make one cease being either a Luo or black.

15   For background on the issues involved, see David William Cohen and E. S. Atieno

Odhiambo, eds., *Siaya: the Historical Anthropology of an African Landscape* (Nairobi: Heinemann Kenya, 1983), pp. 133–9; and Sean Egan, ed., *S. M. Otieno: Kenya's Unique Burial Saga* (Nairobi: Nation Newspapers, 1987). The lawyer for Otieno's clan gave the other side of the case, the gist of which was that a Kikuyu woman who married a Luo had irreversibly walked out of her ethnic group and had become a Luo, thenceforth to be governed by Luo customs. Among those customs was the practice of patrilineage, and the axiom that choice or circumstance did not put a man outside the control of clan and tradition. The latter axiom did not apply to women because of their "migratory nature" and so left them free to change ethnic affiliations whenever they married. There are clearly a number of issues intertwined here, not least of which is the issue of different rights accorded men and women by these traditions. However, on the crucial question of whether a man is voluntarily bound by tradition, the verdict of the court was clear. At the conclusion of the trial after five months the highest court in Kenya endorsed the clan's position that such actions as S. M. Otieno was reported to have undertaken did not remove the man from the operation of the customary law of the Luo.

16 Ifeanyi A. Menkiti, "Person And Community In African Traditional Thought," in Richard A. Wright, ed., *African Philosophy: An Introduction*, (Lanham, Mass.: University Press of America, 1984), pp. 171–81.

17 Ibid., p. 80.

18 Julius Nyerere, *Ujamaa: Essays in Socialism* (New York: Oxford University Press, 1968).

19 See Kenneth Baynes's detailed discussion of these specific areas of Liberal/communitarian dispute in "The Liberal/Communitarian Controversy and Communicative Ethics," in David Rasmussen, ed., *Universalism Vs. Communitarianism: Contemporary Debates in Ethics* (Cambridge, Mass.: MIT Press, 1990), pp. 61–81. Also see Allen E. Buchanan, "Assessing the Communitarian Critique of Liberalism," *Ethics* 99 (July 1989): 852–82.

20 Hajime Nakamura, *Ways of Thinking of Eastern Peoples: India, China, Tibet, Japan*, ed. Philip E. Wiener (University of Hawaii Press, 1964).

21 Chie Nakane, *Japanese Society* (Berkeley: University of California Press, 1970).

22 Joel Feinberg, *Doing and Deserving: Essays in the Theory of Responsibility* (Princeton: Princeton University Press, 1970), p. 236.

23 Quoted from Gempei Seisuiki, XXI (Record of the Rise and Fall of the Minamoto and Taira clans, 857–1185) in Hajime Nakamura, *Ways of Thinking of Eastern Peoples*, p. 418.

24 Ibid., p. 425.

25 Chie Nakane, *Japanese Society*, p. 96.

26 Robert Bellah et al., eds., *Habits of the Heart: Individualism and Commitment in American Life* (Berkeley: University of California Press, 1985).

27 Ibid., pp. 152–5.

28 For a detailed discussion of the ways in which cyberspace communities may be considered models for traditional communities, see Samuel Oluoch Imbo, "Cyberspace: An Effective Virtual Model for Communities," in Paula Smithka and Alison Bailey, eds., *Community, Diversity, and Difference: Implications for Peace*, (Netherlands: Rodopi, 2001).

17

The University as a Universe of Communities

Mary Hawkesworth

Commencement ceremonies at many universities welcome those embarking upon academic careers to the "ancient and honorable community of scholars." The notion of community invoked in this greeting incorporates traces of ancient and medieval educational practices replete with a shared conception of truth, a common metaphysics, and a commitment to an intellectual life in which the range of tolerable diversity was narrowly construed. At the outset of the twenty-first century, universities bear little resemblance to their ancient and medieval antecedents. They exist as complex organizations in which scholarly endeavors and structures of collegial governance coexist with administrative hierarchies characteristic of large bureaucracies, entrepreneurial initiatives and marketing overtures typical of the corporate sector, and stratified work regimens typical of divisions of labor within the service sector. This chapter will interrogate the meaning of community within these hybrid organizations. It will examine the systems of stratification rooted in age, sex, race, class, and discipline that lie at the heart of contemporary universities, and the power/knowledge constellations advanced to legitimate these hierarchical orders. It will also consider challenges to the established order within universities and the prospects for new modes of community that arise in the context of the politics of knowledge.

The Specter of Hegel

The classical model of the academy, as well as medieval models of the university, fit well with a Hegelian notion of community that presupposes shared ideals and purposes, collective projects, and clear criteria of success.[1] The classical model conceives faculty and students in a common project that links individual and civic goods. Seeking to cultivate intellectual and moral excellence, the curriculum was designed to initiate the student to modes of analysis, domains of inquiry, and qualities of character requisite for an educated citizenry. Within the confines of the ancient polis, where education was restricted to the sons of propertied citizens, the success of the academy could be measured by the quality of public life.

In the twelfth century, two different models of university emerged. One form, typically associated with Italian schools such as Bologna and Salerno, which became the prototype for universities in Italy, Spain, and Portugal, conceived the university as a guild of students who hired masters to teach what the students wished to learn. Common intellectual interests among students with remarkably similar class and family backgrounds thus structured the curriculum, the mode of instruction, and bonds of friendship. The second model, typically associated with the universities of Paris, Oxford, and Cambridge, construed the university as a guild of masters, all of whom were clerics, whose entitlement to teach was rooted in the possession of theological expertise. In the context of intense debates over Christian doctrine, theological expertise was closely tied to religious orthodoxy and to established political institutions. The language of instruction and scholarly discourse, as well as the content of the curriculum, manifested the imprint of the Holy Roman Empire, and the purposes of education were closely linked to the needs and interests of the dominant religious orders. Such early institutions, designed to open minds to the pursuit of truth, were at once closed worlds carefully policed to preserve doctrinal compliance.

Contemporary research universities bear little resemblance to their ancient and medieval antecedents. Shared understandings about the nature and purposes of education have been supplanted by the proliferation of academic specializations and increasing divisions of labor within and across academic disciplines, fields, and subfields. Doctrinal concordance has been displaced by fissures within departments concerning the appropriate methods of research and objects of inquiry. At the end of the twentieth century, the metaphor of multiple solitudes captures a dynamic in higher education that C. P. Snow's "two cultures" began to chart in the 1960s.[2] Isolated in an office/study/laboratory, the contemporary academic shares his or her thoughts more readily with virtual communities on-line than with colleagues on campus. What remains of the university as a scholarly community would appear to be nothing more than a common geographical site within which disparate worlds coexist and occasionally collide.

A quick inventory, by no means exhaustive or systematic, gestures toward the range of diversity within contemporary universities. Complex organizational forms, physical facilities, and pedagogic practices proliferate. Departments of Fine Arts or Performing Arts, for example, may house museums and galleries, studios, conservatories, practice rooms, rehearsal and concert halls, theatres, as well as film production technology. Pedagogy may range from private tutorials to mass lectures and entail public performances such as dance recitals, plays, concerts, juried exhibitions, and the half-time shows by the marching band during athletic events. Other humanities disciplines requiring less varied physical spaces may yet embrace enormous pedagogical diversity such as Socratic method and computer-assisted logic courses, rote memorization, self-directed language labs, and overseas language immersion programs, textual analysis, cultural studies, creative writing, and business composition. Social science departments may encompass police training institutes, leadership programs, mock legislatures, global war simulations, psychology clinics, counseling centers, social work placements, service learning and internships, urban planning and renewal projects, radio and television studios, computer labs, wireless classrooms, philosophical argument, statistical analysis, deconstruction, ethnography, social biology, and archaeological digs. The science departments typically require offices, laboratories, clinics, hospitals, human subjects committees, and frequently give rise to inventions, patents, spin-off companies, research parks, and private practice plans.

In addition to academic programs, contemporary universities typically include residence halls, dining facilities, and transportation systems, campus police, hotels and conference centers, sports complexes and athletic teams, publication facilities that produce brochures, stationery, newspapers, alumni magazines, professional journals, and academic books. University development offices raise millions of dollars through diverse marketing strategies, cultivation of alumni and potential donors, corporate solicitation, and government grants and set-aside programs. University foundations operate like professional investment firms, shepherding endowment and grant funds to maximize return on investment while simultaneously regulating the disbursement of accrued interest.

If the constitutive units of the university seem to have little in common, the various segments of the university population might also be said to exist in parallel universes. Student experience may range from an idyllic encounter with the world of ideas in which intellectual horizons expand, understandings deepen, and career paths open on the basis of newly cultivated academic interests, to the "Animal House" stereotype of four years of fraternity parties and athletic events that culminate in a public issuance of credentials certifying labor force readiness. Faculty experience may vary from the privileged existence of the research scholar whose attention is seldom diverted from scholarly pursuits, to the harried world of the gypsy scholar who cobbles together a poverty-level income by teaching four courses per semester at a number of local institutions. University administrators can run the gamut from visionaries who inspire confidence and transform their institutions into models of educational excellence, to morale-destroying muddlers who spin strategic plans designed to maximize efficiency without concern for the unique demands of education. University staff includes celebrity coaches who have multimillion dollar contracts and custodial workers whose hourly wage is pegged to a minimum wage, professionals who understand their vocation as deeply intertwined with the institution's educational mission, as well as employees for whom the university's august status does little to offset low pay and poor working conditions.

If images of parallel universes and organized complexity suggest that the contemporary university falls far short of the shared values central to a Hegelian conception of community, are there other conceptions of community that might be invoked to depict a contemporary university as a community?

Communities: Transient, Exclusionary and Intentional

At the end of a student's university experience in a peculiar ceremony called a "Commencement," doctoral candidates undergo a ritual transformation. Given a hood, a handshake, and a diploma, the now accredited intellectual is welcomed into the "ancient and honorable community of scholars" just as he or she is ejected from the institution. Lest "ejection" seem too harsh a term, it is useful to keep in mind the employment prospects of the newly minted Ph.D. who aspires to enter a professorate in which barely one-fourth of the faculty teaching in universities holds a tenured/tenure-track line. Rather than construing the university as a place of permanence, as a home or a refuge for a community of scholars committed to the intrinsic values of the life of the mind, it is helpful to begin an interrogation of the possible meaning of university as community with the more disruptive image of a transitional space into which one is welcomed only as one leaves. Such a construal, I believe, may help move us closer to an understanding of the kinds of community that exist within universities and the activity of community-making that can and does occur within universities, while also affording insights into a particular form of political contestation ongoing in universities.

Any attempt to construct the university as a universe of communities must necessarily be false to the historical record. Whether one traces its historical antecedents to the academies of classical Athens, to the medieval *universitates* in Bologna and Paris, to the nineteenth-century model for the production of scholars perfected in Germany, or to the American research institutions cultivated in the twentieth century, universities have neither encompassed nor sought to encompass "the whole of existing or created things regarded collectively" – the *OED* definition of a universe. Ancient, medieval, modern, and postmodern universities are sites of exclusion far more than inclusion. If Crispin Sartwell is correct that "communities are made by exclusion,"[3] then universities have been and continue to be communities in this peculiar sense.

The grounds for exclusion have varied markedly over time, encompassing distinctions based on caste, class, sex, religion, race, ethnicity, age, intellectual ability, discipline, and methodological commitments, among others. What has remained remarkably constant, however, is the process of exclusion. Those who are already members of the academic community "do the choosing, in accordance with [their] own understanding of what membership means and of what sort of a community [they] want to have."[4] As the primary agents of exclusion, university faculty have vigilantly policed institutional borders through hiring and tenure decisions, as well as through admissions policies. In the quest to create a community of like-minded individuals, universities have been the prototype of the gated community. As a consequence, universities remain elite institutions that allege to take "the whole of existing or created things" as objects of study, on the assumption that certain knowers can grasp universal truth. Indeed, it is precisely this grasp of truth that affords members of the university faculty their distinctive role. In the words of Jeffrie Murphy:

> the university faculty is not a miniature civil society but is rather a service profession, (a noble calling, I once would have said) whose reason for existence is defined, not by the interests of its own present and future members, but by external goals and an external constituency . . . the pursuit of truth and the education of students.[5]

Murphy's quote embodies what might be called the received view of universities, at least among university professors and administrators, who frequently present versions of this view to students, parents, legislators, and the public to vindicate the institution's existence and to legitimate tuition and funding increases. Yet even in this benign representation, boundaries are drawn in a remarkably exclusionary fashion. Students, who under certain descriptions might be taken to be the *sine qua non* of higher education, are depicted as an "external constituency" rather than as members of the university community. The pursuit of truth, a value intrinsic to academic inquiry understood as a process of discovery, is cast as an "external goal."

The received view of the university as a faculty engaged in the tripartite mission of teaching, research, and service constructs the university as an "intentional community." In this sense, the faculty share a unifying purpose that overrides the marked differences in life circumstances and activities that differentiate faculty by academic rank and specialization. Constituted as a locus of intention rather than as a physical space or lived experience, this university community has a peculiarly disembodied existence. Like their rationalist predecessors, this intentional community of scholars is committed to the life of the mind and their intellectual pursuits remain unencumbered by the demands of the body. In keeping with Aristotelian conceptions, it is assumed that the quest for knowledge can be undertaken only by those who exist within the "realm of freedom" – a realm defined in opposition to the "realm of necessity," which involves the production of goods and services essential to survival. To paraphrase Tim Kaufman-Osborn, the minds of [such] men (and historically these scholars have been overwhelmingly male) are dependent on the bodies of women[6] – or, more accurately, upon the invisible labor of other subordinated groups. Such a vision of the university as an intentional community of scholars necessarily excludes the physical conditions of existence from its rhetorical frame. The disembodied community of the mind renders invisible the custodial workers whose shifts begin at 4 a.m. and whose mandate is to erase the traces of human habitation so that scholars' thought processes will not be impeded by the sight of their own refuse. It renders invisible the food service staff who work long hours at minimum wage to have food at the ready to accommodate the disavowed subsistence needs of scholars. It renders invisible the vital work of the clerical and support staff without whose assistance the university would grind to a halt.

The university as intentional community of scholars purchases its fictive unity at a high price, by replicating the disdain for the body and the contempt for manual labor characteristic of an ancient world-view. Illuminating this cost may help to tarnish idyllic images of shared strivings, a single purpose, a harmony of interests in academic life. Perhaps it can help to slay the specter of Hegel, repudiating a unity grounded in exclusion and oppression and helping to conceive a form of community more suited to complexity, more welcoming to difference.

Recognizing the existence of those who do necessary labor and accepting that labor as essential to the functioning of a university does not in itself resolve the issue of what kind of community can be said to exist within such a complex organization. From the vantage point of the necessary laborers, the university is a hierarchical order that replicates, and concentrates, the race/class/gender privileges of the prevailing society. Within this frame, the university is a hierarchically structured organization in which different groups are accorded different rights, responsibilities, and remuneration on the basis of their employment status. The structure of the university conforms to the pyramid shape familiar within liberal capitalist societies: a small decision-making elite at the pinnacle (the administration) structures the conditions of life for the privileged tenured and tenure-track faculty, as well as for contract workers (part-time and temporary faculty), support staff, custodial workers, and service workers.

Those who inhabit the higher strata of the pyramid receive not only higher wages and better benefits, but have rights of participation and possibilities for self-determination unknown to those at the pyramid's base. Indeed, the rules governing different segments of the university are constitutive of different forms of organization – and one might say, different orders of life. University administration operates in accordance with a bureaucratic model that aspires to rational comprehensive decision-making but more typically functions like feudal fiefdoms – patronage systems bound by ties of fealty to administrative lords who have arbitrary power over those who fall within their jurisdictions. Tenured faculty assert some degree of independence from bureaucratic rule by clinging to vestiges of collegial governance. Maintained through appeals to academic freedom, these vestigial rights support eruptions of participatory decision-making in the realms of faculty hiring and promotion, curriculum, and scholarly activity. Within particular institutions different models of faculty governance may coexist. Participatory decision-making within department meetings and faculty assembly often coexists with delegate democracy within a committee system and representative democracy within faculty senates or faculty unions. Far from instantiating any ideal of self-determination, these vestiges of collegial governance tend to be preoccupied with efforts to fend off bureaucratic encroachments and strategic interventions designed to co-opt faculty governance through the appearance of consultation in forums that allow no substantial determination of outcomes.

Unless unionized, those who comprise the pyramid's base tend to have no rights of self-determination, low pay, and few prospects for upward mobility. As the class that provides the underlabor, they have the status of tacit consenters in a Lockean liberal democracy. Denied any meaningful rights of participation within the university, they can vote with their feet. Their freedom lies in their ability to leave the institution. Within this frame, as within capitalist markets more generally, the hypothetical freedom of the worker diverts attention from persistent inequalities in the conditions of work and the absence of meaningful rights of participation. The university instantiates the principles of neo-liberalism.

In keeping with the individualist premises of neo-liberalism, universities provide some mechanisms for upward mobility and status change for some individuals. Many universities provide free tuition for employees enabling some of those who work at the base of the pyramid to complete college degrees and take advantage of career ladders. In response to the dearth of doctorates among people of color in the United States, some universities have adopted "grow your own" programs that pledge financial assistance to talented students of color and employees of color to enable them to complete their doctoral studies and assume faculty positions. With the increasing emphasis on entrepreneurialism within universities, some schools are rewarding those who launch "spin-off" ventures that translate scientific discoveries into revenue-generating enterprises, allowing salary supplements for enterprising faculty and staff. Universities have also embraced celebrity culture, rewarding those within the university who produce revenue through entertainment. Coaches and student athletes may be far more famous than the most accomplished academics, creating mechanisms for those with celebrity status to write different rules for themselves than are binding on other members of the university. The encroachment of consumer metaphors upon the academic terrain has also shifted power relations somewhat from the traditional norms of academic dyad, teacher/student, to market norms pertaining to service providers/customers, or knowledge producers/consumers. Technology, too, has introduced dramatically new possibilities for faculty/student relations as demands for distance learning and virtual universities give rise to modes of interaction that can be mass-marketed at substantial cost savings, since they require no embodied interactions and no shared physical space.

Attention to the complex and changing practices of contemporary universities sustains a far more diverse view of the university than the received view of an intentional community of scholars. Different classes of people, different organizational forms, different modes of interaction, different disciplines, different interests within and across disciplines, and different economies coexist on university territory as they do within the larger communities in which universities are situated. Is there a conception of community that encompasses such diversity?

In *Community Without Unity*, William Corlett advances a conception of community designed to avoid exclusionary norms, presumptions of disembodiedness, and unifying rhetorics that mask inequalities. Corlett argues that much of the fixation on unity that undergirds exclusionary communities is linked to mistaken etymology. Where many derive their notions of community from the Latin terms "com" (with) and "unus" (oneness or unity) and thereby posit commonality as the foundation for community, Corlett suggests an alternative derivation. Combining the Latin "com" (with) and "munus" (gifts or service) affords an interpretation of community that places mutual service and free gift-giving at the heart of the relationship. According to Corlett, the notion of mutual service "presupposes that we are fully implicated in the infinite differences of fellow beings,"[7] without necessitating any appeal to non-existent unity. Individuals embedded in time and space, coexisting amidst manifold inequalities, providing services, and occasionally giving freely of the self to friends or to strangers is sufficient to make a community. Corlett's conception of community accepts plurality, difference, and mulitplicity as given and the obligation to provide services as unshakeable. But the nature of those services, the conditions under which they are rendered and by whom, depend upon the members of the community. On these terms, the university is a community, but the nature and quality of that community is necessarily institution specific.

Community-Making

To this point, I have suggested that the university can conform to at least three conceptions of community: communities made by exclusion, intentional communities of scholars, and Corlett's community without unity. In these various formulations, there is little to distinguish the university from other modes of community life. To conclude the analysis at this point would be to miss an important aspect of the university, what might be called "community-making," the role of the university in building a world we share in common, by structuring shared expectations and understandings. Community-making suggests that communities are neither fixed nor given, but are called into being through particular kinds of activities. According to Hannah Arendt, human communities are constituted in part by the creation of a common world, which includes the production of artifacts that bind us to one another in physical space (e.g., buildings, roads, parks, art), and the production of understandings about the past, present, and future that make particular modes of life possible.[8] I want to argue that universities play a crucial role in community-making in this latter sense. Universities create and accredit ways of knowing and bodies of knowledge that sustain specific modes of life. Community-making in universities involves educational practices that entrench tacit presuppositions, establishing parameters for what is taken to be known and what is taken to be knowable, accrediting notions of the "given," as well as the possible.

Perhaps the most profound contribution of universities to community-making is the production of a common past and the concomitant erasure of the traces of that production. The "Western Tradition" – philosophical/historical/literary – replete with canonical texts – is a product of particular universities over the past 200 years.[9] Similarly, modern science, with its emphasis upon induction, experimentation, and codification of "natural laws" is an invention of the past few centuries.[10] Higher education in the twenty-first century creates a global community by inculcating commitments to a particular narrative of civilization, including assumptions about reason and progress, the Western tradition, the unfolding of the scientific "quest for truth," and, more recently, certain notions about the internal relations of capitalism and (what is euphemistically called) democratization.

While a systematic discussion of the university's role in community-building would require volumes, several examples may help illuminate the process. Education scholars have provided extensive discussions of the "hidden curriculum" that permeates education (kindergarten through university). On this view, part of what universities create is the ability to mis/take instrumental reasoning for common sense and commodification of all aspects of human life as unproblematic. For more than 40 years, critics of the liberal democracy have argued that universities shore up class, race, and gender hierarchies through constant reiteration of the rhetoric of meritocracy and inculcation of the belief that the "intellectually gifted" (however that may be defined) deserve privileges because of their contributions to the society. Foucaultians have suggested that higher education is complicitous in the production of power/knowledge constellations that individuate even as they desensitize individuals to increasing surveillance by juridico-medical regimes, thus creating a community of individuals who applaud the process of their own subjection. Feminist scholars have argued that universities are deeply involved in reproducing oppressive gender relations through accreditation of defective sociobiological accounts of sex differences under the guise of "science" and through seemingly boundless tolerance for rape in college residences, as well as inadequate efforts to address sexual harassment in university classrooms and faculty offices. Scholars of color have demonstrated that universities not only produced, circulated, and accredited a bogus "science" of race, but continue to reinforce unwarranted racist distinctions by accrediting certain quantitative tests as legitimate markers of "intellect." Rather than merely reflecting the hierarchies of contemporary societies, community-making within universities produce what Arendt called "the sensus communis" – educated minds who accept such hierarchies as the natural order of things.

A recent report by the Association of American Colleges and Universities, *American Pluralism, American Commitments and the College Curriculum*, provides more subtle examples of university community-making through the core curriculum of a "liberal arts" education. Committed to a liberal "ethos, distinctive for its determination to transcend history and align itself with universal processes and principles," the core curriculum of liberal education is assimilationist. It seeks to liberate students from the "parochialism of personal experience. . . . By fostering qualities of mind – rationality, skepticism, critical analysis, humanistic vision – that are supposed to make students citizens of the world, makers of a universal community."[11] But this model of "universal community" is both raced and gendered. By "privileging the universal over the particular, the transhistorical over the contextual,"[12] the university may be creating modes of "rational" community in which women and people of color feel neither welcome nor at home. The very rhetoric of inclusion – universality may unwittingly exclude.

If the core curriculum can be understood as a site of community-making, then the stakes in the "culture wars" in higher education become easier to grasp. At issue is precisely what world we will have in common; what past we will recognize as our own, what practices will govern our daily life, what future we will envision for ourselves. Proponents of the traditional canon seek to vindicate the legitimacy of past exclusions in order to naturalize continuing exclusions and to inscribe an inequitable future as inevitable "given" human nature. Those who have been variously characterized as "radicals," "multiculturalists," and sometimes the "barbarians at the gates" wish to construct a different narrative history, more faithful to the lives of non-elites, that is, to the vast majority of the human population. At stake is not simply an understanding of a more inclusive past, but the prospects for a different mode of collective life. Accepting exclusions and injustices of the past to be as much our legacy as the narrative of the progressive accretion of civilization creates the possibility for a different kind of community, for a more inclusive "we," for a less inequitable future that such a "we" could build together.

The existence and the virulence of the culture wars proves that community-making within universities need not replicate the exclusions of our historical antecedents. In this sense, universities are sites of community contestation in which the struggle continues over what is representable, who will be represented, and who will do the representing of our collective past, present, and future. Such political contestation helps us to make sense of the image of university community with which we began. Within this interpretation of the politics of knowledge, the university as a transitional space, into which one is welcomed only as one leaves, takes on a more positive cast. For those committed to an inclusive university, the activities of teaching and learning are transformative. In this sense, the university we leave is not the one we entered. Through our own participation in transformative practices, we build a university community in which we are welcome and into which members of formerly excluded groups will also be welcome. Given the difficulties of such social change, it is not surprising that even the most modest welcome occurs only at the moment of our departure from a particular institution. But within this frame, the logic of commencement also fits, for community-building within university is prolegomena to transformative work in the world.

Notes

1   In *The Philosophy of Right*, trans. T. M. Knox (Oxford: Clarendon Press, 1952), Hegel drew a clear distinction between a community as a moral entity and the self-interested and amoral civil society of liberalism. For Hegel, community consists in a group of free individuals who choose to make a life in common because they share moral values and they seek to instantiate those values in their community projects and institutions. The hallmark of a Hegelian community is not only that moral commitments shape collective action, but that community members succeed in achieving the moral goals they set for themselves.
2   C. P. Snow, *The Two Cultures: And a Second Look* (Cambridge: Cambridge University Press, 1964).
3   Crispin Sartwell, "Community at the Margin," ch. 2 in this volume.
4   Michael Walzer, *Spheres of Justice* (New York: Basic Books, 1983), p. 32.
5   Jeffrie Murphy, "Faculties as Civil Societies: A Misleading Model," in Steven M. Cahn, ed., *Affirmative Action and the University: A Philosophical Inquiry* (Temple University Press, 1993), p. 166.
6   Tim Kaufman-Osborn, *Creatures of Prometheus* (Lanham, MD: Rowman and

Littlefield, 1997), p. 159.

7   William Corlett, *Community Without Unity: A Politics of Derridean Extravagance* (Durhaj, NC: Duke University Press, 1989), p. 22.

8   Hannah Arendt, *The Human Condition* (Chicago: University of Chicago Press, 1958).

9   John Gunnell, *Philosophy, Science, and Political Inquiry* (Morristown, NJ: General Learning Press, 1975); and *Political Theory: Tradition and Interpretation* (Cambridge, Mass.: Winthrop, 1979).

10   Charles Bazerman, *Shaping Written Knowledge* (Madison: University of Wisconsin Press, 1988); Gerd Gigerenzer et al., *The Empire of Chance: How Probability Changed Science and Everyday Life* (Cambridge: Cambridge University Press, 1989); Robert Olby et al., *Companion to the History of Modern Science* (London: Routledge, 1990); Theodore Porter, *The Rise of Statistical Thinking* (Princeton: Princeton University Press, 1986).

11   Association of American Colleges and Universities, *American Pluralism, American Commitments and the College Curriculum* (Washington, DC, 1994), p. 8.

12   Ibid., p. 10.

Index

moral anchoring 270
moral community 99, 107–9
moral relations, binding force of 12–13,
    117–27
moral values 104–5
moral virtues 19–20, 209–30
morality,
    and art 260–1
    and commitment to the social
        315–16
Mouffe, Chantal 24, 270–1, 283, 286
Moynihan, Daniel Patrick 75
Mulisch, Harry 262
Mulroney, Brian 187
multicultural movement 5, 7, 34, 167,
    174
multiculturalism,
    Canadian policy 19, 186, 192–5,
        197
    resistance to 79–80
multidimensionality 66–7
multilinguistic capacity 107
Murphy, Jeffrie 327
mwa 90
Myrdal, Gunnar 154
myths 124, 145–6, 259–60

Nagel, Thomas 62
Nakamura, Hajime 313
Nakane, Chie 313, 315
naming, as dangerous 135
Napoleon Bonaparte 164
narrative art, ethical function of 257
narratives 259–60
    of civilization 331
    colonial 25
    emplacing 124–5
    equations as 69
    linear of freedom 79
    travel 290
nation-states 93–8, 307
national community 41, 102–5, 161
    Canadian 19
    myths and 145–6
National Congress of American Indians
    (NCAI) 178
national identity, shared sense of 39

nationalism 2, 18, 102, 104, 112,
    189–92
    Canadian 18–19, 182–208
    ethnic or civic 182–208
    "tri"-nationalism 197–201
nationality, American 145–6
nationhood,
    conditions for 191
    definition of 182, 185, 195
nations,
    and nation-states 93–8
    and nationalism 189–92
Native American Church 175
Native Americans 15, 141, 143–8,
    147, 152
    cosmic communities and spiritual
        autonomy 16–18, 167–81
Navajo 178
    court system 176
needs,
    from art 260, 261
    of individuals 20, 221–2
neighborhoods 38, 41, 90, 95–6
neo-liberalism 329
New York City,
    Chinatown 25, 289, 290, 294–7
    Rainbow Curriculum 132
New Zealand 167
news broadcasting, Princess Diana's
    funeral 273, 279–80
Niebuhr, H. Richard 42
Nietzsche, Friedrich 116, 121
Nigeria 98
Nisga'a 195
Nkrumah, Kwame 309
nomos 20–1, 232–4
non-governmental organizations 202
non-voluntary associations 232–4
noninterference, principle of 118
nonlinear dynamics, identities and
    65–87
normality,
    assumption of heterosexual 131,
        139
    images of 24, 272
    and scapegoating 48
    stasis of 56